RECENT
ECONOMIC CHANGES

A Da Capo Press Reprint Series

THE AMERICAN SCENE
Comments and Commentators

GENERAL EDITOR: WALLACE D. FARNHAM
University of Illinois

RECENT
ECONOMIC CHANGES

AND THEIR EFFECT ON
THE PRODUCTION AND DISTRIBUTION OF WEALTH
AND THE WELL-BEING OF SOCIETY

BY DAVID A. WELLS

DA CAPO PRESS · NEW YORK · 1970

A Da Capo Press Reprint Edition

This Da Capo Press edition of
Recent Economic Changes
is an unabridged republication of the
first edition published in New York in 1889.

Library of Congress Catalog Card Number 69-16654
SBN 306-71143-5

Published by Da Capo Press
A Division of Plenum Publishing Corporation
227 West 17th Street, New York, N.Y. 10011

RECENT

ECONOMIC CHANGES

AND THEIR EFFECT ON
THE PRODUCTION AND DISTRIBUTION OF WEALTH
AND THE WELL-BEING OF SOCIETY

BY

DAVID A. WELLS, LL. D., D. C. L.

MEMBRE CORRESPONDANT DE L'INSTITUT DE FRANCE ; CORRESPONDENTE
REGIA ACCADEMIA DEI LINCEI, ITALIA ; HONORARY FELLOW
ROYAL STATISTICAL SOCIETY, G. B. ; LATE UNITED STATES
SPECIAL COMMISSIONER OF REVENUE, AND PRESIDENT
AMERICAN SOCIAL SCIENCE ASSOCIATION, ETC.

NEW YORK
D. APPLETON AND COMPANY
1889

TO

D. WILLIS JAMES,

THE ENTERPRISING AND SUCCESSFUL MERCHANT,

THE PUBLIC-SPIRITED CITIZEN,

THE WISE AND GENEROUS PHILANTHROPIST,

THIS VOLUME IS RESPECTFULLY

Dedicated

BY THE AUTHOR.

PREFACE.

THE economic changes that have occurred during the last quarter of a century—or during the present generation of living men—have unquestionably been more important and varied than during any former corresponding period of the world's history. It would seem, indeed, as if the world, during all the years since the inception of civilization, has been working up on the line of equipment for industrial effort—inventing and perfecting tools and machinery, building workshops and factories, and devising instrumentalities for the easy intercommunication of persons and thoughts, and the cheap exchange of products and services; that this equipment having at last been made ready, the work of using it has, for the first time in our day and generation, fairly begun; and also that every community under prior or existing conditions of use and consumption, is becoming saturated, as it were, with its results. As an immediate consequence the world has never seen anything comparable to the results of the recent system of transportation by land and water; never experienced in so short a time such an expansion of all that pertains to what is called "business"; and has never before been able to accomplish so much in the way of production with a given amount of labor in a given time.

Concurrently, or as the necessary sequence of these changes, has come a series of wide-spread and complex disturbances; manifesting themselves in great reductions of the cost of production and distribution and a consequent remarkable decline in the prices of nearly all staple commodities, in a radical change in the relative values of the precious metals, in the absolute destruction of large amounts of capital through new inventions and discoveries and in the impairment of even greater amounts through extensive reductions in the rates of interest and profits, in the discontent of labor and in an increasing antagonism of nations, incident to a greatly intensified industrial and commercial competition. Out of these changes will probably come further disturbances, which to many thoughtful and conservative minds seem full of menace of a mustering of the barbarians from within rather than as of old from without, for an attack on the whole present organization of society, and even the permanency of civilization itself.

The problems which our advancing civilization is forcing upon the attention of society are, accordingly, of the utmost urgency and importance, and are already occupying the thoughts, in a greater or less degree, of every intelligent person in all civilized countries. But, in order that there may be intelligent and comprehensive discussion of the situation, and more especially that there may be wise remedial legislation for any economic or social evils that may exist, it is requisite that there should be a clear and full recognition of what has happened. And to simply and comprehensively tell this—to trace out and exhibit in something like regular order the causes and extent of the industrial and social changes and accompanying disturbances which have especially characterized the last fifteen or twenty years of the world's history—has been the main purpose of the author. At the same time the presentation of whatever in the way of deduction from the record of experience has seemed legitimate and likely to aid in correct conclusions, has not been disregarded.

In the main the following pages are a reproduction of a series of papers originally contributed to and published in "The (New York) Popular Science Monthly," and in part in "The (London) Contemporary Review" (1887 and 1888). These have, however, in great measure been rewritten, carefully revised, and brought up to a later date.

Norwich, Connecticut, *August, 1889.*

CONTENTS.

IV.

V.

VI.

VII.

RECENT ECONOMIC CHANGES.

I.

THE existence of a most curious and, in many respects, unprecedented disturbance and depression of trade, commerce, and industry, which, first manifesting itself in a marked degree in 1873, has prevailed with fluctuations of intensity up to the present time (1889), is an economic and social phenomenon that has been everywhere recognized. Its most noteworthy peculiarity has been its universality; affecting nations that have been involved in war as well as those which have maintained peace; those which have a stable currency, based on gold, and those which have an unstable currency, based on promises which have not been kept; those which live under a system of free exchange of commodities, and those whose exchanges are more or less restricted. It has been grievous in old communities like England and Germany, and equally so in Australia, South Africa, and California, which represent the new; it has been a calamity exceeding heavy to be borne, alike by the inhabitants of sterile Newfoundland and Labrador, and of the sunny, fruitful sugar-islands of the East and West Indies; and it has not enriched those at the centers of the world's exchanges, whose gains are ordinarily the greatest when business is most fluctuating and uncertain.*

One of the leading economists and financiers of France, M. Leroy Beaulieu, claims that the suffering has been greatest in his country, humiliated in war, shorn of her territory, and paying the maximum of taxation; but not a few stand ready to contest that claim in behalf of the United States, rejoicing in the maintenance of her national strength and dominion, and richer than ever in national resources.

Commenting upon the phenomena of the industrial depression subsequent to the early months of 1882, the Director

---

* The poverty in Australia, in 1885, was reported to be more extreme than at any former period in the history of the colonies; multitudes at Adelaide, South Australia, surrounding the Government House and clamoring for food —the causes of distress assigned being failure of the harvest, drought, and general commercial depression. This depression, especially of the agricultural interests, continued in a marked degree through the year 1885, the exports of the colonies declining thirteen per cent and the imports six per cent as compared with those of the preceding year. With an increase of three per cent in population for the year, the colonial revenues of 1886 also showed a marked decline as compared with 1885. Since 1887, however, business in Australia has greatly improved.

"The close of the year 1884 brought with it little, if any, improvement, in the material condition of South Africa. Commercial disasters may not have been so frequent as during the previous year, but this may be explained by the fact that trade has reached so low a level that very little room existed for further failures. No new enterprises have been set on foot, and the suspension of many of the public works has tended to further reduce the commercial prosperity of the country. Consumption has been upon the lowest possible scale, retrenchment universal, and want of employment, and even of food, among the laboring-classes, a grave public difficulty."—*United States Consul* SILER, *Report to State Department*, 1885.

January, 1885. The price of mackerel in 1884 (Boston) was lower than at any time since 1849; and, in the case of codfish, the lowest since 1838. On the other hand, the price of mackerel in December, 1888, in the same market, was so high as to almost render the consumption of this article of food a matter of luxury. In all countries dependent in a great degree on the production of cane-sugar, the depression of industry in recent years has also been very great, and still (1889) continues.

of the United States National Bureau of Labor, in his report for 1886, considers the nations involved, in respect to their relations to each other and to severity of experience, to stand in the following order: Great Britain, the United States, Germany, France, Belgium. The investigations of the director also indicated a conclusion (of the greatest importance in the consideration of causes); namely, that the maximum of economic disturbance has been experienced in those countries in which the employment of machinery, the efficiency of labor, the cost and the standard of living, and the extent of popular education are the greatest; and the minimum in countries, like Austria, Italy, China, Mexico, South America, etc., where the opposite conditions prevail. These conclusions, which are concurred in by nearly all other investigators, apply, however, more especially to the years prior to 1883, as since then " depression " has manifested itself with marked intensity in such countries as Russia, Japan, Zanzibar, Uruguay, and Roumania.

The business of retail distribution generally—owing, probably, to the extreme cheapness of commodities—does not, moreover, appear to have been less profitable than usual during the so-called period of depression; in contradistinction to the business of production, which has been generally unprofitable.

It is also universally admitted that the years immediately precedent to 1873—i. e., from 1869 to 1872—constituted a period of most extraordinary and almost universal inflation of prices, credits, and business; which, in turn, has been attributed to a variety or sequence of influences, such as excessive speculation; excessive and injudicious construction of railroads in the United States, Central Europe, and Russia (1867-'73); the opening of the Suez Canal (1869); the Franco-German War (1870-'71); and the payment of the enormous war indemnity of fifty-five hundred million francs (eleven hundred million dollars) which Germany exacted from France (1871-'73). The contemporary comments of

two English journals, of recognized authority, on the course
of events in 1872, constitute also an important contribution
to our information on this subject. Under date of March,
1873, the London "Economist," in its review of the commercial history of the preceding year, says:

> Of all events of the year (1872) the profound economic changes
> generated by the rise of prices and wages in this country, in Central
> and Western Europe, and in the United States, have been the most
> full of moment.

And the London "Engineer," under date of February,
1873, thus further comments on the situation:

> The progress of events during 1872 will not soon be forgotten by
> engineers. The position assumed by the working-classes, and the un-
> precedented demand for iron and machinery, combined to raise the
> cost of all the principal materials of construction to a point absolutely
> without parallel, if we bear in mind that the advance of prices was
> not localized, but universal, and that the duration of the rise was not
> limited to a few months or weeks, but, having extended already over
> a period of some months, shows little sign at this moment of any sen-
> sible abatement. *In 1872 scarcely a single step in advance was made
> in the science or practice of mechanical engineering. No one had time
> to invent, or improve, or try new things.* The workingman is setting
> spurs to his employers with no gentle touch, and already we find that
> every master with capital at stake is considering how best he can dis-
> pense with the men who give him so much trouble. Of course, the
> general answer always assumes the same shape—use a tool whenever
> it is possible instead of a man.

The period of economic disturbance which commenced
in 1873 appears to have first manifested itself almost simultaneously in Germany and the United States in the latter
half of that year. In the former country the great and
successful results of the war with France had stimulated
every department of thought and action among its people
into intense activity. The war indemnity, which had been
exacted of France, had been used in part to pay off the
debt obligations of the Government, and ready capital became so abundant that banking institutions of note almost

begged for the opportunity to place loans, at rates as low as one per cent, with manufacturers, for the purpose of enlarging their establishments. As a legitimate result, the whole country projected and engaged in all manner of new industrial and financial undertakings. Thousands of new concerns were called into existence, the management of which did not give the slightest attention to sound commercial principles. In Prussia alone six hundred and eighty-seven new joint-stock companies were founded during the year 1872 and the first six months of 1873, with an aggregate capital of $481,045,000. The sudden growth of industries, and the temptations of cities and towns (the sudden augmentation of which is so striking a feature in the history of Germany after the year 1870), had also induced hundreds of thousands of men and women to desert agricultural pursuits and to seek employment in trades. Such a state of things, as is now obvious, was most unnatural, and could not continue; and the reaction and disaster came with great suddenness, as has been already stated, in the fall of 1873, but without anticipation on the part of the multitude. Great fortunes rapidly melted away, industry became paralyzed, and the whole of Germany passed at once from a condition of apparently great prosperity to a depth of financial, industrial, and commercial depression that had never been equaled.

In the United States the phenomena antecedent to the crisis were enumerated at the time to be, " a rise of prices, great prosperity, large profits, high wages, and strikes for higher ; large importations, a railway mania, expanded credit, over-trading, over-building, and high living." The crisis began on the 17th of September, 1873, by the failure of a comparatively unimportant railway company — the New York and Oswego Midland. On the 18th, the banking-house of Jay Cooke & Co. failed. On the 19th, nineteen other banking-houses failed. Then followed a succession of bankruptcies, until in four years the mercantile failures had aggregated $775,865,000; and on January 1, 1876, the amount of American railway bonds in default amounted to $789,367,655.

The period of economic disturbance which thus began in Germany and the United States soon extended to France and Belgium; and thereafter, but with varying degrees of severity, to Great Britain (i. e., in the latter months of the succeeding year), to the other states of Europe, and ultimately to the commercial portions of almost every country. The testimony before the British Parliamentary Commission (1885–'86), however, shows that the depression in Great Britain was not at once universal; but that, on the contrary, production, employment, and profits, at such great manufacturing centers as Birmingham and Huddersfield, were above the average until 1875.

By many writers on this subject, the depression and disturbance of industry, which commenced in 1873, are regarded as having terminated in 1878–'79; but all are agreed that they recommenced, with somewhat modified conditions, and even with increased severity, in 1882–'83. A full consideration of the larger evidence which is now (1889) available would, however, seem to lead to the conclusion that there really was no termination of the abnormal course of events, and the marked definite commencement of which is assigned to 1873, but that what has been regarded as a "termination" was only an "interruption," occasioned by extraordinary causes, varying locally, and by no means universal. Thus, a failure during the years 1879, 1880, and 1881, of the cereal crops of Europe and most other countries of the world, with the exception of the United States— a failure for which, in respect to duration and extent, there had been no parallel in four centuries—occasioned a remarkable demand on the latter country for all the food-products it could supply at extraordinary prices—the exportations of wheat rising from 40,000,000 bushels in 1877 to 122,000,000 in 1879, 153,000,000 in 1880, and 150,000,000 in 1881; while the corresponding values of the amount exported rose from $47,000,000 in 1877 to $130,000,000 in 1879, $190,000,000 in 1880, and $167,000,000 in 1881.   There was also a corresponding increase in the quantity and value of the American exports of other cereals, and also of most meat products and provisions.*

Such a demand at extraordinary prices for crops, beyond the average in quantity and quality, brought temporary prosperity to American producers, and indúced great industrial and commercial activity throughout the United States; and although the crops of other countries were notably far below the average, yet the great advance in prices undoubtedly went far to alleviate the distress of the foreign agriculturist, even if it did not in some cases actually better his condition and increase his purchasing power of other than food-products.   The extent to which the American producer availed himself of his increased purchasing power during the years under consideration is indicated by the increase which occurred in the importation of foreign merchandise on the part of the United States, namely, from $437,051,000 in 1878 to $667,954,000 in 1880, and $722,-639,000 in 1882.   Such an increase represented payment in part for American exports ($110,575,000 in gold and silver being imported in addition in 1881), and a corresponding demand for the products of foreign industries—the special effect on British industry being characterized by a statement from one of the witnesses before the Royal Commission (a representative of one of the districts of Liverpool) that " the depression continued until 1880, when there occurred an American boom, which temporarily lifted prices and induced

---

* No. 1 spring wheat, which commanded $1.05 per bushel in the New York market on the 1st January, 1878, was quoted at $1.60 at a corresponding date in 1879 ; and at $1.39 in 1881.   The corresponding advance in corn was from 45 cents per bushel in 1878 to 63 cents in 1879, and 70 cents in 1881 ; while the advance in mess-pork was from $7.05 per barrel in 1878 to $12.62½ in 1879, and $17 in 1881.

activity." The testimony of other witnesses was, however, to the effect that in many branches of British industry there was no improvement of condition either in 1878, 1880, or in any subsequent year; the Commission itself reporting (in December, 1886) that there was a general agreement among those whom it consulted that the depression under consideration, " so far as Great Britain was concerned, dates from about the year 1875, and, with the exception of a short period enjoyed by certain branches of trade in the years 1880 to 1883, it has proceeded with tolerable uniformity, and has affected the trade and industry of the country generally, especially those branches connected with agriculture." The Commission further reported that the information received by them leads to the conclusion that " in Belgium, France, Russia, Scandinavia, Spain, and the United States," the depression has been " almost identical in its leading features with that existing in the United Kingdom."

In Germany and Belgium the reaction experienced in 1879, it is admitted, did not extend beyond 1882.

In France the condition of agricultural and other laborers continued so deplorable that the French Chamber of Deputies appointed a special commission of inquiry in 1884 with a view to devising measures for relief; while in Great Britain the condition of trade and industry has uninterruptedly been regarded since 1882–'83 with great anxiety. There is a very general agreement of opinion in England and on the Continent of Europe that the years 1879, 1885, and 1886 were the worst that have been experienced in the period commencing with 1873. In England, France, and Germany, the increase or decrease in exports is popularly regarded as an indication of the condition of business, and, assuming 100 to represent the exports for 1883, the decline in the value of the exports of these several countries since that year may be represented as follows: England, 1883, 100; 1884, 92·2 ; 1885, 88·5, a falling off in two years of 11·5 per cent. The record of France is better—1883, 100;

1884, 93·1; 1885, 92·3, a falling off of 7·7 per cent; while Germany falls behind both countries: 1882, 100; 1883, 98; 1884, 89; 1885, 87·5, a falling off of 12·5 per cent. The transport of merchandise on all the French railways, calculated in tons carried one kilometre, fell progressively from 11,064,000,000 in 1883 to 8,804,000,000 in 1886; the water-carriage of France for the same period, calculated in the same manner, remaining stationary.

The extreme depression of business in the United States in 1884–'85 showed itself very curiously in the diminution of the receipts of the postal service of the country. In October, 1883, the rates of letter-postage were reduced from three to two cents per half-ounce. The aggregate receipts fell off—as was to be expected—but the deficiency for the second year under the reduced rate was largely in excess of what was experienced the first year, although population had increased by at least a million during the second period.

For the year 1887 there was a general concurrence of opinion that the world's business experienced a marked improvement.

Reviewing the condition of British trade and industry, the London "Economist," in its "Commercial History and Review of 1887," says:

That we did a distinctly bigger business than in 1886 there can be no doubt. Whether it was a more profitable business is another question, and one which it is more difficult to answer. In certain branches of trade manufacturers did undoubtedly improve their position. It was so in the finished iron trade, in ship-building, in the spinning branches of the cotton trade, in the jute trade, and probably in the woolen trade as a whole. And in other branches, if there is no improvement to record, there was certainly little, if any, retrogression. It appears somewhat anomalous that a year which has witnessed these changes for the better in the general condition of (British) trade should also have been characterized by louder complaints of lack of employment for and of distress among our working population.

For 1887 the foreign trade of France, calculated on the returns for 1886, showed a small improvement.

On the other hand, the condition of trade and industry in Russia, which is almost exclusively an agricultural and pastoral country, continues, as it has been for recent years, to be one of extreme depression.   In the production of wheat she has had to compete with two great competitors, the United States and India, both of which have had decided advantages in the contest.   Both the United States and India, too, have gained more by the great reduction in the cost of ocean carriage than has Russia, which, moreover, has suffered from many special difficulties ; her political and economical position having necessitated a considerable increase in taxation, which has added to the cost of production, while some of her best and most accessible customers have shut out her cereal produce as far as possible by the imposition of high customs duties.*

In Spain and Portugal the economic condition of affairs during 1887 and 1888 was reported as most deplorable. In the former country emigration was assuming alarming proportions ; and with a depression alike of agriculture and manufactures, the disposition to gain relief by the exclusion of all foreign competing products, or by further restrictions on foreign trade, was becoming almost universal.

During the year 1888, owing to an undoubted expansion of trade and a marked rise in the prices of a few commodities, " which bulk largely in the eyes of the public, there was a general disposition in England to believe that there had been a distinct rise in the general level of prices."   According, however, to the London " Economist," an examination of all available data failed to confirm any such conclusion ; but, on the contrary, showed that, eliminating from the discussion a marked advance in the prices of the two

---

* A striking illustration of the condition of Russian cultivators is supplied by the fact that some 80,000 of them have surrendered their land, finding the costs incidental to ownership surpass the profits thereof, while the army of beggars includes in its ranks landowners numbered by tens of thousands.—*Correspondence London " Economist," November,* 1887.

metals lead and copper—which was wholly due to speculative influences—the general level of prices for 1888 was not materially different from what it was in 1887. For the United States, according to the New York " Commercial Bulletin," there was no recovery of prices, the year 1888 closing with prices fully six per cent lower than at its commencement.

One point of interest which is here specially worthy of note from its bearing on the discussion of causes, is that the recurrence of the period of depression in 1882, after the favorable reaction which occurred to a greater or less extent in 1879, was quiet and gradual, as if matters were naturally again assuming a normal condition, and was not preceded or accompanied by any marked financial or commercial disturbances. On the contrary, the money markets of the world remained " easy," and were characterized, as they have ever since been, by a plethora of capital seeking investment and a low rate of interest; so that the economic disturbance since 1882 has been mainly in the nature of a depression of industry, with a renewed and remarkable decline of prices; with absolutely no decline, but rather an increase in the volume of trade, and certainly no falling off in production, as compared with the figures of 1880 and 1881, which years in the United States, and to some extent in other countries, were regarded as prosperous.

The following presentation, chronologically arranged, of brief extracts from various publications since 1872–'73, will further assist to a recollection and comprehension of the course of events since that period, and also exhibit the opinions which have been expressed at different times, respecting the " influence," " causes," and duration of the so-called " depression of trade and industry," by those who, by position or investigation, have assumed to speak with more or less of authority on the subject. And, with this intent, attention is first asked to the following retrospect of the curious experience of the iron and steel industry of the

United States, as exhibited by quotations from the reports
of the American Iron and Steel Association from 1873 to
1887 :

1873. The year 1872 opened with an increased demand for iron in
nearly all civilized countries.   Prices advanced rapidly in all markets.
The supply was unequal to the demand, although production was
everywhere stimulated.—*Report of the American Iron and Steel Association, November, 1873.*

1874. The reaction (in the world's demand for iron) in 1874 has
been as general and decided as the advance in 1872 was unexpected
and bewildering.   It has been felt most severely in the United States;
but in the United Kingdom, and in France and Germany, the iron
industry has been so much depressed, all through the year, that many
iron-works have been closed, and many others have been employed
but a part of the time.   The testimony of statistics, and of all calm
observers, shows that prostration is greater at the close of 1874 than
it was at the close of 1873, and that the general distress is greater.
At least a million of skilled and unskilled workingmen and working-
women in this country are out of employment to-day, because there is
no work for them to do.—*Report, December 31, 1874.*

1877. Since 1873 each year has shown a decrease in the production
of pig-iron in the United States, as compared with the preceding year,
the percentage of decrease being as follows : 1874, six per cent; 1875,
fifteen per cent; 1876, eight per cent.   This is a very great shrinkage,
and indicates, with concurrent low prices, a very great depression in
the pig-iron industry of the country.   If the rate of decrease which
marked the period from 1873 to 1876 were to be continued, the production of pig-iron in the United States would entirely cease in 1884,
less than eight years from the present time, and our furnace-stacks
would only be useful as observatories for the study of astronomy.—
Report, June, 1887.

1878. More than one half of the furnaces, and many of the rolling-
mills, were idle the whole year.   Prices were so low as to warrant the
impression that they could be no lower.—*Report, July, 1878.*

1879. In nearly all the branches of the domestic iron and steel industries there has been an increased production in 1878 over 1877; but
this increase in production has been accompanied by a decrease in
prices.   At no time in the history of the country have prices for iron
and steel been as low as they were in 1878, excepting in colonial days,
when the price of pig-iron was lower.—*Report, May 6, 1879.*

1880. Near the close of 1878 it became evident that the business depression which had succeeded the panic of 1873 was slowly disappearing, and that a general revival of prosperity was at hand.   In the closing months of 1879 excitement and speculation took the place of the gloom and discouragement with which the American iron-trade had been so familiar scarce one year before, and the business of buying and selling iron became close neighbor to that of gambling in stocks. —*Report, May, 1880.*

No. 1 pig-iron, which sold for $53 per ton at Philadelphia in September, 1872, sold for $24 in 1874, $21.25 in 1876, $16.50 in 1878, $41 in February, 1880, and $25 in May, 1880.

1882. The year 1881 was the most prosperous year American iron and steel manufacturers have ever known.—*Report, June, 1882.*

1883. The extraordinary activity in our iron and steel industries, which commenced in 1879, culminated early in 1882.   The reaction was not sudden, but was so gradual and tranquil that for some time it excited no apprehension.   In November and December the market was greatly depressed.   At the beginning of December, 1881, the average price of steel rails at the (American) mills was $60 per ton, but in December, 1882, the average price was only $39.*   In all the fluctuations of iron and steel that have taken place in this country, we know of none so sweeping as this decline in the price of steel rails, if we except in 1879 and 1880, and many of these were entirely speculative.— *Report, May, 1883.*

The cause of this serious reaction was attributed, in the same report, in great measure to the circumstance that " we had increased our capacity for the production of most forms of iron and steel much faster than the consumptive wants of the country had increased."

1884. Since the publication of the last annual report, in May, 1883, the unsatisfactory condition of the American iron-trade, as it then existed, has not improved.   It has steadily grown worse.—*Report, May, 1884.*

1887. The year 1886 was one of the most active years the American

---

* The average price of Bessemer steel rails, which commanded $39 per ton at American mills in December, 1882, declined to $28.50 in 1885.   For 1886 it was $34.50; for January, 1887, $31.50.

iron-trade has ever experienced. The improvement in demand which had commenced in the latter part of 1885 was well maintained throughout the whole of 1886. The production of the year in all the leading branches of the trade was much the largest in our history. The remote causes of the revival in the prosperity of the American iron-trade which began in the last half of 1885, and still continues, may be difficult to discover; but one influential immediate cause is directly traceable to the meeting of the Bessemer steel-rail manufacturers in August, 1885, at which meeting a restriction of production for one year to avoid the evils of over-production and ruinous prices was agreed upon. This action was almost immediately followed by beneficial results to the iron-trade of the whole country, and to many other branches of domestic industry. An incident of our industrial history for 1886 was the large number of strikes among workingmen. More American workingmen were voluntarily out of employment in that year than in any previous year.—*Report for April, 1887.*

The year 1887 was the most active year in the history of the American iron-trade, far exceeding all previous years, including the remarkable year 1886, in the production and consumption of iron and steel in all their leading forms. In two years, from 1885 to 1887, we increased our production of pig-iron fifty-eight per cent; our production of Bessemer steel ingots, ninety-three per cent; our production of Bessemer steel rails, one hundred and nineteen per cent; and our production of open-hearth steel ingots, one hundred and forty-one per cent. These figures tell a story of truly wonderful progress, such as has been witnessed in no other great industry in this country, and in no other iron-making country.—*Report for May, 1888.*

The report for January, 1889, may be regarded as in the nature of a natural sequence from the antecedent conditions above reported.

There was a decline in the aggregate production of iron and steel in 1888 as compared with 1887, and there was a shrinkage in prices; so that the year was not a prosperous one for our iron and steel manufactures, although production was still very large. We did not consume as much pig-iron as in 1887. The shrinkage in consumption of Bessemer steel rails in 1888, as compared with 1887, was 790,180 gross tons; the greatest that has occurred since the collection of the statistics of these industries was undertaken. No. 1 anthracite pig-iron at Philadelphia declined within the year from $21 to $18 per ton; steel rails from $31.50 to $27.50.

The following extracts from published statements and opinions are more general in their nature, but not less instructive :

1876. Our country is now passing through a period of unusual depression, both in its industries and its business. The present depressed condition of business and of financial affairs exists over all countries having a high civilization. — *Facts and Observations addressed to the Committee on Finance of the Mutual Life-Insurance Company of New York, July, 1876. Printed for the Private Convenience of the Trustees.*

1876. The inquiry has been sufficiently broad to enable them (the committee) to point out with a considerable degree of accuracy the causes which have immediately operated to produce the present depression in the commerce of the country, and in some branches of its manufacturing and mining industries. These causes are quite beyond legislative control in this country.—*Report of Select Committee of the House of Commons, Dominion of Canada, 1876.*

1877. Hard times! For four years this sober pass-word has gained in gravity of import. For a time it was panic; but suppositions of speedy recovery have given place to a conviction of underlying facts that these hard times are more than a panic; that the existing depressions of trade and dearth of employment are not, in popular apprehension, exaggerated, but are the serious results of causes more permanent in their nature than is generally considered.—*Hard Times, by Franklin W. Smith, Boston, 1877, James R. Osgood & Co.*

CONGRESS OF THE UNITED STATES,
HOUSE OF REPRESENTATIVES, *June* 17, 1878.

1878. Mr. Thompson submitted the following resolution, which was agreed to :

Whereas, labor and the productive interests of the country are greatly depressed, and suffering severely from causes not yet fully understood, etc. : Therefore,

Resolved, That a committee of seven members of this House be appointed, whose duty it shall be to inquire into and ascertain the causes of general business depression, etc., and report at the next session.

1878. Commercial depression is the universal cry—a commercial depression probably unprecedented in duration in the annals of trade, except under the disturbing action of prolonged war. . . . Ample evidence abounds on all sides to show its extent and severity in England.

Have other countries bowed their heads in suffering under the commercial depression? Let America be the first to speak. In 1873 she experienced a shock of the most formidable kind. She has not recovered from the shock at this very hour. Let us visit Germany—Germany the conqueror in a great war, and the exactor of an unheard-of indemnity. What do we find in that country? Worse commercial weather at this hour than in any other. Nowhere are louder complaints uttered of the stagnation of trade. Austria and Hungary repeat the cry, but in a somewhat lower voice. And so we come round to France, the people whose well-being has been so visited with the most violent assaults. Her losses and sufferings have surpassed those endured by any other nation. Yet the deep, heavy pressure of her commercial paralysis has weighed upon her the least oppressive of all. Such a depression, spread over so many countries, inflicting such continuous distress, and lasting for so long a period of time, the history of trade has probably never before exhibited.—BONAMY PRICE, *Contemporary Review, 1878.*

1879. The prevailing depression in business from which this country has suffered for six years, and from which nearly every country in Europe is suffering still, has probably furnished support to a greater number of conflicting economical theories than any other occurrence of ancient or modern times. . . . The result, we need hardly say, has not been to raise the reputation of political economy as a science. In fact, it has never seemed so little of a science as during the past five years, owing to the extraordinary array of proof and illustration which the holders of the most widely divergent views have been able to produce.—*The Nation (New York), May, 1879.*

1879. We have just passed through a period of depression, of which, though it came in perfect agreement with all past experiences, was complicated by such an exceptional conglomeration of untoward circumstances, and protracted to such a weary length, that men seemed to lose faith in the revival which was almost certain to come sooner or later, and began to ask whether the commercial supremacy of this country was not permanently undermined. And now, with the new decade, the revival is really here.—*The Recent Depression of Trade, being the Oxford Cobden Prize Essay for 1879, by Walter E. Smith, London, Trübner & Co., 1880.*

1881. The industrial depression is generally thought to have commenced in the closing months of 1874, and it increased in intensity throughout 1876 and 1877.—*Prof.* HENRY FAWCETT, " *Free Trade and Protection,*" *London, 1881.*

1885. The present depression of trade is remarkable, not so much for its intensity or for its extent—in both of which respects it has been equaled or surpassed on previous occasions—but for its persistence during the long period of eleven years. The industrial depression is generally thought to have commenced in the closing months of 1874; and, during every succeeding year, it has continued to be felt with more or less severity, and its remarkable persistence has been commented on by politicians and public writers. Usually a period of depression is quickly followed by one of comparative prosperity. Such a reaction has been again and again predicted in this case, but, up to the present time, there are no satisfactory indications that the evil days are passing away. It is evident, therefore, that we are suffering in an altogether exceptional manner; that the disease of the social organism is due to causes which have not been in action on former occasions, and that the remedial agencies which have been effective on former occasions have now failed us.—*Bad Times, an Essay on the Present Depression of Trade, by Alfred Russel Wallace, London, October, 1885.*

The following are notable extracts from the testimony presented to the Royal (British) Commission, appointed August, 1885, to inquire into the depression of trade and industry, and embodied in their reports submitted to Parliament in 1885–'86 :

1885. At the present time a general depression of trade and industry is stated to exist throughout Italy. While, however, depression is general, it does not act uniformly on all industries.—*Testimony of Ellis Colnaghi, Her Majesty's Consul-General at Florence, October 8, 1885.*

The depression began full ten years ago, and still continues.—*Testimony of the Linen Merchants' Association of Belfast, Ireland, November, 1885.*

The origin of the depression from which we suffer, and which is at the lowest point yet reached, seems to be a reaction from the coal-famine period of 1872–'74, and which was perhaps due to the inflation consequent on the Franco-German War in 1870. The progress of depression has been irregular, but with a persistent downward tendency since 1874. The present tendency is still downward.—*Testimony of the North of England Iron Manufacturers' Association, September, 1885.*

The depression has been increasing in intensity during the last four years. It was probably never greater than at present at this season of the year.—*Testimony of the British Paper-Makers' Association, September, 1885.*

Trade began to be depressed in 1876, and has continued so until the year 1883, with intermittent spurts of improvement. But from the end of 1883 the depression has become increasingly acute.—*Testimony of North Staffordshire Chamber of Commerce, October 21, 1885.*

As a proof of the deplorable state this trade [woolen-yarn spinning, Huddersfield, England] has been in for the last ten or fifteen years, we most respectfully beg to inform you, we hold the list of fifty firms of spinners who have been ruined and brought into bankruptcy court during that period. Another proof of the very serious state of trade here is to be found in the depreciated value of carding and spinning machinery. Good machines, and for all practical purposes equal to new, if brought into the market will only realize some thirty or forty per cent of their cost price. Mill property is also in a similar position.—*Report of the Huddersfield (England) Chamber of Commerce, October, 1885.*

1886. Out of the total number of establishments, such as factories, mines, etc., existing in the country [the United States], about eight per cent were absolutely idle during the year ending July 1, 1885, and perhaps five per cent more were idle a part of such time; or, for a just estimate, seven and a half per cent of the whole number of such establishments were idle, or equivalent to idle, during the year named. . . . Making allowance for the persons engaged in other occupations, 998,-839 constituted "the best estimate" of the possibly unemployed in the United States during the year ending July 1, 1885 (many of the unemployed, those who under prosperous times would be fully employed, and who during the time mentioned were seeking employment), that it has been possible for the Bureau to make. . . . A million people out of employment, crippling all dependent upon them, means a loss to the consumptive power of the country of at least $1,000,000 per day, or a crippling of the trade of the country of over $300,000,000 per annum.—*Report on Industrial Depression, United States Bureau of Labor, 1886.*

1886. The present crisis has a much more general character than any of the crises which have preceded it; because it is a part of an abrupt transformation in the production and circulation of the whole world. For the same reason, it is destined to last longer.—M. LEROY BEAULIEU, *Revue des Deux Mondes, 1886.*

Summarizing very briefly the answers which we received to our questions and the oral evidence given before us, there would appear to be a general agreement among those we consulted:

a. That the trade and industry of the country are in a condition which may be fairly described as depressed.

b. That by this depression is meant a diminution, and, in some cases, an absence of profit, with a corresponding diminution of employment for the laboring-classes.

c. That neither the volume of trade nor the amount of capital invested therein has materially fallen off, though the latter has in many cases depreciated in value.

d. That the depression above referred to dates from about the year 1875, with the exception of a short period of prosperity enjoyed by certain branches of trade in the years 1880 to 1883.—*Report of British Commission, December, 1886.*

There is one condition revealed—i. e., by the statistics of 1885-'86—that is very noticeable : which is, that prices in general touched the lowest point in a quarter of a century. There were those who supposed that the shrinking processes had been arrested in the preceding year, and yet the figures for 1885-'86, in nearly all departments of business, show lower prices than the previous year.—*Report of the Chamber of Commerce, Cincinnati, 1886.*

It is of interest to note how few, relatively, of the staples, raw materials or finished products, have left the year 1886 with any special gain in price as compared with one year or with two years ago, and it is even more striking to enumerate the list of those which show actually no gain at all, or a loss in price.—*Bradstreet's Journal, January, 1887.*

Wheat, oats, sugar, butter, tobacco, and petroleum were lower in price at the close of 1886 than at the close of 1885. Corn, oats, pork, lard, and cotton were lower at the close of 1876 than at the beginning of 1885.—*Ibid.*

For conditions of trade for the year 1887 and 1888, see Chapter IV.

It is almost unnecessary to say that a subject of such transcendent importance, and affecting so intimately the material interests alike of nations and individuals, has naturally attracted a great and continually increasing attention throughout the whole civilized world, entailing at least one notable result, namely, that of a large and varied contribution to existing economic literature. Thus, state commissions for inquiring into the phenomena under consideration have been instituted by Great Britain, the United States,

France, Italy, and the Dominion of Canada, all of which
have taken evidence and reported more or less voluminously;
the report of the Royal British Commission (1885–'86),
comprising five folio volumes of an aggregate of about 1,800
pages; while the books, pamphlets, magazine articles, and
review's on the same subject, including investigations and
discussions on collateral matters regarded as elements or
results of the economic problem (such as the wide-spread
ferment and discontent of labor, and the changes in the
monetary functions of gold and silver), which have ema-
nated from individuals or commissions, have been sufficiently numerous to constitute, if collected, a not inconsiderable library.

In all these investigations and discussions, the chief objective has been the recognition or determination of causes;
and most naturally and legitimately, inasmuch as it is clear
that only through such recognitions and determinations can
the atmosphere of mystery which to a certain extent envel-
ops the phenomena under consideration be dispelled, and
the way prepared for an intelligent discussion of remedies.
And on this point the opinions or conclusions expressed
have been widely and most curiously different.   Nearly all
investigators are agreed that the wide-spread and long-continued " depression of business " is referable not to one but
a variety of causes, which have been more or less influential;
and among such causes the following are generally regarded
as having been especially potential : " Over-production ";
" the scarcity and appreciation of gold," or " the depreciation of silver, through its demonetization "; " restrictions of
the free course of commerce " through protective tariffs on
the one hand, and excessive and unnatural competition
occasioned by excessive foreign imports contingent on the
absence of " fair " trade or protection on the other; heavy
national losses, occasioned by destructive wars, especially
the Franco-Prussian War; the continuation of excessive
war expenditures; the failure of crops; the unproductive-

ness of foreign loans or investments; excessive speculation and reaction from great inflations; strikes and interruption of production consequent on trades-unions and other organizations of labor; the concentration of capital in few hands, and a consequent antagonizing influence to the equitable diffusion of wealth; "excessive expenditures for alcoholic beverages, and a general improvidence of the working-classes." A Dutch committee, in 1886, found an important cause in "the low price of German vinegar." In Germany, in 1886-'88, the continuance of trade depression has been assigned in a great measure to the "inflammable condition of international affairs," and to "looming war"; although the great decline in the price of beet-root sugar, and the "immigration of Polish Jews," are also cited as having been influential.

In the investigations undertaken by committees of Congress in the United States, the causes assigned by the various witnesses who testified before them were comprised under no less than one hundred and eighty heads; and an almost equal diversity of opinion was manifested by the witnesses who appeared before the Royal (British) Commission.* The special causes to which a majority of the Commission itself attached any great degree of importance, stated in the order presented by them, are as follows : 1. Changes in the distribution of wealth i. e., in Great Britain; 2. Natural tendency to diminution in the rate of profit consequent on the progressive accumulation of capital; 3. Over-production; 4. Impairment of agricultural industry consequent on bad seasons, and the competition of the products of other

---

* The Birmingham Chamber of Commerce attributed it in great part to German and Belgian competition, to foreign import duties on home-manufactured goods exported abroad, and exorbitant railway rates ; the Hartlepool Chamber to foreign competition ; Manchester, the same ; Leeds, "to foreign tariffs " ; Liverpool, to a loss in a once large re-export trade in cotton ; Wolverhampton, to changes in the hours of labor resulting from the operation of the Factory, Workshop, and Education Acts, and the action of the various trades-unions.

soils which can be cultivated under more favorable conditions; 5. Foreign tariffs and bounties and the restrictive commercial policies of foreign countries; 6. The working of the British Limited Liability Act. In addition to these special causes, others of a general character were mentioned; such as "the more limited possibilities of new sources of demand throughout the world, and the larger amount of capital seeking employment"; "the serious fall in prices"; "the appreciation of the standard of value" so far as connected with the fall of prices and foreign competition. A respectable minority of the commission also included, in the list of principal causes, the effect of British legislation, regulating the hours and conditions of labor on the cost of production as compared with other countries; and the discriminations given by British railways to foreign producers in the conveyance of goods.

It would seem as if one could not acquaint himself to any considerable extent with the great body of literature on this subject of the recent depression of trade, without becoming impressed with the tendency of many writers and investigators of repute, and of most of the persons who have given testimony before the commissions of different countries, to greatly magnify the influence of purely local causes. "The real and deep-seated cause of all our distress," says the "Oxford Prize Essay" for 1879, "is this: the whole world is consuming more than it has produced, and is consequently in a state of impoverishment, and can not buy our wares."

Nearly all British writers dwell upon the immense losses to British farming capital, contingent upon deficient crops since 1875, and the decline in the value and use of arable land in the United Kingdom, and concurrent decline in the price of agricultural produce, due to foreign competitive supplies, as prime factors in accounting for trade depression; while, throughout much of the testimony given before the British Commission by British manufacturers and merchants, the injurious influence of hostile foreign tariffs on the exports of British manufactures, and the competition of foreign manufactures in the British home market, are continually referred to as having been especially productive of industrial disturbance. In France, the principal assigned causes are, excessive speculation prior to 1873, followed by bad crops; the great falling off in the production of wine through the destruction of vineyards by the phylloxera; * a serious depression of the silk-trade industry; the disappearance of sardines and other fish from the coast of Brittany; excessive taxation; excessive increase in manufactured products; and restricted markets due to the competition of foreign nations paying less wages. In Italy a succession of bad crops, a disease among the silk-worms, and a stagnation of the silk industry, are prominently cited; in Denmark, bad harvests, a disturbed state of internal politics, an alteration in the metallism of the country in 1873, and general over-production of manufactured products, are popularly assigned as sufficient causes; and in Germany, in recent years, to fears of international disturbances and decline in the prices of beet-root sugar.

Excessive taxation upon trade and industry, as a leading cause of trade depression, has also found strong advocacy, and the evidence brought forward is certainly impressive. The annual burden of taxation in Europe for military and

---

* A writer in the " Economiste Français " (1888) estimates the total loss to France from the ravages of the phylloxera since 1875, when this scourge of the French vineyards first made its appearance, at the enormous sum of 10,000,000,000 francs, or about $2,000,000,000; a sum nearly double the amount of the war indemnity of 1871. This estimate is based upon French official statistics giving the aggregate area of vineyards destroyed in the country about 2,500,000 acres, and, on the assumption that, in addition to the acreage of vines thus utterly destroyed, the extent of vineyards more or less infested with the phylloxera amounts to about 500,000 acres, making thus together 3,000,000 acres. This calamity has followed very closely upon the losses of the war, which, in addition to the indemnity, were very great; and has also been concurrent with a great increase in public expenditures and in national taxation every year since that period.

naval purposes at the present time is estimated as at least £200,000,000 ($1,000,000,000). In France, the complaints as to the pressure of taxation on industry are universal. The imperial taxation in 1884 was reported at £120,000,000 ($600,000,000) on a population of 37,000,000. Local taxation in France is also very heavy, the *octroi* duties for Paris alone for the year 1884 having amounted to 139,000,000 francs ($27,800,000), in addition to which were other heavy municipal taxes, as, for example, on carriages, horses, cabs, dogs, market-stalls, funerals, clubs, canals, the keeping of shops, and other commodities and occupations.—*Testimony of J. A. Crowe, British Commission.*

In Italy, according to the British consul-general at Florence (British Commission), the income-tax in 1884 was above thirteen per cent, and the land-tax in some instances as high as twenty-five per cent upon the gross rental. These are independent of local taxation, included in which is the *octroi*, which is also described as " very onerous, and, not being confined to articles of food only, have raised a quantity of small internal barriers, which, in a minor degree, replace the customs barriers of the several small states into which the country was formerly divided."

In respect to Great Britain, the British Commission, as the result of their investigations into this matter, says: " Of the fact of the increase, especially of local taxation, there is no doubt. At the same time it will probably be found that, relatively to the population and wealth of the country, the burden of taxation is now far lighter than in any previous periods."

The published opinions of certain persons of note on the subject are also worthy of attention. Mr. Alfred Russel Wallace, in his book entitled " Bad Times," London, 1885, expresses the opinion that among the most efficient causes for the current depression of trade are " wars and excessive armaments, loans to despots or for war purposes, and the accumulation of vast wealth by individuals."

Dr. Wirth, of Vienna, finds a like explanation in the excessive conversion, or rather perversion, of private wealth for public purposes. Dr. Engel, of Berlin, regards the millions wasted in war by France and Germany, from 1870 to 1871, and continued and prospective expenditures for like purposes, as culminating causes of almost universal business calamities; while, in the opinion of Prof. Thorold Rogers, the scarcity and consequent dearness of gold have been the factors of chief importance.

But side by side with all the theories that the "depression" has been occasioned by the destruction or non-production of vast amounts of property by wars, bad harvests, strikes, loss of capital by employment in worthless enterprises, the conversion of an undue amount of circulating capital into fixed capital, and extravagant consumption, should be placed the facts that statistics not only fail to reveal the existence of any great degree of scarcity anywhere, but, on the contrary, prove that those countries in which depression has been and is most severely felt are the very ones in which desirable commodities of every description—railroads, ships, houses, live-stock, food, clothing, fuel, and luxuries—have year by year been accumulating with the greatest rapidity, and offered for use or consumption at rates unprecedented for cheapness. If lack of capital, furthermore, by destruction or perversion, had been the cause, the rate of profit on the use of capital would have been higher; but the fact is, that the rate of profit on even the most promising kinds of capital during recent years has been everywhere exceptionally low.

Another notable tendency among investigators is to assign to clearly secondary causes or results, positions of primary importance. Thus (general) over-production,* or an amount

---

* No term has been used more loosely in the discussion of this subject of trade depression than that of " *over-production*." The idea that there can be such a thing as a general production of useful or desirable commodities in excess of what is wanted is an absurdity ; but there may be, as above stated, an amount of production in excess of demand at remunerative prices, or, what

of production of commodities in excess of demand at remunerative prices, finds greater favor as an agency of current
economic disturbance than any other. But surely all nations
and people could not, with one accord and almost concurrently, have entered upon a course of unprofitable production without being impelled by an agency so universal and
so irresistible as to almost become invested with the character of a natural law; and hence over-production obviously,
in any broad inquiry, must be accepted as a result rather
than a cause. And so, also, in respect to "metallism" and
the enactment of laws restrictive of commerce; for no one
can seriously suppose that silver has been demonetized or
tariffs enacted inadvertently, or at the whim and caprice of
individuals, with a view of occasioning either domestic or
international economic disturbances; but, on the contrary,
the only reasonable supposition is, that antecedent conditions or agencies have prompted to action in both cases, by
inducing a belief that measures of the kind specified were
in the nature of safeguards against threatened economic
evils, or as helps to, at least, local prosperity. And as crop
failures, the ravages of insects, the diseases of animals, the
disappearance of fish, and maladministration of government, are local and not necessarily permanent, they must all
clearly, in any investigation, be regarded as secondary and
not primary agencies. In short, the general recognition, by
all investigators, that the striking characteristic of the economic disturbance that has prevailed since 1873 is its universality, of necessity compels a recognition of the fact that the
agency which was mainly instrumental in producing it could
not have been local, and must have been universal in its influence and action. And the question of interest which next
presents itself is, Can any such agency, thus operative and
thus potential, be recognized? Let us inquire.

---

is substantially the same thing, an excess of capacity for production ; or the
term may be properly used to indicate a check on the distribution of products
consequent on the existence of such conditions.

II.

The place in history of the years from 1860 to 1885 inclusive—New conditions of production and distribution—The prime factors of economic disturbance—Illustrative examples—The Suez Canal—Influences of the telegraph on trade—Economy in the construction and management of vessels—Disappearance of the sailing-vessel — Revolution in the carrying-trade on land—The annual work service of the railroad—The Bessemer steel rail—Future supply of food commodities—Cheapening of iron—Displacement of labor by machinery—Natural gas—Application of machinery to the production and transportation of grain—Adam Smith and the manufacture of pins—The epoch of efficient machinery production—Influence of labor disturbances on inventions—Prospective disturbing agencies—Displacement of the steam-engine.

WHEN the historian of the future writes the history of the nineteenth century he will doubtless assign to the period embraced by the life of the generation terminating in 1885, a place of importance, considered in its relations to the interests of humanity, second to but very few, and perhaps to none, of the many similar epochs of time in any of the centuries that have preceded it; inasmuch as all economists who have specially studied this matter are substantially agreed that, within the period named, man in general has attained to such a greater control over the forces of Nature, and has so compassed their use, that he has been able to do far more work in a given time, produce far more product, measured by quantity in ratio to a given amount of labor, and reduce the effort necessary to insure a comfortable subsistence in a far greater measure than it was possible for him to accomplish twenty or thirty years anterior to the time of the present writing (1889). In the absence of sufficiently complete data, it is not easy, and perhaps not possible, to estimate accurately, and specifically state the average saving in time and labor in the world's work of production and distribution that has been thus achieved. In a few departments of industrial effort the saving in both of these factors has certainly amounted to seventy or eighty per cent; in not a few to more than fifty per cent.* Mr. Edward Atkinson, who has made this matter a special study, considers one third as the minimum average that can be accepted for the period above specified.† Other authorities are inclined to assign a considerably higher average. The deductions of Mr. William Fowler, Fellow of University College, London, are to the effect that the saving of labor since 1850 in the production of any given article amounts to forty per cent;‡ and the British Royal Commission

---

* According to the United States Bureau of Labor (report for 1886), the gain in the power of production in some of the leading industries of the United States "during the past fifteen or twenty years," as measured by the displacement of the muscular labor formerly employed to effect a given result (i. e., amount of product) has been as follows: In the manufacture of agricultural implements, from fifty to seventy per cent; in the manufacture of shoes, eighty per cent; in the manufacture of carriages, sixty-five per cent; in the manufacture of machines and machinery, forty per cent; in the silk-manufacture, fifty per cent, and so on.

† In a print-cloth factory in New England, in which the conditions of production were analyzed by Mr. Atkinson, the product per hand was found by him to have advanced from 26,531 yards, representing 3,382 hours' work in 1871, to 32,391 yards, representing 2,695 hours' work, in 1884—an increase of twenty-two per cent in product, and a decrease of twenty per cent in hours of labor. Converted into cloth of their own product, the wages of the operatives in this same mill would have yielded them 6,205 yards in 1871, as compared with 9,737 yards in 1884—an increase of $56\frac{22}{100}$ per cent. During the same period of years the prices of beef, pork, flour, oats, butter, lard, cheese, and wool in the United States declined more than twenty-five per cent.

A like investigation by the same authority of an iron-furnace in Pennsylvania showed that, comparing the results of the five years from 1860 to 1864 with the five years from 1875 to 1879, the product per hand advanced from 776 tons to 1,219 tons; that the gross value of the product remained about the same; that the number of hands was reduced from seventy-six to seventy-one; and that consumers gained a benefit of reduction in price from $27.95 per ton to $19.08.

‡ " Wages have greatly increased, but the cost of doing a given amount of

(minority report, 1886) characterizes the amount of labor required to accomplish a given amount of production and transport at the present time as *incomparably* less than was requisite forty years ago, and as " being constantly reduced."

But be this as it may, out of such results as are definitely known and accepted have come tremendous industrial and social disturbances, the extent and effect of which—and more especially of the disturbances which have culminated, as it were, in later years—it is not easy to appreciate without the presentation and consideration of certain typical and specific examples. To a selection of such examples, out of a large number that are available, attention is accordingly next invited.

Let us go back, in the first instance, to the year 1869, when an event occurred which was probably productive of more *immediate* and serious economic changes—industrial, commercial, and financial — than any other event of this century, a period of extensive war excepted. That was the opening of the Suez Canal. Before that time, and since the discovery by Vasco da Gama, in 1498, of the route to India by the Cape of Good Hope, all the trade of the Western hemispheres with the Indies and the East toiled slowly and uncertainly around the Cape, at an expenditure in time of from six to eight months for the round voyage. The contingencies attendant upon such lengthened voyages and service, as the possible interruption of commerce by war, or failure of crops in remote countries, which could not easily be anticipated, required that vast stores of Indian and Chinese products should be always kept on hand at the one spot in Europe where the consumers of such commodities could speedily supply themselves with any article they required ; and that spot, by reason of geographical position

---

work has greatly decreased, so that five men can now do the work which would have demanded the labor of eight men in 1850. If this be correct, the saving of labor is forty per cent in producing any given article."—*Appreciation of Gold*, WILLIAM FOWLER, *Fellow of University College, London*, 1886.

and commercial advantage, was England. Out of this condition of affairs came naturally a vast system of warehousing
in and distribution *from* England, and of British banking
and exchange. Then came the opening of the canal. What
were the results? The old transportation had been performed by ships, mainly sailing-vessels, fitted to go round
the Cape, and, as such ships were not adapted to the Suez
Canal, an amount of tonnage, estimated by some authorities
as high as two million tons, and representing an immense
amount of wealth, was virtually destroyed.* The voyage, in
place of occupying from six to eight months, has been so
greatly reduced that steamers adapted to the canal now
make the voyage from London to Calcutta, or *vice versa*, in
less than thirty days. The notable destruction or great impairment in the value of ships consequent upon the construction of the canal did not, furthermore, terminate with
its immediate opening and use; for improvements in marine
engines, diminishing the consumption of coal, and so enabling vessels to be not only sailed at less cost, but to carry
also more cargo, were, in consequence of demand for quick
and cheap service so rapidly effected, that the numerous and
expensive steamer constructions of 1870-'73, being unable
to compete with the constructions of the next two years, were
nearly all displaced in 1875-'76, and sold for half, or less
than half, of their original cost. And within another decade
these same improved steamers of 1875-'76 have, in turn,
been discarded and sold at small prices, as unfit for the
service of lines having an established trade, and replaced
with vessels fitted with the triple-expansion engines, and
saving nearly fifty per cent in the consumption of fuel.
And now " quadruple-expansion " engines are beginning to

---

* " The canal may therefore be said to have given a death-blow to sailing-
vessels, except for a few special purposes."—From a paper by Charles Mag-
niac, indorsed by the "London Economist" as a merchant of eminence and
experience, entitled to speak with authority, read before the Indian Section of
the London Society of Arts, February, 1876.

be introduced, and their tendency to supplant the "triple expansion" is "unmistakable."

In all commercial history, probably no more striking illustration can be found of the economic principle, that nothing marks more clearly the rate of material progress than the rapidity with which that which is old and has been considered wealth is destroyed by the results of new inventions and discoveries.*

Again, with telegraphic communication between India and China, and the markets of the Western world, permitting the dealers and consumers of the latter to adjust to a nicety their supplies of commodities to varying demands, and with the reduction of the time of the voyage to thirty days or less, there was no longer any necessity of laying up great stores of Eastern commodities in Europe; and with the termination of this necessity, the India warehouse and distribution system of England, with all the labor and all the capital and banking incident to it, substantially passed away. Europe, and to some extent the United States, ceased to go to England for its supplies. If Austria wants anything of Indian product, it stops *en route*, by the Suez Canal, at Trieste; if Italy, at Venice or Genoa; if France, at Marseilles; if Spain, at Cadiz. How great has been the disturbance thus occasioned in British trade is shown by the following figures: In 1871 the total exports of India were £57,556,000, of which £30,737,000 went to the United Kingdom; but in 1885, on a total Indian export of £85,-087,000, the United Kingdom received only £31,882,000. During the same time the relative loss on British exports to India was less than a million and a half sterling.

As a rule, also, stocks of Indian produce are now kept,

---

* "In the last analysis it will appear that there is no such thing as fixed capital; there is nothing useful that is very old except the precious metals, and all life consists in the conversion of forces. The only capital which is of permanent value is immaterial—the experience of generations and the develment of science."—EDWARD ATKINSON.

not only in the countries, but at the very localities of their
production, and are there drawn upon as they are wanted
for immediate consumption, with a greatly reduced employment of the former numerous and expensive intermediate
agencies.*   Thus, a Calcutta merchant or commission agent
at any of the world's great centers of commerce contracts
through a clerk and the telegraph with a manufacturer in
any country—it may be half round the globe removed—to
sell him jute, cotton, hides, spices, cutch, linseed, or other
like Indian produce.†   An inevitable steamer is sure to be
in an Eastern port, ready to sail upon short notice; the
merchandise wanted is bought by telegraph, hurried on

---

* In illustration of this curious point, attention is asked to the following
extract from a review of the trade of British India, for the year 1886, from the
"Times," of India, published at Bombay : "What the mercantile community "—i. e., of Bombay—"has suffered and is suffering from, is the very narrow margin which now exists between the producer and consumer.   Twenty
years ago the large importing houses held stocks, but nowadays nearly everything is sold to arrive, or bought in execution of native orders, and the bazaar
dealers, instead of European importers, have become the holders of stocks.
The cable and canal have to answer for the transformation ; while the ease
with which funds can be secured at home by individuals absolutely destitute
of all knowledge of the trade, and minus the capital to work it, has resulted in
the diminution of profits both to importers and to bazaar dealers."

† Familiar as are the public generally with the operations of the telegraph
and the changes in trade and commerce consequent upon its submarine extension, the following incident of personal experience may present certain features with which they are not acquainted: In the winter of 1884 the writer
journeyed from New York to Washington with an eminent Boston merchant
engaged in the Calcutta trade.   Calling upon the merchant the same evening,
after arrival in Washington, he said : "Here is something, Mr. ——, that may
interest you.   Just before leaving State Street, in Boston, yesterday forenoon,
I telegraphed to my agent in Calcutta, ' If you can buy hides and gunny-bags
at — price, and find a vessel ready to charter, buy and ship.'   When I arrived
here (Washington), this afternoon (4 P. M.), I found awaiting me this telegram
from my partner in Boston, covering another from Calcutta, received in answer
to my dispatch of the previous day, which read as follows : ' *Hides and gunny-
bags purchased, vessel chartered, and loading begun.*' "

Here, then, as an every-day occurrence, was the record of a transaction on
the other side of the globe, the correspondence in relation to which traveled a
distance equivalent to the entire circumference of the globe, all completed in a
space of little more than twenty-four hours !

board the ship, and the agent draws for the price agreed upon, through some bank with the shipping documents. In four weeks, in the case of England, and a lesser time for countries intermediate, the shipment arrives; the manufacturer pays the bill, either with his own money or his banker's; and, before another week is out, the cotton and the jute are going through the factory; the linseed has been converted into oil, and the hides in the tannery are being transformed into leather.

Importations of East Indian produce are also no longer confined in England and other countries to a special class of merchants; and so generally has this former large and special department of trade been broken up and dispersed, that extensive retail grocers in the larger cities of Europe and the United States are now reported as drawing their supplies direct from native dealers in both China and India.

Another curious and recent result of the Suez Canal construction, operating in a quarter and upon an industry that could not well have been anticipated, has been its effect on an important department of Italian agriculture—namely, the culture of rice. This cereal has for many years been a staple crop of Italy, and a leading article of Italian export— the total export for the year 1881 having amounted to 83,598 tons, or 167,196,000 pounds. Since the year 1878, however, rice grown in Burmah, and other parts of the far East, has been imported into Italy and other countries of Southern Europe in such enormous and continually increasing quantities, and at such rates, as to excite great apprehensions among the growers of Italian rice, and largely diminish its exportation—the imports of Eastern rice into Italy alone having increased from 11,957 tons in 1878 to 58,095 tons in 1887. For France, Italy, and other Mediterranean ports east, the importation of rice from Southern Asia (mainly from Burmah) was 152,147 tons in 1887, as compared with about 20,000 tons in 1878.

That the same causes are also exerting a like influence

upon the marketing of the cereal crops of the United States is shown by the circumstance that the freight rates on the transport of grain from Bombay to England, by way of the Suez Canal, declined from 32·5 cents per bushel in 1880, to 16·2 cents in 1885; and, to the extent of this decline, the ability of the Indian ryot to compete with the American grain-grower, in the markets of Europe, was increased.

How great was the disturbance occasioned in the general prices of the commodities that make up Eastern commerce by the opening of the Suez Canal, and how quickly prices responded to the introduction of improvements in distribution, is illustrated by the following experience: The value of the total trade of India with foreign countries, exclusive of its coasting-trade, was estimated, at the time of the opening of the canal in 1869, at £105,500,000 ($527,500,000). In 1874, however, the value was estimated at only £95,500,000, or at a reduction of ten per cent; and the inference might naturally have been that such a large reduction as ten millions sterling ($50,000,000) in five years, with a concurrent increase in the world's population, could only indicate a reduction of quantities. But that such was not the case was shown by the fact that 250,000 tons more shipping (mainly steam, and therefore equivalent to at least 500,000 more tons of sail) was employed in transporting commodities between India and foreign countries in 1874 than in 1869; or, that while the value of the trade, through a reduction of prices had notably declined during this period, the quantities entering into trade had so greatly increased during the same time, that 250,000 tons more shipping were required to convey it.

In short, the construction of the Suez Canal completely revolutionized one of the greatest departments of the world's commerce and business; absolutely destroying an immense amount of what had previously been wealth, and displacing or changing the employment of millions of capital and thousands of men; or, as the London "Economist" has expressed it, " so altered and so twisted many of the existing modes and channels of business as to create mischief and confusion " to an extent sufficient to constitute one great general cause for a universal commercial and industrial depression and disturbance.

The deductions from the most recent tonnage statistics of Great Britain come properly next in order for consideration. During the ten years from 1870 to 1880, inclusive, the British mercantile marine increased its movement, in the matter of foreign entries and clearances alone, to the extent of 22,000,000 tons; or, to put it more simply, the British mercantile marine exclusively engaged in foreign trade did so much more work within the period named; and yet the number of men who were employed in effecting this great movement had decreased in 1880, as compared with 1870, to the extent of about three thousand (2,990 exactly). What did it? The introduction of steam hoisting-machines and grain-elevators upon the wharves and docks, and the employment of steam-power upon the vessels for steering, raising the sails and anchors, pumping, and discharging the cargo; or, in other words, the ability, through the increased use of steam and improved machinery, to carry larger cargoes in a shorter time, with no increase—or, rather, an actual decrease—of the number of men employed in sailing or managing the vessels.

Statistical investigations of a later date furnish even more striking illustrations to the same effect from this industrial specialty. Thus, for 1870, the number of hands (exclusive of masters) employed to every one thousand tons capacity, entered or cleared of the British steam mercantile marine, is reported to have been forty-seven, but in 1885 it was only 27·7, or seventy per cent more manual labor was required in 1870 than in 1885 to do the same work. In sailing-vessels the change, owing to a lesser degree of improvement in the details of navigation, has been naturally smaller, but nevertheless considerable; twenty-seven hands being required in 1885 as against thirty-five in 1870 for the same tonnage entered or cleared.* Another fact of interest is, that the recent increase in the proportion of large vessels constructed has so greatly increased the efficiency of shipping, and so cheapened the cost of sea-carriage, to the advantage of both producers and consumers, that much business that was before impossible has become quite possible. Of the total British tonnage constructed in 1870, only six per cent was of vessels in excess of two thousand tons burden; but in 1884 fully seventeen per cent was of vessels of that size, or larger. Meanwhile, the cost of new iron (or steel) ships has been greatly reduced; from $90 per ton in 1872-'74 to $65 in 1877, $57 in 1880, while in 1887 first-class freighting screw-steamers, constructed of steel, fitted with triple compound engines, with largely increased carrying capacity (in comparison with former iron construction) and consequent earning power, and capable of being worked at less expense, could have been furnished for $33.95 per ton.†

---

* The official statistics do not show in the British mercantile marine whether the economy of labor which was effected prior to 1886 has continued to be progressive; inasmuch as the totals for 1886-'88 include Lascars and Asiatics under Asiatic articles of agreement; allowing for this, however, the proportion of men employed to every one thousand tons of shipping was considerably smaller in the years 1886-'87 than in 1884-'85.

† The following is a copy of a circular issued in October, 1887, by the representatives in New York of a well-known iron-ship-building firm at Newcastle-on-Tyne, England:

"Inviting your attention to the inclosed particulars of two steel screw freight steamers building to our order, by the well-known builders, Messrs. ——, of Newcastle-on-Tyne, we beg to give you some additional details:

"The contract price is £34,250 each, which is just about £6 17s. (six pounds seventeen shillings sterling) a ton dead-weight capacity, and including all expenses up to time of delivery, will not exceed £7 a ton dead weight, or at present rate of exchange, $33.95 American money.

"Thus it will be seen that as regards the cost of these vessels, while of large carrying capacity and consequent earning power, and fitted as they will be with engines of the newest type and with all modern appliances which have been tried and found conducive to quick and economical working (while avoiding all innovations of an experimental character), the present price of

Prior to about the year 1875 ocean-steamships had not been formidable as freight-carriers. The marine engine was too heavy, occupied too much space, consumed too much coal. For transportation of passengers, and of freight having large value in small space, they were satisfactory; but for performing a general carrying-trade of the heavy and bulky articles of commerce they were not satisfactory. A steamer of the old kind, capable of carrying three thousand tons, might sail on a voyage so long that she would be compelled to carry twenty-two hundred tons of coal, leaving room for only eight hundred tons of freight; whereas, at the present time, a steamer with the compound engines and all other modern improvements, can make the same voyage and practically reverse the figures—that is, carry twenty-two hundred tons of freight with a consumption of only eight hundred tons of coal. The result of the construction and use of compound engines in economizing coal has been illus-

---

not over £7 per ton, dead-weight capacity, as against £12 to £13 a few years ago, renders the difference in values relatively even greater than appears at first sight."

A brief examination of what is embraced in the construction of these vessels is not a little interesting and instructive, especially to those who recall what was deemed but a comparatively few years ago the very best conditions for ocean steam navigation: Triple-expansion engines—three cylinders—of the latest and most approved type. Horse-power, 1,700. Propeller shifting blades and spare set; each part of engines interchangeable. Two double-ended steel boilers, in the corrugated furnaces, to work at one hundred and fifty pounds pressure. Four steam winches of most approved pattern and large power. Steam steering-gear forward, and powerful hand gear aft. Patent stockless anchors, working direct into hawser pipes, effecting great saving in time, labor, and gear. Water-ballast in double bottom. Lighthouses on forecastle. Decks of steel throughout; height, seven feet, nine inches, being the suitable height for passengers, horses, and cattle. Ventilation of holds specially provided through automatic exhaustion by means of the funnel. Hatches of large dimensions capable of taking in locomotives or other large pieces of machinery. Six steel bulkheads, with longitudinal bulkheads throughout holds and between decks. Coal consumption, twenty-two tons per day. Coal-bunkers sufficient for forty days' steaming; outfit in sails, steel hawsers, oil and water tanks, loading and discharging gear, cutlery, plate, china, and glass, and optician's stores—all of the best makers and full supply.

trated by Sir Lyon Playfair, by the statement that "a small cake of coal, which would pass through a ring the size of a shilling, when burned in the compound engine of a modern steamboat would drive a ton of food and its proportion of the ship two miles on its way from a foreign port."* Another calculator, says the London "Engineer," has computed that half a sheet of note-paper will develop sufficient power, when burned in connection with the triple-expansion engine, to carry a ton a mile in an Atlantic steamer. How, under such circumstances, the charge for sea-freights on articles of comparatively high value has been reduced, is shown by the fact that the ocean transport of fresh meats from New York to Liverpool does not exceed 1 cent ($\frac{1}{2}d$.) per pound; and including commissions, insurance, and all other items of charge, does not exceed 2 cents ($1d$.) per pound. Boxed meats have also been carried from Chicago to London as a regular business for 50 cents per 100 pounds. In 1860 6d. (12 cents) per bushel was about the lowest rate charged for any length of time for the transportation of

---

* An interesting example of the comparative economy of the old and more modern style of oscillating marine engines was lately furnished by an instance quoted by Mr. J. W. T. Harvey, before the Engineering Section of the Bristol (England) Naturalists' Society. The Juno was originally worked with a jet condenser; after a time this was replaced by a surface condenser, and finally the engines were compounded. Thus we have the same vessel working under three different conditions, and any alteration of coal consumption must be due to the changes in her machinery. The engines originally worked at thirty pounds per square inch, and indicated 1,605 horse-power; they drove the vessel at 14·1 knots, using ninety-two tons of coal per voyage. Subsequently new boilers and a surface condenser were fitted to the ship, the pressure being thirty pounds; the same horse-power and speed were then maintained with a consumption of eighty-two and a half tons of coal per voyage—a saving of nine and a half tons, or nine per cent. As competition in the carrying-trade became keener, this coal consumption could not be afforded, and it was determined to compound the engines as inexpensively as possible. This was done, and the engines now gave 1,270 horse-power, or 335 horse-power less than before, and drove the ship at 13·4 knots, or 0·7 knot slower, on a consumption of forty-nine tons of coal per voyage. The coal consumption per horse-power, therefore, varied under the three conditions as 100, 91, 67. The consumption per voyage varied as 100, 91, 53.

bulk grain from New York to Liverpool, and for a part of that year the rate ran up as high as $13\frac{1}{2}d$. (27 cents) per bushel. But for the year 1886 the average rate for the same service was $2\frac{1}{2}d$. (5 cents) per bushel; while in April, 1888, the rate on grain from New York to Liverpool by steam declined to as low a figure as $\frac{1}{8}d$. per bushel of 60 pounds; $\frac{3}{8}d$. to Antwerp, and $\frac{1}{4}d$. to Glasgow. It seems almost needless to add that these rates were much below the actual cost of carriage. In like manner, the cost of the ocean transportation of tea from China and Japan, or sugar from Cuba, or coffee from Brazil, has been greatly reduced by the same causes.

The above are examples on a large scale of the disturbing influence of the recent application of steam to maritime industries. The following is an example drawn from comparatively one of the smallest of the world's industries, prosecuted in one of the most out-of-the-way places : The seal-fishery is a most important industrial occupation and source of subsistence to the poor and scant population of Newfoundland. Originally it was prosecuted in small sailing-vessels, and upward of a hundred of such craft, employing a large number of men, annually left the port of St. John's for the seal-hunt. Now, few or no sailing-vessels engage in the business; steamers have been substituted, and the same number of seals are taken with half the number of men that were formerly needed. The consequence is, a diminished opportunity for a population of few resources, and to obtain " a berth for the ice," as it is termed, is considered as a favor.

Is it, therefore, to be wondered at, that the sailing-vessel is fast disappearing from the ocean;* that good authorities estimated in 1886 that the tonnage then afloat was about twenty-five per cent in excess of all that was needed to do

---

* The statistics of the world's shipping show that in 1885 there were 25,766 sailing-vessels, of 11,216,618 tons; in 1886 there were 25,155, of 10,411,-807 tons; and in 1887 there were 23,310, of 9,820,492. The decrease in two years was therefore 1,396,123, or 12·4 per cent.

the then carrying-trade of the world ; and that ship-owners everywhere were unanimously of the opinion that the depression of industry was universal?

[During the year 1888, from causes that must be regarded as exceptional (and which will be hereafter noticed), an increased demand for shipping accommodation suddenly sprang up, and which, not being readily supplied, was followed by an almost continued advance in freight rates, until in many directions—i. e., in the Russian grain and Eastern trade—the rise was equal to one hundred per cent advance upon the rates current in 1887 and the early months of 1888. This condition of affairs in turn gave a great impulse to ship-building, especially in Great Britain, where the construction for 1888 amounted to 903,687 tons, as against 637,000 in 1887; an extent of annual increase that, except in two instances, has never been exceeded. The additional tonnage thus supplied proving in excess of the world's demand, the advance in freights in 1888 was in a great measure lost in the first six months of 1889.]

Great, however, as has been the revolution in respect to economy and efficiency in the carrying-trade upon the ocean, the revolution in the carrying-trade upon land during the same period has been even greater and more remarkable. Taking the American railroads in general as representative of the railroad system of the world, the average charge for moving one ton of freight per mile has been reduced from about 2·5 cents in 1869 to 1·06 in 1887; or, taking the results on one of the standard roads of the United States (the New York Central), from 1·95 in 1869 to 0·68 in 1885.* To grasp fully the meaning and significance of these figures, their method of presentation may be varied by saying that two thousand pounds of coal, iron, wheat, cotton, or other commodities, can now be carried on the best managed railways for a distance of one mile, for a sum so small, that outside of China it would be difficult to find a coin of equiv-

---

* On certain of the railroads of the United States an even lower average rate of freight has been reported. Thus, for the year 1886 the Michigan Central Railroad reported 0·56 cent as their average rate per ton per mile for that year, and the Lake Shore and Michigan Southern Railroad 0·55 cent for like service.

alent value to give to a boy as a reward for carrying an ounce package across a street, even if a man or boy could be found in Europe or the United States willing to give or accept so small a compensation for such a service.

The following ingenious method of illustrating the same results has been also suggested : The number of miles of railroad in operation in various parts of the world in 1885 was probably about 300,000.* Reckoning their capacity for transportation at a rate not greater than the results actually achieved in that same year in the United States, it would appear that the aggregate railroad system of the world could easily have performed work in 1885 equivalent to transporting 120,000,000,000 tons one mile. " But if it is next considered that it is a fair day's work for an ordinary horse to haul a ton 6·7 miles, year in and year out, it further appears that the railways have added to the power of the human race, for the satisfaction of its desires by the cheapening of products, a force somewhat greater than that of a horse working twelve days yearly for every inhabitant of the globe."

In the year 1887 the freight-transportation by the railroads of the United States (according to Poor's " Manual ") was equivalent to 60,061,069,996 tons carried one mile ; while the population for that year was somewhat in excess of 60,000,000. The railroad freight service of the United States for 1887 was therefore equivalent to carrying a thousand tons one mile for every person, or every ton a thousand miles. The average cost of this service was about $10 per annum for every person. But if it had been entirely performed by horse-power, even under the most favorable of old-time conditions, its cost would have been about $200 to each inhabitant, which in turn would represent an expendi-

---

* The world's railway mileage for January, 1889, was probaly in excess of 350,000 miles. At the same date the telegraph system of the world comprised at least 600,000 miles of length of line.

ture greater than the entire value of the then annual product of the country; or, in other words, all that the people of the United States earned in 1887 would not pay the
cost of transportation alone of the amount of such service rendered in that year, had it been performed by horse-
power exclusively.*

Less than half a century ago, the railroad was practically
unknown.† It is, therefore, within that short period that
this enormous power has been placed at the disposal of
every inhabitant of the globe for the cheapening of transportation to him of the products of other people and countries, and for enabling him to market or exchange to better
advantage the results of his own labor or services. As the
extension of the railway system has, however, not been equal
in all parts of the world—less than thirty thousand miles
existing, at the close of 1887, in Asia, Africa, and Australia
combined—its accruing benefits have not, of course, been
equal. And while all the inhabitants of the globe have undoubtedly been profited in a degree, by far the greater part
of the enormous additions that have been made to the
world's working force through the railroad since 1840, have
accrued to the benefit of the people of the United States,
and of Europe—exclusive of Russia, Turkey, and the former
Turkish provinces of Southeastern Europe—a number not
much exceeding two hundred millions, or not a quarter part
of the entire population of the globe. The result of this
economic change has therefore been to broaden and deepen

---

* One further interesting corollary of this exhibit is, that the average return, in the form of interest and dividends, on the enormous amount of capital
which has been actually expended in order that the present railway service in
the United States may be performed, can not be estimated as in excess of
four per cent per annum as a maximum.

† As late as 1840 there were in operation only about 2,860 miles of railway
in America, and 2,130 in Europe, or a total of 4,990 miles. For practical purposes, it may therefore be said that the world's railway system did not then
exist; while its organization and correspondence for doing full and efficient
work must be referred to a much later period.

rather than diminish the line of separation between the civilized and the semi-civilized and barbarous nations.

Now, while a multiplicity of inventions and of experiences have contributed to the attainment of such results under this railroad system of transportation, the discovery of a method of making *steel cheap* was the one thing which was absolutely essential to make them finally possible; inasmuch as the cost of frequently replacing rails of iron would have entailed such a burden of expenditure as to have rendered the present cheapness of railway transportation utterly unattainable. Note, therefore, how rapidly improvements in processes have followed the discovery of Bessemer, until, on the score of relative first cost alone, it has become economical to substitute steel for iron in railroad construction. In 1873 Bessemer steel in England, where its price has not been enhanced by protective duties, commanded $80 per ton; in 1886 it was profitably manufactured and sold in the same country for less than $20 per ton!* Within the same time the annual producing capacity of a Bessemer converter has been increased fourfold, with no increase but rather a diminution of the involved labor; and, by the Gilchrist-Thomas process, four men can now make a given product of steel in the same time and with less cost of material than it took ten men ten years ago to accomplish. A ton of steel rails can now also be made with five thousand pounds of coal, as compared with ten thousand pounds in 1868.

"The importance of the Bessemer invention of steel can be best understood by looking at the world's production of that metal in 1887.

---

* The average price of iron rails in Great Britain for the year 1883 was £5 per ton; steel rails in the same market sold in 1886 for £4 5s. per ton; and in 1887 sales of steel rails were made in Belgium for £3 16s. ($18.75) per ton, deliverable at the works. The average price of steel rails in Pennsylvania (U. S.) at the works, for 1886, with a tariff on imports of $17 per ton, was $34½ per ton. Since the beginning of 1883 the manufacture of iron rails in the United States has been almost entirely discontinued, and during the years from 1883 to 1888 there were virtually no market quotations for them. The last recorded average price for iron rails was $45½ per ton in 1882.

The production of Bessemer steel in the eight chief iron and steel producing countries of the world amounted in that year to 7,269,767 tons, as compared with 6,034,115 tons in 1886, showing an increase of 1,260,094 tons, or twenty per cent. The saving effected by railway companies by the use of Bessemer metal and the additional security gained thereby is shown by the fact that a locomotive on the Great Northern Railway has accomplished, with a moderate train-load of passenger-coaches, a statute mile in fifty seconds, or at the rate of seventy-two miles per hour, and makes a considerable continuous run at a speed of one mile per minute—a rate of railway traveling almost beyond the dreams or anticipations of the renowned George Stephenson." The use of steel in place of iron in ship-construction may be said to date from 1878, and the rapidity with which the former has replaced the latter metal is very remarkable. Thus, in 1878 "the percentage of steel used in the construction of steamships in Great Britain was only 1·09, but in 1887 the percentage of iron used in proportion to steel was only 0·93; or, in other words, in 1878 there was ninety times as much iron as steel used for steamers, but in 1887 there was more than eight times the quantity of steel used as compared with iron for the same purpose, and, as regards sailing-ships, the quantity of steel used in 1887 amounted to practically one half that of iron."—*Address of the President (Mr. Adamson) of the British Iron and Steel Association, May, 1888.*

The power capable of being exerted by the steam-engines of the world in existence and working in the year 1887 has been estimated by the Bureau of Statistics at Berlin as equivalent to that of 46,000,000 horses, representing approximately 1,000,000,000 men; or at least three times the working population of the earth, whose total number of inhabitants is probably about 1,460,000,000. The application and use of steam alone up to date (1889) has accordingly more than trebled man's working power, and by enabling him to economize his physical strength has given him greater leisure, comfort, and abundance, and also greater opportunity for that mental training which is essential to a higher development. And yet it is certain that four fifths of the steam-engines now working in the world have been constructed during the last quarter of a century, or since 1865.

One of the most momentous and what may be called humanitarian results of the recent great extension and cheapening of the world's railway system and service is, that there is now no longer any occasion for the people of any country indulging in either excessive hopes or fears as to the results of any particular harvest; inasmuch as the failure of crops in any one country is no longer, as it was, no later than twenty years ago, identical with high prices of grain; the prices of cereals being at present regulated, not within any particular country, but by the combined production and consumption of all countries made mutually accessible by railroads and steamships. As a matter of fact, indeed, the granaries for no small portion of the surplus stock of the world's cereals are at the present time ships and railroad-cars in the process of movement to the points of greatest demand for consumption. Hence it is that, since 1870, years of locally bad crops in Europe have generally witnessed considerably lower prices than years when the local crops were good, and there was a local surplus for export.*

In short, one marked effect of the present railroad and steamship system of transportation has been to compel a

---

* A century ago every nation of Europe raised in ordinary years enough grain to supply the needs of its own population, and the circulation of food from country to country, and from province to province, was restricted and even generally prohibited. After the middle of the eighteenth century there were indications that the domestic growth of wheat in England was falling below the consumption of the people; but this unpleasant fact was studiously concealed by the enormously expensive corn laws, which on the one hand artificially stimulated agriculture and kept poor lands in cultivation, and, on the other, restricted through high prices the consumption of bread—and was not openly recognized for nearly half a century later. Subsequently the other nations of Europe, with the exception of Russia and Austria-Hungary, have experienced the same alteration in their food-producing capacity—in part due to natural influences, and in part to artificial factors—which have turned the attention of the people away from the cultivation of cereals into employments that promised to be more profitable; and they have found it cheaper to import food than to grow it themselves. So that there are now no countries in Europe save the two above mentioned that have a surplus product of wheat available for export.

uniformity of prices for all commodities that are essential
to life, and to put an end forever to what, less than half a
century ago, was a constant feature of European commercial experience, commerce, namely, the existence of local markets, with widely divergent prices for such commodities.

How much of misery and starvation a locally deficient
harvest entailed under the old system upon the poorer
classes, through the absence of opportunity of supplying the
deficiency through importations from other countries and
even from contiguous districts, is shown by the circumstance
that in the English Parliamentary debates upon the corn
laws, about the year 1840, it was estimated upon data furnished by Mr. Tooke, in his "History of Prices," that a
deficiency of one sixth in the English harvest resulted in a
rise of at least one hundred per cent in the price of grain ;
and another estimate by Davenant and King, for the close
of the seventeenth century, corroborates this apparently excessive statement.   The estimate of these latter authorities
was as follows :

For a deficit equal to—	There will be a rise in price of—
1-10	3-10
2-10	8-10
3-10	16-10
4-10	28-10
5-10	45-10

As late as 1817 the difference in France between the
highest and the lowest prices of grain in different parts of
the country was 45 francs per hectolitre.   In 1847 the average difference was 26 francs.   Since 1870 the greatest difference at any time has not been in excess of 3·55 francs.   The
following table, given on German authority, and representing the price (in silver gulden per hectolitre) of grain for
various periods, exhibits a like progress of price equalization
between nations :

PERIOD.	England.	France.	Belgium.	Prussia.
1821–'30.............	10·25	7·35	6·44	5·65
1831–'40.............	9·60	7·61	7·31	5·27
1841–'50.............	9·15	7·89	7·99	6·41
1851–'60.............	9·40	7·84	9·65	8·07
1861–'70.............	8·80	8·59	9·24	7·79

For grain henceforth, therefore, the railroad and the steamship have decided that there shall be but one market —the world; and that the margin for speculation in this commodity, so essential to the well-being of humanity, shall be restricted to very narrow limits; the speculator for a rise in wheat in any one country finding himself practically in competition with all wheat-producing countries the moment he undertakes to advance prices; while abnormal values in one country or market, or excessive reserves at one center or another, are certain to be speedily neutralized and controlled by the influence of all countries and markets.

The movement and prices of wheat for the year 1888 furnish a most remarkable illustration and confirmation of the above statements, and also (as Sir James Caird has pointed out) " of the smoothness (at the present time) of the operations of trade under natural conditions." During the eleven months of 1888, ending November 30th, Great Britain imported a little more than sixty-seven million hundred-weight of wheat and flour. In the corresponding eleven months of 1887 the foreign supply was practically the same. There was, however, a very great change in the sources of supply. Thus, in 1887, North and South America furnished *forty-nine* million hundred-weight out of the *sixty-seven* million hundred-weight that Great Britain required; but in 1888 the harvests of America were comparatively meager, and supplied Great Britain with but *twenty-nine* million hundred-weight, leaving a deficiency of twenty millions to be obtained from other sources. Eastern Europe, and especially Russia, which were favored during the year

1888 with splendid weather and enormous crops, were able
to promptly make good the missing twenty millions; but
the market changes and vicissitudes of trade consequent
on such an extensive transfer of the British supplies of
wheat were something extraordinary. Twenty years ago,
had Russia in any one year harvested a surplus of wheat
as large as she did in 1888, such surplus, through an inability to cheaply and promptly move it to a market, would have
been not only of little monetary value to the producer, but
would probably by its unsalable presence in the country have
considerably lowered the market price of so much of the
crop as was required for home consumption. Under existing conditions, however, great gain accrued to the Russian
farmer and to all the interests and nationalities employed
in the movements of his product. A demand for shipping
for this special trade, which could not at once be fully supplied, also occasioned a quick advance in ocean freights in
all quarters of the globe, in some instances to the extent of
one hundred per cent, and concurrently a revival of the industry of ship-building. On the other hand, this transfer
of the wheat-supply of Great Britain represented an immense change in the carrying-trade and business of the
United States ; while the American speculator, recognizing
the *local* deficiency of the wheat-crop for 1888, and assuming that the American supply of this cereal was the prime
factor in determining its European price, largely advanced
prices (the average price of No. 2 red winter wheat in
New York for the six months ending December, 1888, having been $1.01 per bushel, as compared with 84.2 cents for
the corresponding period of 1887). But in this they were
disappointed. The European prices did not materially advance ; * and as a consequence, while the American public
suffered, " the British consumer was enabled to eat his loaf

---

* English wheat sold December 25, 1888, at £1 11s. 3d. a quarter, against
£1 11s. 2d., or 2½ cents a bushel more than at the corresponding date in 1887,
and 1s. 10d. less than in December, 1886.

at the same price or a less price than he did in the previous year." And if the consumer was not a student of statistics, he would not have been in the least conscious that it was Russian rather than American grain from which his bread was manufactured. In short, under the system of commercial freedom which Great Britain has established, all the farming interests on the earth grow with an eye to the possible advent of the British people as customers; and while the latter, on their part, have so provided themselves with the best equipment for annihilating time and distance, that it is a matter of indifference to them whether the wheatfields, which for the time being shall have their preference, are located in India, Russia, Dakota, South America, or Australia.

The world's total product of pig-iron increased slowly and regularly from 1870 to 1879, at the rate of about $2\frac{1}{4}$ per cent per annum, but after 1879 production increased enormously, until in 1883 the advance among all nations was 82·2 per cent in excess of the make of 1870, the increase in the product of the United Kingdom being 43 per cent, and that of other countries 139·1 per cent (*Testimony of Sir Lowthian Bell, British Commission, 1886*). Such an increase (after 1879), justified perhaps at the moment, was far in excess of the ratio of increase in the world's population, and for a term of years greatly disproportionate to any increase in the world's consumption, and finally resulted, as has been before shown (see Chapter I), in an extreme depression of the business, and a remarkable fall of prices.

By reason largely of the cheapening of iron and steel, the cost of building railroads has also in recent years been greatly reduced. In 1870–'71, one of the leading railroads of the Northwestern United States built 126 miles, which, with some tunneling, was bonded for about $40,000 per mile. The same road could now (1889) be constructed, with the payment of higher wages to laborers of all classes, for about $20,000 per mile.

The power to excavate earth, or to excavate and blast rock, is from five to ten times as great as it was when operations for the construction of the Suez Canal were commenced, in 1859–'60. The machinery sent to the Isthmus of Panama, for the excavation of the canal at that point, was computed by engineers as capable of performing the labor of half a million of men.

The displacement of muscular labor in some of the cotton-mills of the United States, within the last ten years, by improved machinery, has been from thirty-three to fifty per cent, and the average work of one operative, working one year, in the best mills of the United States, will now, according to Mr. Atkinson, supply the annual wants of 1,600 fully clothed Chinese, or 3,000 partially clothed East Indians. In 1840 an operative in the cotton-mills of Rhode Island, working thirteen to fourteen hours a day, turned off 9,600 yards of standard sheeting in a year; in 1886 the operative in the same mill made about 30,000 yards, working ten hours a day. In 1840 the wages were $176 a year; in 1886 the wages were $285 a year.

The United States census returns for 1880 report a very large increase in the amount of coal and copper produced during the ten previous years in this country, with a very large comparative diminution in the number of hands employed in these two great mining industries; in anthracite coal the increase in the number of hands employed having been 33·2 per cent, as compared with an increase of product of 82·7; while in the case of copper the ratios were 15·8 and 70·8, respectively. For such results, the use of cheaper and more powerful blasting agents (dynamite), and of the steam-drill, furnish an explanation. And, in the way of further illustration, it may be stated that a car-load of coal, in the principal mining districts of the United States, can now (1889) be mined, hoisted, screened, cleaned, and loaded in one half the time that it required ten years previously.

The report of the United States Commissioner of Labor for 1886 furnishes the following additional illustrations :

" In the manufacture of agricultural implements, specific evidence is submitted, showing that six hundred men now do the work that, fifteen or twenty years ago, would have required 2,145 men—a displacement of 1,545.

" The manufacture of boots and shoes offers some very wonderful facts in this connection. In one large and long-established manufactory the proprietors testify that it would require five hundred persons, working by hand processes, to make as many women's boots and shoes as a hundred persons now make with the aid of machinery—a displacement of eighty per cent.

" Another firm, engaged in the manufacture of children's shoes, states that the introduction of new machinery within the past thirty years has displaced about six times the amount of hand-labor required, and that the cost of the product has been reduced one half.

" On another grade of goods, the facts collected by the agents of the bureau show that one man can now do the work which twenty years ago required ten men.

" In the manufacture of flour there has been a displacement of nearly three fourths of the manual labor necessary to produce the same product. In the manufacture of furniture, from one half to three fourths only of the old number of persons is now required. In the manufacture of wall-paper, the best evidence puts the displacement in the proportion of one hundred to one. In the manufacture of metals and metallic goods, long-established firms testify that machinery has decreased manual labor $33\frac{1}{3}$ per cent."

In 1845 the boot and shoe makers of Massachusetts made an average production, under the then existing conditions of manufacturing, of 1·52 pairs of boots for each working day. In 1885 each employé in the State made on an average 4·2 pairs daily, while at the present time in Lynn and Haverhill the daily average of each person is seven pairs per

day, " showing an increase in the power of production in
forty years of four hundred per cent."*

The business of making bottles has been arduous and
unhealthy, with a waste of about thirty-three per cent of
the " melting "; and, although this waste is used afterward,
there is a deterioration in its quality from its employment a
second time. For many years this specialty of industrial
production experienced little improvement; but it finally
commenced in the substitution in 1885 of the so-called
Siemens " tank " furnace, in place of the old-fashioned
" coal " furnace for the melting of glass; one of the former supplanting eight of the latter; requiring four men
in place of twenty-eight to feed it, producing 1,000,000
square feet of glass per month, in place of a former product
of 115,000 feet, and working continuously, while the coal-
furnaces work on an average but eighteen days per month.
Such an improvement in the methods of manufacture, as
might be expected, revolutionized the former equilibrium,
in this department of the glass industry as respects the
supply and demand of both labor and product, and occasioned serious riots among the glass-workers of Charleroi, in
Belgium, where it was first introduced.   The process of
producing the bottle by " blowing " was not, however, affected by the above-noticed improvement; but within the
last year (1888) a practical method of producing bottles is
reported as having been invented and practically applied in
England, which now bids fair to entirely do away with the
process of " blowing," with an accompanying immense increase of daily product and a corresponding reduction in
the former cost of labor.

The following are other notable results, in what may be
termed the minor industries :

In the manufacture of jewelry, one skilled workman,

---

* Address by Mr. F. W. Norcross, November, 1888, before the Boston
Boot and Shoe Club.

paid at the rate of two and a half to three dollars per day, and working according to ante-machine methods in use a few years ago, could make up three dozen pairs of sleeve-buttons per day. Now, one boy, paid five dollars per week, and working on the most modern machinery, can make up nine thousand pairs in a day. In gold (or imitation gold) chain-making, the United States now exports the cheapest grade of such jewelry produced by machinery to Germany, where cottage hand-labor, in the same vocation, can be had for a pittance, and finds a ready sale for them as against German manufacturers.

In connection with a new (1889) issue of notes by the Bank of France, for which superiority over anything of this kind heretofore achieved is claimed, and which engravers and chemists believe can not be imitated except at such an expenditure of time and money as would effectually check all effort in this direction, it is also added that they have been produced in a twentieth part of the time spent on those which are now being withdrawn from circulation.

Nothing has had a greater influence in making possible the rapidity with which certain branches of retail business are now conducted, as compared with ten years ago—more especially the sale of groceries—than the cheap and rapid production of paper bags. At the outset, these bags were all made by hand-labor; but now machinery has crowded out the hand-workers, and factories are in existence in the United States which produce millions of paper bags per week, and not unfrequently fill single orders for three millions. Paper sacks for the transportation of flour are now (1889) used to the extent of about one hundred millions per annum; and to this same extent have superseded the use and requirement of cotton sacks and of barrels. With machinery have also come many improvements: square bags that stand up of themselves, and need only when filled from a measure to have the top edges turned over to make the package at once ready for delivery. A purchaser can now also take his butter or lard in paper trays that are brine and grease proof; his vinegar in paper jars that are warranted not to soak for one hour; a bottle of wine wrapped in a corrugated case that would not break if he dropped it on the pavement, and his oysters in paper pails that will hold water overnight. A few years ago, to have furnished gratuitously these packages, would have been deemed extravagance; but now it is found to pay as a matter of business.

The increase in the producing capacity of the United States in respect to the manufacture of paper during the years from 1880 to 1887 inclusive, was also very striking, namely : in number of mills, twenty-five per cent; in product, sixty-seven per cent; in value of product, twenty-seven per cent. The reduction in the prices of paper in the United States under such circumstances has been very great, and since 1872, for all qualities, full fifty per cent.*

The *sobriquet* of an apothecary was formerly that of a pill-maker; but the modern apothecary no longer makes pills, except upon special prescriptions; inasmuch as scores of large manufactories now produce pills by machinery according to the standard or other formulas, and every apothecary keeps and sells them, because they are cheaper, better, and more attractive than any that he can make himself.

Certain branches of occupation formerly of considerable importance under the influence of recent improvements seem to be passing out of existence. Previous to 1872, nearly all the calicoes of the world were dyed or printed with a coloring principle extracted from the root known as *madder*;

---

* In 1880, according to the census, there were 692 paper-mills in the United States, producing 904,216,000 pounds of paper annually, valued at $55,109,914. In 1887 there were 866 mills, with an annual product of 1,514,469,000 pounds, valued at $70,000,000. In addition to this annual product, paper and manufactures of paper to the *net* value of $866,726 were imported. A calculation of the relative amount of paper consumed per capita in the United States in 1887 gives a total of $1.16 of domestic and $1^{4}/_{10}$ cent of foreign manufacture. The tariff on the importation of paper for that year was twenty-five per cent *ad valorem* on " writing," and fifteen per cent on unsized " printing" papers.

the cultivation and preparation of which involved the use of thousands of acres of land in Holland, Belgium, eastern France, Italy, and the Levant, and the employment of many hundreds of men, women, and children, and of large amounts of capital; the importation of madder into the United Kingdom for the year 1872 having been 28,731,600 pounds, and into the United States for the same year 7,786,000 pounds. To-day, two or three chemical establishments in Germany and England, employing but few men and a comparatively small capital, manufacture from coal-tar, at a greatly reduced price, the same coloring principle; and the former great business of growing and preparing madder—with the land, labor, and capital involved—is gradually becoming extinct; the importations into Great Britain for the year 1887 having declined to 1,934,700 pounds, and into the United States to 1,049,800 pounds.

The old-time business of making millstones—entitled to rank among the first of labor-saving inventions at the very dawn of civilization—is rapidly passing into oblivion, because millstones are no longer necessary or economical for grinding the cereals. The steel roller produces more and better flour in the same time at less cost, and as an inevitable consequence is rapidly taking the place of the millstone in all countries that know how to use machinery.* And, as the art of skillfully grooving the surface of a hard, flinty rock for its conversion into a millstone is so laborious, so difficult of accomplishment (four or five years of service being required in France from an apprentice before he is allowed to touch a valuable stone), and to a certain extent so dangerous from the flying particles of steel and stone, humanity, apart from all economic considerations, may well rejoice at its desuetude.

---

* Under the new system, seventy-four per cent of the wheat goes into flour and twenty-six per cent into offal or bran, against thirty-three and a third per cent of bran under the old system.

With the substitution of steamers for sailing-vessels upon
the broad ocean, the former extensive business of sail-making,
and the demand upon factories for heavy cloth as material
for sails, experienced a notable depression, which in later
years has continued and increased, because commerce along
coast-lines now no longer moves exclusively by sail, but
largely in barges dragged or propelled by steam. For the
four years next previous to 1886 the demand for sails in the
United States is estimated to have decreased to the extent
of about twenty-five per cent, although the carrying-trade
of the country by ocean, coast, and inland waters, has, during the same time, increased very considerably.

Cotton-seed oil—an article a few years ago absolutely
unknown in commerce, and prepared from what was formerly regarded almost in the light of a waste product, is
now manufactured in the United States, and has come into
such extensive use as a substitute for lard, olive, and other
oils, for culinary and manufacturing purposes, that its present annual production and sale are estimated to be equivalent to about 70,000,000 pounds of lard ; and has contributed
not only to notably reduce the price and the place of that
important hog-product in the world's markets, but also to
impair the production and depress the price of almost all
other vegetable oils—the product of the industries of other
countries.

Another matter of great industrial importance which a
very few years ago also was practically unknown is the fuel
use in the United States of natural gas, which, during the
year 1887, is estimated by the United States Geological Survey to have displaced the use of 9,867,000 tons of coal, having a value of $15,838,500, as compared with a displacement
of 6,453,000 tons in 1886 and 3,131,000 tons in 1885. The
total mileage of pipes for the conveyance of natural gas in
1887 was estimated at about 2,500 miles. In November of
the same year the whole number of rolling-mills and steel-
works in the United States completed or in the course of

erection was four hundred and forty-five, of which nearly one fourth used natural gas as fuel.

One prime factor in the use of this new agency is the small expense attending its application. Thus in one of the large steel-works of Pittsburg, Pa., three men do all the service required in the boiler-room, each one being on duty for eight hours. When coal was used as fuel, the same firm required the services of ninety men in the boiler-room for every twenty-four hours. Another saving is found in a diminished degree of deterioration in the boilers when the gas is carefully used. For household use the advantage of natural gas is equally evident, a single turn of a cock being substituted in place of the former necessarily dirty work of kindling a fire when coal was employed.

"Natural gas is, however, not now supplied at as cheap rates as a few years ago. It has, too, strange as it may appear, a rival as a cheap and cleanly fuel in water-oil gas produced from petroleum, which is steadily growing in popularity among American iron and steel and a few other manufacturers. It is claimed that this fuel is cheaper than coal, or than gas made from it, and that it possesses all the desirable qualities of natural gas, and is far safer. This new fuel possesses also the advantage that it can be produced and used where natural gas can not be obtained, and even where coal may be too expensive for use."— *Report of* Mr. James M. Swank, *1888.*

But in respect to no other one article has change in the conditions of production and distribution been productive of such momentous consequences as in the case of wheat. On the great wheat-fields of the State of Dakota, where machinery is applied to agriculture to such an extent that the requirement for manual labor has been reduced to a minimum, the annual product of one man's labor, working to the best advantage, is understood to be now equivalent to the production of 5,500 bushels of wheat. In the great mills of Minnesota, the labor of another one man for a year, under similar conditions as regards machinery, is in like manner equivalent to the conversion of this unit of 5,500 bushels of wheat into a thousand barrels of flour, leaving 500 bushels for seed-purposes; and, although the conditions for analysis of the next step in the way of results are more difficult, it is reasonably certain that the year's labor of one and a half men more—or, at the most, two men—employed in railroad transportation, is equivalent to putting this thousand barrels of flour on a dock in New York ready for exportation, where the addition of a fraction of a cent a pound to the price will further transport and deliver it at almost any port of Europe.*

Here, then, we have the labor of three men for one year, working with machinery, resulting in the producing all the flour that a thousand other men ordinarily eat in a year, allowing one barrel of flour for the average consumption of each adult. Before such a result the question of wages paid in the different branches of flour production and transportation becomes an insignificant factor in determining a market; and, accordingly, American flour grown in Dakota, and ground in Minneapolis, from a thousand to fifteen hundred miles from the nearest seaboard, and under the auspices of men paid from a dollar and a half to two dollars and a half per day for their labor, is sold in European markets at rates which are determinative of the prices which Russian peasants, Egyptian "fellahs," and Indian "ryots," can obtain in the same markets for similar grain grown by

---

* "When the wheat reaches New York city, and comes into the possession of a great baker, who has established the manufacture of bread on a large scale, and who sells the best of bread to the working-people of New York at the lowest possible price, we find that one thousand barrels of flour can be converted into bread and sold over the counter by the work of three persons for one year. Let us add to the six and a half men already named the work of another man six months, or a half a man one year, to keep the machinery in repair, and our modern miracle is, that seven men suffice to give one thousand persons all the bread they customarily consume in one year. If to these we add three for the work of providing fuel and other materials to the railroad and the baker, our final result is that ten men working one year serve bread to one thousand."—"*Distribution of Products*," EDWARD ATKINSON.

them on equally good soil, and with from fifteen to twenty cents per day wages for their labor.

On the wheat-farms of the Northwestern United States it was claimed in 1887 that, with wages at twenty-five dollars per month and board for permanent employés, wheat could be produced for forty cents per bushel; while in Rhenish Prussia, with wages at six dollars per month, the cost of production was reported to be eighty cents per bushel.

How much more significantly differences manifest themselves in the results of mechanical production, when long periods of time are taken for comparison, is illustrated by an exhibit in parallel columns of a statement made by Adam Smith in his "Wealth of Nations" (first published in 1776, Vol. I, Chapter I), respecting the manufacture of pins, and which then seemed to him as something extraordinary, and a similar statement of the present condition of this business, as set forth in an official report to the United States Department of State in the year 1888 :

"To take an example, therefore, from a very trifling manufacture, but one in which the division of labor has been very often taken notice of—the trade of the pin-maker. A workman not educated to this business (which the division of labor has rendered a distinct trade), nor acquainted with the use of the machinery employed in it (to the invention of which the same division of labor has probably given occasion), could scarce, perhaps, with his utmost industry make one pin a day, and certainly could not make twenty. But in the way in which this business is now carried on, not only the whole work is a peculiar trade,

"The relative indifference of high day wages when brought side by side with such astonishing results is more apparent yet when we deal with industries where automatic machinery is employed almost exclusively — screw-making, nail-making, pin-making, etc. In the latter industry the coil of brass wire is put in its proper place, the end fastened, and the almost human piece of mechanism, with its iron fingers, does the rest of the work. One machine makes 180 pins a minute, cutting the wire, flattening the heads, sharpening the points, and dropping the pin in its proper place. One hundred and eight thousand pins

but it is divided into a number of branches, of which the greater part are likewise peculiar trades. One man draws out the wire, another straightens it, a third cuts it, a fourth points it, a fifth grinds it at the top for receiving the head. To make the head requires two or three distinct operations; to put it on is a peculiar business, to whiten the pin is another. It is even a trade by itself to put them into the paper, and the important business of making a pin is, in this manner, divided into about eighteen distinct operations, which, in some manufactories, are all performed by distinct hands, though in others the same man will sometimes perform two or three of them. I have seen a small manufactory of this kind where ten men only were employed, and where some of them consequently performed two or three distinct operations. But though they were very poor, and therefore but indifferently accommodated with the necessary machinery, they could, when they exerted themselves, make among them about twelve pounds of pins in a day. There are in a pound upward of four thousand pins of a middling size. Those ten persons, therefore, could make among them upward of forty-eight thousand pins in a day." — ADAM SMITH, *Wealth of Nations*, A. D. 1776.

a day is the output of one machine. A factory visited by me employed seventy machines. These had a combined output per day of 7,500,000 pins, or 300 pins to a paper, 25,000 papers of pins; allowing for stoppages and necessary time for repairs, say 20,000 papers. These machines are tended by three men. A machinist with a boy-helper attends to the repairing. It will not materially influence the price of pins whether the combined earnings of these five men be $7.50 or $10 per diem. The difference would amount to one eighth of a cent on a paper of pins. The likelihood is that when cheaper help is employed a greater number of hands would be employed for the same work and the same output."—*Influences bearing on Production. Report on Technical Education to the United States State Department, by U. S. Consul Schoenhof, 1888.*

In other words, in the time of Adam Smith it was regarded as a wonderful achievement for ten men to make

48,000 pins in a day, but now three men can make 7,500,000 pins of a vastly superior character in the same time.

A great number of other similar and equally remarkable experiences, derived from almost every department of industry except the handicrafts, might be presented; but it would seem that enough evidence has been offered to prove abundantly, that in the increased control which mankind has acquired over the forces of Nature, and in the increased utilization of such control—mainly through machinery—for the work of production and distribution, is to be found a cause sufficient to account for most if not all the economic disturbance which, since the year 1873, has been certainly universal in its influence over the domain of civilization; abnormal to the extent of justifying the claim of having been unprecedented in character, and which bids fair in a greater or less degree to indefinitely continue. Other causes may and doubtless have contributed to such a condition of affairs, but in this one cause alone (if the influences referred to can be properly considered as a unity) it would seem there has been sufficient of potentiality to account not only for all the economic phenomena that are under discussion, but to occasion a feeling of wonder that the world has accommodated itself so readily to the extent that it has to its new conditions, and that the disturbances have not been very much greater and more disastrous.

A question which these conclusions will naturally suggest may at once be anticipated. Have not these same influences, it may be asked, been exerted during the whole of the present century, and in fact ever since the inception of civilization; and are there any reasons for supposing that this influence has been different during recent years in kind and degree from what has been heretofore experienced? The answer is, Certainly in kind, but not in degree. The world has never seen anything comparable to the results of the recent system of transportation by land and water, never experienced in so short a time such an expansion of all that pertains to what is called business, and has never before, as was premised at the outset of this argument, been able to accomplish so much in the way of production with a given amount of labor in a given time. Thus it is claimed in respect to the German Empire, where the statistics of production and distribution have doubtless been more carefully studied by experts than elsewhere, that during the period from 1872 to 1885 there was an expansion in the railroad traffic of this empire of ninety per cent; in marine tonnage, of about a hundred and twenty per cent; in the general mercantile or commercial movement, of sixty-seven per cent; in postal matter carried, of a hundred and eight per cent; in telegraphic dispatches, of sixty-one per cent; and in bank discounts, of two hundred and forty per cent. During the same period population increased about eleven and a half per cent, and from such data there has been a general deduction that, "if one unit of trade was the ratio to one unit of population in Germany in 1872, the proportion in 1885 was more than ten units of trade to one of population." But, be this as it may, it can not be doubted that whatever has been the industrial expansion of Germany in recent years, it has been at least equaled by England, approximated to by France, and certainly surpassed by the United States.*

There is very much that contributes to the support of the idea which has been suggested by M. Laveleye, editor of the "Moniteur des Intérêts Matériels," at Brussels, that the industrial activity of the greater part of this century has been devoted to fully equipping the civilized countries of

---

* A statistical exhibit of the growth of British industrial interests during the reign of Queen Victoria (fifty years), published in 1887, in connection with the "Queen's Jubilee," showed that the production of coal has increased in Great Britain during this period from 36,000,000 tons to 147,000,000 tons per annum; and that manufactures had increased in about an equal ratio with the output of coal—that is to say, had about quadrupled (four hundred per cent). Meanwhile, the population of the United Kingdom increased only thirty-three per cent.

the world with economic tools, and that the work of the future, in this same sphere, must be necessarily that of repair and replacements rather than of new constructions. But a more important inference from this same idea, and one that fully harmonizes with and rationally explains the phenomena of the existing situation is, that the equipment having at last been made ready, the work of using it for production has in turn begun, and has been prosecuted so efficiently, that the world has within recent years, and for the first time, become saturated, as it were, under existing conditions for use and consumption, with the results of these modern improvements.

Again, although the great natural labor-saving agencies had been recognized and brought into use many years prior to 1870, their powers were long kept, as it were, in abeyance; because it required time for the instrumentalities or methods, by which the world's work of production and distribution was carried on, to adjust themselves to new conditions; and until this was accomplished, an almost infinite number and variety of inventions which genius had produced for facilitating and accelerating industrial evolution were matters of promise rather than of consummation. But, with the extension of popular education and the rapid diffusion of intelligence, all new achievements in science and art have been brought in recent years so much more rapidly " within the sphere of the every-day activity of the people " —as the noted German inventor, Dr. Werner Siemens, has expressed it—" that stages of development, which ages ago required centuries for their consummation, and which at the beginning of our times required decades, now complete themselves in years, and not unfrequently present themselves at once in a state of completeness."

It should also be remembered that fifty years ago the " sciences " were little more than a mass of ill-digested facts or " unassorted laws," and that in the departments of physics and chemistry comparatively little had been accomplished in the way of industrial application and direction. To say, indeed, what the world did not have half a century ago is almost equivalent to enumerating all those things which in their understanding, possession, and common use the world now regards as constituting the dividing lines between civilization and barbarism. Thus, fifty years ago the railroad and the locomotive were practically unknown. The ocean steam marine dates from 1838, when the Sirius and Great Western—the two pioneer vessels—crossed the Atlantic to New York. Electricity had then hardly got " beyond the stage of an elegant amusement," and the telegraph was not really brought into practical use before 1844. The following is a further partial list of the inventions, discoveries, and applications whose initial point of " being " is not only more recent than the half-century, but whose fuller or larger development in a majority of instances is also referable to a much more recent date : The mechanical reapers, mowing and seeding machines, the steam-plow and most other eminently labor-saving agricultural devices ; the Bessemer process and the steel rail (1857) ; the submarine and transoceanic telegraph cables (1866) ; photography and all its adjuncts ; electro-plating and the electrotype ; the steam-hammer, repeating and breech-loading fire-arms, and rifled and steel cannon ; gun-cotton and dynamite ; the industrial use of India-rubber and gutta-percha ; the steam-excavator and steam-drill ; the sewing-machine ; the practical use of the electric light ; the application of dynamic electricity as a motor for machinery ; the steam fire-engine ; the telephone, microphone, spectroscope, and the process of spectral analysis ; the polariscope ; the compound steam-engine ; the centrifugal process of refining sugar ; the rotary printing-press ; hydraulic lifts, cranes, and elevators ; the " regenerative " furnace, iron and steel ships, pressed glass, wire rope, petroleum and its derivatives, and analine dyes ; the industrial use of the metal nickel, cotton-seed oil, artificial butter, stearine-candles, natural gas, cheap postage, and the postage-stamp. Electricity, which a very few years ago was regarded as something wholly immaterial, has now acquired a sufficiently objective existence to admit of being manufactured and sold the same as pig-iron or leather. In short, to one whose present memory and life-experiences do not extend over a period of time more extensive than what is represented by a generation, the recital of the economic experiences and industrial conditions of the generation next preceding is very much akin to a recurrence to ancient history.

It will be interesting also here to call attention to some of the agencies productive of further extensive economic changes which are now in the process of development, or which are confidently predicted as certain to occur in the not very remote future.

Thus, notwithstanding the immense service which the steam-engine has rendered to humanity, and its present continuing necessity as a prime factor in all civilization, it is at the same time certain that as a machine it is most imperfect, inasmuch as the very best steam-engines only utilize about one sixth of the power (work) which resides in the fuel which is consumed in the generation of steam. The entire displacement of the steam-engine as it now exists is, therefore, not only essential to further great material progress, but is confidently expected to happen at no very distant period by those eminently qualified to express an opinion on this subject. Thus, at the meeting of the British Association for the Advancement of Science in 1888, the president, Sir Frederick Bramwell, after expressing his belief that the days of the steam-engine for small powers were already numbered, further predicted that those who should attend the centenary of the Association in 1931—

"Would see the present steam-engines in museums, treated as things to be respected and of antiquarian interest, by the engineers of those days, such as are the open-topped steam cylinders of Newcomen and of Smeaton to ourselves, and that the heat-engine of the future will probably be one independent of the vapor of water." Indeed, " the working of heat-engines, without the intervention of the vapor of water by the combusion of the gases arising from coal, or from coal and from water," he continued, " is now not merely an established fact, but a recognized and undoubted commercially economical means of obtaining motive power. Such engines, developing from one to forty horse-power, and worked by ordinary gas supplied by gas-mains, are in most extensive use in printing-works, hotels, clubs, theatres, and even in large private houses, for the working of dynamos to supply electric light. But, looking at the wonderful petroleum industry, and at the multifarious products which are obtained from the crude material, is it too much to say that there is a future for motor-engines worked by the vapor of some of the more highly volatile of these products—true vapor—not a gas, but a condensable body capable of being worked over and over again? Numbers of such engines, some of as much as four horse-power, are now running, and are apparently giving good results—certainly excellent results as regards the compactness and lightness of the machinery."

In connection with this subject, the rapidity with which electric motors for stationary power are supplanting the steam - engine should not be overlooked. Thus, in the United States alone it is estimated that between seven thousand and eight thousand such motors for driving machinery were in operation at the close of the year 1888. Notwithstanding, furthermore, the present wide utilization of telegraphy and the telephone as a means of annihilating time and space, there is much to justify the opinion that both of these instrumentalities are really in their infancy, and that it would not be surprising if, before the commencement of the twentieth century, the present comparatively cumbersome and slow methods of postal communication should be superseded to almost as great an extent as the locomotive has supplanted the stage-coach or the ocean-steamer the sailing-ship, and that ultimately the business and social correspondence of the people of every highly civilized country will be mainly transacted upon an electric basis. How extensive the movement is in this direction may be illustrated by a statement made in the annual report (1888) of the Western Union (United States) Telegraph Company (and which popular opinion indorses), that " there is no business in the country that has developed and is developing such rapid growth and increase as the service of the telegraph." And in support of this assertion, and as showing how the existing system approximates to universality, the same report states that of this company's toll revenue for the years 1887–'88 about ninety-two per cent was derived from commercial, family, and social messages, and only eight per cent from the press. But the measure of this comparatively small proportion of eight per cent is shown by the fact that the mere " news " service delivered from its wires for the year in question—counting one delivery at each place served—comprised 740,000,000 words; and if to this aggregate what is known as " special reports " are added, the total amounted to 1,467,000,000 words transmitted for publication alone.

Speaking generally, moreover, there is no reason for doubting that the wonderful material evolution of recent years will be continued, unless man himself interposes obstacles, although the goal to which this evolution tends can not be predicted or possibly imagined. " The deeper the insight we obtain into the mysterious workings of Nature's forces," says Werner Siemens, an authority most competent to express an opinion, " the more we are convinced that we are still standing only in the vestibule of science, that an immeasurable field still lies before us, and that it is very questionable whether mankind will ever arrive at a full knowledge of nature."

One influence which has been more potent in recent years than ever before in stimulating the invention and use of labor-saving machinery, and which should not be overlooked in reasoning upon this subject, has been undoubtedly the increasing frequency of strikes and industrial revolts on

the part of the large proportion of the population of all civilized countries engaged in the so-called mechanical occupations; which actions in turn on the part of such classes have
been certainly largely prompted by the changes in the conditions of production resulting from prior labor-saving inventions and discoveries. As the London " Engineer " has
already pointed out (see page 4, Chapter I), the remedy
that at once suggests itself to every employer of labor on
the occasion of such trouble with his employés is, " to use a
tool wherever it is possible instead of a man." And one
significant illustration of the quickness with which employers carry out this suggestion is afforded by the well-authen-
ticated fact that the strike among the boot and shoe factories
of one county in the State of Massachusetts, in the year
1885, resulted in increasing the capacity for production by
the same factories during the succeeding year of a fully
equal product, with reduction of at least fifteen hundred
operatives ; one machine improvement for effecting an operation called " lasting " having been introduced which is capable of doing the former work of from two hundred to two
hundred and fifty men, with a force not exceeding fifty men.

Another fact confirmatory of the above conclusion is,
that all investigators substantially agree that the depression
of industry in recent years has been experienced with the
greatest severity in those countries where machinery has
been most extensively adopted, and least in those countries
and in those occupations where hand-labor and hand-products
have not been materially interfered with or supplanted.
There is no evidence that the mass of the people of any
country removed from the great lines of the world's commerce, as in China, India, Turkey, Mexico, and the states
of Northern Africa, experienced any disturbance prior to
1883, except from variations in crops, or civil commotions ;
and if the experience of a few of such countries has been
different since 1883, the cause may undoubtedly be referred
to the final influence of long-delayed extraneous or foreign

economic disturbances; as has been the case in Mexico in respect to the universal depreciation of silver, and in Japan from an apparent culmination of a long series of changes in the civilization and social economy of that country. There have, moreover, been no displacements of labor, or reduction in the cost of labor or of product, in all those industries in *civilized* countries where machinery has not been introduced or increased; as, for example, in domestic service, in amusements, carriage-fare, and horse-hire, in hotel charges, in remuneration of authors, artists, teachers, and for legal or medical services, in house-rents; in such departments of agriculture as the raising and care of stock, the growing of cotton, of flax, hemp, and of tropical fibers of like character, or in such mechanical occupations as masonry, painting, upholstering, plastering, and cigar-making, or those of engineers, firemen, teamsters, watchmen, and the like.

Finally, it is of the first importance to note how all the other causes which have been popularly regarded as having directly occasioned, or essentially contributed to, the recent depression of trade and industry—with the exception of such as are in the nature of natural phenomena, as bad seasons and harvests, diseases of plants and animals, disappearance of fish, and the like, and such as are due to excessive taxation consequent on war expenditures, all of which are local, and the first temporary in character—naturally group themselves about the one great cause that has been suggested, as sequences or derivatives, and as secondary rather than primary in their influence; and to the facts and deductions that are confirmatory of these conclusions, attention is next invited.

III.

OVER-PRODUCTION.—The most popular alleged cause of recent economic disturbances, that to which the Royal Commission of Great Britain in its final report* (December, 1866), and the United States Bureau of Labor † (1886), have

---

* "One of the commonest explanations of this depression or absence of profit is that known under the name of over-production ; by which we understand the production of commodities, or even the existence of a capacity for production, at a time when the demand is not sufficiently brisk to maintain a remunerative price to the producer, and to afford him an adequate return on his capital. We think such an over-production has been one of the most prominent features of the course of trade during recent years ; and that the depression under which we are now suffering may be partially explained by this fact."—*British Commission, majority report.*

" By over-production we understand the production of commodities (or existence of the agencies of production) in excess, not of the capacity of consumption if their distribution was gratuitous, but of the demand for export at remunerative prices, and of the amount of income or earnings available for their purchase in the home market. The depression under which we have so long been suffering is undoubtedly of this nature."—*British Commission, minority report.*

† "Machinery—and the word is used in its largest and most comprehensive sense—has been most potent in bringing the mechanically-producing nations of the world to their present industrial position, which position constitutes an epoch in their industrial development. The rapid development and adaptation of machinery in all the activities belonging to production and trans-

assigned a prominent place, and which the "Trades-Union Congress of England has by resolution accepted as being, in the opinion of the workmen of England," the most prominent cause, is "*over-production*." In a certain sense there can be no over-production of desirable products so long as human wants for such products remain unsatisfied. But it is in accordance with the most common of the world's experiences that there is at times and places a production of most useful and desirable things in excess of any demand at remunerative prices to the producer. This happens, in some instances, through lack of progress or enterprise, and in others through what may be termed an excess of progress or enterprise. An example of the first is to be found in the circumstance that in the days of Turgot, the French Minister of Finance under Louis XVI, there were at times in certain departments of France such abundant harvests that wheat was almost unmarketable, while in other and not far-distant sections of the country there was such a lack of food that the inhabitants perished of hunger; and yet, through the absence of facilities for transportation and communication of intelligence, the influence of bad laws, and the moral inertia of the people, there was no equalization of conditions.*

---

portation have brought what is commonly called over-production; so that machinery and over-production are two causes so closely allied that it is difficult to discuss the one without taking the other into consideration. . . . The direct results, so far as the present period is concerned, of this wonderful and rapid extension of power-machinery are, for the countries involved, over-production, or, to be more correct, bad or injudicious production; that is, that condition of production of things the value of which depends upon immediate consumption, or consumption by that portion of the population of the world already requiring the goods produced."—*Report of the United States Commissioner of Labor*, 1886, pp. 88, 89.

* This experience of France in the last quarter of the eighteenth century is repeating itself at the present day in China. General Wilson, in his recent "Study of China" (1887), states that "over ten million people died from starvation about ten years ago in the provinces of Shansi and Shensi alone, while abundance and plenty were prevailing in other parts of the country. Every

An example of the second, intensified to a degree never before experienced, is to be found in the results of the improvements in production and distribution which have been made especially effective within the last quarter of a century. A given amount of labor, operating through machinery, produces or distributes at least a third more product on the average, in given time, than ever before. Note the natural tendency of human nature under the new conditions. The machinery which thus cheapens and increases product is, as a rule, most costly, and entails a like burden of interest, insurance, and care, whether it is at work or idle ; and the possessor of it, recognizing this fact, naturally desires to convert outlay into income by utilizing it to the greatest extent possible. Again, a man who has learned by experience that he can dispose of a certain amount of product or service at a profit, naturally reasons that a larger amount will give him, if not a proportionally greater, at least a larger aggregate profit; and as the conditions determining demand are not only imperfectly known, but to a certain extent incapable of exact determination, he discards the idea of any risk, even if he for a moment entertains it, and pushes industrial effort to its maximum. And as this process is general, and, as a rule, involves a steady increase in the improved and constantly improving instrumentalities of production and distribution, the period at length arrives when the industrial and commercial world awakens to the fact that there is a product disproportionate to any current remunerative demand. Here, then, is one and probably the best explanation of the circumstance that the supply of very many of the great articles and instrumentalities of the world's use and commerce has increased, during the last ten or fifteen years, in a far greater ratio than the contemporaneous in-

---

effort was made to send food into the stricken regions, but owing to the entire absence of river and canal navigation, as well as of railroads, few of the suffering multitudes could be reached."

crease in the world's population, or of its immediate consuming capacity.

Another interesting feature of the situation, and one which has been especially pointed out by Prof. Lexis, of Göttingen, is, that "over-production" in recent years has resulted largely from the establishment of many new industrial enterprises whose capacity for production far exceeds any concurrent market demand; as is especially exemplified in the case of the manufacture of iron. "When the conditions of production are favorable, each of these establishments strives to bring to market a quantity corresponding to its actual power of production; and even if this can not be done, the recognition of tendencies and possibilities results in causing a depression of prices, under which the less favored undertakings can earn no profit, or, indeed, suffer loss." It was formerly a general assumption that, when price no longer equaled the cost of production and a fair profit on capital, production would be restricted or suspended; that the less favored producers would be crowded out, and by the relief thus afforded to the market normal prices would be again restored. But this doctrine is no longer applicable to the modern methods of production. Those engaged in great industrial enterprises, whether they form joint-stock companies or are simply wealthy individuals, are invested with such economic powers that none of them can be easily pushed to the wall, inasmuch as they can continue to work under conditions that would not permit a small producer to exist. Examples are familiar of joint-stock companies that have made no profit and paid no dividends for years, and yet continue active operations. The shareholders are content if the plant is kept up and the working capital preserved intact, and even when this is not done, they prefer to submit to assessments, or issue preference shares and take them up themselves rather than go into liquidation, with the chance of losing their whole capital. Another feature of such a condition of things is, that

the war of competition in which such industrial enterprises
are usually engaged is mainly carried on by a greater and
greater extension of the market supply of their products.
An illustration of this is afforded in the recent history of
the production of copper. When in 1885 the United States
produced and put on to the market seventy-four thousand
tons, as against forty thousand tons in 1882, the world's
prices of copper greatly declined. A large number of the
smaller producers were compelled to suspend operations, or
were entirely crushed; but the great Spanish and other important mines endeavored " to offset the diminution of profit
on the unit of quantity " by increasing their production;
and thus the price of copper continued to decline until it
reached a lower figure than ever before known in history.

Under such circumstances *industrial over-production*—
manifesting itself in excessive competition to effect sales, and
a reduction of prices below the cost of production—may become chronic ; and there appears to be no other means of
avoiding such results than that the great producers should
come to some understanding among themselves as to the
prices they will ask ; which in turn naturally implies agreements as to the extent to which they will produce. Up to this
point of procedure no exception on the part of society can
well be taken. But such an agreement, once perfected and
carried out, admits of an almost entire control of prices and
the establishment of monopolies, in the management of
which the rights of the public may be wholly ignored. Society has practically abandoned—and from the very necessity
of the case has got to abandon, unless it proposes to war
against progress and civilization—the prohibition of industrial concentrations and combinations. The world demands
abundance of commodities, and demands them cheaply; and
experience shows that it can have them only by the employment of great capital upon the most extensive scale.* The

* Adam Smith, in his " Wealth of Nations," published in 1776, in dis-

problem, therefore, which society under this condition of affairs has presented to it for solution is a difficult one, and twofold in its nature. To the producer the question of importance is, How can competition be restricted to an extent sufficient to prevent its injurious excesses? To the consumer, How can combination be restricted so as to secure its advantages and at the same time curb its abuses?

Another cause of over-production is undoubtedly due to an agency which has never before in the history of the world been operative to the extent that it is at present. With the great increase of wealth that has followed the increased control over the forces of nature and their utilization for production and distribution, there has come a desire to convert this wealth into the form of negotiable securities paying dividends or interest with regularity, and on the recipiency of which the owner can live without personal exertion or risk of the principal. Hence a stimulus for the undertaking of new enterprises which can create and market such securities; and these enterprises, whether in the nature of new railroad, manufacturing, or mining corporations, once developed, must go on producing and selling their products or services with or without a profit in order to meet their obligations and command a share of previously existing trade. Production elsewhere as a consequence, is, interfered with, displaced, and in not a few cases, by reason of better conditions, permanently undersold. And the general result is appropriately recognized by the term " over-production."

Furthermore, in anticipation of such consequences, the tendency and the interest of every successful manufacturing

---

cussing the effect of legislation and corporate regulations in limiting competition, clearly recognizes the tendency of combinations to advance prices, and the difficulty of limiting or preventing their influence by statute enactments. " People of the same trade," he says, " seldom meet together, even for merriment and diversion, but the conversation ends in a conspiracy against the public, or in some contrivance to raise prices." He, however, admitted that it was "impossible to prevent such meetings by any law which either could be executed or would be executed with liberty and justice."

combination is to put the prices of its products down to a
figure where it will not pay for speculators to form new competitive stock companies to be bought off or crushed by it.
For, if it did keep up high profit-assuring prices, one of two
things would eventually happen : either new factories would
be started ; or the inventive spirit of the age would devise
cheaper methods of production, or some substitute for the
product they furnished, and so ruin the first combination
beyond the possibility of redemption. And hence we have
here another permanent agency, antagonistic to the maintenance of high and remunerative prices.

But although such is substantially a correct general
exposition of the recent course of industrial events, and
although all the agencies concerned in reducing the time
and labor necessary to effect a given result in the world's
work have undoubtedly acted to a certain extent and in all
cases in unison, the diversity of method, under which the
supply in excess of remunerative demand, or the so-called
over-production, has been specially effected, is not a little
curious. Thus, in the case of crude iron and steel, cotton
fabrics and textiles generally, coal, most articles of metal
fabrication, ships, and the like, the increase and cheapened
supply have been brought about mainly through improvements in the machinery and economy of production ; while
in the case of wheat, rice, and other cereals, wool, cotton-
fibers, meats, and petroleum, like results have been mainly
occasioned by improvements in the machinery and economy
of distribution. On the other hand, in the case of copper,
tin, nickel, silver, quicksilver, quinine, and some important
chemicals, over-production, in the sense as above defined,
has been almost entirely due to the discovery or development of new and abundant natural sources of supply. It is
also not to be overlooked that other factors, which can not
properly be included within the sphere of the influence of
recent discoveries and inventions, have also powerfully contributed to bring about the so-called phenomenon of over-

production. Thus the changes in the consumption of some commodities is entirely dependent upon the increase in the tastes and intelligence of the masses. In the case of wheat, there is some evidence to the effect that the consumption of those who eat wheat bread habitually does not indefinitely expand with increasing means, but, on the contrary, that it decreases with the ability to procure a greater variety of food. It is also undeniable that the culture of the manual laborers of the world has not advanced concurrently, in recent years, with the increased and cheapened production of such articles. Many things, consequently, have been, as it were, showered upon these classes which they do not know how to use, and do not feel that they need, and for which, therefore, they can create no market. A man who has long been contented with one shirt a week is not likely to wish to use seven immediately, even if he can buy seven for the price that he formerly paid for one, and his wife takes pleasure in doing his washing.

Experience shows that the extremely high wages which were paid in Great Britain and in Belgium in the coal and iron business from 1868 to 1873 did nothing to permanently raise the standard of living among the laborers directly concerned. They spent their increased earnings in expensive food, and even in wines of high cost and quality; and did not make the slightest attempt to improve their style of living in respect to dress, furniture, or dwellings. That a continuance of such wages would eventually give the "coal" and "iron" miner the wants and habits of merchants and professional men, is possible; but it would require considerable time—probably more than one generation—to effect it. "The comforts accessible to the workingman, and which he makes use of and considers necessaries, have certainly been greatly multiplied during the last hundred years; but they have become necessaries very slowly, and anybody who undertook to furnish many of them even fifty years ago would probably have been ruined in the experiment."

One of the inevitable results of a supply of product or service in excess of remunerative demand (i. e., over-production) is a decline of price; and as the power of production and distribution has been increased in an unexampled degree since 1873 (as has been already shown), the prices of nearly all the great staple commodities of commerce and consumption have declined within the same period (as will be hereafter shown) in manner altogether without precedent in all former commercial history. That this experience has been altogether natural, and what might have been expected under the circumstances, will appear from the following considerations :

If production exceeds, by even a very small percentage, what is required to meet every current demand for consumption, the price which the surplus will command in the open market will govern and control the price of the whole; and if it can not be sold at all, or with difficulty, an intense competition on the part of the owners of accumulated stocks to sell will be engendered, with a great reduction or annihilation of all profit. Mr. John Bright, of England, in one of his recent speeches, relates the following incident of personal experience: "I know," he said, "a company manufacturing chemicals of some kind extensively, and one of the principal persons in it told me that in one of those high years, 1872, 1873, and 1874, the profits of that concern were £80,000, and he added that when the stock-taking and its results were communicated to the leading owner in the business, he made this very wise observation: 'I am very sorry to hear it, for you may depend upon it in the years that are to come we shall have to pay the whole of it back'; and in speaking to me of it he said, 'It is quite true, because for several years we have been able to make no dividend at all.' Well, why was that? The men who were making so large incomes at that time reinvested their money in increasing their business. Many of the concerns in this trade doubled their establishments, new companies were formed, and so the produce of their manufacture was extended to such a degree that the prices went down and the profits vanished."

The recent history of the nail-trade in the United States furnishes also a chapter of analogous experience. From 1881 to 1884 the American nail manufacture was exceedingly profitable; and during those years, as a natural consequence, most of the existing mills increased their capacity, and some more than doubled it. New mills also were built East and West, until the nail-producing power of the country nearly doubled, while the consuming capacity increased only about twenty per cent. The further result was that prices were forced down by an overstocked market, until nails were sold at from ten to fifteen per cent below cost, and in some instances mills that " could stand alone " were accused of intentionally forcing down prices in order to bankrupt weaker competitors. In the end prices were in a measure restored by a combination and agreement among manufacturers to restrict production.

Another illustration to the same effect is to be found in the present remarkable condition of the milling (flour) interest of the United States, which was thus described in an address before the " National Millers' Association " by its vice-president, at their annual meeting at Buffalo, in June, 1888 :

" A new common enemy," he said, " has sprung up, which threatens our property with virtual confiscation. . . . Large output, quick sales, keen competition, and small profits are characteristics of all modern trade. We have the advantage in our business of always being in fashion; the world requires so much bread every day, a quantity which can be ascertained with almost mathematical accuracy. . . . But our ambition has overreached our discretion and judgment. We have all participated in the general steeple-chase for pre-eminence; the thousand-barrel mill of our competitor had to be put in the shade by a two-thousand-barrel mill of our own construction; the commercial triumph of former seasons had to be surpassed by still more dazzling figures. As our glory increased our profits became smaller, until now the question is not how to surpass the record, but how to maintain our position and how to secure what we have in our possession. . . . In the general scramble we have gradually lost sight of the inexorable laws of supply and demand. We have been guilty of drifting away from sound trade regulations until our business has not only ceased to be profitable but carries with it undue commercial hazard."

As prices fall and profits shrink, producers working on insufficient capital, or by imperfect methods, are soon obliged, in order to meet impending obligations, to force sales through a further reduction of prices; and then stronger competitors, in order to retain their markets and customers, are compelled to follow their example; and this in turn is followed by new concessions alternately by both parties, until gradually the industrial system becomes depressed and demoralized, and the weaker succumb (fail), with a greater or less destruction of capital and waste of product. Affairs now having reached their maximum of depression, recovery slowly commences. Consumption is never arrested, even if production is, for the world must continue to consume in order that life and civilization may exist. The continued increase of population also increases the aggregate of consumption; and, finally, the industrial and commercial world again suddenly realizes that the condition of affairs has been reversed, and that now the supply has become unequal to the demand. Then such producers as have "stocks on hand," or the machinery of production ready for immediate and effective service, realize large profits; and the realization of this fact immediately tempts others to rush into production, in many cases with insufficient capital (raised often through stock companies), and without that practical knowledge of the detail of their undertaking which is necessary to insure success, and the old experience of inflation and reaction is again and again repeated.

Hence the explanation of the now much-talked-of "periods" or "cycles" of panic and speculation, of trade activity and stagnation. Their periodical occurrence has long been recognized, and the economic principles involved in them have long been understood.* But a century ago or more, when such economic changes occurred in any country, the resulting disturbances were mainly confined to such country—as was notably the case in the "Mississippi Scheme" of John Law in France, and the English "South-Sea Bubble," in the last century, or the severe industrial and financial crises which occurred in Great Britain in the earlier years of the present century—and people of other countries, hearing of them after considerable intervals, and then vaguely through mercantile correspondence, were little troubled or interested. During recent years, however, they have

---

* The theory, more or less widely entertained, that there is some law governing and occasioning the regular recurrence of periods of commercial and financial disaster or prosperity, has thus far not been sustained by investigation. Scarcity and high prices tend to cause increased production and induce speculation; but the supply of different commodities is governed by different laws, and it would be difficult to name any two classes of products that are controlled by the same natural conditions. In the case of some commodities it requires but a brief time to secure an increased production; in the case of others, months, and even years, are requisite. As respects agricultural productions, no locality accessible by modern means of transportation is dependent on its own supplies, or makes its own prices; and the influences which afflict one part of the world with disaster bring bountiful supplies to others. Hence it follows that any periodical cause, common in its effects upon all products, is impossible. Neither can it be conceived how periodical changes in prices can result from any possible law of nature, unless it can be shown that such laws exist and operate with uniformity on the human mind and on the development of the human intellect, which has not yet been done. One of the most noted, and at the same time one of the most empirical, attempts to found predictions as to future conditions of business and prices upon past commercial experiences, is embodied in a little book entitled "Benner's Prophecies," the work of an Ohio farmer named Benner, which, first published about 1875, has since passed through several editions and been widely circulated and quoted. Its prophecies relate mainly to the prices of pig-iron and hogs, and to the next period of commercial and financial disaster. In the case of pig-iron, it is claimed that the prophecies have been in a measure fulfilled; but in the case of hogs, not one has been. A careful analysis of the book has furthermore proved that it is not of sufficient account or correctness to warrant any serious attempt at the refutation of its conclusions, which seem to be based on little more than the assumption that what has been in respect to prices will again happen; and that the cause of periodicity of panics is to be found "in our solar system."

become less local and more universal, because the railroad, the steamship, and the telegraph have broken down the barriers between nations, and, by spreading in a brief time the same hopes and fears over the whole civilized world, have made it impossible any longer to confine the speculative spirit to any one country. So that now the announcement of any signal success in any department of production or mercantile venture at once fires the imagination of the enterprising and reckless in every country, and quickly incites to operations which without such a stimulus would probably not be undertaken. At the same time, the command through the telegraph of instantaneous information throughout the world of the conditions and prospects of all markets for all commodities has also undoubtedly operated to impart steadiness to prices, increase the safety of mercantile and manufacturing operations, and reduce the elements of speculation and of panics to the lowest minimum.

One universally recognized and, to some persons, perplexing peculiarity of the recent long-continued depression in trade is the circumstance, that while profits have been so largely reduced that, as the common expression goes, " it has not paid to do business," •the volume of trade throughout the world has not contracted, but, measured by quantities rather than by values, has in many departments notably increased. The following are some of the more notable examples of the evidence that can be offered in confirmation of this statement :

The years 1879, 1880, and 1881 for the United States were years of abundant crops and great foreign demand, and are generally acknowledged to have been prosperous; while the years 1882, 1883, and 1884 are regarded as having been years of extreme depression and reaction. And yet the movement of railroad freights throughout the country greatly increased during this latter as compared with the former period; the tonnage carried by six railroads centering at Chicago in 1884 having been nearly thirty-three per cent greater than in 1881; and the tonnage carried one mile by all the railroads of the United States in 1884—a year of extreme depression—having been 5,000,000,000 in excess of that carried in 1882; and this, notwithstanding there was a great falling off, in 1884, in the carriage of material for new railroad construction. Again, the foreign commerce of the United States, measured in dollars, largely declined during the same later period; but, measured in quantities, there was but little decrease, and in the case of not a few leading articles a notable increase. Thus, for the year 1885 the total value of the foreign commerce of the country in merchandise was $93,251,921 less than in the preceding year (1884), but of this decrease $90,170,364, according to the estimates of the United States Bureau of Statistics, represented a decline in price. An export of 70,000,000 bushels of wheat from the United States in 1884 returned $75,000,-000; while an export of 84,500,000 in 1885 gave less than $73,000,000. An export of 389,000,000 pounds of bacon and hams in 1884 brought in nearly $40,000,000; but shipments of 400,000,000 pounds in 1885 returned but $37,000,000, or an increase of foreign sales of about 11,000,000 pounds was accompanied by a decline of about $3,000,000 in price. In 1877, 216,287,891 gallons of exported petroleum were valued at $44,209,360; but in 1886, 303,911,698 gallons (or 87,623,-000 gallons more) were valued at only $24,685,767, a decline in value of $19,683,000. But the most remarkable example of changes of this character is to be found in the case of sugar. Thus, in 1883 the United States imported 2,023,-000,000 pounds of sugar, for which it paid $91,959,000. In 1885, 2,548,000,000 pounds were imported, at a cost of $68,-531,000; or a larger quantity by 525,000,000 pounds was imported in 1885, as compared with 1883, for $23,428,000 less money.

The statistics of the recent foreign trade of Great Britain also exhibit corresponding results. For example, the declared aggregate value of British exports and imports for

1883 were £667,000,000 as compared with £682,000,000 in 1873, an apparent decline of no little magnitude. But if the aggregate of the foreign trade of Great Britain for 1883 had been valued at the prices of 1873, the total, in place of £667,000,000, would have been £861,000,000, or an increase for the decade of about thirty per cent.

Again, the declared value of British imports retained for home consumption for the year 1887 was £302,828,000; but had they been valued at the same prices as were paid in 1886, their cost would have been £308,145,000. The saving in the purchases of foreign products by Great Britain in 1887, owing to the fall of prices, as compared with 1886, was, therefore, £5,317,000. On the other hand, if the value of the British exports for 1887, namely, £221,398,000, had been sold on the same terms as in 1886, their value would have amounted to £222,559,000, showing a comparative loss for the year of £1,161,000. Comparing quantities, however, the volume of the British foreign trade for 1887, in comparison with that of 1886, was about five per cent larger in respect to imports and 4·8 per cent in respect to exports.

An explanation of this economic phenomenon of recent years, namely, a continuing increase in the volume of trade, with a continuing low rate or decline in profits, may be found in the following circumstances: One constant result of a decline in prices is an increase (but not necessarily proportional or even universal) in consumption. Evidence on this point, derived from recent experiences, will be referred to hereafter; but the following example illustrates how this economic principle manifests itself even under unexpected conditions: In 1878 sulphate of quinine ruled as high for a time on the London market as $3.96 per ounce, in bulk. In 1887 the quotation was as low as thirty cents per ounce. Quinine is used mainly as a medicine, and is so indispensable in certain ailments that it may be presumed that its cost in 1878 was no great restriction on its consumption, and that no great increase in its use from a reduction in price was to be expected, any more than an increase in the use of coffins for a similar reason—both commodities being used to the extent that they are needed, even if a denial of the use of other things is necessary in order to permit of their procurement. And yet, that increase in the cheapness of quinine has been followed by a notable increase in its consumption, is shown by the fact that the importation of cinchona-bark —from which quinine is manufactured—into Europe and the United States during recent years has notably increased, 4,787,000 pounds having been imported into the United States in 1887, as compared with an import of 2,580,000 in 1883, the imports of quinine itself at the same time increasing from 1,055,764 ounces, valued at $1,809,000, in 1883, to 2,180,157 ounces, valued at $1,069,918, in 1887. The following statement also illustrates even more forcibly the ordinary effect of a reduction of price on the consumption of the more staple commodities : Thus, a reduction (saving) of 6d. (twelve cents) per week in the cost of the bread of every family in Great Britain (a saving which, on the basis of the decline in the wholesale prices of wheat within the last decade, would seem to have been practicable) has been estimated as equivalent to giving a quarter of a million pounds sterling, or $1,250,000 per week, to the whole people of the kingdom to spend for other things.

The evidence is also conclusive that the ability of the population of the world to consume is greater than ever before, and is rapidly increasing. Indeed, such a conclusion is a corollary from the acknowledged fact of increased production—the end and object of all production being consumption. Take, for example, the United States, with its present population of sixty-five millions—a population that undoubtedly produces and consumes more per head than any other equal number of people on the face of the globe, and is producing and consuming very much more than it did ten or even five years ago. The business of exchanging the products or services, and of satisfying thereby the wants of such a people is, therefore, necessarily immense, and with the annual increase of population, and with consuming power increasing in an even larger ratio, the volume of such business must continue to increase. And what is true of the United States is true, in a greater or less degree, of all the other nations of the globe. There is, therefore, nothing inconsistent or mysterious in the maintenance or increase in the volume of the world's business contemporaneously with a depression of trade—in the sense of a reduction of profits—occasioned by an intense competition to dispose of commodities, which have been produced under comparatively new conditions in excess of a satisfactory remunerative demand in the world's markets. And, apart from this, it is now well understood that the aggregate movement and exchange of goods is little if any less in times of the so-called " depression of trade " than in times of admitted prosperity. Again, if depression of business does not signify less business, it can only signify less profits. In fact, a reduction of profits is the necessary consequence of falling prices, since all the calculations, engagements, and contracts of the employing classes, including wages, are based upon the expectation that the prices of their products will remain substantially unchanged, or no worse than before. If there is a progressive fall of prices without a corresponding fall of wages, profits must fall progressively, and interest also, since the rate of interest is governed by the profits which can be made from the use of capital. Now this is exactly what has happened in recent years. Profits and prices of commodities have fallen, but wages have not fallen, except in a few special departments. Consequently the purchasing power of wages has risen, and this has given to the wage-earning class a greater command over the necessaries and comforts of life, and the purchases of all this great class have supplemented any forced economizing of the employing and well-to-do classes. " The latter are the ones who make the most noise in the newspapers, and whose frequent bankruptcies

most fill the public eye. But they are not those whose consumption of commodities most swells the tonnage of the
railways and steamships. They occupy the first cabin, and
their names are the only ones printed in the passenger lists,
but the steerage carries more consumers of wheat, sugar, and
pork than all the cabins together."

The popular sentiment which has instinctively attributed
the remarkable disturbance of trade within recent years to
the more remarkable changes which have taken place concurrently in the methods of production and distribution has,
therefore, not been mistaken. The almost instinctive efforts
of producers everywhere to arrest what they consider " bad
trade " by partially or wholly interrupting production has
not been inexpedient; and the use of the word " over-production," stripped of its looseness of expression, and in the
sense as defined by the British Commission (and as heretofore shown), is not inappropriate in discussing the economic
phenomena under consideration. It would also seem as if
much of the bewilderment that is still attendant upon this
subject, and the secret of the fruitlessness of most of the
elaborate inquiries that have been instituted concerning it,
have been due mainly to an inability to distinguish clearly
between a causation that is primary, all-sufficient, and which
has acted in the nature of unity, and causes which are in the
nature of sequences or derivatives. An illustration of this
is to be found in the tendency of English writers and investigators to consider the immense losses which British
farming capital has experienced since 1873, as alone sufficient to account for all the disturbances to which trade and
industry in the United Kingdom have been subjected during the same period. That such losses have been extensive
and disastrous without precedent, is not to be questioned.
Sir James Caird estimates this loss in the purchasing power
of the classes engaged in or connected with British agriculture, for the single year 1885, as having amounted to £42,-
800,000 ($214,000,000); and as the losses for several preced-

ing years are believed to have been equal or even greater than this, an estimate of a thousand million dollars decline in the value of British farming capital since 1880, from depreciation of land-values, rentals, and prices for stock and cereals, is probably an *under* rather than an *over*-estimate.

Wheat-growing, which was formerly profitable in Great Britain, is reported as not having been remunerative to the British farmer since 1874; a fact that finds eloquent expression in the acknowledged reduction in British wheat acreage from about 4,000,000 acres (3,981,000) in 1869 to 2,317,324 acres in 1887, or more than 40 per cent. And as the English farmers have decreased their production of cereals by reason of the small amount of profit accruing from their labor, the English agricultural laborer has from necessity been compelled to seek other employments, or emigrate to other countries.

[According to a recent report of Major Cragie to the British Farmer's Club, the wages of farm laborers in England after 1860 advanced on the average thirty per cent; but since 1881 the average decline in wages " over the farmed surface of England " has been at least fourteen per cent; and in some sections of the country the whole of the rise in the mean wage of ordinary agricultural labors since 1860 has entirely disappeared. The decline in the rents of farm lands in England in recent years has been estimated by the London " Economist," on the authority of Mr. Clare Read, as not less than thirty per cent, or 10s. per acre on the wheat area—about $8,700,000 yearly. These results may, and probably do, furnish an explanation of the fact that the increase of wheat acreage in Great Britain in 1888 as compared with 1887 was 280,708 acres, or 11·8 per cent.]

That the agricultural populations of the interior states of Europe, which have hitherto been protected in a degree by the barrier of distance against the tremendous cheapening of transportation, are also at last feeling the full effects of its influence, is shown by the statement (United States Consular Reports, 1886) that farming land in Germany, remote

from large cities, where the demand for milk and other
perishable products is small, can now be purchased for fifty
per cent of the prices which prevailed at the close of the
Franco-German War in 1870–'71. And yet such startling
results, in the place of being prime factors in occasioning a
depression of British trade and industry, are really four removes from the original causes, which may be enumerated
in order as follows: *First*, the occupation and utilization of
new and immense areas of cheap and fertile wheat-growing
land in the United States, Canada (Manitoba), Australia,
and the Argentine Republic. *Second*, the invention and application of machinery for facilitating and cheapening the
production and harvesting of crops, and which on the wheat-
fields of Dakota (as before pointed out) have made the labor
of every agriculturist equivalent to the annual production of
5,500 bushels of wheat. *Third*, the extension of the system
of transportation on land through the railroad, and on sea
through the steamship, in default of which the appropria-
tion of new land and the invention and application of
new agricultural machinery would have availed but little.
Fourth, the discovery of Bessemer, and the invention of
the compound (steamship) engine, without which transportation could not have cheapened to the degree necessary
to effect the present extent of distribution. Now, from
the conjoined result of all these different agencies has come
a reduction in the world's price of wheat to an extent sufficient to make its growing unprofitable on lands taken at
high rents, and under unfavorable climatic conditions; and
legislation is powerless to make it otherwise. In short, the
whole secret of the recent immense losses of the British
and to a lesser extent also of the Continental agriculturist,
and the depression of British trade and industry, so far
as it has been contingent on such losses, stands revealed in the simple statement that American wheat sold
for export at the principal shipping ports of the United
States in 1885 for 56 cents less per bushel than in

1874, 32 cents less than in 1882, and 20 cents less than in 1884.*

"I have calculated that the produce of five acres of wheat can be brought from Chicago to Liverpool at less than the cost of manuring one acre for wheat in England."—*Testimony of* W. J. HARRIS, *a leading farmer in Devonshire, England, before the British Commission, 1886.*

---

* The average value of the wheat exported from the United States in 1885, according to the tables of the United States Bureau of Statistics, was 86 cents per bushel at the shipping ports. This was a decline of 20 cents from 1884, 26¼ cents from 1883, 32 cents from 1882, 56 cents from 1874, and 61 cents from 1871.

The export value of corn was 54 cents in 1885, showing a decline of 7 cents from 1884, 14 cents from 1883, 12 cents from 1882, 30 cents from 1875, and 15 cents from 1872.

The export value of oats was 37 cents in 1885, showing a decline of 2 cents from 1884, 13 cents from 1883, 7 cents from 1882, 20 cents from 1875, and 14 cents from 1871.

The export price of lard was 7 cents in 1885, showing a decline of 2 cents from 1884, 4 cents from 1883, 6 cents from 1875, 3 cents from 1872, and 9 cents from 1870.

How closely the decline in recent years in the export prices of American cereals has been followed by corresponding reductions in the prices of cereals in the markets of Great Britain is exhibited by the following table (published in the British "Farmer's Almanac" for 1886), showing the average prices per quarter of wheat, barley, and oats, in Great Britain for two periods of ten years, commencing with 1865, with a separate estimate for 1885:

CEREALS.	Price per quarter. Average for the ten years, 1866–1875.		Price per quarter. Average for the ten years, 1876–1885.		Average price per quarter for 1885.	
	s.	*d.*	*s.*	*d.*	*s.*	*d.*
Wheat	54	7¾	43	9¼	32	10
Barley	39	2	36	5	30	1
Oats	25	10½	22	8¼	20	7

Similar tables given by the same authority show the gross value per annum of the product of wheat, barley, oats, beef, mutton, and wool, in Great Britain, to have been £35,000,000 ($175,000,000) less in 1885 than were the mean returns for the ten years 1866–1875. According also to data given in the returns of the British Registrar-General, the average prices of beef by the carcass in the London market were £58 5s. 7d. per ton during the ten years from 1866–1875, £57 5s. 8d. for 1876–1885, and £49 17s. 6d. for the year 1885.

Indian corn can be successfully and has been extensively raised in Italy. But Indian corn grown in the valley of the Mississippi, a thousand miles from the seaboard, has been transported in recent years to Italy and sold in her markets at a lower cost than the corn of Lombardy and Venetia, where the wages of the agriculturist are not one third of the wages paid in the United States for corresponding labor. And one not surprising sequel of this is that 77,000 Italian laborers emigrated to the United States in 1885.

Now, what has happened in the case of wheat and corn has happened also, in a greater or less degree, as respects meats and almost all other food products; increased supplies having occasioned reduction of prices, and reduction of prices, in turn, ruinous losses to invested capital and revolutionary disturbances in old methods of doing business. The Bessemer rail, the modern steamship, and the Suez Canal have brought the wheat-fields of Dakota and India, and the grazing-lands of Texas, Colorado, Australia, and the Argentine Republic, nearer to the factory operatives in Manchester, England, than the farms of Illinois were before the war to the spindles and looms of New England.

CHANGES IN THE RELATIONS OF LABOR AND CAPITAL.—Consider next how potent for economic disturbance have been the changes in recent years in the relations of labor and capital, and how clearly and unmistakably these changes are consequents or derivatives from a more potent and antecedent agency.

Machinery is now recognized as essential to cheap production. Nobody can produce effectively and economically without it, and what was formerly known as domestic manufacture is now almost obsolete. But machinery is one of the most expensive of all products, and its extensive purchase and use require an amount of capital far beyond the capacity of the ordinary individual to furnish. There are very few men in the world possessed of an amount of wealth sufficient to individually construct and own an extensive line of railway or telegraph, a first-class steamship, or a great factory. It is also to be remembered that for carrying on production by the most modern and effective methods large capital is needed, not only for machinery, but also for the purchasing and carrying of extensive stocks of crude material and finished products.

Sugar can now be, and generally is, refined at a profit of an eighth of a cent a pound, and sometimes as low as a sixteenth; or, in other words, from eight to sixteen pounds of raw sugar must now be treated in refining in order to make a cent; from eight hundred to sixteen hundred pounds to make a dollar; from eighty thousand to one hundred and sixty thousand pounds to make a hundred dollars, and so on. The mere capital requisite for providing and carrying the raw material necessary for the successful prosecution of this business, apart from all other conditions, places it, therefore, of necessity beyond the reach of any ordinary capitalist or producer. It has been before stated that, in the manufacture of jewelry by machinery, one boy can make up nine thousand sleeve-buttons per day; four girls also, working by modern methods, can put together in the same time eight thousand collar-buttons. But to run an establishment with such facilities the manufacturer must keep constantly in stock thirty thousand dollars' worth of cut ornamental stones, and a stock of cuff-buttons that represents nine thousand different designs and patterns. Hence from such conditions have grown up great corporations or stock companies, which are only forms of associated capital organized for effective use and protection. They are regarded to some extent as evils; but they are necessary, as there is apparently no other way in which the work of production and distribution, in accordance with the requirements of the age, can be prosecuted. The rapidity, however, with which such combinations of capital are organizing for the purpose of promoting industrial and commercial undertakings on a scale heretofore wholly unprecedented, and the tendency

they have to crystallize into something far more complex
than what has been familiar to the public as corporations,
with the impressive names of syndicates, trusts, etc., also
constitute one of the remarkable features of modern business methods. It must also be admitted that the whole
tendency of recent economic development is in the direction of limiting the area within which the influence of competition is effective.

And when once a great association of capital has been
effected, it becomes necessary to have a master-mind to manage it—a man who is competent to use and direct other men,
who is fertile in expedient and quick to note and profit by
any improvements in methods of production and variations
in prices. Such a man is a general of industry, and corresponds in position and functions to the general of an army.

What, as a consequence, has happened to the employés?
Coincident with and as a result of this change in the methods of production, the modern manufacturing system has
been brought into a condition analogous to that of a military organization, in which the individual no longer works
as independently as formerly, but as a private in the ranks,
obeying orders, keeping step, as it were, to the tap of the
drum, and having nothing to say as to the plan of his work,
of its final completion, or of its ultimate use and distribution.
In short, the people who work in the modern factory are, as
a rule, taught to do one thing—to perform one and generally a simple operation ; and when there is no more of that
kind of work to do, they are in a measure helpless. The result has been that the individualism or independence of the
producer in manufacturing has been in a great degree destroyed, and with it has also in a great degree been destroyed
the pride which the workman formerly took in his work—
that fertility of resource which formerly was a special characteristic of American workmen, and that element of skill
that comes from long and varied practice and reflection and
responsibility. Not many years ago every shoemaker was or

could be his own employer.   The boots and shoes passed directly from an individual producer to the consumer.   Now this condition of things has passed away.   Boots and shoes are made in large factories; and machinery has been so utilized, and the division of labor in connection with it has been carried to such an extent, that the process of making a shoe is said to be divided into sixty-four parts, or the shoemaker of to-day is only the sixty-fourth part of what a shoemaker once was.*   It is also asserted that " the constant employment at one sixty-fourth part of a shoe not only offers no encouragement to mental activity, but dulls by its monotony the brain of the employé to such an extent that the power to think and reason is almost lost." †

---

* The following is a reported enumeration of the specialties or distinct branches of shoemaking at which men, women, and children are kept constantly at work in the most perfect of the modern shoe-factories, no apprentices being needed or taken in such establishments : " Binders, blockers, boot-liners, beaters-out, boot-turners, bottomers, buffers, burnishers, channelers, counter-makers, crimpers, cutters, dressers, edge-setters, eyeleters, finishers, fitters, heelers, lasters, levelers, machine-peggers, McKay stitchers, nailers, packers, parters, peggers, pressers, rosette-makers, siders, sandpaperers, skinners, stitchers, stringers, treers, trimmers, welters, buttonhole-makers, clampers, cleckers, closers, corders, embossers, gluers, inner-sole-makers, lacers, leather-assorters, riveters, rollers, seam-rubbers, shank-pressers, shavers, slipper-liners, sole-leather-cutters, sole-quilters, stampers, stiffeners, stock-fitters, strippers, taggers, tipmakers, turners, vampers, etc."

† The position taken by Prince Krapotkin, who represents to some extent the extreme socialistic movement in Europe, is, " that the division and subdivision of functions have been pushed so far as to divide humanity into castes almost as firmly established as those of old India.   First, the broad division into producers and consumers : little-consuming producers on the one hand, little-producing consumers on the other hand.   Then, amid the former, a series of further subdivisions—the manual worker and the intellectual worker, sharply separated ; and agricultural laborers and workers in manufactures. Amid little-producing consumers are numberless minute subdivisions, the modern ideal of a workman being a man or a woman, a boy or a girl, without the knowledge of any handicraft, having no conception whatever of the industry in which he or she is employed, and only capable of making all day long and for a whole life the same infinitesimal part of something—from the age of thirteen to that of sixty pushing the coal-cart at a given spot of the mine, or making the spring of a pen-knife, or the eighteenth part of a pin.   The working classes have become," he says, " mere servants to some machine of a given

As the division of labor in manufacturing—more especially in the case of textiles—is increased, the tendency is to supplement the employment of men with the labor of women and children. The whole number of employés in the cotton-mills of the United States, according to the census of 1880, was 172,544; of this number, 59,685 were men, and 112,859 women and children. In Massachusetts, out of 61,246 employés in the cotton-mills, 22,180 are males, 31,496 women, and 7,570 children. In the latter State certain manufacturing towns, owing to the disparity in the numbers of men and women employed, and in favor of the latter, are coming to be known by the appellation of " *she-towns.*" *
During recent years the increase in the employment of child-labor in Germany has been so noticeable, that the factory inspectors of Saxony in their official report for 1888 have suggested that such labor be altogether forbidden by the State, and that the hours during which youths between the ages of·fourteen to sixteen may be legally employed in factories should be limited to six.

---

description; mere flesh-and-bone parts of some immense machinery, having no idea about how and why the machinery is performing its rhythmical movements. Skilled artisanship is swept away as a survival of a past which is condemned to disappear. For the artist who formerly found æsthetic enjoyment in the work of his hands is substituted the human slave of an iron slave," etc., etc.

* " The tendency of late years is toward the employment of child-labor. We see men frequently thrown out of employment, owing to the spinning-mule being displaced by the ring-frame ; or children spinning yarn, which men used to spin. In the weave-shops, girls and women are preferable to men, so that we may reasonably expect that, in the not very distant future, all the cotton-manufacturing districts will be classed in the category of ' she-towns.' But people will naturally say, What will become of the men ? This is a question which it behooves manufacturers to take seriously into consideration, for men will not stay in any town or city where only their wives and children can be given employment. Therefore, a pause at the present time might be of untold value in the future ; for, just as sure as the world goes round, women and children will seek fresh pastures, where work can be found for the husband and father, in preference to remaining in places where he has to play the part of the ' old woman,' while they go to work to earn the means of subsistence."—WADE's *Fiber and Fabric.*

Another exceedingly interesting and developing feature of the new situation is that, as machinery has destroyed the handicrafts, and associated capital has placed individual capital at a disadvantage, so machinery and associated capital in turn, guided by the same common influences, now war upon machinery and other associated capital. Thus the now well-ascertained and accepted fact, based on long experience, that power is most economically applied when applied on the largest possible scale, is rapidly and inevitably leading to the concentration of manufacturing in the largest establishments, and the gradual extinction of those which are small. Such also has already been, and such will continue to be, the outcome of railroad, telegraph, and steamship development and experience; and another quarter of a century will not unlikely see all of the numerous companies that at present make up the vast railroad system of the United States consolidated, for sound economic reasons, under a comparatively few organizations or companies.* In

---

* "There are in England eleven great companies, but these were formed of two hundred and sixty-two companies, while the six great companies of France have absorbed forty-eight companies. When the New York Central Railway was formed in 1853, it consisted of a union of eleven railways. It takes twenty-five pages in 'Poor's Manual of Railroads for 1885' merely to give a list of railways in the United States which have been merged in other lines. This shows in marked manner the tendency toward consolidation. There is no exception. It is a phenomenon common to all countries.

"By means of combination and concentration of railway property the railway business of the country can be conducted most effectively. It is an improvement in economic methods of large proportions. The experience of the world has demonstrated this so conclusively that it admits of no doubt, and a very little reflection on the nature of the economic functions of the railway will render it clear to the reader. When the general public and the press resist this tendency, or cry out in childish indignation because Mr. Vanderbilt bought the West Shore Railway in the interest of the New York Central and Hudson River Railway, they are more foolish than laboring-men who resist the introduction of new and improved machinery. The latter have at least the excuse that changed methods of production often occasion the bitterest distress, and injure permanently some few laboring men; and it is hard to appreciate a permanent advantage which must be acquired by severe present suffering. The impulse to such great economies as can be secured by com-

this respect the existing situation in Great Britain (which corresponds to that in all other countries) has thus been represented :

" Trade after trade is monopolized, not necessarily by large capitalists, but by great capitals. In every trade the standard of necessary size, the minimum establishment that can hold its own in competition, is constantly and rapidly raised. The little men are ground out, and the littleness that dooms men to destruction waxes year by year. Of the (British) cotton-mills of the last century, a few here and there are standing, saved by local or other accidents, while their rivals have either grown to gigantic size or fallen into ruin. The survivors, with steam substituted for water-power, with machinery twice or thrice renewed, are worked while they pay one half or one fourth per cent on their cost. The case of other textile manufactures is the same or stronger still. Steel and iron are yet more completely the monopoly of gigantic plants. The chemical trade was for a long time open to men of very moderate means. Recent inventions threaten to turn the plant that has cost millions to waste brick and old lead. Already nothing but a trade agreement, temporary in its nature, has prevented the closing of half the (chemical) factories of St. Helen's and Widnes, and the utter ruin of all the smaller owners. Every year the same thing happens in one or another of our minor industries."

" The president of one of the largest cotton corporations in New England in a recent annual report stated that ' competition is so sharp that the profits of a mill are generally only the savings made on the general expenses caused by increased production, so that a mill with a small production finds it impossible to live. Unless the smaller cotton-mills have a monopoly of some fancy business, they have all gone under or must fail.' "

bination is so strong as to be irresistible. It is one of those forces which overwhelm the man who puts himself against them, though they may be guided and directed, will one but put one's self in the stream and move with it."— *The Reform of Railway Abuses.* ELY.

" The railroads of the country are rapidly moving toward some great system of consolidation. . . . The movement is to-day going forward more rapidly—much more rapidly—under the artificial stimulus given to it by the Inter-State Commerce Act than ever before. The next move will be in the direction of railroad systems of twenty thousand miles, each under one common management."—*Speech of* MR. CHARLES FRANCIS ADAMS, *President Union Pacific, before the Commercial Club, Boston, December,* 1888.

Such changes in the direction of the concentration of production by machinery in large establishments are, moreover, in a certain and large sense, not voluntary on the part of the possessors and controllers of capital, but necessary or even compulsory. If an eighth or a sixteenth of a cent a pound is all the profit that competition and modern improvements will permit in the business of refining sugar, such business has got to be conducted on a large scale to admit of the realization of any profit. An establishment fitted up with all modern improvements, and refining the absolutely large but comparatively small quantity of a million pounds per annum, could realize, at a sixteenth of a cent a pound profit on its work, but $625. Accordingly, the successful refiner of sugars of to-day, in place of being as formerly a manufacturer exclusively, must now, as a condition of full success, be his own importer, do his own lighterage, own his own wharfs and warehouses, make his own barrels and boxes, prepare his own bone-black, and ever be ready to discard and replace his expensive machinery with every new improvement. But to do all this successfully requires not only the command of large capital, but of business qualifications of the very highest order—two conditions that but comparatively few can command. It is not, therefore, to be wondered at that, under the advent of these new conditions, one half of the sugar-refineries that were in operation in the seaboard cities of the United States in 1875 have since failed or discontinued operations.

In the great beef slaughtering and packing establishments at Chicago, which slaughter a thousand head of cattle and upward in a day, economies are effected which are not possible when this industry is carried on, as usual, upon a very small scale. Every part of the animal—hide, horns, hoofs, bones, blood, and hair—which in the hands of the ordinary butcher are of little value or a dead loss, are turned to a profit by the Chicago packers in the manufacture of glue, bone-dust, fertilizers, etc.; and accordingly the great packers can afford to and do pay more for cattle than would otherwise be possible—an advance estimated by the best authorities at two dollars a head. Nor does this increased price which Western stock-growers receive come out of the consumer of beef. It is made possible only by converting the portions of an ox that would otherwise be sheer waste into products of value.

The following statements have recently been made in California, on what is claimed to be good authority ("Overland Monthly"), of the comparative cost of growing wheat in that State on ranches, or farms of different sizes. On ranches of 1,000 acres, the average cost is reported at $92\frac{1}{2}$ cents per 100 pounds; on 2,000 acres, 85 cents; on 6,000 acres, 75 cents; on 15,000 acres, 60 cents; on 30,000 acres, 50 cents; and on 50,000 acres, 40 cents. Accepting these estimates as correct, it follows that the inducements to grow wheat in California by agriculturists with limited capital and on a small scale are anything but encouraging.

The following are other illustrations pertinent to this subject: " It is a characteristic and noteworthy feature of banking in Germany," says the London " Statist," " that the bulk of the business is gradually shifting from the small bankers, who used to do a thriving business, to the great banking companies, leaving quite a number of small customers almost without any chance to prosper in legitimate operations—concentration of capital and business in the hands of a limited number of powerful customers being the rule of the day."

The tendency to discontinue the building and use of small vessels for ocean transportation, and the inability of such vessels to compete with vessels of larger tonnage, is shown by the statement that while a steamer of from 200 to 300 tons requires one sailor for every 19·8 tons, a steamer of from 800 to 1,000 tons requires but one sailor for every 41·5 tons. In like manner, while a sailing-vessel of from 200 to 300 tons requires one sailor for every 28·9 tons, a sailing-vessel of five times the size, or from 1,000 to 1,600 tons, requires but one sailor for every 60·3 tons. And as it is also claimed that other economies in the construction of the hull or the rigging, and in repairing, are concurrent with the reduction of crews, it is not difficult to understand why it is that large vessels are enabled to earn a percentage of profit with rates of freight which, in the case of small vessels, would inevitably entail losses.

It was a matter of congratulation after the conclusion of the American war in 1865, that the large plantation system of cotton-raising would be broken up, and a system of smaller crops, by small and independent farmers or yeomanry, would take its place. Experience has not, however, verified this expectation; but, on the contrary, has shown that it is doubtful whether any profit can accrue to a cultivator of cotton whose annual crop is less than fifty bales.

"Cotton (at the South) is made an exclusive crop, because it can be sold for cash—for an actual and certain price in gold. It is a mere trifle to get eight or nine cents for a pound of cotton, but for a bale of 450 pounds it is $40. The bale of cotton is therefore a reward which the anxious farmer works for during an entire year, and for which he will spend half as much in money before the cotton is grown, besides all his labor and time. And the man who can not make eight or ten bales at least has almost no object in life, and nothing to live on."—*Bradstreet's Journal.*

About fifteen years ago the new and so-called "roller process" for crushing and separating wheat was discovered and brought into use. Its advantages over the old method of grinding by millstones were that it separated the flour more perfectly from the hull or bran of the berry of the wheat, gave more flour to a bushel of wheat, and raised both its color and strength (nutriment). As soon as these facts were demonstrated, the universal adoption of the roller mills and the total abolition of the stone mills became only a question of time, as the latter could not compete with the former. The cost of building mills to operate by the roller process is, however, much greater than that of the old stone mills. Formerly, from $25,000 to $50,000 was an ample capital with which to engage in flour-milling in the United States, where water-power only was employed; but at the present time from $100,000 to $150,000 is required to go into the business upon a basis with any promise of success, even with a small mill; while the great mills of Minneapolis, St. Louis, and Milwaukee cost from $250,000 to $500,000 each, and include " steam " as well as water-power. The consequence of requiring so much more capital to participate in the flour business now than formerly is that the smaller flour-mills in the United States are being crushed, or forced into consolidation with the larger companies, the latter being able, from dealing in such immense quantities, to buy their wheat more economically, obtain lower rates of freight, and, by contracting ahead, keep constantly running.* At the same time there is a tendency to drive the milling industry from points in the country to the larger cities, and central grain and flour markets where cheap freights and large supplies of wheat are available. As might have been anticipated, therefore, the Milwaukee " Directory of American Millers," for 1886, shows a decrease in the number of flour-mills in the United States for that year, as compared with 1884, of 6,812, out of a total in the latter year of 25,079, but an increase at the same time in capacity for flour production. These new conditions of milling have been followed by a movement in England for the consolidation in great cities of the flour-mills and bakeries into single establishments, where the bread-making of the whole com-

---

* What has happened in this business in the United States is true also of Great Britain. In both countries the new system of milling and the concentration of the business in great establishments has led to over-production, undue competition, and minimized profits ; and in both countries great milling syndicates or trusts have been formed to regulate production and prices.

munity may be done in immense ovens, under the most scientific conditions, and at a material saving in cost.

The improvements in recent years in the production of sugar from the beet, and the artificial encouragement of this industry in the continental states of Europe through the payment of large bounties, has in turn compelled the *large* producers of cane-sugars in the tropics to entirely abandon their old methods of working, and reorganize this industry on a most gigantic scale as a condition of continued existence. Thus, for example, although the business of cane-sugar production was commenced more than three hundred years ago on the island of Cuba, the grinding of the cane by animal or " wind " power, and the boiling and granulating by ancient, slow, and wasteful methods, was everywhere kept up until within a very recent period, as it still is by small planters in every tropical country. But at the present time, upon the great plantations of Cuba and some other countries, the cane is conveyed from the fields by a system of railroads to manufacturing centers, which are really huge factories, with all the characteristics of factory life about them, and with the former home or rural idea connected with this industry completely eliminated. In these factories, where the first cost of the machinery plant often represents as large a sum as $200,000 to $250,000, with an equally large annual outlay for labor and other expenses, all grades of sugar from the " crude " to the " partially refined " are manufactured at a cost that once would not have been deemed possible. In Dakota and Manitoba the employment on single wheat estates of a hundred reapers and an aggregate of three hundred laborers for a season has been regarded as something unprecedented in agricultural industry ; but on one sugar estate in Cuba—" El Balboa "—from fifteen hundred to two thousand hands, invariably negroes, are employed, who work under severe discipline, in watches or relays, during the grinding season, by day and night, the same as in the large iron-mills and furnaces of the United States and Europe. At the same time there are few village communities where a like number of people experience the same care and surveillance. The male workers occupy quarters walled and barricaded from the women, and the women from the men. There is in every village an infirmary, a lying-in hospital, a physician, an apothecary, a chapel, and priest. At night and morning mass is said in chapel, and the crowds are always large. There is of a Sunday less restraint, though ceaseless espionage is never remitted. On these days and in parts of holidays there is rude mirth, ruder music, and much dancing. This picture is given somewhat in detail, because it illustrates how all-pervading and tremendous are the forces that are modifying society everywhere, in civilized, partially civilized, and even barbarous countries, conjointly with the new conditions of production and consumption.

The experience of the co-operative societies of Great Britain—the inception and practical working of which have been hopefully looked upon as likely to furnish a solution of the labor problem—as recently detailed by Mr. Thomas Hughes (" Tom Brown "), does not, moreover, seem likely to constitute any exception to the general tendency of great aggregated capital, employed in production or distribution, to remorselessly disregard any sentiment on the part of the individual workman in respect to his vocation, and to crush out or supersede all industrial enterprises of like character that may be compelled to work at relative disadvantage by reason of operating upon a smaller scale, or inability to employ a larger aggregate of capital. This experience, as related by Mr. Hughes at a recent congress (1887) of the co-operative societies of Great Britain, has been as follows: Co-operation in Great Britain, so long as it has confined itself to distribution—that is, to the purchase of commodities at the lowest rates at wholesale and without the intervention of middle-men, and their subsequent sale to members of the societies at the minimum of cost and profit—

has been a very great success; but co-operation in production, so far as it has been attempted by these same societies, appears to have succeeded only by abandoning co-operation in the original and best sense of the term. For example, some of the great and most successful co-operative distribution societies of England, in order to increase their dividends, have recently undertaken to manufacture a portion of the goods which they require, and thus secure for themselves the profits they have heretofore paid to the manufacturers; and, with this view, the manufacture of boots and shoes has been commenced on a large scale by two of the largest of such societies in Glasgow and Manchester respectively—the English society employing a thousand operatives, and disposing of goods to a present aggregate value of more than a million dollars per annum. " These manufacturing enterprises have not, however, been conducted on co-operative lines. . . . The work-people in their factories are not co-operators. They do not share in the profits of the business. They receive simply the market rate of wages." They are on just as bad terms with their co-operative employers as they would be with individual capitalists, and they have endeavored to better their condition by entering upon strikes; or, in other words, the great Co-operative Distribution Society managers in Great Britain, finding that it was essential to their success as manufacturing producers, have adopted without scruple all the methods and rules that prevail in similar establishments which have been incorporated and are managed solely with a view to the profit of their individual capitalists or stockholders."

But this is not the whole story. Besides these great wholesale co-operative distribution societies which have engaged in manufacturing, there are a large number of smaller and weaker similar societies in Great Britain which are also attempting to manufacture the same description of goods for the profit of their more limited circle of members, and these last now complain that they are absolutely unable to withstand the competition of the larger wholesale societies, which, purchasing labor at the lowest rate in the open market, denying any participation of profit to their workmen, and working upon the largest scale, are enabled to produce and sell cheaper. " So that all the disastrous effects of unlimited and unscrupulous competition, for which co-operation was expected to be a cure, are showing themselves among the co-operators, and another example is to be added to the record of modern economic experience, of the strong industrial and commercial organizations devouring the weak."

An element of international character and importance, growing out of the improvements in production through machinery, should also not be overlooked. Whatever of advantage one country may have formerly enjoyed over another by reason of absolute or comparative low wages, is now, so far as the cost of machine-made goods is concerned, through the destruction of handicrafts and the extended use and improvements in machinery, being rapidly reduced to a minimum. For, apart from any enhancement of cost by taxes upon imports, there is at present but very little difference in all countries of advanced civilization in the cost of machinery, of the power that moves it, or of the crude materials which it converts into manufactures. The machine, therefore, which enables the labor of one man to dispense with the cheap labor of ten men, practically reduces any advantage which the manufacturer in France, Germany, or other countries, paying nominally low wages, has heretofore had over the manufacturer of England or of the United States, to the simple difference in the cost of the labor of the operative who manages the machine in different places; and all experience shows that the invariable concomitant of high wages, conjoined with the skillful management of machinery, is a low cost of production.

Attention is next asked to the economic—industrial, commercial, and financial—disturbances that have also re-

sulted in recent years from changes, in the sense of improvements, in the details of the distribution of products; and
as the best method of showing this, the recent course of
trade in respect to the practical distribution and supply of
one of the great articles of commerce, namely, tin-plate, is
selected.

Before the days of the swift steamship and the telegraph,
the business of distributing tin-plate for consumption in the
United States was largely in the hands of one of the great
mercantile firms of New York, who brought to it large enterprise and experience. At every place in the world where
tin was produced and tin-plate manufactured they had their
confidential correspondent or agent, and every foreign mail
brought to them exclusive and prompt returns of the state
of the market. Those who dealt with such a firm dealt with
them under conditions which, while not discriminating un-
favorably to any buyer, were certainly extraordinarily favorable to the seller, and great fortunes were amassed. But
to-day how stands that business? There is no man, however
obscure he may be, who wants to know any morning the
state of the tin-plate market in any part of the world, but
can find it in the mercantile journals. If he wants to know
more in detail, he joins a little syndicate for news, and then
he can be put in possession of every transaction of importance that took place the day previous in Cornwall, Liverpool, in the Strait of Sunda, in Australia, or South America.
What has been the result? There are no longer great warehouses where tin in great quantities and of all sizes, waiting
for customers, is stored. The business has passed into the
hands of men who do not own or manage stores. They have
simply desks in offices. They go round and find who is
going to use tin in the next six months. They hear of a
railroad-bridge which is to be constructed ; of a certain
number of cars which are to be covered ; that the salmon-
canneries on the Columbia River or Puget's Sound are likely
to require seventy thousand boxes of tin to pack the catch

of this year, as compared with a requirement of sixty thousand last year—a business, by the way, which a few years
ago was not in existence—and they will go to the builders,
contractors, or business-managers, and say to them : " You
will want at such a time so much tin. I will buy it for you
at the lowest market price, not of New York, but of the
world, and I will put it in your possession, in any part of
the continent, on a given day, and you shall cash the bill
and pay me a percentage commission "—possibly a fraction
of one per cent ; thus bringing a former great and complicated business of importing, warehousing, selling at wholesale and retail, and employing many middle-men, clerks,
book-keepers, and large capital, to a mere commission business, which dispenses to a great extent with the employment
of intermediates, and does not necessarily require the possession or control of any capital.*

Let us next go one step farther, and see what has happened at the same time to the man whose business it has
been not to sell but to manufacture tin-plate into articles
for domestic use, or for other consumption. Thirty or forty
years ago the tinman, whose occupation was mainly one of
handicraft, was recognized as one of the leading and most
skillful mechanics in every village, town, and city. His

---

* During the year 1887 one of the oldest, most extensive, and successful
firms in the United States (New York) engaged in the importation and sale of
teas—owning their own vessels, having their own correspondents in China,
and possessed of extensive capital—retired from business, and gave to the
public the following reason for so doing, namely, " a conviction that in the
present condition of the tea-market it was impossible for a firm to do sufficient
business to guarantee a commensurate return in form of profit for the volume
of monetary outlay and the anxiety and care of management." It was also
stated that the conditions of the tea-importing business were now such as not
to allow of successful operations on a large scale, involving as formerly the
carrying of large quantities of the commodity itself, which deteriorates rapidly
with age, and demands for profitable handling a rise of value unknown to the
present market. Jobbers, also, it was found, who once bought of houses like
the firm in question, now purchase direct from the foreign growers, and
thereby deprive the large importer in his own market of a very necessary element of patronage.

occupation has, however, now well-nigh passed away. For example, a townsman and a farmer desires a supply of milk-cans. He never thinks of going to his corner tinman, because he knows that in New York and Chicago and Philadelphia, and other large towns and cities, there is a special establishment fitted up with special machinery, which will make his can better and fifty per cent cheaper than he can have it made by hand in his own town. And so in regard to almost all the other articles which the tinman formerly made. He simply keeps a stock of machine-made goods, as a small merchant, and his business has come down from that of a general, comprehensive mechanic to little other than a tinker and mender of pots and pans. Where great quantities of tin-plate are required for a particular use, as, for example, the canning of salmon or lobsters, of biscuit, or of fruit and vegetables, the plates come direct from the manufactory to the manufacturer of cans or boxes, in such previously agreed-upon sizes and shapes as will obviate any waste of material, and reduce to a minimum the time and labor necessary to adapt them to their respective uses. And by this arrangement alone, in one cracker (biscuit) bakery in the United States, consuming forty thousand tin boxes per month, forty men are now enabled to produce as large a product of boxes in a given time as formerly required fifty men; and, taken in connection with machinery, the labor of twenty - five men in the entire business has become equivalent to that of the fifty who until recently worked by other methods. And what has been thus affirmed of tin-plate might be equally affirmed of a great variety of other leading commodities; the blacksmith, for example, no longer making, but buying his horseshoes, nails, nuts, and bolts; the carpenter his doors, sash, blinds, and moldings; the wheelwright his spokes, hubs, and felloes; the harness-maker his straps, girths, and collars; the painter his paints ground and mixed, and so on; the change in methods of distribution and preparation for final consumption having been equally radical in almost every case, though varying somewhat in respect to particulars.

The same influences have also to a great degree revolutionized the nature of retail trade, which has been aptly described as, "until lately, the recourse of men whose character, skill, thrift, and ambition won credit, and enabled them to dispense with large capital." Experience has shown that, under a good organization of clerks, shopmen, porters, and distributors, it costs much less proportionally to sell a large amount of goods than a small amount, and that the buyer of large quantities can, without sacrifice of satisfactory profit, afford to offer to his retail customers such advantages in respect to prices and range of selection as almost to preclude competition on the part of dealers operating on a smaller scale, no matter how otherwise capable, honest, and diligent they may be. The various retail trades, in the cities and larger towns of all civilized countries, are accordingly being rapidly superseded by vast and skillfully organized establishments—and in Great Britain and Europe by co-operative associations—which can sell at little over wholesale prices a great variety of merchandise, dry-goods, manufactures of leather, books, stationery, furs, ready-made clothing, hats and caps, and sometimes groceries and hardware, and at the same time give their customers far greater conveniences than can be offered by the ordinary shop-keeper or tradesman. In London, the extension of the "tramway" or street-railroad system is even advocated on the single ground that the big stores need quicker access to their branch establishments, in order to still further promote the economy of goods distribution.

The spirit of progress conjoined with capital, and having in view economy in distribution and the equalization of values, is therefore controlling and concentrating the business of retailing, in the same manner as the business of wholesale distribution and transportation, and of production by machinery, is being controlled and concentrated, and all to an extent never before known in the world's experience. And in both wholesale and retail operations the reduction of profits is so general that it must be accepted as a permanent feature of the business situation, and a natural result of the new conditions that have been noted.

Keeping economy in distribution constantly in view as an essential for material progress, the tendency is also everywhere to dispense to the greatest extent with the "middleman," and put the locomotive and the telegraph in his place. Retail grocers, as before shown, now buy their teas directly of the Chinaman, and dispense with the services of the East Indian merchant and his warehouses. Manufacturers deal more directly with retailers, with the result, it is claimed, of steadying supply and demand, and preventing the recurrence of business crises. The English cotton-spinner at Manchester buys his raw cotton by cable in the interior towns of the cotton-growing States of North America, and dispenses with the services of the American broker or commission-merchant. European manufacturers now send their agents with samples of merchandise to almost every locality in America, Asia, and the Pacific islands, where commerce is protected and transportation practicable, and offer supplies, even in comparatively small quantities, on better terms than dealers and consumers can obtain from the established wholesale or retail merchants of their vicinity. A woolen manufacturer, for example, prepares a set of patterns for an ensuing season, sends his agent around the world with them, and makes exactly as many pieces as his customers want, not weaving a single yard for chance sale. A great importing house will take orders for goods to be delivered two or three months afterward, and import exactly what is ordered and no more. Rent, insurance, handling, and profits are thus minimized. Before the days of railroad extension, country buyers used to have to come to the centers of trade in spring and fall to lay in their supplies; now they come every month, if they wish, to assort a stock which is on an average much less heavy than it used to be, and can be replenished by the dealer at very short notice by telegraph to the manufacturer, whether he resides at home or beyond an ocean. The great dry-goods houses of the large commercial cities are in turn reducing their storage and becoming mere sales-rooms, the merchandise marketed by them being forwarded directly from the point of manufacture to that of distribution. A commission house may, therefore, carry on a large business, and yet not appear to the public to be extensively occupied. One not inconsiderable gain from such a change in goods distribution accrues from a consequent reduction in the high rates and aggregates of city fire insurances.

From these specimen experiences it is clear that an almost total revolution has taken place, and is yet in progress, in every branch and in every relation of the world's industrial and commercial system. Some of these changes have been eminently destructive, and all of them have inevitably occasioned, and for a long time yet will continue to occasion, great disturbances in old methods, and entail losses of capital and changes of occupation on the part of individuals. And yet the world wonders, and commissions of great states inquire, without coming to definite conclusions, why trade and industry in recent years have been universally and abnormally disturbed and depressed.

There is one curious example in which improvement is being sought for at the present time, though what at first seems to be retrogression. With the great extension and perfecting of the railway system, and the consequent great reduction in the cost of merchandise carriage through its agency, it has been generally assumed that there was no longer any necessity for long lines of canals, or profit in their maintenance and operation ; and, as a matter of fact, many canals of expensive construction in England and the United States have been absolutely abandoned. But at the present time there is a tendency—especially in Europe—to return to the use of inland navigation—canals and rivers —for the purpose of still further cheapening transportation.

There is no question that goods can be carried much cheaper by water than by rail. The original cost per mile of an ordinary canal in England has been estimated at not more than one fourth the cost of building a railway in that country; and the expense of managing and maintaining a canal in good workable order is not in excess of one fifth of the charges of a corresponding railway company. The average canal charges in England are, therefore, only about one half as much as railway rates for the same description of traffic; and, for the transportation of imperishable goods, when the time occupied in transit is not a prime factor, cheapness of carriage, in these days when keen competition is reducing the margin of profit on the production of commodities to a minimum, has become more than ever a matter of the first importance. The attention of English commercial men and manufacturers is, accordingly, largely directed at the present time to the necessity of again using and improving existing inland water-ways, and of constructing additional canals, as a means of transporting merchandise at lower rates than those charged by railways; and one practical outcome of this interest has been the chartering and constructive commencement of an immense ship-canal between Liverpool and Manchester, which, it is predicted, "will effect a sort of revolution in the Lancaster cotton-trade," and the inception of which, moreover, was significantly opposed by all the railway companies with which the canal is likely to come into competition. Propositions for the construction of other important British ship-canals, as from Sheffield to the Humber, and with a view of cheapening transportation from Birmingham, are also under consideration. It is also to be noted that a very considerable number of the British canals, that have been kept up and not allowed to become useless, continue to pay good, and, in a few cases, large dividends ; and that the price of their stocks is often largely in excess of their par value.

In 1880 the French Government, acting upon the assumption that the canals and river transportation of France were likely to be crushed out by railway competition, exempted the former from all taxation. The result has been, that the total tonnage moved (per kilometre) upon the canals and rivers of France increased sixty-three per cent between 1880 and 1887, while during the same period the transportation by the main lines of the French railway system fell off to the extent of nearly thirteen per cent. The French railways are, accordingly, demanding a reimposition of the tolls taken off the canal and river traffic in 1880.

In the United States the resuscitation of the decayed canal system of transportation has not as yet been considered as desirable, and probably because the average charges for railroad freight service is considerably below the average rates of any other country in the world ; although other nations have nominally cheaper labor and far denser populations.

IV.

DEPRESSION of prices has, to a large extent, been accepted as a prime cause of the "economic disturbance"
which has prevailed since 1873. Indeed, Mr. Robert Giffen,
the well-known English economist and officer of the British
Board of Trade, in an article contributed to the "Contemporary Review," June, 1885, does not hesitate to express the
opinion that "it is clearly unnecessary to assign any other
cause for the gloom of the last year or two"; and, continuing, he further says :

"The point to which I would draw special attention is, that . . .
the most disastrous characteristic of the recent fall of prices has been
the descent all round to a lower range than that of which there had
been any previous experience. It is this peculiarity which—more than
anything else—has aggravated the gloom of merchants and capitalists
during the last few years. Fluctuations of prices they are used to.
Merchants know that there is one range of prices in a time of buoy-
ancy and inflation, and quite another range of prices in times of dis-
credit. By the customary oscillations, the shrewder business people
are enabled to make large profits, but during the last few years the
shrewder, as well as the less shrewd, have been tried. Operations they
ventured on when prices were falling to the customary low level have
failed disastrously, because of a further fall which is altogether with-

out precedent. The change is more like a revolution in prices than anything which usually happens in an ordinary cycle of prosperity and depression in trade."

Here, then, is a description of the extent of the recent fall in prices, and its influence in producing and aggravating the gloom of merchants and capitalists, by one well competent to appreciate and describe what has happened. The point of novelty and most significance, however, in Mr. Giffen's statement is, not that a depression of prices has been productive of gloom and a depression of business—for no fact is better recognized than that nothing is more productive of gloom to the industrial and mercantile community owning or carrying stocks of merchandise than losses experienced or anticipated through a fall in prices; but that the recent fall in the prices of the great staple commodities of the world has been in extent and character without precedent in the world's history.*

A further fact of the highest importance, and one that is not disputed, is, that no peculiarity of currency, banking,

---

* " Many who discuss this question, and whose opinions generally command deference, appear scarcely to realize the enormous extent of the fall, and it is only by means of very extensive statistics and of a comparison of various periods that a clear insight into the details and a broad view of the whole can be gained."—AUGUSTUS SAUERBECK's *Journal of the Statistical Society of London, September*, 1886.

" It is hardly possible to gain an adequate conception of the change in the condition of man except through the development of the system of prices. We may compare Abraham, in the first recorded monetary transaction, buying the field of Ephron for four hundred shekels of silver, ' current money of the merchants,' with his latest descendants the Rothschilds, bringing the enterprises of nations and of kings to the tribunal of the money market. The prices of corn and mutton were matters of small concern to the men of Abraham's day. They made their own arrangements for food independent of their neighbors' wants. They planted their fields, tended their flocks and defended them, and according to their success in these pursuits did they and their children have much or little to eat. But now in Rothschild's time each minute want of Jew or Gentile is conceived on a money scale. It is attainable, or impossible, according to its price. Almost every action of a very large part of mankind is controlled by considerations of price."—*Congested Prices, by* M. L. SCUDDER, Jr., *Chicago*, 1883.

or standard of value, or form of government, or incidence
and degree of taxation, or military system, or condition of
land tenure, cr legislation respecting trade, tariffs, and bounties, or differences in the relations between capital and labor
in different countries, have been sufficient to guard and save
any nation from the economic disturbances or trade depression which has been incident to such changes in prices.

The question which here naturally suggests itself, as to
what in general has been the extent of the recent fall in
prices, is perhaps best answered from the basis of English
figures, by M. Augustus Sauerbeck, who, as the result of an
exhaustive inquiry into the price movements of thirty-eight
leading articles of raw produce since 1818–'27 (communicated to the Statistical Society of London and published in
the journal of their "Proceedings" for September, 1886,
and March, 1887), has arrived at the following conclusions:
There was a persistent decline in the average prices of general commodities in England from the beginning to the
middle of the present century; or, more exactly, to 1849.
From thence there was an advance, which culminated in
1873. But leaving out of consideration a remarkable speculative period from 1870 to 1874, coincident with the Franco-
German War and the payment of the war indemnity by
France, during which period prices rose with great rapidity
from 1870 to 1873, and fell in the succeeding year (1874)
below their average starting-point in 1870, the decline of
prices may be regarded as having been continuous from
1864 to 1886. Compared with the average prices of general
commodities from 1867–'77, the period from 1878–'85 shows
a depreciation of eighteen per cent. But if the average
prices of 1885 alone be taken, the decline from the average
for 1867–'77 is twenty-eight per cent; or, continuing the
comparison through 1886 and embracing a somewhat larger
number of articles, the average depreciation, in the opinion
of M. Sauerbeck, has amounted to thirty-one per cent. Furthermore, the average level of prices for 1886, according to

the tables of M. Sauerbeck, was considerably below the average for the year 1848, which in turn appears to have been the lowest previous point for the century subsequent to 1820.

Many similar inquiries, embracing in some instances a much larger number of articles than were selected by M. Sauerbeck, have been instituted in recent years by other investigators in England, France, Germany, and the United States; and while there is much of agreement as respects results in a majority of cases, no figure representing the average decline during the periods under investigation would probably be universally accepted as every way satisfactory and conclusive. For example, an analysis of the exports and imports of the United Kingdom for the years 1873 and 1883 respectively, according to the returns of the British Board of Trade—prices and quantities being taken into consideration—has led the London "Economist" to the following conclusions: In respect to *articles of food*, which constitute nearly two thirds of British imports, and which being of the most staple nature and least subject to wide variations of supply and demand are the most steady in price, the valuation—the quantities compared being the same—for 1873 was about fifteen per cent higher than in 1883. Of *raw materials* for manufacture, which constitute the bulk of other British imports, the valuation for 1873 was higher than in 1883 to the extent of about thirty per cent. On the other hand, an analysis of the exports of the United Kingdom, consisting chiefly of what may be called commercial articles—manufactures, metals, etc.—which are more directly dependent upon the fluctuations in commercial conditions, speculation, supply and demand, etc., and which, therefore, are always far more sensitive to depreciatory conditions than are food products, or even raw materials, for the latter can be carried for an improvement in prices where manufactures can not, showed a valuation in 1873 higher by about forty-eight per cent than 1883. As the values compared in these analyses embrace the transactions of the leading commercial nation in every kind of commodity and with all the countries of the world, they probably reflected with approximative accuracy the condition and changes of universal values in all markets for the period under consideration.

A similar analysis of British imports and exports for the years 1885 and 1886 (also instituted by the " Economist ") furnished evidence, almost in the nature of a demonstration, of the continued tendency of prices to decline during the two (later) years mentioned, and also of the continued universality of such tendency. Thus, looking first at exports, it appears that there was an increase during the year 1886 in the quantities of British and colonial commodities exported of 6·02 per cent, as compared with similar aggregates for 1885 ; or Great Britain sent out 106,020 pounds, tons, or other quantities in 1886, in place of 100,000 in 1885. Comparing, however, the sum which the quantities actually exported in 1886 would have cost at the prices of 1885, a decline in price is indicated of 6·34 per cent; or while sending away 106,020 pounds, tons, or other quantities in 1886, as compared with 100,000 in 1885, Great Britain received back in money value only $93,660 for the same quantities which in the previous year brought $100,000.

A similar examination of British imports for 1886 also brought out the further interesting fact that the average decline in the prices of the goods imported was almost precisely the same as in prices of goods exported. The increase in quantities of imports was less than one per cent ; or the country brought in 100,796 pounds, tons, or other quantities, in place of every 100,000 in 1885. But the decline in prices was 6·373 per cent; so that the country paid only $93,627 for the same quantities for which it paid $100,000 in the previous year. The decline in the general range of prices for the year 1886, as compared with 1885, and as measured again by the actual exports and imports of the greatest exporting and importing nation of the world, would therefore appear to have been in excess of six per cent; and this decline would seem to have occurred during the same period in all those countries in which Great Britain dealt as a seller equally with those in which she dealt as a buyer; or, in other words, this decline was practically universal.

An investigation of American prices, instituted by Mr. William M. Grosvenor, in which quotations of some two hundred staple articles were compared, and the quantities of the same which the same amount of money (gold) would purchase were also taken into account, led to the conclusion that the general average of prices in New York, at the close of the year 1885, was 77·43 as against 100 in 1860.

During the year 1888 there was a considerable expansion and improvement in trade throughout the world, and a significant advance in the prices of many great staple commodities—cereals and meats excepted. In the case of twenty-two selected commodities, this advance, calculated according to the index system of the London "Economist," was a trifle over two per cent (2·150). Such an evident lack of elasticity in prices, coincident with a decided improvement in trade, would seem to show that the causes, whatever they may be, which occasioned the marked depression of prices since 1873 was still influential and operative down to the close of the year 1888.*

* The following table, according to Mr. Robert Giffen, represents the comparative wholesale prices of leading commodities on the English market for January, 1873, 1879, 1883, 1885, and for December, 1888:

ARTICLES.	1873.	1879.	1883.	1885.	1888.
Scotch pig-iron, per ton	127s.	43s.	47s. 8d.	41s. 9d.	41s. 11d.
Coals, per ton..............	30s.	19s.	17s. 6d.	18s.	17s. 9d.
Copper, Chili bars, per ton .	91l.	57l.	65l.	48½l.	78l.
Wheat, Gazette average, per qr	55s. 11d.	39s. 7d.	40s. 4d.	34s. 11d.	31s. 9d.
Beef, prime small, per 8 lbs.	5s. 3d.	4s. 9d.	6s.	5s. 4d.	4s. 2d.
Cotton, midland, per lb....	10d.	5⅜d.	5¹¹/₁₆d.	6d.	5⁷/₁₀d.
Wool, per pack	23l.	13l.	12l.	11l.	11l.
Sugar, Muscovado, per cwt.	21s. 6d.	16s.	16s. 6d.	10s.	13s. 3d.
Coffee, Ceylon, per cwt.....	80s.	65s.	78s. 6d.	71s.	91s.
Pepper, black, per lb.......	7d.	4½d.	5¾d.	8d.	7⅝d.
Saltpeter, per cwt..........	29s.	19s.	19s.	15s. 3d.	16s. 6d.

The usual method employed by European economists in order to form a correct idea of the changes of prices in one period as compared with another, is to take the prices of certain selected commodities in a given year, or the average prices of a series of years, as the standard; represent this by the figure 100 or 1,000, and then note the increase or decrease in price in the case of each article in each subsequent year in proportion to this standard. Combining the percentage of price alterations among all the articles, a total of the variations experienced become known, and the number thus obtained is termed an *index number* for the year, or other period under consideration; or a number expressive of the ratio of price at a given date to the average of some former period. Thus, for example, if the average price of forty articles in the year 1880 were to be taken at 100, and the average decline in the prices of these same articles for the year 1810 was found to be 20 per cent, the index number for the year 1800 would be 100, and for the year 1810, 80.*

The difficulties in the way of obtaining satisfactory averages from comparisons of prices at different periods by the above or any other methods are, however, almost insuperable; so that it may well be doubted whether the determination of an average of general prices is ever within the bounds of possibility. Quotations for a given day or month do not necessarily show the average for the year; and, in like manner, the selection of a limited number of articles

---

Commenting upon this exhibit of prices, Mr. Giffen remarks: "Although some prices are higher now (December, 1888) than in 1885, they are in a very few cases higher than in 1883. They are," on the average, "far below the level of 1873, and a good deal below the level of 1879. It is also well to bear in mind that the latter year was one of depression of trade, while 1888 was one of expansion."

* For a full exhibit and discussion of these tables, reference is made to a paper in the Harvard "Quarterly Journal of Economics" (vol. i, No. 3, Boston, 1887), by Prof. J. Laurence Laughlin, and to the "Final Report of the (British) Gold and Silver Commission," pp. 16, 17, 1888.

for comparison can not insure correct conclusions respecting the movement of prices in general. All methods of comparing price variations which content themselves with mere average quotations of different articles, and which do not pay due regard to the relative importance of each article in the domestic and foreign commerce of a country; which, for example, allows a change of eighty per cent in the price of an article like cochineal, of which the value sold in any one year is small, to balance a change of two per cent in an article, like sugar, the value of which annually sold is enormous, are also in a great degree deceptive and worthless; * and even when, in the comparison of prices, the importance of considering relative quantities is fully recognized, the data for ascertaining these relations are extremely uncertain and questionable. The utmost of service that all such tabular comparisons of prices, even when prepared with all desirable qualifications, are capable of rendering, would, therefore, seem to be limited to certain broad general results, or to the affording of important inferences respecting the tendencies and variations of prices. In all other respects they are little other than curiosities; inasmuch as if some articles in a given period have risen and others have fallen in price, and if the fall of some and the rise of others can be undoubtedly traced to the action of entirely different causes, the grouping of these facts into the form of tables, and the endeavor to reduce the sum of the respective changes to a common average, can prove nothing whatever as to the cause or causes which have been operative in producing the

---

* One of the best-known tables of this character, embracing twenty-two different articles, has been kept by the London "Economist" for many years as a constituent element of current British commercial history, and by many is regarded as about the most reliable indication of the movements in the prices of wholesale commodities that can be obtained. The results of this table are, in brief, as follows: If the index number 2,947 be taken to represent the combined prices of twenty-two leading commodities at the close of 1872, the combined prices of the same commodities at the close of 1886 was 2,059, a decline of over thirty per cent.

changes. And between such discordant results effected by entirely diverse influences, there would, furthermore, seem to be no possibility of establishing an average; for the price of some articles, whose use has been superseded or impaired by change of fashion or new inventions, may fall nearly or quite to zero, while the price of others, by reason of increased demand or interrupted supply, may rise almost to infinity by comparison; and between such extremes there may be any number of gradations.*

All, therefore, that can be confidently affirmed in respect to the extent of the recent depression of prices is, that comparing the data for 1885–'86 with those of 1866–'76, the decline in the wholesale prices of most of the staple commodities of the world's commerce has been extraordinary, and has extended to most countries; and that the estimate of M. Sauerbeck (before referred to) of thirty-one per cent, as the average measure or extent of this decline, is not excessive.

It seems almost unnecessary to remark that a fall of prices, although commonly so considered, can not, in any comprehensive discussion, be regarded as in any sense a pri-

---

* The objections inherent in this system have been forcibly illustrated by a recent occurrence, to which attention has been called by the " New York Commercial Bulletin ": Thus, a comparison of index numbers for January and July, 1886, and for January, 1887, as deduced from the " Economist's " tables of prices, indicated a small advance for the latter month in the general level of British prices. But the first article on the " Economist's " list of prices is coffee, which advanced from July 1, 1886, to January, 1887, to a degree sufficient to alone add 50 to the index number of January ; while the entire increase for the whole twenty-two articles was only 36 ; or, in other words, if coffee alone were omitted from the list of articles compared, the net result would show an apparent decline instead of any advance in the general level of prices. " Certainly," as the " Commercial Bulletin " remarks, " it is difficult to attach much importance to results having no better basis than this. For coffee is by no means one of the most important articles compared ; it is greatly exceeded in importance by at least twelve of them. But the change in that one article happens to have been surprisingly great, and it thus outweighs far more important changes in other articles, such as iron or meats."

mary cause of economic disturbances; but that here again something antecedent in the nature of causes, more or less general, must be sought for in explanation. What these causes or agencies have been, how they have acted, and what disturbing influences they have exerted on the world's prices, on the world's industries, commerce, and consumption, and on pre-existing relations of labor and capital, will, when fully told, constitute one of the most important and interesting chapters of political economy and commercial history. Such a complete statement, for lack of sufficiently reliable and comprehensive data, can not now be made ; or, in other words, the time for making it has not yet come. And in default thereof it is sufficient for the present to say, that all economists and financial authorities have substantially agreed that while many circumstances may and doubtless have been contributory, the extraordinary movements in prices under consideration must *in the main* be referable to one of two causes : *First*, a great multiplication and cheapening of commodities *through new conditions* of production and distribution, which in turn have been *mainly* (but not exclusively) due to the progress of invention and discovery ; and, *second*, that the precious metal used for standard money, viz., gold, has, through relative scarcity, owing to diminished production and increased demand, greatly appreciated in value ; in consequence of which a given amount of gold buys more than formerly, or, what is the same thing, the price or purchasing power of commodities, in comparison with gold, has fallen.

As to which of these two causes has been most influential, the best authorities who have investigated the subject widely differ. It is also well recognized that the determination of this question is almost fundamental in the so-called bimetallic controversy ; the plea for an increased use of silver as money being wholly predicated on an alleged insufficiency in the supply of gold for effecting the world's exchanges, while ample evidence of the scarcity of gold is claimed to be found in the remarkable fall of prices which has been recently experienced.

Preliminary to entering upon any review of this vexed question, a consideration of the following general propositions may possibly help to a determination of opinion in respect to it: *First.* It is a universally accepted canon, alike in logic and common sense, that extraordinary and complex agencies should never be invoked for the explanation of phenomena, so long as ordinary and simple ones are equally available and satisfactory for the same purpose. *Second.* The most natural presumption, and the one which the commercial world most readily accepts, is, that when an article under free competition declines in price, the supply has outrun the demand; not of demand in the abstract, for in a certain sense there is no limit to the demand for useful and desirable things, but of demand at the pre-existing price. If this presumption is not correct, then the hitherto universally accepted influence of the law of supply and demand on prices has been entirely misunderstood, and belief even in any such law may as well be abandoned. On the other hand, if the presumption is correct, then any cause, other than a disturbance of pre-existing relations of supply and demand, capable of occasioning a decline in prices, must of necessity be an extraordinary one, and demanding evidence, not general, but specific and clear in the highest degree, as a prerequisite to a belief in its actual occurrence and influence. Now, as to the character of the evidence that can be adduced in support of the two great causes respectively to which the decline in prices has been mainly attributed, it is not to be denied that the evidence pertaining to the first can, either with or without statistics, be stated with precision; while the evidence pertaining to the second is at best indefinite, and mainly conjectural. In other words, the " HOW of the depression of prices," as Prof. Lexis, of Göttingen, has happily expressed it, through a lowering of the cost of production and transportation, and a widening of the area of cultivation, is clear to all; but the *how* of the effect of the enhancement in value of one description of money no one has, thus far, proved to us *in concreto*.* If any one "affirms a connection between the prevalent low prices and the assumed appreciation of gold arising from scarcity, let him explain the *modus operandi*; let him set forth the process of reasoning; the motive which impels a seller to accept, except upon the issue of the struggle between supply and demand, a lower price for his goods in the face of an abundance of capital and a low rate of interest." †

With these premises, attention is next asked to the evidence confirmatory of the predominating influence of the first cause, which is to be found in the history of the recent separate or individual economic experiences of 'the world's great staple commodities; ‡ and for the purpose of making such an exhibit, it is expedient to group such commodities for consideration under *two* heads; namely, those in respect

---

* "Least of all has Mr. Gibbs done so, although he was examined long on this point [by the British Gold and Silver Commission]. After all, he had no argument, except that the formation of prices depends on the quantity of commodities, and on the quantity of money as compared with those commodities. Hence if the quantity of money diminishes, prices must fall; as if the quantity of money stands like a dead mass over against the commodities; as if the efficient purchasing power did not appear only to the slightest extent at the present day, except in the form of cash money; as if in almost every instance, in which the debtor possesses the necessary circulating or personal property, the employment of real money in payment may not be avoided. In England, as compared with France, perhaps twice the quantity of goods are sold every year; although the former country has less than one half, perhaps less than one third, of the quantity of money to be found in the latter."—PROF. LEXIS, *of Göttingen, Review of the Report of the British Gold and Silver Commission.*

† Paper by Lord Addington, a Director of the Bank of England; final report (British) "Gold and Silver Commission," p. 211.

‡ "A general movement in prices is the resultant of a number of particular movements, and in these particular movements, again, we find the proximate causes of the distribution of the industrial forces of the world and of the wealth which these forces create."—PROF. J. S. NICHOLSON, *Professor of Political Economy, University of Edinburgh, etc.*

to which the evidence that decline in price has been the direct resultant of new conditions of production and distribution is full, clear, and unimpeachable; and those in respect to which, through lack mainly of universally accepted statistical data, the evidence is more or less inferential or circumstantial. Under the *first* group would be comprised *sugar, petroleum, or mineral oils, copper, iron, quicksilver, tin, tin-plates, nickel, lead, coal, quinine,* paper, rags, *chemicals, meats, cheese, fish, and freights ;* under the *second, wheat, cotton, wool, silk, jute.*

SUGAR.—Adopting this grouping, the commodity whose recent economic experience will be first related will be *sugar ;* which, commencing to decline in price in 1880–'81, fell to lower rates in 1887 than has ever been known in the history of modern commerce; the wholesale price of fair refining sugars having been more than one hundred and fourteen per cent higher in 1880 than in the first half of the year 1887.*

Now, while improved methods of manufacture and greater and cheaper facilities for transportation have undoubtedly contributed to such a result, it has been mainly due to an apparent desire, as M. Leroy-Beaulieu has expressed it, on the part of the Governments of France, Germany, Austria, Belgium, Holland, Italy, and Russia, " to make their national sugar industry the greatest in the world " by stimulating the domestic production of this commodity by the payment of what is equivalent to extraordinary bounties on its exportation to other countries; or, in other words, by competing with one another in paying large

---

* How continuous and regular was the decline in the price of sugars is shown by the following table, which exhibits the average price of fair refining sugars in bond (or free of duty) in New York from 1880 to July, 1887, inclusive :

1880, 5·08 cents.	1885, 3·06 cents.
1882, 4·53 cents.	1886, 2·92 cents.
1884, 3·31 cents.	1887 (lowest to July), 2·37½ cents.

sums for the purpose of speedily getting.rid of one of the most valuable and highly-desired products of the earth conjoined with human industry.*

On the other hand, in order to neutralize to some extent the exceptional advantages enjoyed through such an economic policy by the producers of beet-sugar in Europe, some of the cane-growing countries have felt obliged to encourage, by subsidies or tax-exemptions, their own sugar-production. In both Brazil and the Argentine Republic the manufacturers of cane-sugar have obtained a guarantee from the state of a five to six per cent return on their capital invested, while all the machinery needed in this industry may be im-

---

* The payment of direct bounties in Europe for stimulating the production of sugar is now and always has been an exception, and the existing system, as a matter of fact, has grown up from the repayment, on the exportation of sugars, of an excise duty which had been charged upon them. But this repayment in reality constitutes a bounty " in its primitive and most insidious form. Let us suppose that one hundred tons of beet-root have been estimated, for purposes of taxation, as yielding eight tons of sugar, and that the duty has been fixed on that basis. If, by improved manipulation, from this amount of beet-root are extracted ten tons, the extra two tons will, if consumed in the country, pay no excise duty whatever ; but, if they are exported, the duty which all home sugar is supposed to have paid will be returned. The money given back as duty returned on the two tons which did not pay any duty, is a bounty.

" It is obvious that this repayment of unpaid duty forms a substantial help to the sugar-trade. It is not merely so much cash given as a present to the producer, but it is a great incentive to the manufacturer to select the richest roots to make his sugar from, and to exercise his ingenuity in extracting the fullest possible yield from the beets. He only pays on an estimate of eight tons of sugar from a hundred tons of beets. He will not be satisfied with the two tons in excess of this ; he will torture his invention to squeeze eleven or even twelve tons of sugar out of his measure of beets, and the more he makes the greater the direct gift he receives from the Government on exportation. Germany is a striking instance of this, since during the last ten years, through the improvement in machinery, the average yield of sugar has increased from eight tons to nearly twelve on every hundred tons of roots. To the ordinary tax-payer in Germany this is not altogether a matter of congratulation, since out of a large revenue collected as excise the state regularly pays back about four fifths in the form of export bounties, with a result that the sugar is immensely cheapened—not, however, to the German, but to the foreign consumer."

ported free of duty. In the Spanish West Indies the home
Government has (1887) felt compelled to relinquish the export duties on sugars—the produce of Cuba and Porto Rico
—which have long been regarded as almost indispensable on
account of revenue necessities; while in South Africa and
Australia the production of sugar has also been encouraged
to such an extent that both of these countries will hereafter
be undoubtedly included among the number of important
sugar-exporting regions. In Central America, the British
and Dutch West India Islands, Guiana, and India (which
last produces more sugar than any other country), production has not as yet been artificially encouraged, and, with
the exception of the levying of export taxes in certain localities, neither have any impediments been placed in the
way of the natural growth of production. But at the same
time it can not be doubted that the recent increased facilities for transportation and communication have, as before
pointed out, been in the nature of a stimulus to the production of sugar, in common with all other commodities, and
have opened up large and fertile sections of the earth which
a quarter of a century ago were practically inaccessible.

Under such conditions the increase in the production of
sugar entering into the world's commerce and available for
general consumption has been extraordinary. Mr. Sauerbeck estimates the increase from 1872–'73 to 1885–'86 to
have been sixty-eight per cent. Other authorities estimate
the increase from 1853 to 1884, exclusive of the product of
India and China, to have been at the rate of thirty per cent
for each decade, or about one hundred per cent compounded.
Between 1882–'83 and 1888–'89 inclusive the increase was
in excess of twenty-three per cent. In the Hawaiian Islands,
where a remission of duties on sugars exported to the United
States is equivalent to an export bounty of about eighty-five
per cent (and amounting for the year 1888 to over $6,000,-
000), the domestic production of sugar has increased from
about 12,000 tons in 1875 (the year before the duties were

remitted) to 114,000 tons in 1888, an increase (nine hundred per cent) that has no parallel in the history of the sugar industry. The part that beet-root sugar has played in this increase is shown by the circumstance that while in 1860 the proportion of this variety to the whole sugar-product of the world was less than twenty per cent, its product for 1886–'87 was estimated as about fifty-six per cent; Germany alone having increased her product from about 200,-000 tons in 1876 to 594,000 tons in 1880–'81, and to 1,155,-000 tons in 1884–'85, while the increase of the beet-sugar product in the other bounty-paying states of Europe was not disproportionate.

Of this extraordinary increase of product, as large a proportion as foreign markets would take was, as a matter of course, exported in order to obtain the benefit of the Government bounties on exports, the sugar-export of Germany alone increasing from about 500,000 hundred-weight in 1876 to over 6,000,000 hundred-weight in 1885, and, with every increase of exportation, the Government disbursements on account of export bounties increased proportionately. The export bounty paid by Russia is estimated to have been as high at one time as $31.25 (£6 8s.) per ton, and that of France at between $35 and $40 (£7 and £8), representing, in the case of the latter country, an estimated money loss to the treasury and a bounty to the manufacturer of 43,955,000 francs in 1886 and 92,077,000 francs ($18,555,000) in 1887. In 1887 the French Government somewhat reduced the bounty, but the margin left to the manufacturer is still very effective.

In Germany the amount paid in the way of subsidies on sugar was estimated by Deputy Gehlert, in a speech in the German Reichstag in 1886, as having up to that time approximated $40,000,000, while for the year 1887–'88 about $7,000,000 it was claimed would be necessary, or an amount equal to the total wages paid to all workmen in all the German sugar-refineries. As might also have been expected, the profits of producers, and more especially of the sugar-refiners, working under the bounty (export) system, were at the same time enormously increased. In Germany the largest and best-managed beet-sugar manufactories divided for a series of years dividends to the extent of sixty, seventy, ninety, and in one instance one hundred and twenty-five per cent per annum on the capital invested,* and corresponding results were also reported in Austria, Russia, France, and Belgium. How rapidly and extensively sugar has declined in price consequent upon such an extraordinary and unnatural increase in production has already been pointed out. How much of disaster this decline has brought to great business interests and to the material prosperity and even the civilization of large areas of the earth's surface, will be made a subject of future notice.†

During the year 1888 a marked change occurred in the supply and prices of sugars. The beet-root manufacturers on the Continent of Europe, alarmed at an apparent glut of the sugar market, reduced

---

* " By a law passed in 1869 it was assumed that it took 12½ centners of beet-roots to give one centner of crude sugar, and a tax was levied on this basis and a corresponding drawback allowed on exported sugar. Since then great improvements have been made in the process of manufacturing, so that but 10½ centners of roots are necessary to produce one centner of sugar instead of 12½ as formerly ; but the Government continued to grant a drawback on the basis of 12½. The export drawback thus became an enormous premium to the producers, and the German manufacturers have been enabled to supply all Europe with cheap sugar ; till, to protect themselves, the other states have had to increase their duties on the imports of foreign sugar."—*Report to United States Department of State by Commercial Agent* SMITH, *Mayence, January*, 1887.

† " It has almost bankrupted the sugar-producing interests in the West Indies and the Dutch East Indies, and threatens the continuance of productive industries and even of civilization in these countries. In consequence of the low prices of sugar in Europe and America, owners of plantations and their lessees have speculated to such an extent that they have placed themselves on the brink of an abyss, and it is feared that this will totally stop the production of sugar in Java. This event would in every way be a great catastrophe. It would at once throw half a million of Javanese laborers out of employment, who would increase the already enormous number of Malay pirates."—*Journal des Fabricants de Sucre, October*, 1886.

production. The world's population and consumption continued to increase, and the stock of raw sugars at the principal markets of the world rapidly decreased, the stock at the port of London being reported, for example, as comparatively smaller, at the close of the year 1888, than at any former period. As a consequence, prices everywhere materially advanced. An interesting feature of the world's sugar-supply in 1888 was the change in the relative proportions of cane and beet, the result of a reduced beet-crop on the Continent of Europe. Taking the British Board of Trade returns as a standard, the importations of beet-sugar into Great Britain for 1888 as compared with 1887 decreased 278,000,000 pounds, but with an increase in price. Cane-sugars, mainly the product of Java and the British West Indies, immediately flowed in to nearly supply the deficiency.

PETROLEUM (MINERAL OIL).—The economic history of petroleum and its principal derivative, kerosene-oil, since the year 1872, is in many respects more interesting and remarkable than that of any other staple commodity, because the decline in its price has been absolutely greater than in the case of any other article, and the agencies which have been concerned in producing such a result are capable of statement with accuracy and completeness.

In the first place, the annual product of crude petroleum in the United States—the chief source of supply—increased from 9,893,786 barrels in 1873 to 28,249,597 in 1887. The price of *crude* oil during this period declined from 9·42 cents to 1·59 cents per gallon, and of *refined* oil from 23·59 cents to 6¾ cents per gallon. The decline in the price of crude oil was unquestionably due to its enormous supply, which at one time amounted to nearly 100,000 barrels per day, " while the stock of crude oil rose from 3,500,000 barrels in 1876 to the stupendous figures of 41,000,000 barrels in 1884." Had refined oil declined only at the same rate, its minimum price would have been 15·75 cents per gallon. But the fall in refined oil has been 9·01 cents per gallon greater than the fall in crude oil ; and as over 1,000,000,000 gallons were consumed in 1887, this saving of 9·01 cents per gallon to the public amounted to nearly $100,000,000

for that same year.̄ Here, then, some agency other than increased supply and diminished cost of the crude oil has unquestionably come in and operated to reduce the price of a
manufactured product in a given period disproportionally
to that experienced by the raw material from which it was
derived. What was that agency? Did any concurrent
change in the relative values of the precious metals used as
money contribute in any degree toward effecting such a result? It is claimed, and without doubt correctly, to be
largely due to the fact that the whole business of refining
petroleum in the United States and the distribution of its
resulting products has gradually passed, since 1873, into the
ownership and control of a combination or "trust"—the
Standard Oil Company—which, commanding millions of
capital, has used it most skillfully in promoting consumption, and in devising and adopting a great number of ingenious methods whereby the cost of production has been reduced to an extent that, at the outset, would not have seemed
possible. The methods in detail by which this "trust"
has achieved results in the way of reducing prices which
find no parallel in the history of industry have been thus
recently told by one of its principal managers:

"1. They have used capital, which only a large combination could use, in opening markets for petroleum throughout the civilized and uncivilized world. Through their ex-
ertions it is now used wherever steamers, or vessels, or cars,
or carts, or camels, or coolies can carry it. The exports
from the United States have been in excess of $44,000,000
per annum in value. The value of the domestic consumption is much greater, and from this immense output at low
prices great aggregate gains have been realized from small
profits.

"2. By using capital in cheapening methods of transportation, building cars for carrying oil in bulk, erecting
tank stations for holding oil in bulk, and constructing pipe-
lines, or lines by which the crude oil is transmitted hun-

dreds of miles, with great rapidity and at small expense, by a system of underground pipes. In this way the rate of transportation has been reduced about two thirds in fourteen years, a saving of not far from $20,000,000 per year.

" 3. All the persons concerned in the management of the combination (or " trust ") have the benefit of combined knowledge and experience, and the best and cheapest methods of manufacture, as well as the use of patents; in consequence of which the actual cost of manufacturing refined oil has been reduced sixty-six per cent in fourteen years.

" 4. The same cheapening has taken place in the manufacture of barrels, tin cans, boxes for inclosing cans, paint, glue, and acids. The company use 3,500,000 barrels per annum. The saving in cost of manufacture since 1873 amounts to $4,000,000 per annum. Thirty-six million cans are used per year. The cost of making has been reduced about one half. The saving amounts to $5,400,000 per annum. The cost of making wooden cases has been reduced one third. The saving amounts to $1,250,000 per annum. The public has had the benefit of all these savings in a cheaper product, and it is in this way that the reduction of former prices, equivalent to $100,000,000 per year, has been effected." *

Extremely low as is the present price of mineral oils, yet, with the recently recognized ability of Russia to supply apparently unlimited quantities of it at low rates, and the determination of the great American company, at the same

---

* Although the "trust" has undoubtedly greatly contributed to these cheapening results, it would be an error to suppose that it is entitled to exclusive credit for the same. Thus, for example, the reduction of freights since 1873 has been universal for all classes of commodities—on the Pennsylvania Railroad to an average of fifty-two per cent—and the improved methods of manufacturing barrels, cans, etc., speedily came into common use. It is no less certain that the economies effected in the refining of mineral oils have not resulted in benefiting consumers to anything like the extent that was possible, without interfering with the realization of large profits by the manufacturing combination.

time, to vigorously compete with the Russian product in the world's markets, there seems no probability that any advance in price is likely to occur in the immediate future.

COPPER.—This metal touched the lowest price on record in 1886, Lake Superior copper in New York falling from twenty-five cents per pound in 1880 to nine and four fifth cents in May, 1886; and in the case of only a very few commodities is the connection between a decline in price and an increase of production and supply so well established and so significant. The increase in the copper product of the world is estimated by Mr. Sauerbeck to have been ninety-seven per cent in the thirteen years from 1873 to 1885, inclusive; while according to the report of the United States Geological Survey, 1886, the increase from 1879 to 1885 was nearly forty-seven per cent (46·8). The countries which have most notably contributed to this increased product have been the United States, Spain, and Portugal; the increase in the case of the former having been from 23,000 tons in 1879 to 74,053 tons in 1885; and in that of the latter, from 32,677 tons to 45,749 in the same period. As in all other like cases, the disturbing effect on the industries involved—mining and smelting—contingent on this rapid and remarkable fall of prices, was very great, and in all quarters of the world. In Montana, the Montana Copper Company, with an annual product of 8,000,000 pounds of pure copper, entirely suspended operations; and the Anaconda Company, with an annual product of 36,000,000 pounds, shut down twenty out of twenty-eight furnaces, and discharged most of its hands at the mine. In Chili, production during the year 1885 was diminished to the extent of about ten per cent. In Germany the great Mansfield mine, which reported gross profits in 1884 of 5,675,000 marks, sustained a loss in the operation of 1885 of 653,338 marks; and its managers sought relief by petitioning the Imperial Government for the imposition of a higher tariff on the imports of copper into the empire. For the years

1881–'83 the great San Domingo mine in Portugal paid annual dividends of twelve and a half per cent; in 1885 the annual rate was reduced to three and three fourths per cent.

It is important to note, as throwing light on this phenomenal decline in the price of a great staple commodity, that while the increase in the product of copper was admitted to be immense and primarily influential, three other agencies may be regarded as having concurrently contributed to this result :

The *first* is, that there has been a reduction in the cost of mining, smelting, and marketing copper at the principal mines of the world, owing to improved processes, and reduced rates of transportation contingent on railroad construction. In the case of the Lake Superior mines, this reduction has been very remarkable; thus, in one of the leading mines, $5.50 per ton was paid in 1867 for stamping and washing; in 1876 the same processes cost only 83·89c. per ton, and in 1885 the expense had been still further reduced to 47·31c. Between 1876 and 1885, in like manner, the cost of manipulating the rock was reduced from 3·45c. per ton to 1·95c. For the same concern the cost of refined copper per pound at the mine was stated at 15·42c. in 1876 and 8½c. in 1885; and since then there has been further progress in the application of economical methods. The annual report of the "Tamarack" (Lake Superior) Company for the year ending June, 1888, shows the total cost of its annual product of over 10,000,000 pounds of refined copper at the mine to have been 3·97c. per pound. The addition of charges for smelting, freight, commission and office expenses brought up the total cost per pound of refined copper, laid down in New York and sold, to 5¾c. per pound. This is probably as cheap as any company produces; and in comparison with 1867, or even with 1876 or 1885, the cheapness of the processes appears phenomenal.

Second. The recent discovery and rapid development of

new and rich mines in Montana, Arizona, the Dominion of
Canada, and elsewhere, have engendered a feeling in the
metal-trade that the supply of copper is practically illimit-
able.

Third. During the year 1886 the previous decline in
prices was intensified by the circumstance that the consumption of copper in Europe fell off 14,000 tons below the
average for the two preceding years—a result attributed
mainly to the dullness of ship-building, and the various
metal industries.

In short, the great decline in the price of copper subsequent to 1880 and down to 1887 was mainly a normal
movement, and any advance in its price since then has been
in defiance of the conditions of production.

The state of affairs for the producers of copper up to
the close of the year 1887 was therefore a gloomy one; relieved only by the circumstance that the low price of this
metal tended to enlarge the sphere of its uses, and although
the visible supply of copper had not fallen off materially,
it was being generally recognized that consumption was
gradually gaining on production, and that the stocks of raw
material in the hands of smelters and manufacturers, and
of finished goods in the hands of dealers and consumers,
were very greatly reduced. The opportunity thus presented was seized upon, in the autumn of 1887, by the
Société des Métaux of France to " corner " the copper
market, and advance prices. At the outset it is probable
that no very extensive operations were contemplated, but
the movement soon acquired such an impetus that those
who initiated it were able to perfect, and for a time successfully carry out, a scheme for the control of the price and
supply of copper which hardly finds a parallel in modern
commercial experience. In the short space of three months
the syndicate advanced the price of copper more than one
hundred per cent—Chili bars, which sold in London on
the 1st of October, 1887, for £39 15s. per ton, being quoted

on the 1st of January, 1888, at £85; at the same time the market price of the shares of many of the principal copper-mining companies were greatly advanced; from seventy to one hundred per cent, and to even higher premiums. These high prices for copper naturally stimulated its production everywhere throughout the world; new mines, which the completion of new lines of railroad had brought within easy reach of the market being opened, while old mines, which the competition of stronger companies had kept partially undeveloped, were worked to their utmost capacity; the total mining output increasing from 224,000 tons in 1887 to 255,000 in 1888. Indeed, for the latter year the world's aggregate production is believed to have surpassed the world's aggregate consumption to the extent of 80,000 tons, or one third of the year's product. Two other influences also virtually contributed to greatly increase the supply of copper. Old and scrap copper, unavailable at eight and nine cents per pound, became important at sixteen cents; and large quantities were collected and pressed upon the market. Consumers also strove for the greatest economy of material under the higher prices; dispensed with the use of copper altogether in many cases, and in others substituted different materials, especially zinc and iron. Under such circumstances the syndicate in March, 1889, finding itself not only with an immense stock of metal which it could not sell at the current prices which it had established, but also under obligations to take at a high price all that the leading mines of the world could continue to produce for a lengthened period, broke down, and carried with it to ruin the Société des Métaux of France, and also one of the largest banking institutions of that country—the Comptoir d'Escompte—the price of copper falling in less than thirty days from £80 per ton to £35 and £40 per ton, or to about the point before the advance under the operations of the syndicate began.

IRON.—Sir Lowthian Bell, recognized as one of the best

authorities on the production of iron and steel, in his testimony before the Royal British Commission on the Depression of Trade in 1885, estimated the increase in the world's production of pig-iron from 1870 to 1884 at eighty-two per cent. The tables of the American Iron and Steel Association, prepared by Mr. James M. Swank, indicate an increase in the pig-iron product of the world, from 1870 to 1886 inclusive, of about one hundred per cent. All authorities are therefore substantially agreed that the increase in the production of this commodity within the period mentioned was not only far in excess of the increase of the world's population in general, but also of the increase of the population of the principal iron-producing countries. This abnormal augmentation of product was not, however, equally distributed over all the years from 1870 to 1886. From 1870 to the end of 1879 it was very small, averaging, according to Mr. Bell, but about two and a quarter per cent per annum; but after 1879 the production of iron increased all over the world in a most rapid and most extraordinary manner—the product of 1880 over 1879 having been thirty per cent greater in Great Britain, thirty-six per cent in the United States, and thirty-two per cent in Belgium, while in all other iron-producing countries the increase in production was also very notable. The years 1881, 1882, and 1883 were also characterized by continual extraordinary production; so that at the end of the latter year the annual product of the world was about fifty per cent (49·9) greater than in 1879; the increase in Great Britain and the United States for the same period having been forty-one and sixty-seven per cent respectively.

Attention is next asked to the price experiences of iron subsequent to 1870. In Great Britain the average prices from 1870 to 1876 rated high, and for part of the time—from 1872 to 1876—might be fairly characterized as extravagant, and even as famine prices. In the United States prices were also well maintained until after 1875, and the reason for a lack of greater correspondence between British and American pig-iron prices for the period in question is undoubtedly due to the fact that the depression of trade, which commenced in the United States in 1873 and prevailed with great severity in 1874 and 1875, did not manifest itself to a corresponding extent in Great Britain until 1876. After 1877 prices continued to decline in both countries, but not to a greater extent than might have been expected, considering the extreme depression of trade which had then become almost universal; and some descriptions of British iron, as "Staffordshire bars," were even higher in 1879 than in 1870. In 1880 there was a marked advance in the price of iron, both British and American, but after the enormous increase in the world's product in the years 1880–'82 had been experienced the prices of iron began to decline in an extraordinary manner; and in the case of some varieties touched in 1885–'86 the lowest figures ever recorded. Thus, American anthracite pig, which sold in February, 1880, for $41 per ton, declined almost continuously until July, 1885, when the low point of $17¾ was reached; while in Great Britain, Cleveland pig, which sold for £4 17s. 1d. in 1872, and £2 5s. in 1880, declined to £1 10s. 9d. in 1886. The decline in Bessemer steel rails in the English market was from £12 1s. 1d. in 1874 to less than £4 in 1887. In the United States, Bessemer steel rails, which commanded $58 per ton at the mills in 1880, fell to $28.25 at the close of the year 1884, reacting to $39½ in March, 1887.

Reviewing, specifically, the causes which contributed to the above-noted extraordinary decline in the prices of iron, the following points are worthy of notice :

First. The testimony of Sir Lowthian Bell shows that foreign countries have within recent years, and contrary to former experience, increased their production of iron in a far greater ratio than Great Britain, which was formerly the chief factor in the world's supply; and, in consequence, have become formidable competitors with Great Britain, not only in their own territories, but also in neutral markets. New fields of iron-ore have been discovered in Germany, France, and Belgium, very analogous in point of character to those which by discovery and development, about the year 1850, in the north of England, led to the subsequent great and rapid increase of British iron production.

Second. The power of producing iron with a given amount of labor and capital, and the number of establishments with great capacity for production, have, in recent years, greatly increased. For example, the average product per man of the furnaces of Great Britain, which for 1870 was estimated at 173 tons, is reported to have increased to 194 tons in 1880, and 261 tons in 1884, or fifty-one per cent.* Between the years 1885 and 1888 the number of furnace-stacks in the five States of Ohio, Michigan, Indiana, Illinois, and Wisconsin, was reduced from 139 to 134, but the product of the remainder during the same time nearly doubled.

Third. The substitution of steel for iron has resulted in a notable diminution of the consumption of iron for the attainment of a given result, or, in other words, more work is

---

* The claim has been made that as the decline in the prices of iron in recent years has been greater than the improvement in the efficiency of the labor engaged in producing iron, the inference is warranted that some other influence than the increased efficiency of labor must have come in to occasion such decline. A comparison of the prices of the standard varieties of iron in 1870 and 1887, shows, however, some very curious correspondences between the reduced prices and the reported degree of increase in the efficiency of labor within the same period. Thus, in the United States anthracite pig-iron, which sold at an average in 1871 of $35 per ton, had an average price in 1885 of $18. Cleveland bars, which commanded £6 19s. in 1870, sold for £4 10s. in 1887. At the same time nothing is more certain than that a great many other considerations than immediate labor cost enter into and determine the market prices, not only of iron, but of all other commodities. In the case of American wheat, for example, the evidence is indisputable that its cost in the Liverpool market has been reduced to the extent of thirty cents a bushel in the years from 1870–'72 to 1887, from causes wholly independent of the efficiency or wages of the men who produced it.

attainable from a less weight of material. Sir Lowthian Bell, in his testimony before the Royal British Commission, stated that a ship of 1,700 tons requires seventeen per cent less in weight of pig-iron, in being built of steel rather than of iron, and is capable of doing seven per cent more work.

Again, the quantity of pig-iron requisite for keeping a railroad in repair will depend greatly upon the state in which iron enters into construction; rails of steel, for example, having a far greater durability than rails of iron. *

A further example of recent economic disturbance consequent upon changes in the manufacture of iron—characterized by the Secretary of the British Iron Trade Association, in his report for 1886, as " one of the most remarkable of modern times "—is to be found in the rapid disuse of the system invented about one hundred years ago by Henry Cort for converting pig-iron into malleable iron by the so-called process of " puddling." Twenty years ago the use of

---

* Opinions, as yet, vary greatly as to the comparative durability of iron and steel rails. In the testimony given before the British Royal Commission, Mr. I. T. Smith, manager of the Barrow Steel Company, gave it as his opinion that the life of a steel rail is three times that of an iron rail, adding, " My reason for saying so is, that I know that upon the London and Northwestern Railroad, where steel rails have been now in use more than twenty years, they consider it so."

Sir Lowthian Bell also, in testifying before the commission, on the effect on the iron-trade of Great Britain from the expected longer duration of steel rails, says : " Assuming iron rails to last twelve and steel rails twenty-four years, instead of the railways now in existence in the United Kingdom requiring 465,648 tons annually for repairs, 232,824 tons will suffice for the purpose. Although this only involves the saving of a comparatively small weight of pig-iron, it means less work for remelting and for our rolling-mills, say to the extent of 4,000 to 5,000 tons per week." The difference in duration of iron and steel rails is not, however, in itself a complete measure of the amount of pig-iron required for renewals. This arises from the fact that an iron rail splits up and becomes useless long before the actual wear, as measured by the diminution of weight, renders it unsafe, which often happens when the loss of weight does not exceed four per cent of the original weight. Steel rails, on the other hand, go on losing weight until they are from ten to twenty per cent lighter than when they were laid down, before becoming unsafe.

this process was almost universal, to-day it is almost a thing that has past; and the loss of British capital invested in puddling-furnaces which have been abandoned in the ten years from 1875 to 1885 is estimated to have approximated £4,667,000, or $23,333,000, involving in Great Britain alone a displacement or transfer of workmen to other branches of industry during the same period of about 39,000.

After 1883 the production of iron in all iron-producing countries was for a time notably restricted; the product of the United States, for example, declined from 4,595,000 tons in 1883 to 4,044,000 tons in 1885, and that of Great Britain from 8,490,000 tons to 7,250,657 tons in the corresponding years; and as the decline in prices continued, and subsequently reached its extreme in 1885-'86, it has been urged that some other influences than excessive production must have been influential.* This paradoxical circumstance admits, however, of sufficient explanation. The years 1884, 1885, and 1886 were years of almost unprecedented business depression, restricting necessarily the uses and demand for iron for industrial purposes; while at the same time the capacity of every iron-producing country to supply its domestic requirements was greater than ever before. Under such conditions Great Britain, which produces about one half of all the iron and steel that is made in Europe, and more than any other country except Belgium depends on foreign markets to take its surplus of these products, found more difficulty than ever before in disposing of such surplus. The fact that the unsold stocks pressing upon the markets of the United States and of Europe continued to accumulate during the years 1884 and 1885, when production was restricted and declining, would seem also to be equivalent to a demonstration that no other influence than over-production could have operated at that period to occasion a continual decline in prices. Thus, in 1879

---

* "Financial Chronicle" (New York), January 21, 1888.

the unsold stock of all kinds of pig-iron in the United States in the hands of the makers was only 141,674 tons; in 1881, 210,876; in 1883, 533,800; and in 1884, 593,000 tons (the report of the American Iron and Steel Association being authority); while for the United States and Great Britain, conjointly, Sir Lowthian Bell reports the unsold stocks on hand at 1,874,000 tons in 1878, and 2,404,000 in 1884—an increase in these years of 528,000 tons. At the close of 1885 the stock of unsold pig-iron in Great Britain alone amounted to 2,491,000 tons—exactly fifty per cent larger than the stock on hand at the close of 1882, and the largest that had, up to that time, ever been held in Great Britain at the close of any one year. The unsold stock at the close of 1887 was, however, 2,616,000 tons, or 125,000 larger than in 1886.

In consequence of increased demand occasioned by extensive railroad constructions, the reduction in production of pig-iron which commenced in the United States in 1884 terminated in 1885–'86, since when production has augmented in a manner almost without precedent, namely, forty per cent in 1886 in excess of 1885, thirteen per cent in 1887 in excess of 1886, and eleven per cent in 1888 in excess of 1887, the product for 1888 having been the largest in the experience of the country. The causes influencing the increase in iron production in the United States in 1885–'86 not having been concurrently operative in Europe, the revival there of this industry was somewhat later; but for the United Kingdom the production for 1887 was about eight and a half per cent over that in 1886, while for all countries during the same period the increase has been estimated at 9·6 per cent.

With increased demand for iron, prices in the United States quickly advanced—i. e., from $17.75 per ton for anthracite pig in July, 1885, to $21.50 in January, 1887. As production increased, however, prices, in harmony with previous experiences, again declined, and in the first six months of 1889 American pig-iron generally ruled at lower figures than at any former period.

QUICKSILVER.—Excepting petroleum and quinine, the decline in price of this metal seems to have been greater in recent years than that of any other leading commodity—i. e., from £26 per flask (the highest) on the London market in 1874, to £5 2s. 6d. (lowest) in 1884; and from $118 (highest) to $26 (lowest) on the San Francisco market during the same period—a decline of 77.1 per cent. The explanation of this movement of price is to be found mainly in the circumstance that California, which furnishes nearly one half of the world's supply of this metal, increased her production from 30,077 flasks in 1870 to 79,684 in 1877; and although, as the result of low prices, many of the mines of California subsequently suspended operations and none paid dividends in 1885, the generally increased supply of quicksilver, coupled with its diminished use in the reduction of silver-ores—consequent on the introduction and use of cheaper processes—prevented any material augmentation in its price until 1886–'87, when the price advanced in the latter year to £11 5s. per flask in London and to $50 in San Francisco.

SILVER.—The decline in the average annual price of bar-silver per standard ounce in pence upon the London market has been from 59¼ in 1873 to 41⅝ in May, 1888 (the last being the lowest figure in all history), a decline in value in relation to gold in fifteen years of about thirty per cent. Notwithstanding this great decline in price, the annual production of silver during this same period has steadily augmented, or from $64,000,000 in 1873 to $95,000,000 in 1880, $122,000,000 in 1885 and $135,000,000 in 1887, an increase in fifteen years of one hundred and eleven per cent. Such a large and constantly increasing product of silver, while its price is declining, suggests a limitless supply.*

---

* The figures here given are those reported by the Director of the Mint of the United States, the value of silver being taken at the coining rate in the United States of silver dollars of $41.56 to the kilogramme.

TIN.—The production and price experiences of this metal during the last quarter of a century have been very curious. The world's consumption of tin from 1860–'64 constantly tended to be in excess of production, and prices rose from £87 per ton (the lowest figure) in 1864 to £159 (the highest) in 1872. In this latter year the mines of Australia began to produce very largely, and in a short time afforded a supply equal to one third of the world's current consumption. Under such circumstances the price of tin rapidly declined, and in October, 1878, touched £52 10s., the lowest price ever known in history, a decline of sixty-six per cent.

Subsequently the product of Australia declined and that of the " Straits " of Malacca did not materially increase, while that of England (Cornwall) and other countries remained nearly stationary. Meantime the consumption of tin throughout the world continually increased, so that prices advanced concurrently—i. e., from £52 10s. on the London market in 1879 to £105 in May, 1887. Recognizing this tendency of price movement, a French syndicate—the Société des Métaux—undertook to control the market-supply of the metal with a view of still further advancing prices, and for a time were so successful that in December, 1887, " Straits " tin was quoted in London at £167 15s. As a consequence of such inflation, every pound of tin that could be collected was placed on the market, and, as at the same time consumption was greatly checked, stocks accumulated to an unprecedented amount, the year 1887 closing with a visible market-supply full fifty per cent greater than twelve months previous. The syndicate was, nevertheless, enabled for some time to maintain prices at an extremely high level ; but in May, 1888, the receipts of tin from the " Straits " having for the previous five months been increased by upward of 107,000 hundred-weight over the receipts of the corresponding period of the preceding year, its ability to do so ceased. The conditions of supply and demand were too much against it, and in two days the advance in price which it had taken six months to engineer was lost, tin declining on the London market within that time from £166 ($830) per ton to £77 ($485), or over forty per cent. Subsequently an even lower quotation of £76 per ton was reached.

TIN PLATES.—Owing to a tendency of consumption to exceed production, tin plates in common with tin ruled at what were termed "famine" prices in 1874, and for some years previous; the average price for "coke" plates being from 26s. to 27s. per ton. After 1875, prices declined about fifty per cent; or during the year 1887 to 12s. 1½d. to 13s. per box. This remarkable and steady decline during a period of fifteen years is as clearly and certainly understood as in the case of tin, above noticed, and is referable to three causes: *First*, the reduction in the cost of the metal tin. *Second*, to improvements in the manufacture of iron, and the extensive substitution of steel (plates) in place of charcoal and puddled-iron plates. *Third*, to new processes of manufacture and tinning; a modern tin-plate mill turning out every twenty-four hours more than double the product of old-fashioned mills, without any increase in expenditure for motive power or labor. Supply and consumption alike under such circumstances have increased to an enormous extent, and the tin-plate trade, instead of being a minor industry of the world, as was formerly and not remotely the case, has become one of great magnitude.*
These changes in the conditions of production and prices

---

* An attempt on the part of Germany to break in upon the almost complete monopoly of the manufacture of tin plates enjoyed by Great Britain, by imposing a heavy duty on their importation, has been singularly unsuccessful; domestic (German) production and exports having diminished, and exports increased, as will appear from the following table:

YEAR.	Production.	Imports.	Exports.
	Tons.	Tons.	Tons.
1885.................................	4,892	5,798	186
1878.................................	8,582	5,307	1,696

brought, however, nothing of prosperity to the British tin-plate manufacturing industry; and the period under consideration was characterized by very many failures on the part of (South Wales) producers.

NICKEL, not many years ago, was a scarce metal of limited uses, and commanded comparatively high prices. Latterly the discovery of new and cheaper sources of supply have tended to throw upon the market an amount in excess of the world's present average yearly consumption—estimated at between 800 and 900 tons—and, as a consequence, there has been "over-production, and unsatisfactory prices to dealers." There is, moreover, little prospect that prices in respect to this metal will ever revive—one mine in New Caledonia (Pacific Ocean) alone being estimated as capable of producing two or three thousand tons annually, if required; while the discovery of new deposits of ore is frequently reported.

LEAD experienced a decline, comparing the highest market prices in New York, in January, 1880 and 1885, respectively, of about thirty-nine per cent. The world's production of lead since 1876 has increased very rapidly; especially in the United States; the total annual product of which has advanced from 42,540 tons in 1873, to 143,957 in 1883, and 180,555 in 1888. One marked result of this increase has been that the United States, in place of being as formerly a large consumer of foreign lead, now imports but a comparatively insignificant quantity, namely, 7,035,000 pounds in 1888 as compared with 72,423,000 pounds in 1873. Rich and extensive mines of lead have also in recent years been discovered and worked in Australia.

The decline in the price of lead, above noted, occasioned the suspension or bankruptcy of many English lead-mining companies, and during the year 1885 much distress from this cause was reported as existing among English lead-miners. The following is an example of another economic disturbance contingent on changes in the production and price of lead : Formerly the domestic supply in the United States of white-lead and of all paints, the basis of which is oxide of lead, was derived almost exclusively from manufactories located upon the Atlantic seaboard ; but with the discovery and working of the so-called silver-lead mines of the States and Territories west of the Mississippi, and the production of large quantities of lead as a product residual, or secondary to silver, the inducements offered for the manufacture of white-lead and lead-paints, through local reductions in the price of the raw material and the saving of freights, have been sufficient to almost destroy the former extensive white-lead and paint business in the Eastern sections of the United States, and transfer it to the Western.

At present the lead produced in silver-mining constitutes a large proportion of the world's supply of lead ; and most of the mines of lead which do not produce a considerable amount of the more precious metal have been abandoned ; " or, in other words, lead is now produced as a valuable by-product in the mining of silver." At the same time the industrial employment of lead is diminishing, other metals having taken its place—especially in the construction of pipes—to such an extent that the main use of lead is now for small projectiles, and for the making of paint.

COAL.—The decline in the export prices of British coal, comparing the average for 1867–'77 with 1886, was about thirty-three per cent. In the United States, although her present annual production of coal is one fourth that of the world, nothing reliable in the way of average prices for a series of years can be given ; inasmuch as, through combinations of coal-owners and railways, and by reason of frequent labor troubles among miners, the price of coal in recent years has rarely been determined by natural conditions and has fluctuated greatly from year to year. Thus, on the 1st of January, 1876, 1881, 1882, and 1885, respectively, the price of mining 100 bushels of coal on the railroads entering into the city of Pittsburg, Pa., was $2.50, $3.50, $4.00, and $3.00; and the price of coal at Pittsburg, Pa., on the corresponding dates, per 100 bushels, was $5.50, $7.00, $7.50, and $5.50. Again, the decline in the average annual price of anthracite coal (by the cargo at Philadelphia), comparing 1870 with 1880, was thirty-eight per cent; but, as between 1870 and 1886, it was only 6·6 per cent.

According to the returns of the United States Geological Survey, there was a gain in the production of coal in the United States for the year 1886, as compared with the aggregate product of 1885, of 1,785,000 short tons, but a loss in value at the point of production of $4,419,420. For the succeeding year, 1887, on the other hand, there was a gain of 16.333,000 tons over the product of 1886, and a gain in value of $26,483,000.

The increase in the production and also of the consumption of coal within recent years constitutes one of the most remarkable features in economic history. The increase in the product of the five chief coal-producing countries of the world—Great Britain, the United States, Germany, France, and Belgium—from 1870 to 1886 inclusive, has been in excess of eighty per cent : Great Britain increasing her product from 109,000,000 gross tons in 1870 to 159,351,000 in 1885, and 169,935,000 in 1888 ; and the United States from 38,468,000 tons in 1870 to 97,000,000 in 1885, 111,000,000 for 1887, and 123,000,000 in 1888, or eleven per cent in excess of the product of 1887. In Germany, the increase reported was from 36,041,000 tons in 1873 to 55,000,000 in 1883 In 1870 the average output of coal per miner in the British coal-mines—counting in all the men employed—was 250 tons, an amount never before reached. In 1879 this average had increased to 280 tons per man ;* and in 1884, according

---

* See testimony of assistant-keeper (Meade) of the mining records of Great Britain, " Second Report of the British Commission on Depression of Trade," 1886, p. 337.

to Mr. J. S. Jeans, Secretary of the British Iron Association, was 353 tons,* and for the United States 374 tons. For Germany, the increase was from 261 tons in 1881 to 269 tons in 1883; and in Belgium, for corresponding years, from 165 tons to 173 tons per miner, while for 1887 the average product of each coal-mining hand, according to M. Harzé, chief of the Administration of Mines, reached 244 tons, or 15 tons more than in 1886.

Concurrently with the enormous increase in the production of coal and greater efficiency and economy in mining, very much has been done to reduce the amount of coal formerly used to effect industrial results; for example, at blast-furnaces, coal was formerly used for heating the boilers that furnished steam for blowing, hoisting, etc., and for heating the air which was blown into the stacks. Now, a well-ordered set of blast-furnaces does not use a single ounce of coal except what goes in to melt the ore. The whole of the heat used to produce the steam required in connection with the furnace, and for heating the stoves for making the hot blast, is obtained from the gases which rise to the top of the stacks in the process of smelting the iron, and which formerly was all thrown away.† The following short table, based on official statistics, from the London " Economist," October, 1888, shows the progressive economy in the use of coal for the production of pig-iron in Great Britain during the short space of the three years 1885, 1886, and 1887 :

YEAR.	Pig-iron.	Coal used.	Per cent of coal.
	Tons.	Tons.	
1887.....................	7,559,518	15,304,188	202
1886.....................	7,009,754	14,249,715	203
1885.....................	7,415,469	15,287,527	205

* " Journal of the Royal Statistical Society," 1884, pp. 621. 622.
· † Testimony of J. D. Ellis, chairman of John Brown & Co., Sheffield, British Commission, 1886.

The displacement of finished iron by steel, which is rapidly taking place, also tends to reduce the consumption of coal; while in the manufacture of gas, and in all steam appliances—more especially in marine locomotion—it is well known that great economies in the use of coal have been effected, whereby it is possible to do a far greater amount of work with a given quantity of fuel than was the case five or ten years ago. In the United States a new agency has come in, namely, natural gas, which has been largely influential in displacing the use of coal. For the year 1886 the amount of coal thus displaced was estimated by the United States Geological Survey at 6,453,000 tons, valued at $6,847,000, while for 1887 the displacement was about fifty per cent greater, or 9,867,000 tons, having a valuation of $15,838,000. Furthermore, it should not be overlooked that the cost of transporting coal, which constitutes a most important element in determining its price at the point of consumption, has been subject, both by sea and land, to very great reductions.

That the world's consumption of coal during the period under consideration has progressively and enormously increased, and is still increasing, is not to be questioned, and, in the absence of any reliable data for ascertaining the relations between the production and consumption of this commodity, great latitude of opinion on this point is permissible; but, at the same time, the fact that competition for the supply of coal in all the markets of the world has been and is exceedingly keen, goes far to justify the current belief of the trade everywhere that production has for years been augmented at a greater rate than the demand warranted. In addition, the further facts that new, extensive, and readily accessible coal-fields have been and are continually being discovered, that the supply of coal is regarded as practically inexhaustible, and that the slightest increase of demand is sufficient to speedily stimulate production, would of themselves seem to forbid the assumption that any cause except change in supply and demand could have been influential in determining the recent price experiences of coal.

COFFEE AND TEA.—The decline in recent years in the prices of each of these great staple commodities has been almost as remarkable as has been the case with sugar—coffee having touched the lowest prices ever known in commerce in the early months of 1886, the price of "ordinary," or "exchange standard No. 5," having been seven and a half cents in January of that year in the New York market; while, according to Mr. Giffen, of the British Board of Trade, the decline in the price of tea, comparing 1882 with 1861, has been greater than that of sugar, or, indeed, of almost any other article. In both cases the decline would seem to find a sufficient explanation in a common expression of the trade circulars, " Our supplies have far outrun our consumptive requirements." In the case of coffee, the total imports into Europe and the United States, comparing the receipts of the year 1885 with 1873, showed an increase of fifty-seven per cent; while the increase in the crops of Brazil, Ceylon, and Java during the same period has been estimated at fifty-two per cent. Subsequently to January, 1886, the price of coffee, owing to a partial failure of the Brazil crop, rapidly advanced two hundred per cent; "ordinary " or " exchange standards " having been sold in New York in 1886 at twenty-two cents, the highest point in the history of American trade, unless possibly during the war, when entirely abnormal circumstances controlled prices. From these high prices there was a subsequent disastrous reaction and extensive failures. The advance in average prices was, however, maintained in 1887, and for so long a time that the reduction in the world's consumption during that year was very great, and for Europe was estimated at the large figures of 77,000 cwts., or over 1,000,000 bags of " Brazil "; while in the United States the reduction was believed to have been equivalent to two pounds per head of the population, or double the total annual consumption of Great Britain.

In the matter of the supply of tea, the total exports from China and India increased from 234,000,000 pounds in 1873 to 337,000,000 pounds in 1885, or forty-four per cent; the exports from India having increased from 35,000,000 pounds in 1879 to 68,000,000 pounds in 1885; 98,000,000 in 1887, and 113,000,000 in 1888.* In this latter year the imports of Indian and Ceylon tea into Great Britain for the first time on record exceeded the imports of Chinese teas; and herein we have another striking example of the inability of unskilled labor, or labor following old processes, even at extreme low wages, to contend against intelligence and machinery; inasmuch as the English planter in India by skillful cultivation and careful manufacture with machinery is now able to place in Europe a tea of good quality, and greater strength, at a price which the Chinaman, with his old methods, producing an inferior article, can not afford.

SULPHATE OF QUININE, a standard chemical preparation, used extensively all over the world for medicinal purposes, affords another illustration of extraordinary declining price movements in recent years, which are thoroughly capable of explanation.

In 1865 the highest price of sulphate of quinine in the English market was 4s. 4d. ($1.07) per ounce, which gradu-

---

* The British Chancellor of the Exchequer, Mr. Goschen, in his budget speech for 1887, calls attention to the following curious incident of financial disturbance growing out of a change in the quality of tea, which, in turn, has been contingent on a change in the locality or country of its production: "Whereas, ten years ago," he said, "we (Great Britain) received 156,000,000 pounds of tea from China and 28,000,000 pounds from India, in 1886 we received 145,000,000 pounds from China and 81,000,000 pounds from India. In the transfer of consumption of tea from the tea of China to that of India, we have to put up with a loss of revenue owing to the curious fact that the teas of India are stronger than the teas of China, and therefore go further, so that a smaller quantity of tea is required to make the same number of cups of tea." Mr. Goschen further called attention to the fact that "the fall in the price of tea and sugar (in Great Britain) has been so great, that whereas in 1866 a pound of tea and a pound of sugar would have cost 2s. 6d. and in 1876 2s. 1½d., in 1886 they would have cost only 1s. 7½d., or 3d. less than they would have cost in 1866 with all the duties taken off."

ally advanced to 9s. 6d. in 1873, reacting to 6s. 9d. in 1876. In the subsequent year, owing to an interruption in the exportation of cinchona-bark from South America by civil war in New Granada, and by low water in the Magdalena River, the price advanced to the unprecedentedly high figure of 16s. 6d. ($4.70) per ounce, receding to 13s. in 1879, and 12s. ($3) in 1880. In 1883 identically the same article sold in Europe for 3s. 6d. (80 cents) per ounce, in 1885 for 2s. 6d., and in 1887 to 1s. 6d. (30 cents) or less.

The history of the influences that have occasioned such results is as follows : Formerly all cinchona-bark from which quinine is manufactured came from the forests of the northern states of South America; and as the cinchona-trees were not under any system of cultivation, and as the methods of collecting their barks were wasteful and destructive, reasonable apprehensions began to be entertained, as far back as 1855, that the supply of this most important natural product would ultimately, and at no distant day, be exhausted. Moved by such considerations the English and Dutch Governments determined, therefore, to attempt the cultivation of the cinchona-trees in India and Java, and the effort has proved exceedingly successful. The first installment of seeds and plants reached Ceylon and Java from South America in 1861, and the first export of bark, consisting of but twenty-eight ounces, took place in 1869. After that the East Indian product gradually but enormously increased—Ceylon, for example, exporting 6,925,000 pounds in '1882-'83 ; 11,500,000 pounds in 1883-'84; and 15,235,000 pounds in 1885-'86. From Java the exports have been much smaller, but for 1887 were in excess of 2,200,000 pounds. As the world had never before been supplied to such an extent with bark, its price rapidly declined ; and as the cost of quinine is mainly determined by the cost of the crude material from which it is manufactured, its extraordinary price reduction followed, as has been pointed out. Two other circumstances contributed to such a result : the *first* is, that while cinchona-barks from South America—the product of indigenous trees—yield on an average not over two per cent of quinine, the bark of the cultivated tree in the East Indies is reported to yield from eight to twelve per cent. A given quantity of bark, therefore, goes much further in producing quinine than formerly. *Secondly*, owing to the recent discovery and employment of new and more economical processes, more quinine can now be made at less cost in from three to five days than could have been effected by old methods in twenty days.

PAPER AND RAGS.—A quarter of a century ago, or less, paper was made almost exclusively from the fibers of cotton and linen rags; and with an enormous and continually increasing demand, paper and rags not only rapidly increased in price, but continually tended to increase, and thus greatly stimulated effort for the discovery and utilization of new fibrous materials for the manufacture of paper. These efforts have been so eminently successful that immense quantities of pulp suitable for the manufacture of paper are now made from the fibers of wood, straw, and various grasses, and so cheaply that the prices of fair qualities of book-paper have declined since the year 1872 to the extent of fully fifty per cent, while in the case of ordinary " news " the decline has been even greater. Rags, although still extensively used, have, by the competitive supply of substitute materials, and a consequent comparative lack of demand, been also greatly cheapened, and the cotton rags sold in 1887 for a lower price in the London market than over before recorded.

The returns of the American Paper-Makers' Association exhibit the following changes that have taken place in this department of industry in the United States, comparing the years 1880 and 1888 : Increase of capital employed, from $46,000,000 to $80,000,000 ; of product, from 451,000,000 tons to 1,200,000,000 ; of wages, from an average of $1.13 to $1.50 per day. On the other hand, the average value of a pound of paper declined from 6·09c. in 1880 to 3·95c. in

1888; and the per cent of labor per pound, from 94 cents to 77 in the same period. In other words, while the cost (wages) of labor has increased thirty-two per cent, the cost of labor per pound of paper has decreased twenty-two per cent.

NITRATE OF SODA.—The recent price experiences of nitrate of soda (Chilian saltpeter) have been very curious. The supply of this article, which corresponds to the more valuable nitrate of potash (true saltpeter), is practically limited to one locality on the earth's surface—a rainless, desert track—in the province of Tarapacá, which formerly belonged to Peru, but has recently been annexed to Chili. It is cheaply and plentifully obtained, at points from fifty to ninety miles from the coast, by dissolving out the nitrate salt from the desert earth, which it impregnates, with water, and concentrating the solution by boiling to the point where the nitrate separates by crystallization. Up to the year 1845 it was an article so little known to commerce that only 6,000 tons were annually exported; but as its value as a fertilizing agent in agriculture, and as a cheap source of nitrogen in the manufacture of nitric acid, became recognized, the demand for it rapidly increased until the amount exported in 1883 was estimated at 570,000 tons, or more than a thousand million pounds. To meet this demand and obtain the profit resulting from substituting skillful for primitive methods of extracting and marketing the nitrate, foreign capital, mainly English, extensively engaged in the business. A large amount of English-made machinery, and many English engineers and mechanics, were sent out and planted in the desert; additional supplies of water were secured, and a railroad fifty-nine miles in length constructed to the port of Iquique on the sea-coast, for the transportation of coal, provisions, and other material *up*, and the nitrate as a return freight *down*. So energetically, moreover, was the work pressed, that at the last and most complete establishment constructed under English auspices, the business, employing when in full operation six hundred men, was prosecuted unremittingly by night (by the agency of the electric light) as well as by day. The result was exactly what might have been anticipated. The export of nitrate, which was 319,000 tons in 1881, rose to 570,000 tons in 1883; and prices at the close of 1883 declined with great rapidity to the extent of more than fifty per cent, or to a point claimed to be below the cost of production. Such a result, threatening the whole business with disaster, led to an agreement on the part of all the interests concerned, to limit from June, 1884, to January, 1887, the product of every establishment to twenty-five per cent of its capacity. But, notwithstanding these well-devised measures, prices were not immediately restored to their former figures, the average price per cwt. in London having been 10s. in 1886, as compared with an average of 14s. for 1867–'77. Since 1887 the increase in the demand for this commodity, especially by the growers of beet-root on the Continent, has been very marked; and the world's consumption is estimated to have advanced from 502,000 tons in 1887 to 645,000 in 1888. The world's total supply increased, however, during the same period in a greater proportion, namely, from 507,000 tons in 1887 to 715,000 tons in 1888. The almost certainty that the consumption of nitrate of soda is to continue increasing, and the knowledge that its supply is or can be thoroughly controlled, gave rise in 1888 to great speculation in the shares of the various producing companies, and advanced their prices to very high figures. This experience of nitrate of soda seems especially worthy of notice, because it constitutes another example of a great and rapid decline in the price of a standard and valuable commodity in the world's commerce, and for which—all the facts being clearly understood—it is not possible to assign any other cause than that of production in excess of any current demand for consumption, and which in turn has been solely contingent on the employment, under novel conditions, of improved methods for overcoming territorial and climatic difficulties.

Concurrently with the fall in the price of nitrate of soda, saltpeter, or nitrate of potash, also notably declined from 28s. 3d. in 1880 to 21s. in 1887 (for English refined), a fact which seems to find a sufficient explanation in the circumstance that nitrate of soda can be used to a certain extent as a substitute for nitrate of potash, and that the export of the latter from India, the country of chief supply, increased from 352,995 cwt. in 1881 to 451,917 cwt. in 1885, or thirty-six per cent.

The decline in the prices of many chemicals, due to improvements in methods and to excess of production, has also been very great in recent years—the decline in soda-ash from 1872 having been fifty-four per cent, while bleaching-powders (chloride of lime) declined from £10 in 1873 to £6 15s. in 1878, reacting to £9 in 1887; but declined to £7 15s. in 1888.   During 1888 the supply of salt—the crude material out of which soda is manufactured—having passed under the control of an organization or " trust," the price of salt, and consequently the price of soda-ash, materially advanced. Caustic soda in 1887 touched, however, the lowest price on record.

MEATS.—The price of meats, according to the statistics of English markets, exhibits no material decline, comparing the average prices of 1867–'77 and of 1878–'85.   But during the years 1885 and 1886 the decline was very considerable, and extended also to most other animal products.   The percentage of fall in the carcass prices of different kinds and quantities of meat in London, as given by the London " Economist" of November 27, 1885, was, in comparison with the prices for 1879, as follows : For inferior beef, forty-three per cent; prime beef, eighteen per cent; prime mutton, thirteen per cent; large pork, twenty-two per cent; middling mutton, twenty-seven per cent.

In November, 1887, Mr. W. E. Bear, of England, published the following estimates of the meat-supply—home and foreign—of the population of the United Kingdom for the years 1877 and 1885, respectively:

Year.	Population.	Total meat-supply.
1877	33,446,000	30,800,000 cwt.
1885	36,331,000	36,460,000 "
Increase of population, 8·6 per cent.		
" supply, 18 "		

The decline in the average export price of salt beef in the United States was from 8·2 cents per pound in 1884 to 6 cents in 1886 (twenty-six per cent); of salt pork from 8·2 cents to 5·9 cents (twenty-seven per cent); of bacon and hams from 9·6 cents to 7·5 cents; and of lard from 9·4 cents to 6·9 cents. In the case of lard-oil an exceptionally great decline in price in recent years—i. e., from an average of 94 cents per gallon (Cincinnati market) in 1881–'82 to a minimum of 48·8 cents in 1886, is claimed to be due mainly to the large production and more general use of vegetable oils —cotton-seed oil in the United States, and palm and cocoanut oils in Europe. The effect of the increased quantity and cheapness of these vegetable oils has been especially marked in England, France, Italy, and Germany; and has also undoubtedly influenced the price of tallow, the decline of which in English markets, comparing the average prices of 1867–'77 with those of 1886, having been thirty-one per cent, while in the United States the price for 1884–'85 was the lowest on record.

The immediate cause of this decline in the price of meats in the United Kingdom and on the Continent of Europe was undoubtedly the new sources of supply of live animals and fresh meats that have been opened up to Europe, and especially to Great Britain, from extra-European countries: the value of the imports into Great Britain from North America of live animals having increased from $1,085,000 in 1876 to $22,980,000 in 1885; of fresh meat from $1,950,-000 to $11,820,000; and of fresh meat from Australia and the river Plate (transported through refrigeration) from $880,000 in 1882 to $5,850,000 in 1885; a total increase of from $3,025,000 in 1870 to $40,650,000 in 1885. The ability of the three countries named to increase their exports of meat during such a brief period to such an enormous extent, constitutes of itself a demonstration of increased product and of the diminished price that is the invariable accompaniment of a surplus seeking a market.* All these countries, moreover, coincidently with their increased exports of meats, increased their stocks of cattle, sheep, and pigs. Thus, in the United States the increase in the number of cattle between 1870 and 1880 was sixty-six per cent; † in Australia, between 1873 and 1883, forty-three per cent; while the recent increase in the Argentine States is believed to have been in a greater ratio. In respect to sheep, also, their number increased in the United States from 33,783,-000 in 1875 to 50,626,000 in 1884; in Australia, from 57,-144,000 in 1873 to 83,369,000 in 1883, and 97,900,000 in 1887; while in the Argentine States the number at present is estimated to be nearly as great as in all Australia.

It is probable that the number of cattle in Europe has not increased in recent years, and may have declined, although there are no recent accepted statistics on this point. "The Continent of Europe, however, as a whole," according to the London "Economist" (October 15, 1887), "supplies itself with beef and spares a surplus for the United Kingdom. It is true that a few countries (of the Continent) im-

---

* A statement of the late Neumann-Spallart—a recognized authority—that "the total international trade in meat of all kinds had only increased from 1,946,000,000 marks in 1877 to 1,954,000,000 in 1884," has been regarded by some writers as constituting proof that the decline in the price of meats during these years could not have been occasioned by any increased supply. If, however, the greatly increased quantity of meat which a given amount of money (gold) represented in 1884 over 1877 is taken into consideration, the deductions from Mr. Spallart's figures are capable of a very different interpretation.

† In the United States there has been since 1883 a marked decline in the value of prairie cattle on the hoof, which in the main has resulted from oversupply. In 1888 the receipts at the Union Stock Yards, at Chicago, were 230,000 head in excess of what had ever been received before. Besides, there was a large visible unmarketed supply.

port small quantities of beef in one form or other, but there is a net surplus." Commenting on this subject, an elaborate report on "Cattle and Dairy Farming," issued by the United States State Department in 1887, also thus sums up the situation: "It would seem as if the cattle, meat, and dairy producers of the world (that portion at least which prosecutes advanced agriculture) look to the British markets for the consumption of their surplus products." And, in confirmation of this conclusion, the same report makes the following exhibit of the manner in which the exports of "cattle and their products" from the United States in 1885 were distributed according to value : "To the United Kingdom, $54,250,000 ; to all the other countries in Europe, $3,200,000 ; to all the countries outside of Europe, $4,108,-176." And what is true of the distribution of the exports of the surplus meat products of the United States in recent years has been equally true of those of Australia, Canada, and the "river Plate." Or, in other words, the admitted great increase in the export of cattle and cattle products, as well as of other meats from all these countries in recent years, has practically sought but one market, namely, that of Great Britain.

As bearing on the future meat-supply of Europe, it is important here also to call attention to the rise and development of a comparatively new industry, namely, "the frozen-meat trade." In 1860, 400 carcasses of frozen mutton were imported from Australia into Great Britain ; in 1888 the importations from Australia and the river Plate wore close on to 2,000,000 carcasses. One establishment in New Zealand—"The Canterbury Freezing Company"—has, it is stated, contracted with ship-owners for the transportation of frozen mutton to London for the years 1889 and 1890 at a rate not exceeding one penny per pound. This reduction in the charge for freight has been rendered possible by a change in the conditions of trade. At one time only from 10,000 to 12,000 carcasses could be carried in each ship; now the average would be between 24,000 and 30,000 carcasses to each vessel. The London charges are reckoned at $\frac{1}{4}d$. per lb.; in New Zealand they are slightly under $\frac{1}{2}d$.; the total, therefore, will not exceed $2d$. per lb. This, on the minimum price of $3\frac{1}{2}d$. in London, will give the farmer $1\frac{1}{2}d$. per lb., in addition to skin and fat. The Argentine States of South America are also largely engaged in the exportation of frozen meats, and, under the stimulus of a bounty offered by the Government, the business promises to assume large proportions.

CHEESE.—American cheese experienced an extraordinary decline in price from twelve to thirteen cents in 1880 to $8\frac{3}{8}$ and $10\frac{1}{8}$ cents in 1885; and, as the American contribution of this article of food to the world's consumption has constituted in recent years a large factor, the world's prices generally corresponded with those of the American market. This decline in the United States was due mainly to two causes : *First*. The establishment of the cheese-factory, which brought new processes and new machinery— not adapted for economical use by small or individual farmer producers—to the business of manufacturing, and so revolutionized and greatly cheapened production. *Second*. The relative prices of butter and cheese in the United States after 1880–'81 were so much to the advantage of the latter, that large quantities of milk which had previously gone to the creameries to be made into butter, found their way into factories to be made into cheese; and for the years 1883, 1884, and 1885, the annual receipts at New York city averaged twenty-five per cent in excess of the receipts for 1880. Demand for export at the same time largely fell off, and so assisted in the decline of prices; the same influences existing in the United States having also apparently prevailed to a degree in other cheese-producing countries; the amount recognized by the trade as having been supplied to the great cheese-consuming countries, Great Britain, the Continent of Europe, and South America, having increased from 1880 to 1884 to the extent of fourteen per cent.

Among new sources of cheese-supply in recent years is New Zealand, whose product in large and rapidly increasing quantities is becoming a factor in the European market. The unprofitableness of wheat-culture in many countries is also undoubtedly turning the attention of their farming classes to dairy farming in preference, and for this reason the world's supply of cheese has, and is likely to be, largely augmented. One proof of this is to be found in the circumstance that the Swiss agriculturists—the reputation of whose cheese product is proverbial—are complaining of an inability to extend and even hold their existing markets, and are devoting more attention to the raising of cattle with a view to their exportation.

FISH.—The years 1884 and 1885 in the United States were notable for a plethora of all kinds of dry and pickled fish on the one hand, and of extreme low prices of such commodities on the other; mackerel having touched a lower price in the Boston market than for any year since 1849, while for codfish the price was less than at any time since the year 1838. Subsequently to 1885 the price experiences of mackerel have been most interesting. For some reason the American fishermen have not been able to catch as many mackerel as formerly; the catch of the New England fleet declining from 478,000 barrels in 1884 to 50,000 barrels in 1888. Demand in the latter year, accordingly, soon absorbed the supply; prices advanced several hundred per cent, and at the close of the year 1888 there was not only no trade in salted mackerel, but there was none possible.

FREIGHTS.—Although a service and not a commodity, the reduction in recent years of freights, or the cost of transportation and distribution, may be legitimately included in the first group of price experiences, and here considered, as no other one agency has been more influential in occasioning a decline in prices. It has, moreover, acted universally, is without dispute entirely the outcome of new processes, constructions, and machinery, and has no connection whatever with matters pertaining to currency, or standards of value. Its influence has also necessarily manifested itself very unequally, occasioning the greatest price-reductions in the case of articles—like cereals, meats, fibers, ores, and all coarser materials—in respect to which transportation constitutes the largest element of cost at the place of consumption; and least in the case of articles—like textiles, spirits, spices, teas, books, and similar products—where great values are comprised in small bulk. The investigations of Mr. Atkinson show, that had the actual quantity of merchandise moved by the railroads of the United States in 1880 been subjected to the average rate per ton per mile which was charged from 1866 to 1869, the difference would have amounted to at least $500,000,000 (£100,000,000), and perhaps $800,000,000 (£160,000,000), more than the actual charge of 1880.   Comparing 1865 with 1885, Mr. Atkinson further shows that, taking a given weight of goods to be moved from Chicago to New York, one thousand miles, by the New York Central Railroad, fifty-eight per cent of the original value was absorbed in transportation and depreciation of the currency in the former year; while in 1885 only twenty per cent was so absorbed—the charge per ton per mile having fallen from 3·45 cents in 1865 to 1·573 cents in 1873, and to 0·68 of a cent in 1885.

In 1883 the average rate on all classes of freight, on all classes of railways in the United States, was 1·236 cents per ton per mile.   In 1887 it was only a trifle over a cent; a reduction in the short space of three years that is little less than marvelous.

The fall in price for the carriage of commodities by sea has also been as remarkable as the decline in the cost of carriage by land.   Freight, on the average, between Calcutta and England experienced a decline of about fifty per cent in 1885 as compared with 1875. In the case of India wheat transported to England *via* the Suez Canal, the decline in freights was from 71*s.* 3*d.* per ton in October, 1881, to 27*s.* in October, 1885, or more than sixty-three per cent. Between 1873 and 1885 the tolls and pilotage on the Suez Canal were reduced to the extent of about thirty-three per cent.

Freights from New York to Liverpool declined, from 1880 to 1886, as follows (maximum and minimum): On grain, from $9\frac{1}{4}d.$ to 1*d.* per bushel; on flour, from 25*s.* to 7*s.* 6*d.* per ton; on cheese, from 50*s.* to 15*s.* per ton; on cotton, from $\frac{3}{8}d.$ to $\frac{7}{64}d.$ per pound; and on bacon and lard, from 45*s.* to 7*s.* 6*d.* per ton. Ocean freights continued very low until the latter months of 1888. In May of that year, wheat to Antwerp from New York was taken at half a cent per bushel of sixty pounds; a rate which could not have paid for the cost of loading and discharging the cargo. As to the cause of the decline in ocean freights there can be no controversy. Between 1881 and 1883 shipping returned fair dividends on the investment. The ocean shipping of the world, taken as a whole, was operated during 1884, 1885, 1886, 1887, and a great part of the year 1888 without profit. The immediate cause of the change in the situation was an over-production of tonnage. The profits made by cargo-vessels prior to 1883—in some instances very great —stimulated ship-building, and multitudes of men having no practical experience became ship-owners. Capitalists large and small readily furnished the money where investment seemed so promising. Fewer sailing-ships and more steamers were built, largely increasing the capacity for work. In 1875 the business done per ton by British shipping, in active employment, was $10\frac{8}{10}$ tons; in 1886, it was $13\frac{3}{10}$ tons. The transition from wood to iron, and from iron to steel, in the construction of vessels; the improvements in machinery which largely economize fuel and labor; and the bounty system, by which some of the Continental states of Europe offer a premium on ship-building—have also been important factors. Low freights have caused a diminished demand for ship-building materials, and this in turn has depressed the prices of materials for constructing ships, and cheapened them.

Mr. Robert Giffen, in a report to the Royal Commission on Trade Depression, has run an interesting line of comparison between the imports and exports per head, and the entries of shipping per head, in the United Kingdom since 1855-'59. From 1855 to 1874 the values of British imports and exports increased more than the increase of shipping; but after 1874 values increased very slowly, and between 1875-'79 declined, while the increase in shipping went on at very rapid rates.

TELEGRAPH RATES.—The great decline in telegraph rates in recent years, in common with all other agencies that have reduced the expenses of business, has also been an instrumentality of no little potency in influencing a decline of general prices. Taking the experience of the United States as a criterion, the charges for the transmission of dispatches were on the average six times less in 1887 than in 1866. For example, the reductions between 1866 and 1887 in the cost of sending ten words from New York to the following various points, was as follows: To St. Louis, from $2.25 to 40c. ; to Galveston, Texas, from $5.50 to 75c. ; to San Francisco, from $7.45 to $1.00; to Washington, from 75c. to 25c.

Attention is next asked to the *second* group of staple commodities which have experienced a notable decline in price in recent years; and in respect to the causes of which the evidence, although more inferential and circumstantial, through lack of universally accepted data, than in the case of the commodities included in the *first* group, seems, nevertheless, to be sufficiently positive and conclusive.

WHEAT.—The most important commodity in this group

is wheat ; the price experiences of which, in recent years, have been as follows: Comparing the years 1875 and 1882, there was no very marked change in the price of wheat in the English market ; the average for the year 1875 having been 45*s*. 2*d*. per quarter, and for the year 1881, 45*s*. 4*d*. In the United States the average export price was $1.12 per bushel in 1875 and $1.11 in 1881. After 1882 prices declined rapidly ; the average price of British wheat, which was 45*s*. 4*d*. per quarter in that year, falling to 32*s*. 10*d*. in 1885, to 31*s*. 3*d*. in 1886, and to less than 30*s*. in 1887, which last quotation was the lowest since average market prices have been officially recorded.*

The average price of wheat in the English markets for the decade from 1870 to 1880 was forty-three per cent higher than the average of 1886 ; and the average prices from 1859 to 1872 were sixty-eight per cent higher than the average of 1886.

An analysis of the comparative prices of wheat in the United States furnishes corresponding results : the average price of No. 2 spring wheat having declined in the Chicago market from $1.10 (gold) in 1872 to seventy-six and a half cents in 1886 ; and sixty-seven cents in July, 1887 ; a price equivalent to 29*s*. per quarter in the harbor at Liverpool, or eighty-six cents per bushel, cost, freight and insurance included. This is about the lowest price ever reported for the United States since wheat has become an exportable product.

In seeking for an explanation of such price phenomena, we find a factor at the outset which has undeniably been most influential, namely, the great reduction in recent years in the cost of the transportation or distribution of all commodities, and more especially of the commodity wheat. Thus,

---

* The Eaton record gave only 26*s*. 9¼*d*. per quarter as the price for the year 1761, when reduced to Winchester bushels ; but there is no certainty that the average for the entire year was even in that one market as low as that, and still less that the price was as low in more than one hundred and fifty English market towns as it was in 1886.

the freight on wheat from New York to Liverpool declined from 9¼d. per bushel in 1880 to 1d. per bushel in 1886. According to Mr. Edward Atkinson, who has made this matter a special study, the reduction in the cost of the inland transportation of American wheat a distance of fifteen hundred miles, comparing the rates charged in 1870–'72 with those of 1887, was equivalent to a fraction over 11s. per quarter reduction in the delivery cost of such wheat in the English market, and for the reduction in the cost of ocean transportation between the two periods, he estimates 4s. per quarter. In addition, the substitution of sacks costing 13 cents for barrels costing 50 cents (in 1872) is believed to be equivalent to a further reduction, if rated on wheat, of 1s. per quarter; and, finally, for reduction of charges in hauling, elevating, and milling (assuming the wheat to be exported in the form of flour) at least 3s. per quarter more must be allowed; so that, if these estimates of reduction are correct (and they have not been controverted), the American farmer could have sold wheat in England in 1887 for 34s. per quarter, with as much of profit to himself as 54s. per quarter would have afforeded him in the years from 1870 to 1873 inclusive.

In June, 1881, and June, 1886, the prices of Cawnpore wheat at Calcutta were at the same level, namely, 2·9 rupees per maund. The cost of Indian wheat in London in 1881 was 42s. a quarter, and 31s. 6d. in 1886, or 10s. 6d. difference. In 1881 the rate of freight on wheat from India to London was 60s. per ton, and in 1886 30s., a difference of 30s. per ton, or 6s. 6d. per quarter. The decline in freights, therefore, accounts for 6s. 6d. out of the 10s. 6d. per quarter difference between the prices of Indian wheat in London in 1881 and 1886 respectively, leaving 4s. per quarter to be contributed by other agencies. Between 1879 and 1886 the charge for the railway transport of grain between Cawnpore and Calcutta (684 miles) was reduced to the extent of about 2s. per quarter, which represented to the purchaser in Calcutta an equivalent reduction in the cost of Indian production, and in the absence of which the Calcutta and European prices would obviously have been correspondingly increased. A further reduction of 6d. per quarter " is probably owing to a decline, during the same period, in the price of the gunny-bags " in which the wheat is transported; leaving 3s. 6d. per quarter, which may not unreasonably be referred to and fully accounted for by the extraordinary decline of more than 12s. per quarter, between the years 1880 and 1885, in the export price of American wheat; which, as hitherto, the largest factor in determining the world's surplus of this commodity, has also been necessarily the largest factor in determining what shall be the price of this surplus in the world's market.*

Here, then, is an agency which sufficiently accounts for a great part of the recent decline in the price of wheat, and which would have operated all the same, even if the relative values of the precious metals existing in 1870–'73 had remained unaltered.

The next point worthy to be taken into consideration in this inquiry is, that the increase in the supply of wheat in recent years, in many parts of the world, has been very great. The report of the British Gold and Silver Commission (1888) characterizes it "as enormous," and asserts that it " has been due, in a great measure, to the fact that vast territories consisting, in some instances, of virgin soil, have been opened up by the construction of railways, and have become the means of creating supplies largely in excess of the needs of those engaged in their production." †
Thus, in the United States, for example, the increase was from 250,000,000 bushels in 1872, to 512,000,000 in 1884,

---

* See " First Report of the British Commission "—evidence of Henry Waterfield, C. B., Financial Secretary of the India Office, and representing the Government of India, pp. 125, 126.

† " Final Report of the British Gold and Silver Commission," p. 66.

declining in the succeeding year (1885) to 357,000,000, and recovering to 477,000,000 in 1886.

" It is a significant fact, in connection with the rapid increase of population in the United States, and with the decline in proportion of rural population, that its wheat-supply of forty years ago should not only have been sustained but increased. In 1849 the product was 4·33 bushels for each inhabitant: in 1859, 5·5; in 1869, 7·46; in 1879, 9.16; and in 1884, 9·16 per capita. From 1849 to 1884, a period of thirty-five years, the increase of population was 141 per cent, while the increase in the production of wheat was 410 per cent."—*Report of the United States Department of Agriculture, 1887.*

The published results of the investigations of Mr. Edward Atkinson, based on the reports of the United States Agricultural Department, also show that the cereal crops of the United States, measured in bushels, increased from 1873 to 1885 at the rate of nearly one hundred per cent, while the increase of the population of the country during the same period was not in excess of thirty-seven per cent.

In 1881 the Territory of Dakota (U. S.), comprising over 150,000 square miles, had not produced a single bushel of wheat for sale. In 1886 its crop was estimated by the U. S. Department of Agriculture at 30,704,000 bushels, or nearly as great as the average annual export of wheat from India since 1880, and which export, according to a recognized English authority (Mr. William E. Bear), has been primarily responsible for the decline in recent years in the world's average price of wheat. In 1887 the crop was 62,553,000 bushels, or one seventh of the total wheat product of the United States in 1886. In 1888 the wheat-crop of this same Territory, owing to a remarkably unpropitious season, declined to 37,948,000 bushels, and was considered a failure ; but if it was a failure, it was, nevertheless, 37,000,000 bushels in comparison with a product of not even one marketable bushel seven years before, and could not afford the slightest reason for inferring that the future wheat product of

Dakota is not to go on increasing from year to year in a continually augmenting ratio.

During the same period, Australia and New Zealand, in which a rapid growth of population inevitably tends to divert agricultural industry from wool-producing to wheat-growing, largely increased their production of wheat.

Previous to 1873 there was practically no trade or movement in wheat between Europe and India. The high cost of transportation and the existence of an Indian export-duty of above six per cent made it impossible that there should be any. But with a reduction of freights by sea, following the opening of the Suez Canal, and by land, in consequence of the construction of railways in India, coupled with a removal of an export duty, the export of Indian wheat commenced and rose to 18,896,000 bushels in 1880, 19,466,000 in 1885, 36,880,000 in 1886, and 41,588,000 in 1887.

"There is nothing more remarkable in the history of railway enterprise than the development of the traffic that has occurred on Indian railways within the last ten years, to go no further back. In 1876 the total quantity of goods-traffic carried on all the railways of India was 5,750,000 tons. In 1885 the quantity was about 19,000,000 tons. In the year 1876 the mileage open was 6,833 miles, so that the volume of goods-traffic carried per mile was about 800 tons. In 1885 the mileage open was 12,376, so that the average volume of traffic carried per mile was over 1,500 tons. (In 1888 the mileage open was 14,383.) The aggregate volume of traffic in the interval had fully trebled, and the average traffic carried per mile open had almost doubled. Notwithstanding these remarkable results, the traffic which has been developed on the railways of India is less, in proportion to the population, than that of any other country in the world. This is especially the case in reference to goods-traffic, which only represents some ·05 of a ton per head of the population, as compared with three tons per head in Canada, and over seven tons per capita in the United Kingdom. But the goods-traffic of India is likely to develop very rapidly in the future, and especially in agricultural produce, of which only about 4,000,000 tons are now annually transported, as compared with 75,000,000 tons in the United States for less than a fourth of the population.—*Bradstreet's (N. Y.) Journal.*

In 1878 the Argentine States of South America were not reckoned as a factor to the smallest extent in the world's wheat-supply; but in 1885 they exported 4,000,000 bushels of this cereal, and in 1887 over 8,000,000. In the case of Russia her aggregate exports of wheat, comparing the four years from 1873 to 1876 with the four years from 1881 to 1884, increased over thirty-eight per cent; while for the years of 1887–'88 her exports amounted to 112,000,000 bushels. In Austria-Hungary the average annual wheat product for the seven years from 1873 to 1880, was 93,000,000 bushels; but for the seven years from 1880 to 1886, inclusive, it was 133,000,000 bushels.

Finally, it is to be noted that, in very few branches of production, have greater improvements been made and adopted in recent years than in the growing of wheat; the maximum result of which finds expression in the statement, which is well supported by evidence, that in California* wheat can now be grown at a cost of not over seventy cents per one hundred pounds, or forty-two cents per bushel.

Now while the evidence of the recent great increase in the world's production of wheat is not and can not be questioned, it is nevertheless claimed that such increase has not been in excess of the increased demand for this cereal for consumption, in consequence mainly of the increase in the world's wheat-consuming population; and that here, also, some other cause than oversupply must be sought for to explain the phenomenal decline in the price of this commodity. Such a claim has found, however, but very few advocates, and its discussion involves the employment and comparison of statistical data that are in themselves matters

---

* On many of the large ranches of California steam-plows are used, and on others gang-plows which turn four to six furrows and are drawn by from eight to fourteen mules. Not unfrequently the plows are run in a straight line for a distance of six or eight miles. A patent machine for sowing seed is employed, by means of which, it is claimed, one man and a team can sow one hundred acres of grain in a day.

of controversy. On the other hand, the opinion of nearly all investigators in all countries, who are regarded as authorities on this subject, is in the highest degree in favor of the theory of increased supply. Reference has already been made to the opinions of the British Gold and Silver Commission (1888) which was created in great part for the purpose of investigating into the cause of the decline of prices. The opinion of the United States Department of Agriculture, as given in the report for 1887, was as follows :

" Wheat-growing was stimulated greatly between 1875 and 1880 by a series of crop failures in Western Europe, causing a demand which never existed before, and may never again. Meantime, the world's production has kept up, with little change or diminution, depressing prices, and furnishing cheap bread to consumers, and little profit to producers ; and yet the inquiry is made, Why are prices so low ? In view of these facts, the question needs no answer. It is utterly useless to pretend reduction of area, as some do, where there is none. The influence of over-production on prices in the United States is seen in a comparison of the farm prices of wheat per bushel for the two periods from 1870 to 1880, and from 1880 to 1887, viz., $1.049 and $0.833 respectively ; showing a reduction of 20·6 per cent.

In a communication to the "Journal of the Royal Agricultural Society" of England, of May 1, 1888, Mr William E. Bear, a recognized authority on agricultural matters, says :

" The exports of wheat from India were not considerable until 1881–'82, and whether it is merely a coincidence, or more than that, it is a fact that the average price of wheat in England has been permanently below 45s. a quarter only since 1882." And again, speaking of the relative quantities of wheat imported into the United Kingdom from 1881 to 1887, he says : " These figures show that the receipts of wheat from India, which in only one previous year had been as much as five per cent of the total foreign supplies, rose to 10·3 per cent in 1881, to fifteen per cent in 1885, and to 16·7 per cent in 1886. Surely such proportions were large enough to account for a great fall of prices, considering that they represent receipts from a new source of supply. And as we had not felt the want of these new supplies, there was no natural demand for them except at the expense of other importing countries ; and as the other countries had prepared to meet our wants to the full, the large surplus from India produced the effect always to be expected from a glut in the markets."

"But the effect of Indian wheat upon prices is more clearly to be estimated by the supply to Europe, which during the six years ending with 1886–'87 averaged over 4,000,000 quarters per annum—a very large quantity to come on top of supplies already ample, and just after wheat production in the United States had reached its maximum. Of course, the entire fall in the price of wheat is not attributed to the Indian supply, as the decline in the prices of commodities has been general. But it is contended that the Indian supply is the principal cause of the excessive drop in the value of wheat." *

Again, during all the years in which wheat has been declining or ruling at low prices, there has never been any apprehension for any length of time, on the part of grain merchants and dealers, of any scarcity of its supply in the

---

* The following represents the opinions of other recognized authorities :

The German economist, Kleser, writing on this subject, says : " The inquiry whether the cheapness of grain is the result of the specific appreciation of gold, seems to be superfluous in presence of the fact, for instance, that the export of wheat from India grew from an unrecorded minimum in 1870 to 11,-000,000 cwts. in 1883, a similar expansion of the trade in cereals having occurred in Russia and the United States." See " Recent Currency Discussions in Germany," " British Foreign Office Reports," No. 40, p. 13. The distinguished French economist, M. Leroy-Beaulieu, as the result of his investigations, has also indorsed, in the " Revue des Deux Mondes," the opinion that the cause of the decline in the prices of grain has been unmistakably due to an increase and cheapening of product, and believes that, even in Europe, the supply of food in recent years has increased faster than population.

" The decline in the price of English wheat in twelve years has been 26s. 1d. per quarter, and in the last five years 8s. 8d. per quarter, of eight bushels. The principal causes of this large depreciation in prices are the heavy increase in production of wheat in British India, Australasia, and in the United States." —Bradstreet's Journal, N. Y., January, 1888.

" Prices of breadstuffs have not been fully maintained during the past week, for reasons previously explained. Somewhat more favorable reports regarding the growing crops are mentioned as a reason, but the bottom fact in the business is that the supply of wheat continues to exceed by many million bushels the quantity likely to be required."—New York Commercial Bulletin, May 21, 1888.

principal markets of the world.   During all these years,
the complaint, moreover, of the absence of all profit in producing wheat has been almost universal.   Under such circumstances of pressing necessity, it is almost needless to
say that producers, aided by speculators, would have speedily advanced the prices of this cereal if it had been in their
power; and it is equally clear that the only reason why
they have failed to do so is because the trade everywhere
has recognized that the supply of wheat was sufficient to
meet all demands at the current low prices; and that
under such a condition of affairs no material advance in
price was possible.   In short, during all the years in which
the decline in wheat has been phenomenal, the law of
supply and demand has not been violated, and price in the
world's market has conformed strictly to the supply of the
world.

The experience of the years 1888 and 1889 would also
seem to constitute evidence, almost in the nature of a demonstration, of the entire accuracy of the opinion which
ascribes the recent low prices of wheat mainly to a supply
largely in excess of the world's requirements at prices current under old conditions of the production and distribution of this commodity.   Thus, it is agreed that " the
world's product of wheat for 1888 was far below the average; the crops of the United States, Australia, Canada, and
the Argentine Republic being regarded as failures; * and
in September, 1888, recognized English authorities predicted a deficiency in the world's supplies for the year, even
after allowing for reserved stocks, of 50,000,000 bushels.
But this, and all other like predictions, failed to material-

---

* " The continued depression in the wheat trade under circumstances
which might have been expected to bring an improvement in prices is dis-
heartening and calculated to cause growers to despair of remunerative returns
for years to come, as the chances are that it will be a long time before the
world's supply will again be as small as it is for the current cereal year."—
WILLIAM E. BEAR, *Bradstreet's Journal, April,* 1889.

ize; for the world's supply of wheat proved so entirely adequate for meeting all demands that its price movements for the cereal year 1888–'89 in the London market (the representative center of demand) were most inconsiderable; and the year closed with a conceded large unsold surplus.

The future supply and price of wheat are matters of speculation not pertinent to the present inquiry; but one point belonging to the domain of fact has certainly an important bearing on these problems, and that is, that the extraordinary construction of railroads, especially in the United States, the Argentine Republic, India, and Australia, is making available enormous tracts of land eminently fitted for wheat-culture, which hitherto, by reason of inaccessibility, have practically been non-existent; while improvements in methods of cultivation have greatly facilitated and cheapened production. " Each mile of railroad constructed in a new country is a kind of centrifugal pump furnishing for exportation hundreds of tons of the products of such country." * The report of the United States Agricultural Department for 1889 shows an increase in the extent of cultivated land in the United States, and consequent expansion of agricultural possibilities, that is certainly akin to the marvelous. Between 1879 and 1888—a period of nine years —the area occupied by the four principal arable crops of the country—cotton, corn, wheat, and oats—experienced an enlargement of 31,000,000 acres; or from 128,000,000 to 159,000,000 acres. Furthermore, great as is the present wheat product of the United States, Mr. Atkinson has shown that all the land at present in actual use in that whole country for growing maize or Indian corn, wheat, hay, oats, and other food-crops, is less than 300,000 square miles, out of 1,500,000 miles of arable land embraced in its present national domain; and, also, that the present entire

---

* M. F. Bernard, " Journal des Économistes."

wheat-crop of the United States could be grown on wheat-land of the best quality selected from that part of the area of the State of Texas by which that single State exceeds the present area of the German Empire.*

In short, it would seem as if the world in general, for the first time in its history, has now good and sufficient reasons for feeling free from all apprehensions of a scarcity or dearness of bread. But, while from a strictly humani-tarian point of view this is certainly a matter for congratu-lation, the results, viewed from the standpoint of the interests involved, which embraces a large part of the world's popu-lation, appear widely different. The effect of the extensive fall in prices of agricultural products during the last decade has been most disastrous to the agricultural interests and population of Europe. It has reduced farming in England and in most of the states of the Continent to the lowest stage of vitality; and, by reason of the complaints of their agriculturists, the customs duties of many countries have been largely increased, and the conditions of consumers greatly modified. In France the position has been taken, by not a few familiar with the situation, that the only pos-sible means of salvation for the agriculture of central Eu-rope will be for France, Germany, Austria, and Italy to sink all political antipathies and jealousies and form an inter-national customs union to exclude all food-products from Russia, Australia, and America.

The present agricultural condition of Italy is thus de-picted in a report recently made (1888) to the Agricultural Department of the British Privy Council, by Mr. W. N.

---

* Although the prices of grain have seriously fallen in Russia—about twenty per cent in 1888 below those of 1881—yet, according to a recent report to the British Foreign Office from the British consul at Tanganrog, " The present prices of wheat (1888) not only cover the cost of production, but on most estates in wheat-regions yield a moderate profit, owing, no doubt, to the fact that the cost of production is lower in Russia than in any other wheat-growing country, except India."

Beauclerk, a secretary in the British diplomatic service. He says :

"Agriculture in Italy is in the throes of a severe crisis. American competition is strongly felt in the corn-trade, and there are those who even go so far as to predict that the agricultural population must retrograde to the pastoral state, unless things change for the better—a spectacle which might astonish the universe. And with regard to the great question of progress in agricultural production so as to make a stand against the importation from America, and to secure the future existence of the rural population, the verdict of the landholders of Italy is thus given : as long as millions of acres remain unreclaimed and untilled, as long as the majority and the strongest of men are under arms, as long as huge armies entail excessive expenditure, and agriculture is suffocated with a weight of taxation which absorbs from one third to one half of the returns, and so long as education, credit, and manures are wanting, we can not strive with a reasonable prospect of success."

In 1880 forty-four per cent of the entire population of the United States was engaged in agriculture, and less than seven per cent in manufactures ; and since the year 1820, or for a period of sixty-six years, the proportion between the agricultural and non-agricultural exports of this country has been remarkably steady, the average for the former for the whole of this period having been about seventy-eight per cent. Up to the present time there has been little tendency to change in these proportions ; but, if the continued fall of prices of agricultural products in the United States and other countries should compel their farming populations to seek other employments, what other employments are open to them ? That the world will ultimately adjust itself to all new conditions may not be doubted ; but what of the period pending adjustment ?

As bearing upon this subject, certain statements recently (1889) published by the United States Agricultural Department are of the highest interest and importance. From these it appears that Europe is practically the only market that America can have for her surplus wheat. But the wheat-crop of Europe, which has not materially declined within the last ten years, and which "represents more than half of all that is grown in the world," is so nearly sufficient to meet the wants of its people, that "if the surplus of eastern Europe should be distributed only in the Continental states, it would nearly supply all their deficiencies, leaving practically only Great Britain to receive the imports of other continents, and consume alone the surplus of the wheat markets of the world."

The present average wheat-crop of Europe is estimated at 1,200,000,000 bushels, and her average annual deficiency of supply, to be made good by foreign imports, at 144,000,-000 bushels. Of this deficiency the United States, in ordinary years, can supply about 100,000,000 bushels; but in 1880 the United States, Russia, India, Australia, and the Argentine Republic exported a surplus of 208,987,000 bushels, of which the United States contributed sixty-nine per cent. It is obvious, therefore, that with this limitation of market, any enlargement of the surplus wheat-product of the United States must inevitably reduce its price at home and abroad.

For the other cereal products of the United States the European demand is comparatively inconsiderable. The imports of European countries requiring maize, for example, do not make a sum half as large as the products of single States. The deficiency of France could be supplied by single counties, and Germany requires still less.

COTTON declined in price, taking the annual reported * averages of upland middlings in Liverpool, from $9d.$ per lb. in 1873 to $6\frac{15}{16}d.$ in 1880; $5\frac{3}{4}d.$ in 1883, and $5\frac{1}{4}d.$ in 1886; the last being the lowest price on record since 1848, when the average was $4\frac{1}{2}d.$

The world's supply of cotton since 1873 has been as follows: 1872–'73, 6,366,000 bales; 1882–'83, 10,408,000 bales :

---

* See Annual Tables of Liverpool Cotton Association.

an increase in ten years of 63·5 per cent. After 1882 there was a notable decline in the estimated crop of the world, but for 1885–'86 the aggregate crop is believed to have been 9,580,000 bales; or an increase in supply in thirteen years of about fifty per cent. For 1886–'87 the estimate was 9,757,000 bales, and for 1887–'88 10,161,000.* Such an increase in supply, it seems hardly necessary to say, was very far in excess of any increase in the total population of the world during the period of years under consideration, and also in excess of any increase in the population of those countries of the world that are the principal consumers of cotton fabrics. But here, again, as in the case of wheat, it is contended that the consumption of cotton has increased in at least an equal degree, and tables have been published showing that the consumption in a series of recent years has even exceeded production. Hence the decline in the price of cotton, it is argued, must have been due to causes other than those contingent on supply and demand.

That consumption of cotton fabrics has greatly increased can not be questioned. It has followed naturally from the very great increase in the productive power of labor, using improved machinery, and a consequent great decline in the prices of such fabrications; the equivalent of the labor of an operative in the factories of New England having increased, for example, from 12,164 yards in 1850 to 19,293 in 1870, and 28,032 in 1884, while the reduction in the price of standard sheetings from 1850 to 1885 was about ten per cent, and of standard prints and printing-cloths, during the same period, approximately forty per cent.

A curious discrepancy in the rates of decline in the price of raw materials and of the products manufactured from them (to which attention has been called in the case of petroleum) occurs in the price experiences of cotton and cot-

---

* New York " Financial Chronicle," September 10, 1887.

ton fabrications. Thus, comparing 1855 and 1886, the average price of the cotton imported into Great Britain was only five per cent lower in the latter year than in the former; but the decline in the average price of the British exports of cotton cloth during the same period was twenty-one per cent.* The agencies that have operated to occasion ·decline in the two instances would, therefore, seem to have been altogether different.

A comparison of the most reliable statistics of the world's cotton production and consumption for recent years furnishes, however, some information on this subject of a definite character. Thus, comparing 1872–'73 with 1882–'83, production increased from 6,366,000 bales to 10,408,-000, or in the ratio of 63·5 per cent; the world's consumption during the same period increasing from 6,425,000 bales to 9,499,000, or in the ratio of 47·8 per cent. Comparing the years 1872–'73 with 1885–'86, the increase in production was from 6,366,000 bales to 9,580,000, or in the ratio of about fifty per cent; and of consumption from 6,425,000 bales to 9,371,000, or in the ratio of 45·8 per cent.†

At the same time every year closes with a visible unconsumed surplus stock of cotton, which varies from about one sixth of the estimated year's consumption (as in 1883–'84) to about one tenth (as in 1887–'88). But, as the average stocks carried over from year to year are not as large as formerly, it is claimed that herein is to be found proof that reduction in the price of cotton could not have occurred through an excess of supply. A consideration, however, of the great changes which have taken place in recent years in the conditions of supply and demand in respect to cotton, in common with most other stable commodities, deprives the claim of much if not of all significance. Fifteen or twenty years ago the means of determining the present and

---

* Address of Mr. Bertwhistle, Secretary of Lancaster (England) Weavers' Association, 1886.
† " Financial Chronicle," New York, September 15, 1888.

prospective supply of the world's great products were very imperfect, and considerable time was required before reliable information could be collected and disseminated; and, in the case of cotton especially it was a matter of doubt whether the United States would speedily or ever regain and hold its former relative importance as a producer of this commodity. Under such circumstances it was undoubtedly most important, for the stability of production and trade, that great reserves of raw materials should be constantly kept in store, or in sight. But with the marvelous changes in the facilities for collecting and disseminating information which have come in recent years, with the opening of many new sources of supply, with the ability to know from day to day the amount of stock on hand of any article in any quarter of the globe, and its prospective conditions of supply, the same importance no longer attaches to reserve stocks; and, in fact, they are no longer kept at great central points of distribution to anything like the same extent as formerly. In the case of cotton the manufacturers of the world have seen the crop of the United States increasing at the rate of seventy-six per cent between the years 1866 and 1872, forty-nine per cent between 1872–'73 and 1885–'86, and they have also learned that not three per cent of the land of the United States available for the production of cotton has as yet been put under cultivation. Improvements in machinery, by which finer yarns and fabrics can be furnished at no greater, or even at smaller cost, than coarser and less desirable yarns and fabrics were formerly supplied; or, in other words, the new ability to supply to a considerable extent the popular demand for cotton fabrications with a smaller relative consumption of cotton, would also seem to be equivalent to increasing the supply of cotton, or of reducing the necessity of the continued maintenance of the reserve stock at figures that formerly might have been regarded as indispensable.

But, as bearing on prices, the decline in the average of

reserve stocks of cotton carried over from year to year, be the amount of such decline greater or less, has no manner of significance, unless such decline has been regarded by consumers as indicative of prospective scarcity or insufficient supply to meet the demands of immediate or future consumption.   There is not, however, a particle of evidence that any such apprehension has, in recent years, existed.   In point of fact, the evidence all runs to the effect that the apprehension, in recent years, in the minds of the world's great consumers of cotton and all the other staple commodities—sugar, iron, coal, petroleum, copper, lead, etc.—has been of disturbance in their respective industries, from an over-production and increase, rather than from any decrease in the supplies of their crude materials ; and such a frame of mind favors, if it does not directly occasion, low prices.*

---

* The following expression of opinion relative to the supply of cotton, by the " Manchester Examiner," England (no mean authority), may also be read with interest in connection with this discussion.   Writing under date of January 18, 1888, it says: " The invisible supply of actual cotton in spinners' hands all over the world is now the largest on record for this time of the year —English spinners alone holding the unprecedented quantity of 350,000 bales, which has been brought about, to a very large extent, by the fear that the small crop estimates put forth in November would prove correct.   Besides the invisible supply of actual cotton, spinners hold enormous lines of weekly deliveries and futures, which means that they can at any time keep out of our market for three months, and buy only retail lots.   The question is, will they do so when they see plainly for themselves that this crop is about seven millions, and which means abundance ; and not 6,300,000, which meant scarcity ? . . . The fact of the spinner apparently using less American also tends to show that the spinning qualities of the present American crops, which range now far higher in grade and quality than in years past, must be much better than the previous crops—an important fact when crops are grown from six and a half to seven millions.   This has been entirely lost sight of when estimating the prospects of supply and demand for the last three months of the season, and thereby prophesying scarcity, which so far has never yet come off, and which was exemplified again last July, August, and September, by prices falling 1*d.* per pound in the face of prognosticated scarcity, besides leaving a surplus of 250,000 bales at the end of the season, with the price at 5¼*d.*"

Commenting on the decline in the American export price of cotton from an average of 9·9 cents in 1886 to 9·5 cents in 1887, the New York " Commercial Bulletin," October, 1888, says : " This comparison leads to the reflection that

It is interesting to recall in this connection that it was the general opinion in 1859 that the American cotton-crop of the previous year, 1858 (3,994,000 bales), represented a maximum capacity of production, and that a crop of over 4,000,000 bales could not be picked, even if grown. Since then the crop of the United States has been in excess of 7,000,000 bales.

The condition of the cotton-manufacturing industry of Great Britain (which may be considered as typical of the condition of the same industry in all other countries) during the early months of the year 1889, is also not a little instructive. The production of cloths was greater than at any former equal period in history, and concurrently the world's consumption of cotton, judging from the increase in British exports, has been unprecedentedly large. The situation of British manufacturers, under such circumstances, to quote from the London " Economist " (May, 1889), is, however, " anything but encouraging " :

They " have been experiencing a narrow and unprofitable margin for months, and, at the present time, things are becoming seriously worse. Speaking broadly, the enormous production turned off can only be got rid of at a comparatively low price, and, notwithstanding the heavy export, it appears to be too large to allow prices to rise."

The legitimate inference from all this would, therefore, seem to be that the world, in 1889, had got more cotton cloth (and consequently more raw material) than it could consume, at prices so extremely low for the former, as to leave little or no margin of profit to manufacturers working with advantages, as respects cost and product, that a comparatively few years ago were hardly regarded as possibilities.

WOOL.—According to the statistics of M. Sauerbeck

---

perhaps a partial loss of the cotton-crop this year may not prove an unmixed calamity, since the enormous increase of yield for which the enlarged acreage had prepared would probably have depressed prices most disastrously for the producer."

("Journal of the Statistical Society," March, 1887), the price of merino wool (Port Philip, Australia, average fleece), comparing the average of the series of years 1867–'77 and 1878–'85, declined 10·7 per cent; or, comparing the average price of 1867–'77 with that of the single year 1886, when wool "was cheaper than at any time within the memory of the present generation," 27 per cent. Certain fibers classed with wool, and known as "alpaca" and "mohair," and the grade of long-combing English wools known as "Lincoln," experienced a much greater decline after 1874–'75, owing to the curious circumstance that a change in fashion in those years almost entirely and suddenly destroyed any demand for the before popular, stiff, lustrous fabrics manufactured from such wools for female wear, and substituted in their place the soft and pliable cloths that are made from the merino wools.

A striking illustration of the decline in the price of wool since 1872 is found in the experience of the British colonial wools, mainly the product of Australia. Thus, the total product of such wools during the year 1872 was 743,-000 bales, and the price realized was £19,690,000 ($95,821,-385). In 1887 the total product was 1,444,000 bales, nearly double the quantity of that of 1872, but the value showed a slight increase, being only £526,000 ($2,559,779) more than that of 1872, on an aggregate of $98,300,000. It will thus be seen that the increase in production did little to increase the amount of money received by the growers. For making allowance for the circumstance that the proportion of colonial wool shipped in the grease is now much larger than it formerly was, it is considered that the increase in quantity from 1872 to 1887 was equal to about eighty per cent; or, in other words, the colonies were obliged to grow eighty per cent more wool in 1887 than they did in 1872 in order to realize the same amount of money.*

---

* Report to the United States Department of State, 1888, by G. W. Giffin, United States consul at Sydney, Australia.

The increase in the production and world's supply of raw wools, from the years 1860 to 1885 inclusive, was in excess of 100 per cent. According to Mr. Sauerbeck's tables, the increase from 1873 to 1885 inclusive, was 20 per cent; according to Messrs. Helmuth, Schwartze & Co., of London, the increase from 1871–'75 to 1881–'85 was 23 per cent, and from 1871–'75 to 1886, 35 per cent.* The wool-clip of the United States increased from 264,000,000 pounds in 1880 to 329,000,000 in 1885, or 24·6 per cent in six years. Taking "Lincoln hogs" as the standard of English wools, their value (January, 1889) was estimated at 10½d. per pound. This price appears startlingly low compared with that which ruled in 1864, namely, 2s. 6d. per pound; but in that year the import of wool of all kinds into England was only 211,000,000, while for the year 1888 it was not far short of 650,000,000 pounds.

As the increase in the production of wool in recent years has but slightly exceeded the ordinary growth of population, and as the stock of wool on hand in Europe at the end of the year 1885 was only 180,000 bales, as compared with 207,000 in 1880, it has here also been contended that some influences other than those contingent on supply and demand must have been influential in occasioning the decline of prices noted. But every year, nevertheless, has closed with a surplus in excess of any current demand; and it is also to be remembered that when the supply of any commodity exceeds by even a very small percentage what is

---

* The details of this increase are thus stated by Messrs. Helmuth, Schwartze & Co., of London, in their annual review of the production and consumption of wool for 1887 : "Making allowance," they say, "for the increase of population, we find that the principal development in the supply of wool took place from 1860 to 1868, in which period the consumption rose from 2·03 pounds of clean wool per head to 2·47 pounds, or about 22 per cent. From 1868 to 1879 the consumption remained practically unchanged, amounting on the average to 2·41 pounds clean wool per head. It rose to 2·49 pounds for the average of the next four years, and was 2·58 in 1884 and 2·66 pounds in 1886."

required to meet every demand for current consumption
—especially in the case of a staple commodity like wool,
whose every variation in supply and demand is studied every
day, as it were microscopically, by thousands of interested
dealers and consumers—it is the price which this surplus
will command that governs and fixes the price for the
whole; and as this can not be sold readily—as under such
circumstances no one buys in excess of present demand, and
all desire to dispose of accumulated stocks—the result is a
decline of prices, in accordance with no law, and which will
be more or less excessive, or permanent, as opinions vary as
to the extent of the surplus and the permanence of the
causes that have occasioned it.*

Another factor, not to be overlooked, which in recent
years has undoubtedly been most influential in depressing
the prices of wool, has been the increasing use of " shoddy,"
or the product of old woolen rags torn up and reduced to
fibers, or even dust; and also of immense quantities of cow
and other hair for mixing with wool in the manufacture of
fabrics.   Thus, the import of woolen rags into the United
Kingdom, which was only 5,250,000 lbs. in 1855, was returned at 80,750,000 lbs. in 1883.   In the United States,
according to the census of 1880, the amount of scoured
wool that entered into the production of domestic wool-
ens during the previous year was returned at 109,725,-
000 lbs.; of shoddy, 46,583,000 lbs.; and of the hair of
the buffalo and other animals, 4,495,000 lbs.; or, for every
2·1 lbs. of wool used, one pound of something that was

---

* Gregory King, in discussing the law of prices more than two centuries
ago, showed that an increase or diminution in the supply of a necessary of
social life depresses or raises the price to the consumer in a degree which is
far in excess of the quantity in excess or defect. Thus, a deficient supply of
wheat, taken to be a prime necessary of life, to the extent of five per cent in
the customary demand, will raise the price ten per cent; one of ten per cent
may raise it thirty, one of twenty will double it, and so on. Excess of supply
will lower it, but not in the same ratio, because stocks accumulate in hopes of
a turn in the market.

not wool entered into the woolen manufactures of this country.

SILK.—The decline in the price of silk (Tsatlee), according to M. Sauerbeck, from the average price of 1867–'77 to the average of 1886, was about forty per cent; and the average increase in supply of all varieties of silk-fiber, comparing 1873 with 1885, was reported by the same authority as about twelve per cent. According to the most reliable French statistics, the supply of raw silk—domestic and foreign—available for the markets of Europe, increased from 21,837,000 lbs. in 1884 to 25,762,000 in 1887, or in the ratio of above seventeen per cent. No relation between the price movements of this commodity and supply and demand, or any other agencies, can, however, be established, which fails to take into account the great increase in the use of the ramie and other fibers and materials within recent years as substitutes for or adulterations of silk in the manufacture of fabrics. Thus, recent investigations, made under the auspices of the United States revenue authorities, indicate, that in the case of the cheaper silks of extensive consumption, materials other than silk often enter into their composition to the extent of even sixty per cent; and that other methods of adulterating silk, formerly but little known, are now extensively practiced—all of which is equivalent to increasing the supply of silk for manufacturing, far beyond what commercial reports respecting the supply of the fiber would indicate.

JUTE.—Good medium jute declined on the London market from £17 per ton in 1874 to an average of £11 10s. in 1886, or more than fifty per cent. The increase in exports from British India was from 5,206,570 cwt. in 1876 to 10,-348,909 cwt. in 1883, or ninety-eight per cent.

Many other commodities, of greater or less importance, might be included in this investigation, with a deduction of like results; but a further exhibit is not necessary, for it is difficult to see how any one can rise from an examination of the record of the production and price experiences of the commodities which have been specified, which, it must be remembered, represent—considered either from the standpoint of qualities or values—the great bulk of the trade, commerce, and consumption of the world, without being abundantly and conclusively satisfied that the decline in their prices, which has occurred during the last ten or fifteen years, or from 1873, has been so largely due to conditions affecting their supply and demand, that if any other causes have contributed to such a result, the influence exerted has not been extensive; and, further, that if the prices of all other commodities, not included in the above record, had confessedly been influenced by a scarcity of gold, the claims preferred by the advocates of the latter theory could not be fairly entitled to any more favorable verdict than that of "not proven." The philosophy of the experiences which have been collected and recorded is, that the cost of producing the great staple commodities of the world's trade and commerce have, in comparatively recent years, through inventions and discoveries, been materially reduced; that this result is a permanent one, and that every attempt to restore the old-time prices—as has been especially shown in the recent price movements of copper, tin, and wheat—results in disaster.

NOTE.—In the year 1886 the British Government created a "commission" of persons of eminent qualifications, to "inquire into the recent changes in the relative values of the precious metals," embracing causes and results. This commission, after devoting nearly two years to their task, calling to their assistance a large number of persons as witnesses, or experts, whom they regarded as qualified to express opinions, submitted a "final" report in October, 1888, embodying the facts to which their attention had been called; a summary of the arguments, on the one side and the other, touching questions in controversy; and a marked diversity of conclusions on the part of the several members of the commission. There was, however, an entire unanimity of opinion on some points, which the commission express as follows:

"We are of opinion that the true explanation of the phenomena which we are directed to investigate is to be found in a combination of causes, and can not be attributed to any one cause alone. The action of the Latin Union in 1873 broke the link between silver and gold, which had kept the price of the former, as measured by the latter, constant at about the legal ratio; and, when this link was broken, the silver market was open to the influence of all the factors which go to affect the price of a commodity. These factors happen since 1873 to have operated in the direction of a fall in the gold price of that metal."

Six members of the commission, embracing one half of the whole number reporting, thus further summarized their conclusions, in respect to the remarkable fall in recent years in the prices of commodities:

" We think that the fall in the price of commodities may be in part due to an appreciation of gold, but to what extent this has affected prices we think it impossible to determine with any approach to accuracy.

" We think, too, that the fall in the gold price of silver has had a tendency operating in the same direction upon prices; but whether this has been effective to any, and if so, to what extent, we think equally incapable of determination.

" We believe the fall to be mainly due, at all events, to circumstances independent of changes in the production of, or demand for, the precious metals, or the altered relation of silver to gold.

" As regards the fall in the gold price of silver, we think that, though it may be due in part to the appreciation of gold, it is mainly due to the depreciation of silver."

In regard to this same problem, the other six members of the commission, holding dissentient views, express themselves as follows:

" We are not insensible to the fact that facilities for production are habitually increasing, and the cost of production is constantly becoming less. But these factors have always been in operation since the world began; and, while we recognize their tendency to depress the prices of commodities, they are not, in our opinion, sufficient to account for the abnormal fall in prices, which has been apparent since the rupture of the bimetallic par, and only since that time."

V.

THE question which next naturally suggests itself is,
What have been the price movements of such commodities
as have not in recent years experienced in any marked degree
a change in their conditions of supply and demand? Do
they exhibit any evidence of having been subjected to any
influence attributable to the scarcity of gold?

The answer is, that not only can no results capable of any
such generalization be affirmed, but no one commodity can
even be named in respect to which there is conclusive evidence that its price has been affected in recent years by influences directly or mainly attributable to any scarcity of
gold for the purpose of effecting exchanges.

In the first place, all that large class of products or
services, which are exclusively or largely the result of handicrafts; which are not capable of rapid multiplication, or of
increased economy in production, and which can not be
made the subject of international competition—have exhibited no tendency to decline in price, but rather the
reverse. A given amount of gold does not now buy more,

but less, of domestic service and of manual and professional labor generally than formerly;* does not buy more of amusement; not more of hand-woven lace, of cigars, and of flax, which are mainly the products of hand-labor; of cut-glass, of gloves, of pictures, or of precious stones. It buys no more of horses, and other domestic animals; of pepper; of cocoa, the cheap production of which is limited to a few countries, and requires an interval of five years between the inception and maturing of a crop; of malt liquors, eggs, currants, and potatoes; nor also of house-rents, which depend largely upon the price of land, and which in turn is influenced by fashion, population, trade, facilities for access, and the like. Retail prices generally have not fallen in proportion to the decline in wholesale prices; and one explanation that has been given for such a result is, that retail trade is more directly and largely dependent on personal services.

"Any one who thinks about the subject of gold and prices must be struck with the curious fact that it is in the wholesale dealings in the principal articles of commerce that the fall of prices is shown to have taken place, and that, at the same time, in these dealings little or no gold is ever used; while, on the other hand, in the dealings (and in those countries) in which gold is used—such as small retail dealings and wages, no such fall in prices, or no equal fall, has been proved."— *Sir* THOMAS FARRER, *Member of British Gold and Silver Commission.*

---

* "There is no feature in the situation, which the commissioners have been called to examine, so satisfactory as the immense improvement which has taken place in the condition of the working-classes during the last twenty years."—*Report of the Royal (British) Commission on the Depression of Trade,* 1888.

"There does not appear to be any evidence that the salaries of clerks and others, outside of what may be termed the wage-earning classes proper, have decreased; and, although some house-rents have fallen, it seems questionable whether, as except the more expensive houses, which are inhabited by the wealthy, there has been any general diminution of house-rent."—*Report of the British Gold and Silver Commission, Part II,* 1888.

"Instead of an alleged lowering of the price of labor, we have to report, taking a wide extent, rather a rise in wages."—*Report of Factory Inspectors, Germany,* 1886, p. 74.

How little of change in price has come to the commodities of countries of low or stagnant civilization, that have remained outside of the current of recent progress, is strikingly illustrated in the case of a not unimportant article of commerce, namely, the root *sarsaparilla ;* which, with a gradually increasing demand, continues to be produced (collected and prepared) in Central America, by the most primitive methods, and without any change in the conditions of supply, save, possibly, some greater facilities for transportation from the localities of production to the ports of exportation.   Thus, in the case of Honduras sarsaparilla, at New York, which is the principal distributing market of the world, the average price for the best grade was reported as identical for the years 1881 and 1886; while for the " Mexican," the average reported for 1881 was eight cents per pound, and for 1886, with much larger sales, from seven to eight and a quarter cents.

The very slight decline in recent years in the prices of such of the commodities of India as constitute her staple exports is also an illustration to the same effect.*

Now, all of the commodities referred to, including labor

* According to Mr. Robert Giffen, in his testimony before the British Gold and Silver Commission, 1886, the general result of a comparison of India prices shows a fall of only two per cent in 1880-'84, as compared with 1870-'74, or with the period immediately before the fall in silver:

" The general conclusion appears to me to be that the effect of the present relations between gold and silver have not told appreciably on prices in India, or on the relative progress of her import and export trade."—*Testimony of Sir* Louis Mallet, *late Under-Secretary of State for India, Member British Gold and Silver Commission,* 1886.

" In India, in the opinion of nearly all the witnesses whom we have examined, the purchasing power of the rupee continues unimpaired, and the prices of commodities measured in silver remain practically the same.   We have no evidence to show that silver has undergone any material change in relation to commodities, although it has fallen largely in relation to gold; in other words, the same number of rupees will no longer exchange for the same amount of gold as formerly, but, so far as we can judge, they will purchase as much of any commodity or commodities in India as they did before."— *Final Report British Gold and Silver Commission,* p. 95.

and personal service, and many others which might be specified, whose condition in recent years has not been materially influenced by changes affecting their supply and demand, ought to have exhibited evidence, in a decline of prices, of the influence of the scarcity of gold, if any such had been exerted ; but they have not, and the *onus* of showing why they have not clearly rests upon those who deduce from the evidence of price movements the conclusion that the standard of price measurements (gold) has appreciated.

The record of extreme changes in prices, by reason of circumstances that are acknowledged to have been purely exceptional, is also most instructive, and removes not a few commodities from the domain of any controverted economic theory respecting monetary influences.   Thus, from 1862 to 1870, cotton, owing to war influences, ruled so high—from seventy to eight hundred per cent in excess of normal prices—that its inclusion in computations, with a view of determining any average of prices, or generalization of causes affecting prices during the years mentioned, would, vithout proper allowance, completely vitiate any conclusions.

War and interruption of traffic on the upper Nile have increased the prices of "gum-Arabic " and of the drug " senna "in recent years more than a hundred per cent.   The prices for French and other competing light wines and brandies are much higher than the average for 1866–'67, because the phylloxera has so impaired the production of French vineyards that France has of late years imported more wine than she exports.   " Cochineal " and " madder " have greatly declined in price since 1873, because their use as dye-stuffs has been to a great extent superseded by equivalent and cheaper coloring-materials derived from coal-tar; and within a very recent period the discovery of a method of cheaply preparing a chemical preparation from cloves, having all the flavoring qualities of the vanilla-bean, has already diminished the demand, and bids fair to greatly impair the price of this heretofore scarce and costly tropical product. Certain animal products, notably entering into commerce, have greatly advanced in price in recent years by reason of a rapid diminution in the number of the animals affording them, as buffalo-horns, ivory, and whalebone. Ivory has trebled in price since 1845, and whalebone increased from $32\frac{1}{2}$ cents per pound in 1850 to 85 cents in 1870, and $3.50 in 1886.

In October, 1888, according to a circular issued by the "Baker's Guide" at Havana, Cuba, the price of bread in that city was lower than in any country, either in America or Europe, where wheat is produced. The reasons assigned for this were the substitution of free for slave labor, and the depreciation of paper currency in comparison with gold : "flour on the date mentioned selling at $13 per barrel in gold, and paper money at a reduction of two hundred and forty per cent from gold prices."

The price of manufactured Mediterranean coral—the trade in which is extensive—has been greatly depressed in recent years by reason of the discovery of new banks of coral on the coast of Sicily, from which the raw material has been obtained most cheaply, and in large excess of demand. The consequent decline in prices has, however, opened new markets in Africa, where the natives now purchase coral ornaments in place of beads of Venetian and German manufacture.

HOPS.—Few commodities have fluctuated more violently in price in recent years, or more strikingly illustrate the degree to which supply and demand predominates over all other agencies in determining price, than the vegetable product *hops*. In 1881 there was an almost universal crop failure, and the highest grade of English hops (East Kent) commanded 700s. per cwt. In 1886 the German Hop-Growers' Association estimated the quantity grown throughout the world at 93,340 tons, and the annual consumption at only 83,200 tons, so that there was an excess of production over consumption for that year of nearly 10,000 tons. As might have been expected, there was a notable decline in the world's prices for hops, and the same quality of English hops which commanded 700s. per cwt. in 1882 sold for 74s. in 1887, and in June, 1888, for 68s. Later in the year, with unfavorable harvest reports, the price advanced to 147s.

DIAMONDS.—The recent price experience of diamonds is in the highest degree interesting. Diamonds were first discovered in South Africa about the year 1868, and a business of searching (mining) for them immediately sprang up. At the outset the mining was conducted by individuals, but, in consequence of the expense, the work gradually and necessarily passed into the control of joint-stock companies with command of large capital ; and it was not until 1880 that operations on a great scale were undertaken. The result of this improved system, conjoined with underground mining, was such an increase in the output of diamonds that an oversupply to the market and a serious reduction in price became imminent; and the period of 1883–'84 was in fact one of falling prices and intense competition among the various producing companies, during which the leading companies paid little or nothing to their shareholders, and some entirely suspended operations.* Continued disaster was, however, finally arrested through a practical consolidation of all the companies for the purpose of controlling product and prices ; and a revival in demand having occurred about the same time, average prices were advanced between 1885 and 1887 from 20s. 5d. per carat to 23s. 7½d.

The value of the diamonds exported from South Africa

---

* The " Kimberly Central Company "—the leading organization—which from 1880 to 1883 increased its dividend from ten to thirty per cent, paid nothing to its shareholders during 1884 and 1885, and at the close of 1886 was only able to declare a dividend of five per cent. The other great diamond-mining company, the " De Beers," was more fortunate, and paid for 1884 to 1886 an average of about eight and a half per cent ; but most of the companies paid nothing during the same period, and some entirely suspended mining.

since the first discovery of the mines, or from 1868 to 1887, is believed to have been between £40,000,000 and £45,000,000 ($200,000,000 to $225,000,000), of which about £15,500,000 ($77,500,000) represents the value of the output from 1883 to 1887. Very curiously, this large export of value—nearly all in the first instance to England—seems to find no distinctive place in the columns of British imports, although they have served in a large measure to enable South Africa to pay for her imports of British and other foreign products. If the export of diamonds from South Africa to Europe has aggregated £45,000,000 ($225,000,000) in the rough, the process of cutting may be regarded as having increased their market value full one hundred per cent, or to £90,000,000 (or $437,000,000); a greater value than the yield of the world during the two preceding centuries. The aggregate weight of the entire diamond product of the South African mines up to 1887 is estimated at 38,000,000 carats, or over seven and a half tons.*

We have, therefore, in this experience, the phenomenon of the strangely persistent value of a comparatively useless gem, during a period when the prices of most other commodities were diminishing by leaps and bounds, as well as the extraordinary concurrent absorbent power of the world for a greatly increased product. But the demand for diamonds latterly is thought not to have kept pace with their increasing production; and it is said that the stock of dia-

---

* Of this immense product there is good reason for believing that a very large proportion found a market in the United States. According to the customs returns, the value of the unset diamonds which were imported into the United States, and paid duty, from 1877 to 1887, inclusive, was in excess of $50,000,000; and it can hardly be doubted that an equal or larger import in the form of unset stones and jewelry escaped during the same period the cognizance of the revenue officials. The value of the present annual import of precious stones not set—mainly diamonds—is about $10,000,000. In 1868 the annual value of a corresponding import was about $1,000,000. These data, imperfect as they are, afford some indication of the rapid increase in wealth in recent years among the people of the United States.

monds in the hands of dealers in 1888 was fully twenty-five
per cent in excess of their requirements. To meet and neutralize the influence of this condition of affairs, the South
African diamonds-mining companies have limited production, which for the time has advanced prices. But the tendency obviously is for diamonds to decline in value ; and the
wonder, indeed, is that this has not happened at an earlier
date. " One thing, furthermore, seems certain, and that is,
that when the breakdown of speculation and prices does occur, the consequences will be singular and far-reaching. For
it is to be remembered that for the most part the use of diamonds is a mere whim of fashion, that may change at any
time. There is no way of stimulating the demand for them,
except by lowering prices, and, of course, if prices were materially reduced, the wealthy votaries of fashion would inevitably cease to wear diamonds, and would take up some
other form of personal adornment." * The price experiences
of diamonds in the near future promises, therefore, to be
even more interesting than it has been the recent past.

In the United States during recent years there has been
a remarkable decline in the price of hides and in certain
descriptions of leather ; " Buenos Ayres " hides having sold
in May, 1889, at the lowest figures for thirty years, while
the leather-trade generally has been depressed and unsatisfactory. The agency occasioning the first result is ascribed
to the great increase in the supply of domestic hides consequent upon a notable extension of the American (Western)
cattle industry ; and, in the case of the second, to an over-
production and decline in demand for upper leather, in consequence of a change in fashion, whereby lighter grades of
foot-wear have supplemented the use of " leg-boots."

The extreme fluctuation in recent years in the price of
certain drugs from well-recognized and unmistakable causes
is also worthy of notice. For example, " Turkey opium,"

---

* London " Economist," March, 1888.

a standard article of commerce, which in 1878 commanded 17s. per case in the London market, under the influence of subsequent unusually large crops declined in 1886 to 6s. 6d. for prime qualities. In 1876–'78 there was so little demand for the drug known as " balsam Tolu " that it seemed not unlikely that its production and market supply would entirely cease. In later years, however, it was discovered that it could be used for the manufacture of " chewing-gum "— an article in extensive use in the United States—and the demand thus occasioned has not only created a greater market than ever before, but the increased production has been attended with a reduction of from sixty to seventy per cent in price.

The British Gold and Silver Commission call attention, in their " Final Report, 1888 " (pages 67 and 68), to three other causes of an exceptional character that have doubtless been influential in determining prices in a greater or less degree since 1873, and which are in no way connected with any changes in the relative values of the precious metals. The *first* is that " the rise in the price of raw products during the period preceding 1875 exceeded the average rise of the prices of all commodities, while the fall in the prices of raw products since 1875 has been above the average fall. Comparing, therefore, the earlier with the later period, the lower cost of manufacture was in the earlier period counteracted by the higher cost of raw materials, while in the later period not only was this not the case, but the cost of the raw materials has decreased simultaneously with the diminished cost of manufacture." The *second* is that, comparing the years since 1873 with previous periods, " there has been a remarkable freedom from an absorption of the people of the Continent of Europe in occupations of war. Their energies have thus been turned instead to industrial and commercial pursuits, which has led to an increase in their power of production." A *third* cause " which has tended to lower certain prices in the open markets of the world, from which the 'index' numbers of prices are taken, has been the increase in protective tariffs. These tariffs, by enabling manufacturers to demand high prices at home, have, in so doing, enabled them to throw their productions at an unnaturally low price upon foreign markets. In the case of bounties— e. g., those on sugar—the operation of protection upon prices has been more direct; and even in protected countries, while the first effect of protection has been to raise prices, the ultimate effect has been in many cases to produce a glut, and make it difficult for the protected industries to get rid of their stocks."

The divergency in the price movements of different and special commodities has also been very notable—so much so that, out of the long list of articles embraced in the numerous tables that have been prepared by European economists for determining the general average of prices during recent periods, the price movements of no two commodities can be fairly regarded as harmonizing. While in the case of some staple products prices fell immediately and rapidly after 1873, the prices of others, although subjected to the same gold-scarcity influence, and which did not have this influence neutralized by a decline of production concurrent with continuing demand, exhibited for a long time comparatively little or absolutely no disturbance. This was especially the case in respect to wool, the price of which, long after metals, breadstuffs, chemicals, and cotton goods had succumbed to the wave of depression subsequent to 1873, "continued" (to use the language of the trade) "remarkably healthy," notwithstanding a continually increasing product was recognized; and it was not until 1884 that the decline in the general prices of this commodity gave any occasion for anxiety.

In certain tables prepared by Dr. Soetbeer, one hundred leading commodities are divided into seven classes. Comparing the average prices of these classes in 1886 with those of the period of 1871-'75—which last immediately preceded the commencement of the alleged scarcity of gold—the following results were obtained : There was a fall in Class I (agricultural products) of thirty-one per cent; in Class II (cattle and fish products) of twenty-three per cent; in Class III (tropical fruits) of seven per cent; in Class IV (colonial commodities) of twelve per cent; in Class V (mining and smelting products) of forty per cent; in Class VI (textile products) of twenty-four per cent; in Class VII (miscellaneous articles) of thirty-two per cent.

Careful comparisons of price movements in recent years also fail to show any exact correspondence of results as respects different countries, the average fall of prices having been apparently less in France and Germany than in Great Britain during the same period ; while the average fall in prices in the United States, in respect to all those commodities which enter into the general wants of man, have been undoubtedly greater than in any other country.*

---

* The following extract from the " Report of the Chamber of Commerce of Cincinnati, Ohio," for the year ending August 31, 1886, strikingly illustrates the extraordinary decline in the price of staple commodities in this great interior market of the North American Continent :

" There is one condition revealed "—i. e., by the statistics of 1885-'86— " that is very noticeable, which is that prices in general touched the lowest point in a quarter of a century. There were those who supposed that the shrinking processes had been arrested in the preceding year, and yet the figures for 1885-'86, in nearly all departments of business, show lower prices than the previous year. In presence of the low prices of 1884-'85, it seemed almost incredible that so much of market value could be wrung from them as has been during the past year. Thus, commencing near the alphabetical list, bran declined 0 per cent; creamery butter, 20·7 ; butterine, 18 ; candles, 18·7 ; soap, 15·2; cattle, 8; coal, delivered, 7·8; middling cotton, 11·9 ; feathers, 6·7 ; dried apples, 27·4 ; No. 2 mixed (shelled) corn, 14·6 ; No. 2 oats, 5·3 ; New Orleans molasses, 11·6 ; Louisiana rice, 13·1 ; hay, 5 ; hops, 25·2; mess-pork, 21·1 ; prime lard, 10·7 ; lard-oil, 11·7 ; tallow, 22 : white-leaf tobacco, 25 ; flax-seed, 18·4 ; starch, 13·4 ; high wines, not including the taxes, 16·3. In a few articles—tanners' bark, clover-seed, lead, barley, wool, etc.—there was an advance ; yet the number is so small as to make them quite exceptional.

" While the depreciation which has taken place the past year (1885-'86), compared with the prices of 1884-'85, has been marked, it may be interesting

Now, while such results are not in accordance with what might have been anticipated *from* and can not be satisfactorily explained *by* any theory of the predominating and depressing influence of a scarcity of gold on prices, they are exactly the results which might have been expected from and can be satisfactorily explained by the conditions of supply and demand—conditions so varying with time, place, and circumstance as to require in the case of every commodity a special examination to determine its price-experience, and which experience, once recognized, will rarely or never be found to exactly correspond with the experience of any other commodity; the leading factor occasioning the recent decline in the prices of sugars having been an extraordinary artificial stimulus; in quinine, the changes in the sources of supply from natural to artificially cultivated trees; in wheat, the accessibility of new and fertile territory, and a reduction of freights; in freights, *on land*, the reduction in the cost of iron and steel, and *on the ocean* new methods of propulsion, economy in fuel and undue multi-

---

to take a glance at the tremendous reduction which has taken place in the past five years, which, in articles that enter into the every-day wants of man, in not a few instances has been equal to almost one half their value in 1881–'82. The gravitation to a lower plane of value has been so steady as to prevent a full appreciation of the enormous shrinkage to which commodities have been subjected. Thus, in mess-pork the depreciation in the general average price since 1881–'82 has been 48·5 per cent; in prime steam lard, 46; hams, 24·4; shelled corn, 43; oats (which in Europe have shown no tendency in recent years to fall in price), 39·4; rye, 32·6; bran, 33·8; extra butter, 46·9; tallow, 41·4; flour, 34·3; linseed-oil, 30; salt, 18·6; cheese, 17·1; fair to medium cattle, 18·3; middling cotton, 21·7; Louisiana rice, 28·9; barley, 18·6; and wool, 15 per cent."

The report for the year ending August, 1887, thus further states the experience of the Cincinnati market: "Low as were the prices of breadstuffs in the previous year, they touched in the past year (1887) still lower points. The same is true of cattle, sheep, molasses, sugar, rice, sirups, salt, and, during most of the year, potatoes. The food of the people, in general, was cheap, the labor of the country never having received a larger return, in actual necessities and comforts, for wages received. The working forces of the country are so productive that it furnishes either a constant pressure in the direction of lower prices or resistance to advance."

plication of vessels; in iron and steel, new processes and new furnaces, affording a larger and better product with less labor in a given time; in certain varieties of wool, changes in fashion, and in others an increase of production in a greater ratio than population and their consuming capacity; in ores and coal, the introduction of the steam-drill and more powerful explosive agents; in cheese, a disproportionate market price for butter; in cotton cloth, because the spindles which revolved four thousand times in a minute in 1874 made ten thousand revolutions in the same time in 1885; in "gum-arabic" and "senna," a war in the Soudan; in wines, a destruction of the vines by disease; in American hog-products, a plentiful supply of hogs, consequent upon an abundant corn (maize) crop, etc. And yet all these so diverse factors of influence evolve and harmonize under, and at the same time demonstrate, the existence of a law more immutable than any other in economic science—namely, that when production increases in excess of current market demand, even to the extent of an inconsiderable fraction, or is cheapened through any agency, prices will decline; and that when, on the other hand, production is checked or arrested by natural events—storms, pestilence, extremes of temperature—or by artificial interference—as war, excessive taxation, or political misrule or disturbances—prices will advance; and, between these extremes of influence, prices will fluctuate in accordance with the progressive changes in circumstances and the hopes and fears of producers, exchangers, and consumers.*

---

* In new countries, or countries where industry is confined to the production of a few staple products, like wool, wheat, sugar, etc., a decline in prices exerts a wider and much more disturbing influence than in countries where there is great diversity of industry, and where the sources of income and the opportunities for employment are more numerous and more varied. In the latter all branches of industry are rarely depressed at the same time, and prosperity in some compensates to a certain extent for adversity in others. But, in countries of inferior industrial organization and diversification, the interests of the entire community are so common and united that the tendency is

It should also not be overlooked that extraordinary price movements—mainly but not exclusively in the direction of further decline, and as the result of continually changing conditions in the production and supply of commodities— are constantly occurring, and are likely to continue to occur, unless further material progress is in some way to be arrested. Bessemer-steel rails, which commanded £4 5s. in Great Britain in 1886, sold in Belgium in June, 1887, for £3 16s.; sugar, which was thought to have touched the lowest possible price in July, 1886—2·92 cents per pound in New York (for fair refining in bond), sold in July, 1887, in the same market, for 2·37¼ cents, and in 1888 for 3·09; copper, which brought 25 cents per pound in New York in 1880, sold for 9⅜ cents in 1886, 11¼ cents in 1887, and 16¾ cents in 1888; quicksilver, which sold for $118 per flask in San Francisco in 1874, sold for $26 in 1884 and $50 in 1887. Sulphate of quinine, which sold in 1885 for 2s. 6d. per ounce (sixty cents), in 1887, owing to continued cheapening in the production and transportation of cinchona-barks and improvements in manufacture, sold for 1s. 6d. (thirty cents), and one of the largest of the world's manufacturers of quinine, under date of September, 1887, writes, "No one can predict the future prices of this product, as all past experience goes for naught." "Manila" and "Sisal" hemps, on the other hand, with an admitted notable increase in annual market supply, advanced in price fully one hundred per cent between the 1st of January, 1887, and the corresponding period in 1889, because under the new methods of binding the sheaves of American grain the demand for coarse twines has been in excess of supply.

---

always, for a change of price in one commodity—either rise or fall—to unduly influence the prices of all commodities. And this, according to the London "Statist," is what has been particularly noticeable in Australia, where such a sympathy obtains between the three great products of that country—wool, wheat, and copper—that it rarely happens that one of them droops in price without the price of the others rapidly weakening.

Such, then, are the leading and admitted facts illustrative of the nature and extent of the extraordinary and most extensive decline in prices which has occurred in recent years, and which has been the most apparent and proximate (but not the ultimate) cause of the period of economic disturbance which, commencing in 1873, still exists, and seems certain to last for some time longer. Such, also, is a summary of the evidence in support of the view that this recent phenomenal decline of prices is due so largely to the great multiplication and cheapening of commodities through new conditions of production and distribution, that the influence of any or all other causes combined in contributing to such a result has been very inconsiderable, if not wholly inappreciable.

It is not, however, to be concealed that numerous economists and statisticians of high repute—M. Sauerbeck and others—are nevertheless of the opinion that, allowing all that has been claimed for the influence on prices occasioned by reduction of cost through increased and cheapened production and distribution, the decline in recent years is too great to be "simply explained away" by these agencies But these authorities have specified no commodities, the analysis of whose production and price-experiences in recent years furnish any sufficient foundation for such a general conclusion; and it is interesting to note how the experiences of the few—as has been pointed out in the case of wool and silk—which at first thought would seem to indicate the sensible influence of " other " agencies, on analysis prove to the contrary. Reasoning also from what may be termed the gold standpoint, the evidence to the same effect is not less conclusive. It would seem, in the first place, that if the scarcity influence of gold on prices had originated and operated as the advocates of this theory claim, such influence would have been as all-pervasive, synchronous, irresistible, and constant as the influence of gravitation; and that something of correspondence, as respects time and degree, in the resulting price-movements of commodities, would have been recognized. But no such correspondence, as has been shown by examples, has been or can be established. On the contrary, the movement of general prices since 1873—although generally downward—has been exceedingly irregular; declining until 1878–'79; then rising until 1882–'83; then again declining to an almost unprecedented low average in 1886; and in the year 1887 exhibiting, in respect to some commodities, a slight upward tendency, which in 1888–'89 was even more pronounced. It might also have been expected that the influence of a scarcity of gold would have especially manifested itself at or shortly subsequent to the time (1873–'74) when Germany, having demonetized silver, was absorbing gold, and France and the Latin Union were suspending the coinage of silver. But the years from 1875 to 1879, inclusive, taking the English market as the criterion, were characterized generally by an excessive supply of money and currency of all kinds; and the same has been true of the period from 1880 to 1886–'87, when, if the supply of money from gold was constantly diminishing, contrary results would seem to have been inevitable.*

---

* It has, however, been urged in opposition to this view that, when from any causes prices fall, "there will always be an excessive supply of money seeking investments at the money centers," and that "the supply of money may have diminished, but in the face of falling prices the demand for it will naturally have diminished faster still." To this it may be answered that, when falling prices are accompanied or occasioned by diminished trade, the above inferences may be true ; but, in the phenomenal period under consideration, prices have fallen greatly without any diminution of the volume of trade. In fact, the volume of trade, or the quantities of commodities produced, moved, and exchanged, has never been so great in the history of the world as during the last ten or fifteen years ; and the so-called depression of trade during this time has been mainly due to a reduction of profits to such an extent that, as the expression goes, "it has not paid to do business," which in turn has been occasioned by an intense competition in all markets to dispose of an excess of product. Under such circumstances there is no reason to believe that the demand for money has diminished faster than prices have fallen, or to doubt that, if there had been any real scarcity of gold, it would have failed to manifest itself.

But a more interesting question, and one more pertinent to this discussion than any other, is, has gold, in recent years, as an instrumentality for effecting exchanges (by measuring the relation between the various commodities and things exchanged), really become scarce—at least to the extent of occasioning, through its increase of value or purchasing power, a considerable fall in the prices of all commodities? And on this point the following is a summary of the evidence in favor of and in contravention of such a supposition.* The position taken by the advocates or believers in the gold-scarcity theory, is, in brief, that the production of gold in recent years has largely fallen off and become wholly inadequate to meet the demands for coinage contingent on the increase in the world's trade, wealth, and population; and further, and as a direct consequent, that trade everywhere has been obstructed and depressed; that prices, profits, and wages have fallen, and the burden of public debts and of taxation in general has been augmented.

That the world's annual product of gold—consequent mainly upon the exhaustion of the mines of California and Australia—has largely diminished in recent years is not disputed. Opinions as to the extent of this reduction of supply vary somewhat, but the following estimates of Dr. Soetbeer of the total annual average production since 1851 are accepted as approximately accurate:

---

* To avoid confusion of ideas on this subject, it is desirable that the reader should keep clearly in view that *price* is the expression of the value of a commodity in terms of money, and that the expressions, "fall in prices" and "appreciation of gold," for purposes of the present discussion, mean really one and the same thing. "If you have a fall in prices, you have an appreciation of gold; and if you have an appreciation of gold, you have a fall in prices." The problem presented is, therefore, not has gold appreciated in value or purchasing power—for, a fall in prices being admitted, such a result becomes inevitable and coincident—but has its appreciation been due to something that has befallen commodities, or something that has befallen gold itself, such as scarcity of supply or extraordinary demand?

1851–'55.................	£27,815,400	$135,182,844
1856–'60.................	28,144,900	137,784,415
1866–'70.................	27,206,900	132,225,534
1876–'80.................	24,052,200	116,893,692
1881–'85.................	20,804,900	101,111,814

For the year 1888 the estimate is ("New York Financial Chronicle") £19,056,782, or $92,575,000. The estimates of experts as to the proportion of the annual product of gold which is available for coinage purposes vary considerably; the uncertain elements in the case being the amount of gold that is recoined and the proportion that is used in the arts and manufactures.

That trade, in the sense of diminishing volume, has *not* been obstructed, and that the decline in prices in recent years has *not* been occasioned, to any appreciable extent, by reason of the scarcity of gold, would appear to be demonstrated by the evidence that has been herewith presented. For the assertion that wages, generally, have fallen, there is absolutely no foundation, as will be shown hereafter. That profits have fallen must be admitted; but such a result has been due, in almost every case, to the severe competition engendered by the desire to effect sales in face of a continued supply of commodities in excess of any current market demand; while in contravention of the assumption that the supply of gold in recent years has been inadequate to meet the increased demands of the world for coinage, etc., the following facts are in the highest degree pertinent, if not wholly conclusive:

No one doubts that the amount of gold in the civilized countries of the world has largely increased in recent years. According to Dr. Soetbeer,* the monetary stock of gold and gold reserve in the treasuries and principal banks of civilized countries has shown an increase for every decade since 1850, and at the end of 1885 was nearly four times what it was in

---

* Soetbeer's "Materialien," second edition, 1886, p. 47.

1850; so that, instead of there being a reduced supply of gold, as compared with thirty-five years ago, there is a greatly increased supply.

Prof. Laughlin estimates this increase to have been "from $477,000,000 in 1870–'80 to $836,000,000 in 1885." In 1871–'74 there was, according to the same authority, "$1 in gold for every $3.60 of the paper circulation of the banks of the civilized world; in 1885 there was $1 of gold for every $2.40; the total note circulation increasing during the same time to the extent of $464,000,000, or twenty-nine per cent." In 1870–'74 the gold reserves amounted to twenty-eight per cent of the total note circulation, and sixty-four per cent of all the specie reserves; in 1885 "the gold bore a larger ratio to a larger issue of paper, or forty-one per cent of the total note circulation, and seventy-one per cent of the specie reserves. This," as Prof. Laughlin remarks, "is a very significant showing. What it means, beyond a shadow of doubt, is that the supply of gold is so abundant that the character and safety of the note circulation have been improved in a signal manner."

The investigations of Mr. Atkinson have also led him to the conclusion that, while the population of the world since 1849 has increased about forty per cent, the concurrent increase in the volume of the money metals has been fully one hundred per cent, and that the value of the gold, added to the circulation during that period, was more than double that of the silver added.*

---

* "We are substantially certain that the quantity of gold and silver combined which has been added to the circulation of the money metals between the year 1850 and the year 1885 exceeds the total quantity which was in use in 1850. That is to say, that portion of the world's product of gold and silver which has been added to the circulation for use as money between these dates, has increased the total amount in circulation more than *one hundred per cent*. Did the population of the globe increase more than *one hundred per cent* in this period? To this question a negative answer may be given with equal assurance. The increase of population in the civilized states of the world, now numbering only a little over four hundred millions, has been only forty-

Since 1873–'74 Germany has radically modified her metallic circulation, giving preference to and using additional gold, and the United States and Italy have resumed specie payments. But the supply of gold has been sufficient to give to these nations all the gold that they required, without apparently affecting the requirements of other countries. Again, it is not disputed that the rate of interest and discount has declined in all these countries—like Germany, the United States, Scandinavia, Holland, and Italy—which in recent years have increased their demand and use of gold for coinage; whereas a scarcity of money resulting from a scarcity of gold ought to have produced just the contrary effect.

The present annual production of gold is enormous compared with any period antecedent to 1850.* Between 1820–1830 its average annual production was $10,000,000; between 1831–1840 it was $14,151,000; and between 1840–1850, $38,194,000. It was at its highest figure—$170,000,000 to $180,000,000—in 1852; averaged $101,000,000 from 1881 to 1885; and (according to the estimates of the Director of the United States Mint) was $103,000,000 in 1885, and $99,000,000 in 1886.

The production of silver has also largely increased in recent years ($39,000,000 in 1850, $64,000,000 in 1873, and $135,000,000 in 1887), and no evidence can be produced to show that there has been any actual diminution in its aggre-

---

two per cent in this period; can the remainder have increased in greater measure? Surely not. Hence it follows that such an addition of gold and silver has been made to the money metals since 1850 as would have caused them to depreciate between these two dates had the simple quantity or volume of money in circulation per capita been the only element in the problem.

"It is also a well-known and fully ascertained fact that between these two dates the value of the gold added to the circulation of the world very far exceeded the value of the silver, the ratio or valuation of silver being computed at *fifteen and one half pounds* of silver to *one* of gold."—EDWARD ATKINSON.

* "In the last thirty-five years, one and one third times as much gold has been produced as in the three hundred and fifty-eight years preceding 1850." —LAUGHLIN.

gate use by reason of its so-called "demonetization" in any country.

Now, while the supply of the precious metals for money purposes has been amply sufficient to meet all requirements, there is abundant evidence in proof that the use of metallic money for the purpose of effecting exchanges has been greatly supplemented in recent years through numerous and varied agencies. "In America, France, and Germany there are besides gold coins immense sums of silver money, paper money, and uncovered bank-notes; and these media of circulation are fully equivalent to gold in value, owing to public or private credit; and, therefore, in the figures of prices they have the same influence in commerce as a corresponding amount of gold money would have."*

Never before in the history of the world have there been so many and such successful devices invented and adopted for economizing the use of money. Every increase in facilities for banking and for the granting and extension of credits largely contributes to this result; the countries enjoying the maximum of such facilities requiring the smallest comparative amount of coin for their commercial transactions. In the United States the number of national

---

* "In France in latter years we find in the vaults of the Bank of France a cash reserve of 1,100 to 1,200 francs in gold, and a like amount in silver of legal tender. Besides this, the note circulation amounts to 2,600,000,000 to 2,700,000,000 francs, and is, therefore, covered to the extent of nearly half in gold and nearly five sixths in metal. Were there an increased demand for circulation, there could be—political quiet and peace being assured—an issue of 500,000,000 to 600,000,000 francs more in notes covered by the existing cash reserve without causing thereby the least injury to credit.

"In Germany, too, there can be no talk of any dearth of circulation so long as the Imperial Bank holds a cash reserve of 650,000,000 to 750,000,000 marks in gold and silver, which is treble the sum which before 1870 was quite sufficient for the Prussian Bank. Nearly three fourths of the amount of the notes issued by the Imperial Bank and the other banks of issue are usually metallically covered, and therefore the issue of notes could, if it was only a question of the credit of the notes, be increased by the sum of some 100,000,-000 marks on the present cash reserve."—PROF. LEXIS, *Göttingen, Answer to Circular Letter of British Gold and Silver Commission,* 1888.

banks increased from 2,052 in December, 1879, to 3,151 in December, 1888, or in the ratio of over fifty-three per cent. During the same period their capital, surplus, and undivided profits increased 38·5 per cent, and their loans and discounts seventy-nine and a half per cent. In England, Scotland, Ireland, and the Channel Islands there were 2,417 banking offices in 1865, and 3,886 in 1885—an increase which is regarded as extraordinary. The total banking deposits of England, which were estimated (at one moment) at £676,000,000 in 1874, were £760,000,000 in 1884—an increase of £84,000,000 ($408,000,000) in nine years, and this notwithstanding the concurrent great fall in prices. " In Germany, a system of deposit accounts began at the Imperial Bank in 1876; since then they have grown to more than 350,000,000 marks ($85,000,000). Of these deposits, the owners can at any time avail themselves by means of checks, and make their payments throughout the whole empire without any expense." To this must be added the progress made in Germany in recent years in the absorption and utilization of the very smallest reserves of money through the savings-banks system. " There are now scarcely any peasants left in Germany who keep ready money on hand to any considerable amount; and in families, in which a few decades ago, every child possessed his money-box filled with gold and silver pieces, now every child has his savings-bank book."—*Prof.* NASSE, *of Bonn.*

The great reduction in the time and cost of distribution of commodities, and the facility with which purchases can be made and credits transmitted by telegraph, have also resulted, not only in an enormous saving of capital, but also in an ability to transact an increased business with diminished necessity for the absorption and use of actual money. A most striking illustration in proof of this, given by Mr. Fowler ("Appreciation of Gold," London, 1885), is, that while the total British export and import trade, aggregating £6,000,000,000 from 1866 to 1875, was accompanied by an aggregate export and import of £530,000,000 of bullion and specie, an aggregate value from 1876 to 1885 of £6,700,000,-000, was moved with the aid of only £439,000,000 of bullion and specie. The same authority refers to an eminent English firm doing business with the East, as stating that " their business could now be conducted with one fifth of the capital formerly employed," which would seem to warrant the inference that the reduction in the necessity for using so much of their capital as was represented by money had also been proportionate.

For the settlement of international balances—a large function of gold—it is certain that every ounce of this metal —through the great reduction in the time of ocean-transits —is at the present time capable of performing far more service than at any former period ; the time for the transmission of coin and bullion having been reduced in recent years between Australia and England from ninety to forty days, and from New York to Liverpool from twelve or fifteen to eight or nine days. Such an increase of rapidity in doing work is certainly equivalent to increase in quantity.

The very great change which has taken place in the United States in this respect is thus noticed in the report of the United States Controller of the Currency for 1888 :

" Of late years the gold movement across the Atlantic has become much more sluggish, because something has been found to take its place, and to some extent, at least, to serve the purpose of regulating exchanges and transferring capital. Certain securities on the New York stock-list have come to be largely and constantly dealt in at the European monetary centers, and as, by means of cable communication and through the close competition of dealers, their values are generally at a level in all markets, they supply a cheaper means of settlement than gold, and a more convenient basis for exchange operations." These securities " have become the stock in trade of dealers in foreign exchange ; they are shipped back and forth according as exchange quotations fluctuate ; indeed, in many cases they are not even shipped ; the ownership is transferred by a cablegram, and this transfer supplies a basis for bills of credit. Before this new business came in, the dealers in foreign exchange, being dependent wholly upon gold to settle their balances, or to serve as a basis for drafts or credits whenever the supply of commercial bills proved insufficient, were compelled to carry a stock of coin, or bullion, and this constituted a fund apart from the general monetary stock of the country."

The statistics of clearing-houses, which are everywhere multiplying, also show a continued tendency for the settlement of financial obligations without the intervention of either notes or coin. In the United States the exchanges effected through the medium of clearing-houses increased $7,604,000,000 in the single year from 1885 to 1886. In the United Kingdom the daily clearances of its banks amount to nearly one fifth of the whole supply of gold in the country; and for the year 1885, for the three commercial centers of London, Manchester, and Newcastle, amounted to the almost incomprehensible sum of £6,048,000,000 ($29,393,280,000). In Germany the clearing-house system only came into full action in 1884, but in 1886 the business had grown to 12,355,000,000 marks; and the question in this connection is most pertinent—i. e., " What relation does this saving of the use of money bear to the quantity of gold Germany is estimated to have absorbed in her new coinage ? "—Sir Thomas Farrer.

Repeated investigations made in England in recent years prove that only about ·06 per cent of coin is used in settling the transactions of banks and bankers of that country; and the results of an inquiry instituted by the United States Controller of the Currency in 1881 showed that, of all the receipts by 1,966 national banks in one day in that year (June 30th), ninety-five per cent were made up of forms of credit, exclusive of even circulating notes; while for New York city the percentage was 98·7. At all the banks the proportion of gold coin to the whole receipts was only ·65 of one per cent.* A curious indirect illustration of the influ-

---

* In an address before the British Institute of Bankers, November, 1887, by Mr. J. W. Birch, one of the directors of the Bank of England, he stated

ence of the extension of banking facilities, and the use of checks in economizing coin as a medium for effecting exchanges, is afforded by contrasting the monetary condition of France—a country where the check as a means of payment is comparatively little used, and other banking devices have not been extensively adopted—with that of the United States, where all the modern instrumentalities for facilitating exchanges have been quickly adopted and extensively employed. The result is, according to M. Leroy-Beaulieu, that while France has only 38,000,000 inhabitants, as compared with 65,000,000 in the United States, it holds, and seems to require, for the transaction of its business a much larger stock of gold—a stock which bears the same proportion to that held in the United States as five to three. Taking the amount of gold per capita, the disproportion is even much greater; the amount of gold, according to the same authority, held in France being 131 francs (about $25) per capita, while in the United States it is not in excess of $10 (about 52 francs) per capita; or, in other words, the amount of gold money per capita in France is two and one half times that in the United States.

"The transfer by means of checks of the right to the possession of gold, has to a vast extent taken the place of the transfer of gold itself, and it can not be doubted that every day the payments which are made by means of checks greatly exceed the amount of gold which exists available to meet the checks, if every holder were to insist upon receiving the gold which he is entitled to claim. The purchasing power of the people consists, it appears to us, not only of the actual gold which they possess, or of that which their bankers are possessed of and can

---

that he had "asked the head of the Private Drawing Office of the Bank of England to take out the figures of one week's payments hap-hazard, and the result was that instruments of credit were eighty-seven and a quarter per cent of the total, bank-notes twelve and a quarter per cent, while the cash payments amounted to only about three per mille. He had obtained similar statistics for twenty-two days' payments at Messrs. Glyn, Mills & Co., with the result that their average of cash payments was about four and a half per mille."

immediately command, but, to use a popular expression, of the money which they have at their disposal at their bankers', which greatly exceeds the amount of gold which either they or their bankers could at any time at once command. This is indeed an under-statement of the case, for the credit which customers can obtain from their bankers may have as potent an influence upon prices as their cash balances. So long as those who possess commodities are as ready to take checks for them as they would be to take gold, the balance which a man has or can have, at his bankers', influences prices to the same extent as if he were possessed of that amount of gold."—*Final Report of the British Gold and Silver Commission, Part II, p. 70.*

In every country which has adopted the "postal money" system, the rapidity with which the public resort to that method of effecting exchanges is also most surprising.

The number of "postal" orders issued by the British Post-Office in 1887 was 35,198,754, representing £14,228,734 ($69,151,000); while money-orders, domestic and foreign, were issued during the same year to the amount of £27,320,-000 ($132,776,000).

Domestic money-orders were first issued in the United States in 1864. In the fiscal year 1864–'65 the total amount issued represented $1,360,122; but for the fiscal year ending June 30, 1888, the amount of such orders issued had grown to $119,649,064. The growth of the international money-order system has been even more marked. Such orders were first authorized in 1869, and the total amount issued from September 1, 1869, to June 30, 1870, was only $22,189. From 1872, however, the system made rapid strides, and in the fiscal year 1887–'88 the total amount issued had grown to $11,293,870.

In estimating the influence of any diminished production of gold in recent years, it is important to bear in mind a point to which attention has been often heretofore called, and that is, that gold and silver are not like other commodities, of which the greater part of the annual production is annually consumed; but that their use for the purpose of effecting exchanges does not involve consumption, except by loss and wear ; that the work they have once done they are equally ready to do over and over again, and that every addition to their stock is an addition to the fund available for exchanges. It follows, therefore, that in the case of the precious metals, a diminution, or an increase in the new supply is of less importance than in the case of consumable articles, and that an increase or diminution of demand has a smaller effect. Furthermore, the aggregate stock of gold has not diminished, but has continually increased ; although the annual addition to the world's stock has somewhat diminished of late years. Dr. Soetbeer estimates " the production of gold since the end of the fifteenth century to have been £1,553,415,000 ($7,549,596,900). An annual supply of £20,000,000 ($97,000,000) above the present average product would consequently be about one and a quarter per cent on that stock ; while the annual diminution in the supply which has taken place in the last fifteen years would only amount to one quarter per cent per annum." * That such a diminution of supply—even if a much higher estimate is adopted—has for each and every year for a considerable period been far more than supplemented and made good by the reduction in the amount of capital, in the form of money, which the increased facilities for doing business have permitted and effected, is a proposition which it would seem could not well be doubted.†

---

* " Final Report of the British Gold and Silver Commission," p. 13.

† " The trade of the world is carried on by credit and capital, and any causes affecting these essentials have infinitely greater effect on prices than a slight proportionate increase or decrease in the production of gold. A merchant may not hold ten sovereigns, but he may have capital and credit for ten millions. An ingenious statistician has calculated the capital of the world in 1880 at £46,000,000,000 sterling" ($230,000,000,000), " and if credit and capital have had the main voice in the question of prices, how minute must have been the effect on the market of an annual reduction in the production of floating capital of ten (sterling) millions per annum, from a short period of most exceptional production, especially when the falling off has been more than balanced by the increased economy in the use of gold ! "—NATHANIEL CORK, " What is the True Measure of the Alleged Appreciation of Gold? " London, 1883.

The evidence, therefore, seems to fully warrant the following conclusions : That the tendency of the age is to use continually less and less of coin in the transaction of business; and that "so far from there being any scarcity of gold, there never was a period in the world's commercial history when the existing quantity was so large as at present, in proportion to the necessity for its use or the purposes it has to serve."

The present and rapidly increasing indifference of the business public, alike in Europe and the United States, whose interest in this subject is mainly practical, is also significant, as indicating that the importance formerly conceded to the gold-scarcity theory has not been confirmed by experience.

In fact, the changes in recent years in the world's economic condition have essentially changed the relative importance of the two functions, which gold as the leading monetary metal discharges; namely, that of an instrumentality for facilitating exchanges and as a measure of values. As civilization has increased, and as new, quicker, and cheaper methods for the interchange of thought and commodities have been invented and adopted, the function of gold as a medium of exchange—the one that necessitates a large and continually augmenting supply, and entails the greatest wear and loss—is rapidly diminishing in importance by the supplementation of other and better agencies. On the other hand, the function of gold as a measure or verifier of values, by reason of its exemption from value fluctuations to a greater extent than any other product of labor, is becoming of greater and greater importance with the continually increasing volume of the world's production and distribution, and more especially since the other precious metal—silver—has become uncertain and fluctuating in value. But, in discharging this function, the service which gold renders is analogous to that rendered by all other measures, the yard-stick, the bushel measure, or the metal mercury, which in the tube of the thermometer or barometer measures the temperature or pressure of the atmosphere. That is, a given quantity of gold can be used to an indefinite extent with such a minimum of waste that continuous large supplies are not imperative; or, as Sir Thomas Farrer has happily expressed it, " we are returning in the advanced stage of commerce to a state of barter, in which money is merely the measure and language, not the actual medium, of exchange, and in which personal rights and duties take the place of cash." *

Whether in the case of silver, which has been used for currency purposes throughout the world since 1873 to a greater extent than ever before, but which has ceased to maintain its parity with gold as a measure of value, it is possible, or desirable, to restore the latter quality through legislation, is a subject foreign to the present discussion. But it may not be irrelevant to call attention at this point to the manner in which certain admitted facts touching the recent fall in prices have been misunderstood, and, more especially, have been perverted, with a view of sustaining the theory of the appreciation of gold and of creating exaggerated ideas respecting consequent impending disasters, and the power of legislation to provide remedies. Thus, in illustration of the assumption that the quantity of gold in the world, available for use as money, mainly regulates prices, and that, prices having fallen by reason of a scarcity of gold, the ratio of debts to assets, or the burdens upon

---

* " In the original and simplest form of barter, goods and services were exchanged directly against one another : a horse against so many sheep, a day's labor against a day's food, and so on. In the next stage the exchange was effected by the intervention and actual use of money, which was then both the measure of value and the actual medium by the use of which the exchange was actually effected. In the third stage, to which the most advanced nations have now come, the barter is effected not by the use and intervention of money, but by the use and intervention of personal promises, which are made in terms of money, and the value of which is therefore measured by money."

debtors, has been increased, the following statements were made in a memorial signed by ninety-five members of the United States House of Representatives of the Forty-eighth Congress, and presented to the President of the United States in 1885 :

"Eighteen million bales of cotton were the equivalent in value of the entire interest-bearing national debt in 1865 ($2,221,000,000); but it will take thirty-five million bales at the price of cotton now (1885) to pay the remainder of such debt ($1,196,000,000). Twenty-five million tons of bar-iron would have paid the whole debt ($2,674,000,000) in 1865; it will now take thirty-five million tons to pay what remains ($1,375,000,000) after all that has been paid."

The inference, therefore, intended to be conveyed was, that the burden of the national debt of the United States in 1885, notwithstanding the large payments on the same during the previous twenty years, had really been increased, inasmuch as a greater effort of labor, or an increased amount of the products of labor, was now necessary to liquidate it, than when the purchasing power of gold had not been appreciated through its scarcity; and, as with public debts, so also with private debts, especially such as are in the nature of mortgages on land, or on other productive fixed capital.

Now, in reply to this it is to be said, *first*, that the basis assumed for this comparison of prices was, in the case of cotton, entirely unfair and unnatural—the *gold* price of this commodity in the year 1865, owing to a scarcity occasioned by war, having been more than two hundred and fifty per cent higher than the average prices in 1860 before the war; while the price of iron for that same year in the American markets was also inflated on even a gold basis; and, *secondly*, that no consideration is given or allowance made in the above comparisons for the results of labor at the two periods of 1865 and 1885; not more, and probably much less, actual labor in 1865–'86 having produced 6,550,000 bales of cotton in the United States than was required in

1860 to produce 3,800,000 bales;* while in the case of bar-iron the proportion of days' labor to a ton of product has been diminished more than one half since 1865; and the same is true, also, of that more valuable product of iron, namely, steel. Furthermore, no important product of the United States can be named in which the labor cost of production has not decreased very much more than has the gold price of the same between 1865 and 1885. In short, if the debtor has got more to pay at the latter than at the former period, it is not the fault of any change in the relations of the precious metals if he has not at the same time got correspondingly more to pay with.

The monetary experience of the United States since 1879 has been so especially remarkable, and has such a bearing on the economic problem of the relation of money-supply to prices, as to entitle it to extended notice. The following table shows the changes in the circulating media of the United States—bullion, coin, and paper—since January 1, 1879 (when the country resumed specie payments), and January 1, 1889—a period of ten years:

---

* The increase in the cotton product of the United States since 1860 has been due mainly to increased use of fertilizers, better tillage, and better conditions for the employment of labor. In the Brazos alluvial region of Texas, which ranks among the first of cotton-producing regions, the relative increase in cotton product and population between 1870 and 1880, according to the United States census, was 1·8 to 1. In what is termed the " oak-upland" regions of North Carolina, the product of cotton in 1880 had increased over that of 1870 in the ratio of 4·5 to 1, or this region in 1880 produced more cotton than the product of the entire State in either 1870 or 1860. " This remarkable result," according to the special United States census report on cotton for 1880, " was due mainly to the introduction and general use of commercial fertilizers, which not only increase the crop, but hasten its maturity from two to three weeks, and so bring into the cotton belt a strip of plateau country, whose elevation of from 800 to 1,200 feet had placed it just beyond the climatic range of the cotton-plant. This change is in no respect due to altered relations of labor." In truth, there was no one thing in which the American advocates of slavery were more mistaken than in the assumption that slave labor was cheap labor.

CIRCULATION.	Jan. 1, 1879.	Jan. 1, 1889.	Total.
Gold coin and bullion....	$278,310,126	$704,608,169	Inc. $426,298,043
Silver dollars..........	22,495,550	315,186,190	" 292,690,640
Silver bullion..........	9,121,417	10,865,237	" 1,743,820
Fractional silver.......	71,021,162	76,889,983	" 5,863,821
National-bank notes....	323,791.674	233,660,027	Dec. 90,131,647
Legal-tender notes.....	346,681,016	346,681,016	....
Total currency issues...	1,051,420,945	1,687,890,622	Inc. 636,469,677

Of this large increase of $636,469,677, $578,637,368, in coin and paper, were in the hands of the people; and $57,832,309, in bullion, coin, and paper, in the national Treasury.*

It thus appears that, while there has been an increase in the population of the United States during the period of ten years under consideration of about thirty per cent, the increase in the precious metals and paper available for circulation during the same time was 60·05 per cent; while of coin and paper in active use among the people and banks the increase was 69·6 per cent, or much more than double the rate of increase in population. Now, as during this same period there was a great and universal decline in the prices of commodities in the United States (as elsewhere), the interesting question arises, How do these experiences harmonize with the theory that the volume of circulating medium controls prices, and that the movement of the precious metals puts *down* prices in the event of a reduction of the supply, and puts them *up* in the event of an increase of supply? Note, further, that the increase of gold and silver coin and bullion in the United States during the ten years, from 1879 to 1889, was $726,600,000, while the paper circulation diminished. Nor can it be maintained that the fall in the value of silver bullion has affected this circulation, since, for all purposes of internal circulation, silver and its paper representatives have had the same efficiency and

---

* New York "Financial Chronicle," February 9, 1889.

exchangeable value as existed before the depreciation of silver bullion. The availability of silver coin for the settlement on the part of the United States of international balances has been alone affected ; and this, so long as there has been an adequate supply of gold, is an immaterial factor. It would, therefore, seem that the above exhibit furnishes the most complete refutation of the theory that changes in the supplies of the precious metals account for the fall in the prices of commodities.*

* It will add to the understanding of this important economic experience to note the arguments brought forward in the United States in disproof of the above conclusion — the facts, as stated, being indisputable. It has been claimed, in the first instance, that as the United States has a vast quantity of products to sell—the prices of which are regulated by the prices which the surplus of such products will command in foreign markets—the home prices of the same can not escape conformity to the universal cost ; or, in other words, that the influence of the local inflation of currency that has taken place in the United States has been thus neutralized. But the market value of all the products of the United States are not regulated by foreign demand ; and, of such exceptions, not one can be cited that has unmistakably increased in price during recent years by reason of any increase in the volume of the circulating media. It has also been maintained that the increasing importations of the United States since 1879 constitute evidence of the fact and influence of inflation—i. e., by increasing the buying power of her people. But a more rational explanation would seem to be found in a corresponding increase of exports, or an improvement in national credit, or both conjoined ; the occurrence of which would seem to be demonstrated by the fact that the country from 1879 to 1889 has not been under the necessity of exporting its precious metals in payment of its imports, and not only retained but increased its stock of them. Had the expansion of currency in the United States since 1879 occasioned any upward tendency of prices, then exports would have been to a like extent checked, and the nation's ability to import correspondingly restricted. For it is the ability of a country to export that determines its ability to import, and not the *vice versa* proposition. Furthermore, there has been during the period of inflation in the United States no unusual speculation. On the New York Stock Exchange the number of shares sold has been annually decreasing since 1882, and for the year 1888 the aggregate sales were less than for any time during the previous ten years.

VI.

Changes in recent years in the relative values of the precious metals—Subject not generally understood—Former stability in the price of silver—Action of the German Government in 1873—Concurrent decline in the price of silver—Action of the " Latin Union"—Influence and nature of India " Council bills "—Alleged demonetization of silver—Increased purchasing power of silver—Increased product of silver—Economic disturbances consequent on the decline of silver—Increased production of cotton fabrics in India—Industrial awakening in India—Relation of the decline in the value of silver to the supply of India wheat—International trade, a trade in commodities and not in money—Economic disturbances in the Dutch East Indies—Natural law governing the selection and use of metallic money —Experience of Corea—The metal coinage system of the world trimetallic —The gold standard a necessity of advanced civilization—The fall of prices due to more potent agencies than variations in the volumes or relative values of the precious metals.

NOTWITHSTANDING the great attention that has been given to the subject of the change in recent years in the relative values of the precious metals, and the disturbing influences resulting therefrom—with its almost interminable resulting publications and public and private discussions— there is probably no other one economic or fiscal problem concerning which there is so little comprehension on the part of the general public, or so little agreement as to causes and results among those who have made it a matter of special investigation.* It is of the first importance, therefore, for

---

* " From the commencement of our inquiry we have been profoundly impressed with the extreme complexity of the questions submitted for our consideration."—*Final Report of the British Gold and Silver Commission.*

" It has been my experience, that about nine men out of ten, even of those who might be expected to have some definite views upon the subject, when asked their opinion upon the expediency or necessity of adopting a bimetallic

the understanding of the past involved economic disturbances, that a clear and succinct statement of what has happened should be presented; and such a statement it is now
proposed to attempt.

For many years prior to 1873 the bullion price of silver
remained very nearly constant at from 60 to 61 pence per
ounce on the London market, while the market ratio of gold
to silver, or the ratio according to which gold and silver
could be interchanged, was limited in London, from 1851 to
1872 inclusive, to a range of variation of from 1 to 15·10
(the minimum) in 1865 to 1 to 15·79 (the maximum) in
1872.*

In 1873 the new German Empire—recognizing the importance of having a monetary system better suited to her
advanced industrial and commercial situation than that
which she then possessed, and also the desirability of having
a uniform coinage throughout the numerous small states
that had come to be included under the Imperial Government—took advantage of the command of a large stock of

---

monetary system, will reply, ' Oh, that is a very important question, but I do
not pretend to understand it.' "—EDWARD ATKINSON, *British Association
Proceedings*, 1887.

" There never has in this country been any but a very languid interest in
the question of bimetallism, and even that slight interest will not endure if
trade goes on improving. The subject is one which the general public do not
understand. Thanks to the untiring energy of the advocates of a double
standard, a certain number of people have become vaguely impressed with the
idea that somehow or other dull trade and low prices have been caused by a
scarcity of money, and that, in some way or other, if our mint were opened to
the unrestricted coinage of silver, some of it would find its way into their
pockets. This impression, however, would very quickly wear off if trade became really active; and as there is now the prospect of a genuine trade revival,
we are inclined to believe that here, at all events, bimetallism will soon die a
natural death. In any case, it is evident that there is no such strong propel-
ling force behind the agitation as will induce our Government to take any
action in the matter in face of the conflicting report of the Gold and Silver
Commission. And when it is certain that nothing will be done, it is not worth
while to prolong discussion."—*London Economist, November* 17, 1888.

* Pixley and Abell's " Tables," London.

gold, that had accrued through the payment by France of an enormous war indemnity,* to effect reform. An exceedingly miscellaneous system of coinage and currency—consisting of seventeen varieties of gold money; sixty-six different coins of silver, possessing full legal-tender powers and constituting (in 1870) 65·7 per cent of the entire circulation; forty-six kinds of notes issued by thirty-five different banks, besides state paper money of various kinds to the extent of 7·5 per cent of the circulation—was accordingly called in, and replaced by a new system of gold and silver coinage and paper currency. In this new system, gold was established as the sole monetary standard of the empire, unlimited of necessity in respect to legal-tender powers, while to silver was assigned the function of subsidiary service; and for the latter purpose an issue of silver coinage was provided, not to exceed in the aggregate 10 marks ($2.50) for each inhabitant of the empire (a comparatively low figure), with its legal-tender value limited to 20 marks ($5). An issue of new paper currency was also authorized, with a prohibition of the use of notes of a less denomination than 100 marks ($25), to be distributed according to population among the various states, and redeemable in the new imperial coinage. A proportion of the old silver coinage, which, having been supplanted by gold, was not needed for recoinage under the new system, was offered for sale in the open market as bullion, and the amount actually sold between 1873 and the end of May, 1879, when the sales were suspended, realized $141,784,948. Of this aggregate, $45,-644,311 was sold between the years 1873 and 1876, and $96,-140,627 between 1877 and 1879 inclusive.

Concurrently with this action of Germany the bullion price of silver began to decline, and this decline was un-

---

* The amount in gold which France paid to Germany directly was $54,-600,000; but in addition there were French bills of exchange which gave Germany a title to gold in places like London, on which such bills were negotiated.

doubtedly further promoted by the subsequent action of the so-called "Latin Union"—comprising the five countries of Europe using the franc system, namely, France, Belgium, Italy, Switzerland, and Greece—which, fearing lest the silver liberated from use in Germany, and offered for sale, would flow in upon and flood their respective mints, to the entire exclusion of gold if the free coinage of silver was continued; first restricted (in 1874), and finally (in 1877–'78), owing to the continued decline in the value of silver, entirely suspended the coinage of silver five-franc-pieces. The coinage of subsidiary silver, or silver of smaller denominations than five francs, was, however, permitted and continued.

In 1873, also, the Congress of the United States, in revising its coinage system, dropped from the list of silver coins authorized to be thereafter issued from its Mint, the silver dollar of $412\frac{1}{2}$ grains, although providing for the unlimited issue and coinage of silver in pieces of smaller denominations than the dollar; and mainly for the reason that this particular silver coin was not then in circulation in the country, and indeed had not been for a period of more than twenty-five years.*

The extent of the decline in the price of bar-silver per standard ounce, in pence, upon the London market, since 1873, is shown by the following exhibit of annual average quotations:

1873, $59\frac{1}{4}d.$	1883, $50\frac{9}{16}d.$
1874, $58\frac{5}{16}d.$	1885, $48\frac{13}{16}d.$
1875, $56\frac{7}{8}d.$	1886, $45\frac{9}{8}d.$
1876, $52\frac{3}{4}d.$	1887, $44\frac{5}{8}d.$
1879, $51\frac{1}{4}d.$	1888, $42\frac{7}{8}d.$

In May, 1888, the price of silver temporarily fell to $41\frac{5}{8}d.$ per ounce—the lowest price ever known in history.

---

* The statement often made, and to a large extent credited, that the silver dollar was dropped in 1873 from the coinage system of the United States by "stealth, and for a secret and dishonest purpose," has not the slightest foundation in fact, and is simply an oft-exploded falsehood.

During the early years of the decline of silver the opinion was extensively entertained that it was primarily and mainly occasioned by the new supply to the world's market consequent upon the sales of silver by Germany,* and this opinion found so much of favor with leading German bankers that it is understood that Germany suspended her sales of silver in 1879 in accordance with their advice, and with the expectation that a partial or entire recovery of price would thereby ensue.   But no such result, as is well known, followed the suspension of sales thus recommended.   How little, moreover, there was of foundation for this opinion, will appear from the following circumstances :

The aggregate silver product of the world during the years (1873–'79), when Germany was selling her discarded coinage, was about $650,000,000, or more than four and a half times the amount of the sales ($141,781,000) which Germany actually effected.   Again, during the same period of years when Germany was increasing the world's supply of silver, through her sales, to the extent of $141,781,000, the United States drew upon and reduced this same supply by increasing her dollar and subsidiary coinage to the amount of $111,307,187.†   Surely the world's status of sil-

---

* The amount of silver (old coin) which Germany up to 1880 *was able* to sell, as the result of her policy of displacing silver by gold, has been estimated at $270,000,000.   The amount which she *actually did sell* between 1873 and May, 1879 (when the sales were suspended), is believed to have been about $141,781,000 (£28,000,000).   Since then it is understood that only a few additional millions have been marketed—i. e., to Egypt.   In addition, Denmark, Sweden, and Norway, which followed the lead of Germany, and changed their silver circulation to gold, have since thrown upon the market about $9,000.000 of silver.   (*See* LAUGHLIN's *History of Bimetallism in the United States*, pp. 141–145.)

† During the twenty years from 1853 to 1873, the aggregate silver coinage of the United States was $57,137,000, or an average of only $2,856,000 per annum, and of this aggregate but $5,538,948 was in the form of silver dollars. From 1874 to 1879, inclusive, the silver coinage of the United States was 35,859,360 trade-dollars, 35,801,000 standard dollars, 22,899,785 halves, and 16,747,042 quarters and twenty-cent pieces ; total, $111,307,187, or an average of $18,560,000 per annum.

ver during these years must have been one of extraordinarily unstable equilibrium from antecedent causes, threatening serious fluctuations in price even in the absence of anything abnormal, if the addition of so small a net product during six years as $30,473,000 to the current market supply of silver could depress the bullion price of the world's mass of this metal from 59¾ to 48⅝ pence per ounce, or over thirteen per cent.

That the term "unstable equilibrium" is truly expressive of the real status of silver in 1873 would further appear from the following evidence : There was a well-recognized movement in France against silver and in favor of gold from 1853 to 1865, and its influence would probably have shown itself in a fall in value of silver, had it not been for the cotton famine consequent on the American war, which occasioned extraordinary shipments of silver to India, and so counteracted any tendency then existing to a surplus in the European markets. In 1867 an International Monetary Conference at Paris voted almost unanimously in favor of the adoption of a single gold standard by the chief commercial nations. As far back as 1860, the late Prof. Cairnes, who is recognized as a far-seeing economist, ventured the prediction that silver was in the process of depreciation. Another influence tending to powerfully affect the status of silver in 1873 was due to the circumstance that, subsequent to 1868–'69, the India Council greatly increased the sale of their bills (i. e., drawn on India and payable in silver) on the London market, and so virtually increased the stock of marketable silver at that point to the extent of from $20,000,000 to $30,000,000 annually, in excess of what it had been for the years immediately previous.*

---

* The Government of India is under obligation to pay annually in England certain fixed charges in gold, the same being in the nature of reimbursements —principal or interest—to England for loans on account of public works in India, receipts from railroads belonging to the British Government, pensions chargeable to India, etc. India being exclusively a silver-using country, pays

The German "sales" theory being thus untenable, another hypothesis has found wide acceptation—namely, that, notwithstanding any absolute or comparative increase in the supply of silver during recent years, its decline in price and the economic disturbances which are alleged to have followed, would not have occurred, had it not been for the "demonetization" or the general discrediting of this metal for use as money; which has been contingent on the adoption of gold as the sole monetary standard and as a larger instrumentality of exchange by several of the most important commercial countries—notably Germany and the United States; or, as a leading American statesman has expressed it, "but for the striking down of one half of the world's coinage," and "compelling gold to do the work of both gold and silver." But here, also, the evidence in confirmation of this hypothesis is exceedingly unsatisfactory or wholly lacking. If by demonetization is meant that there has been less of silver in use and circulation as money, absolutely or comparatively, throughout the world since 1873 than formerly; or that the people of any country have been inhibited to their disadvantage in its use; or that, in consequence of any restrictions on its use for coinage, production and trade have decreased, and the prices of commodities and wages have fallen—the assumptions are not warranted, and the term demonetization is meaningless. The world's average annual production of silver since 1873 has been greater than ever before. Between 1883 and 1887, inclusive, the aggregate product—measured in dollars of 412½ grains each—has been in excess of $600,000,000, and most of it has passed

---

its taxes and railroad freights and fares, etc., exclusively in silver; and in liquidation of its foreign monetary obligations, silver is remitted to London in the form of bills (exchange) payable in the silver currency of India, namely, rupees, which are drawn by the India Council, or the Government of India residing in London. It must be obvious that to just the amount of such council bills or drafts as are sold in London, to just that same extent the exportation of silver for business purposes is supplemented or made unnecessary.

into circulation as coin, or lies piled up in national depositories awaiting any popular demand for its employment; *
and the greater number of the daily transactions of trade
continue to be settled by the use of silver, just as formerly.
"If you take," says Mr. Robert Giffen, in his testimony before the British Gold and Silver Commission, 1886, "the
fifteen years from 1870, and compare them with the fifteen
years before, you will find that the practical diminution for
the demand for silver in France, and I suppose it has been
the same in other Latin countries, has not been sensible at
all." The continually increasing importation of silver into
India, China, Burmah, and Japan is conclusive also as to
the absence of any restrictions on the use of this metal for
coinage purposes in these countries.† In short, all that is
now claimed by one of the most distinguished economists
who inclines to the view that the monetary use of silver has
been artificially restricted, is that its employment for coinage might possibly have been greater if it had not been for
the action of the Latin Convention countries.‡ But it is

---

* The number of standard silver dollars in the United States in 1879, the
year of the redemption of specie payments by the Federal Government, was
reported at 35,801,000. The number coined between 1878 and 1888, inclusive,
was 299,424,790, and of these 249,979,440 were in the national Treasury on
November 1, 1888. Of this number, however, 229,783,152 were held for the
redemption of a like amount of silver certificates, which circulate as currency.
The Mint estimate of the total amount of silver coin in the United States, June
1, 1888 (dollars and subsidiary coin), was $376,115,166. Of a coinage of
34,484,673 standard silver dollars during the year 1888, 34,445,517 rested at
the end of the year in the vaults of the Treasury, and only 39,156 passed into
the hands of the people.

† During the fifteen years from 1855 to 1870 the annual demand of India
for silver was very nearly £10,000,000. This period embraced the cotton
famine. From 1872 to 1875, just before the drop in silver, the amount that
India annually received was £3,000,000. From 1875 to 1880 it was £7,000,-
000 ; from 1880–'85, £6,000,000 ; and for 1885, £7,108,000.

‡ "The suspension of the free coinage of silver by the Latin Union operated not to diminish the actual employment for silver as compared with what
had been in existence before 1872, but a possible employment which might
have come into existence if the law had not changed." (*See testimony of* Mr.
Robert Giffen, *British Gold and Silver Commission, First Report*, p. 28.)

obvious that this opinion must be necessarily a matter of conjecture.

Again, the world has never made so great progress in respect to all things material in any equal number of years as it has during those which have elapsed since silver began to decline in price in 1873. Never before in any corresponding period of time has labor been so productive; never has the volume of trade and commerce been greater; never has wealth more rapidly accumulated; never has there been so much abundance for distribution on so favorable terms to the masses; never, finally, would an ounce of silver exchange for so much of sugar, wheat, wool, iron, copper, coal, or of most other commodities, as at present. If the fall in the price of all desirable commodities has been an evil, as not a few seem to believe, it can not be conclusively proved, in respect to even one article, that any such fall has been *extensively* due to any decline in the value of silver or any appreciation of gold.

On the other hand, a more rational explanation of the decline since 1873 in the value of silver, and one which the logic of subsequent events is substantiating, would appear to be as follows : Since 1860 * the annual product of silver has been rapidly increasing—i. e., from $40,800,000 in 1860 to $51,900,000 in 1865; $60,000,000 in 1871; $69,000,000 in 1875; $95,000,000 in 1880; $122,000,000 in 1885; and $135,449,000 † in 1887. The continued increase in the production of silver in the United States since 1861 is very noteworthy. " The total production of that year was $2,000,-000, or 1,546,910 fine ounces. In 1873 it had reached $35,750,000, or 27,651,017 fine ounces. Since that date the value of bullion has been steadily declining (i. e., from an average of $60\frac{5}{16}$ in 1872 to $42\frac{3}{8}$ in 1888), but that has in no

---

* The average annual production of silver, according to M. Soetbeer, was $22,474,000 from 1811-'20; $18,140,000, 1820-'31; $24,788,000, 1831-'40; and $35,118,000, 1841-'50.

† Report of Director of the United States Mint, 1888.

measure checked the expansion in production. Each succeeding twelve months has registered further growth, until
in 1888 the total reached over $59,000,000, or 45,783,632
fine ounces. Here, then, is an increase of production of
over sixty-five per cent in the face of a decline in price of
nearly twenty-nine per cent.*

Previous to 1871–'72 neither France nor the Latin Convention states of Europe had been large consumers of silver.
In fact, from about 1850 to 1864, France, instead of being
a consumer, was really a seller of silver, and during that
period disposed of about £75,000,000 ($375,000,000). After
1864 the tide turned, and France began to take back silver,
but up to 1873–'74 her imports had by no means balanced
her previous exports. M. Victor Bonnet, writing in 1873
("Revue des Deux Mondes"), after the greater part of the
French indemnity had been paid, estimated the quantity of
specie remaining in the possession of the French people at
6,000,000,000 francs ($1,200,000,000). China, also, which
previous to 1864 had been a silver-importing country, after
1864, and until up to about the time of the drop in silver,
became a silver-exporting country.† From 1853 to 1873,
inclusive, the United States furthermore coined but very
little silver, and during this whole period drew on the world's
supply of silver for coinage purposes to an extent (measured
in dollars) of only $57,137,000; while, during her long
period of suspension of specie payments, subsequent to 1861,
her stock of silver coin entirely disappeared from circulation, and in great part was doubtless added to the supply of
other countries.

Under such circumstances, which were perfectly well
known to the custodians and dealers in silver everywhere,
Germany entered the world's market as a seller of silver.
The amount offered at first was absolutely very small and

---

* "New York Financial Chronicle," March 2, 1889.

† Testimony of Mr. Robert Giffen, "First Report of the British Gold and
Silver Commission," p. 29.

comparatively insignificant, but it nevertheless probably constituted a supply in excess of any current demand. As the states of Europe and the United States could not at once increase their consumption and import of the products of Asia, Africa, and South America, and so increase their sales (exports) of silver, and, as the price which the surplus of any commodity forced for sale will command determines the price of the whole stock of such commodity, the price of the whole stock of silver bullion naturally began to decline. The general policy of Germany respecting the use of silver for coinage, which was subsequently favored and adopted by Sweden, Norway, Denmark, and Holland, with the concurrent suspension by the states of the Latin Union of the free coinage of the silver five-franc pieces, also unquestionably favored and intensified the decline in the price of silver thus inaugurated, by creating an apprehension (or scare) among the bullion-dealers as to what might further happen.

The continued decline in the value of silver in more recent years may also be rationally referred to a continuance of the same influences. The world's annual product of silver has continued to increase, from $95,000,000 in 1880 to $135,000,000 in 1887, or to an aggregate of over $900,000,000 for the included period. No one knows what is to be the product of silver in the future; but it is reasonable to believe that, if the price of silver were to advance materially, its product would be largely augmented. Recent reports made under the auspices of the Mexican Secretary of the Interior, and published in the " Mexican Economist " (1886), claim that the cost of working the argentiferous lead-ores of Mexico, which " exist in prodigious abundance," has been greatly reduced within recent years, and that under a better system of taxation and with an adequate supply of capital the annual product of the silver-mines of Mexico could be quickly doubled and even trebled.* Furthermore, an aver-

---

* The silver production of Mexico, as a matter of fact, is rapidly increas-

age decrease of at least thirty per cent in the prices of the
commodities that represent the great bulk of the world's
production and consumption (comparing the data of 1885–
'86 with those of 1867–'77) has in itself been equivalent to
largely or entirely supplementing any increased demand for
the use of silver and gold as money, consequent upon any
increase in the volume of the world's business during the
same period. The constantly increasing tendency of the
age to use less and less coin in the transaction of business, and the continued invention and successful application
of numerous and unprecedented devices for economizing
the use of metallic money, must at the same time have been
equivalent to a constant comparative increase in the supply
of precious metals for coinage purposes. Still another factor
exercising a disturbing influence on the price of silver, and
preventing its price recovery, undoubtedly grows out of the
fiscal relations of Great Britain with India. The regular
annual sales at London of India Council bills—the character
of which has been heretofore explained (see page 229)—are
in the nature of forced sales of silver, and at present average about $45,000,000 per annum. How much effect these
sales, at the point where the silver-bullion trade of the world
centers, have had in depressing the market price of silver,
is undetermined; but that it has not been unimportant can
not well be doubted.

Attention is next asked to the character of the economic
disturbances which have resulted from the change since 1873
in the relative values of gold and silver. Omitting from
consideration the extreme views on this subject, in which
silver seems to be regarded in the sense of a personality that
has been unjustly and designedly " outlawed " and deprived
of some ancient prerogative, the disturbances in question
are the same in character as have always accompanied the

---

ing— i. e., from a product of $27,258,000 in 1884 to $33,000,000 in 1886 and
$37,570,000 in 1887.

use of a depreciated, fluctuating currency, with this additional and novel peculiarity—namely, that while heretofore
depreciation of currency has been due to the forced issue of
redundant and irredeemable paper money or debased coin,
and has been local in its influence, the present experience
is due to a depreciation in the value of one of the precious
metals with reference to the other, and extends to many
countries in very different degrees. Let us particularize
these disturbances, and see how serious or otherwise have
been their resulting influence.

In the United States all the evil which has thus far been
experienced has been solely from apprehensions of evil in
the future, which in turn have been occasioned by the circumstance that the United States, in harmony with her
protective policy, buys from the owners of the (present)
most productive and cheaply worked silver-mines in the
world, silver bullion for coinage to the value of $2,000,000
monthly, irrespective of any current demand or necessity
for such coinage on the part of her own people. In the
coinage system of Great Britain the function of silver remains as it has for a long period, almost as unimportant as
that of copper. In Germany, " although the imperial mark
is now everywhere recognized as the standard, all Germans,
whether they live in Bavaria, Prussia, or Hanover, are able
to sell their commodities with the consciousness that the
' marks ' they receive in payment for them are good money,
with the same purchasing power, whether paid out as silver
thalers or as gold crowns." *

In the other states of Europe, the currencies of which
are on a specie-paying basis, the situation is substantially
the same as in Germany. In exclusively silver-using countries, like India and Mexico, the decline in the value of
silver has not appreciably affected its purchasing power in

---

* Speech of Mr. H. H. Gibbs, a director of the Bank of England, before
the Birmingham (England) Chamber of Commerce, 1886.

respect to all domestic products and services; but the silver of such countries will not exchange for the same amount of gold as formerly, and it might be supposed that, owing to this change in the relative value of the two metals, the silver of India, Mexico, and other like countries would purchase correspondingly less of the commodities of foreign countries which are produced and sold on a gold basis. But the people of such countries have not thus far been sensible of any losses to themselves thereby accruing, for the reason that the gold prices of such foreign commodities as they are in the habit of buying have declined in a greater ratio since 1873 than has the silver which constitutes their standard of prices—a condition of things which Don Francisco Bulnes, the distinguished Mexican economist, in a recent official report, has exemplified to his countrymen by the following felicitous illustration :

"Two merchants, named Mexico and Foreigner, exchange annually cotton shirtings for silver dollars : Mexico delivers $100, and receives from Foreigner one hundred pieces of cotton shirting. By the depreciation of silver, it results that Foreigner only wishes to accept the Mexican dollar for eighty-six cents for each one, but gives in exchange each piece of cotton shirting for sixty-six cents. Which of the two will be the loser?" * Nevertheless, if silver had maintained its former relative value to gold, the benefit accruing to silver-using nations from the decline in the prices of commodities through improvements in their production and distribution might have been greater; but, if so, the loss does not appear to have been made by them a cause of complaint.

All the evidence seems to indicate that the economic disturbances contingent on the decline in the value of silver,

---

* In a subsequent part of his report M. Bulnes shows that, if it is certain that Mexican silver is worth less than formerly in foreign markets on exchange, its cost of production has declined to an extent that fully compensates for any such depreciation.

apart from what have been due to the apprehension of evil
(or scare), have thus far been almost exclusively confined to
the trade or financial intercourse between the gold-standard
and the silver-standard nations, or between the states of
Western Europe and the United States, and the nations of
the Eastern hemisphere and of Central and South America;
and that the manifestations of these disturbances have been
greatest in England and Holland, where the foreign trade
of the silver-using countries largely centers.   And it seems
further to be admitted that these disturbances have not
resulted so much from a fall in the value of silver *per se* as
from the uncertainties or fluctuations in its price, or, as
commonly expressed, in the rates of exchange—an eminent
merchant of Manchester, England, largely engaged in trade
with India and the East, being reported as saying, at the
meeting of the British Association (September, 1887), that
with the present excellent telegraph service, and a level
(non-fluctuating) monetary basis, exchange in India would
be as steady as in New York.   In all this there is, however,
nothing unprecedented or in the nature of the unexpected;
nothing which the world has not heretofore repeatedly experienced.   For it is to be remembered that fluctuations in
exchange are the invariable accompaniment of trade with
nations using a depreciated and fluctuating currency; and
that there is no good reason for supposing that the disturbances which have characterized the trade of Europe with
India and the East during recent years, from fluctuations
in the price of silver, have been any different in kind than,
or as great in degree as, those which characterized the trade
of Europe with the United States from 1861 to 1879, or
which characterize to-day the trade of the outside world
with Russia, whose currency is depreciated and fluctuating.
Moreover, the difficulties arising from the uncertainties of
exchange, at least between England and India, appear to
have been greatly exaggerated.   Mr. Lord, a director of
the Manchester (England) Chamber of Commerce, testified

before the Commission on the Depression of Trade, in 1886, that, "so far as India was concerned, it is not necessary to run any risk at all" from the uncertainties of exchange. Mr. Bythell (representing the Bombay Chamber of Commerce) testified before the same commission: "He [Mr. Gibbs] says that commerce with India is paralyzed. I deny the assertion. There is no difficulty in negotiating any transaction for shipping goods to India, and in securing exchange." It is also generally recognized that, owing to telegraph correspondence and rapid steam communication, the risk in transacting business between different countries, contingent on fluctuations in exchange, is being gradually eliminated, inasmuch as sales and purchases, or remittances, and all the incidents of exchange, freights, commission, etc., can be practically arranged between the operators at one and the same time.*

But whatever may have been the disturbances resulting from fluctuations in rates of exchange between Great Britain and the silver-using countries (of which India is the chief), contingent on the fluctuations in recent years in the price of silver, these disturbances do not appear to have had any effect up to 1884–'85 in checking the volume of British trade with Eastern nations, or in changing the relations of exports and imports that previously existed. In fact, there has been an enormous expansion of British trade with such countries as use a silver currency, since the fall in the price of silver commenced. Thus, from returns officially presented to the British Gold and Silver Commission, 1886, it was established that the trade of Great Britain with India since 1874 had relatively grown faster than with any for-

---

* "If trade can go on profitably between countries having an inconvertible paper of a widely fluctuating kind and the rest of the world, *a fortiori*, it can go on between gold and silver countries. The exchange is a hindrance and obstacle, as many other things are hindrances and obstacles, but it is nothing more. . . . Such difficulties are the ordinary incidence of trade and life, and will be dealt with like other difficulties of a far more serious kind by those concerned."—*London Times, September* 14, 1886.

eign country, "except the United States and perhaps Holland." Assuming 100 to represent the trade between the two countries in 1874–'75, the imports from the United Kingdom into India rose from 100 to 154 in 1884–'85, and the exports from India to the United Kingdom from 100 to 149.

Much also has been said respecting the serious injury which the export trade in cotton manufactures from England to India has sustained in recent years in consequence of the " dislocation " of the money of England's Indian customers. But the facts do not bear out such statements. Taking the number 100 as representing the condition of the cotton-fabric export trade of England with India in 1874, the numbers for 1886 were, respectively, 134 for quantity and 96 for value; and this change in value, as was testified to before the Gold and Silver Commission, has " occurred since 1883 "; or was coincident with a recognized increase at that date in the manufacturing capacity of the cotton-factories of Europe and the United States, greatly in excess of any former period.*

In like manner the official returns also show that while India during recent years has largely increased her exports of domestic cotton fabrics—cloth and yarn—to China and Java, the exports of like products from England to these same countries from 1875 to 1884–'85—the period covering the greatest decline in the price of silver (or of the fall in ex-

---

* In 1870 the British export of cotton piece-goods to India was returned at 923,000,000 yards, representing 28·4 per cent of the entire trade of the United Kingdom with India. In 1884 the export of these same goods was 1,791,000,-000 yards, or 40·6 per cent of the entire trade. In respect to cotton yarns the British exports to India for 1870 were 31,000,000 pounds, or 16·5 per cent of the total exports; and in 1884, 49,000,000 pounds, or 18·1 per cent of the total exports. The bulk of the trade of Great Britain is with gold-using countries; and yet, while the trade of India with Great Britain was 8·3 per cent of the whole trade of the kingdom in 1870, it constituted in 1883 as much as 9·9 per cent of the whole trade.—*Testimony before the Gold and Silver Commission of* Mr. HENRY WATERFIELD, *Financial Secretary of the India Office, London.* (See First Report of the Commission, pp. 122, 123.)

change)—also continually increased; or for 1884 were four-teen per cent in the case of piece-goods, and thirty-two per cent in yarn, greater in the aggregate than they were in 1875. Subsequent to 1884–'85 British foreign trade in respect to cotton fabrications was for a time less favorable; but for the year 1888, the export of cloths was 5,038,469,400 yards (the largest on record), and of yarns, 255,820,200 pounds, which amount has been only twice exceeded in previous years—1883 and 1884. Comparing the distribution of 1888 with 1887, India and China increased their purchases of British cotton fabrics in 1888 to the extent of 117,500,000 yards, and of yarns to the extent of 15,500,000 pounds.

It is undoubtedly true that the Government of India, in selling its remittances in silver—India Council bills—to cover its liabilities in England, for a less price in gold than formerly, constantly experiences a degree of financial em-barrassment and perhaps loss. But, on the other hand, it is admitted that the condition of India has never been more prosperous and encouraging than at present.

Another pertinent example of the slight effect the change in the relative values of gold and silver has had upon the volume of the international trade of exclusively silver-using countries, and one not in any way connected with the trade of Europe or India, is afforded by the recent trade ex-periences of Mexico. This country has almost exclusively a silver currency; and the fluctuations in the price of silver since 1873—Mexican exchange having varied in New York in recent years from 114 to 140 * would soom noocssarily to have been a disturbing factor of no little importance in the trade between the United States and Mexico. But the official statistics of the trade between the two countries since 1873 (notoriously undervalued) fail to show that any serious interruption has occurred; but, on the contrary, that

* That is, one hundred and forty Mexican dollars to one hundred dollars of the United States gold standard.

the total volume of trade—exports and imports—continually increases.

In recent years there has been a notable increase in the cotton-manufacturing industry of India—i. e., from eighteen factories, with 450,156 spindles and 4,972 looms in 1873, to seventy factories, with 1,698,000 spindles and 14,635 looms in 1884 ; and the cause of this increase, which is enabling India to compete (as never before) * with Lancashire (England) in supplying cotton yarn and fabrics to the Indian and other Eastern markets, and to the alleged serious detriment of English interests, is popularly believed and asserted to have been occasioned mainly by the decline and fluctuations in the price of silver.

There has been much discussion on this subject in England and India, and much disagreement in opinion among investigators; but a majority of the Board of Directors of the Manchester (England) Chamber of Commerce after an exhaustive inquiry, has reported, that the main cause that has favored the rapid increase of mills in India, and enabled them to a great extent to supply China and Japan with yarns, which formerly were shipped from Lancashire, is their geographical position, which places them in close proximity to the cotton-fields on the one hand, and to the consuming markets on the other. The net advantage to the Indian spinner from these circumstances, over his competitor in England, after allowing for his extra outlay for machinery, and consequently enhanced interest and depreciation, as well as greater expenditure in such items as imported coals, stores, etc., was estimated by the committee as equal to at least $\frac{3}{4}d.$ per pound on the portion of their output that is shipped to China and Japan, and $1\frac{3}{16}d.$ to $\frac{7}{8}d.$ per pound on what is consumed in India itself.† Other circum-

---

* The exports of cotton yarn from India have risen from about 7,000,000 pounds in 1877 to 113,000,000 in 1887.

† A minority of the board, on the other hand, came to the conclusion that the principal cause which has enabled Bombay spinners to supersede those of

stances, such as cheaper labor and longer factory hours, may have also favored the Indian manufacturers; but these differences as respects the condition of labor in England and India have existed from time immemorial; and the real novelty of the present situation is, that India, with railroads and factories, and the advantage of cheap ocean freights, is now emancipating herself from chronic sluggishness and beginning to participate in the world's progress; and under English auspices, and largely with English capital, is, for the first time, extensively utilizing her geographical advantages and her cheap and abundant labor in connection with labor-saving machinery. And it is to be further noted that her progress in cotton manufacturing exhibited itself unmistakably some years before the commencement of the decline in silver; that the first shipment of cotton yarns from India to China, in competition with yarns of English make, was in 1866, and that between 1865 and 1873 the increase in the number of cotton-spindles in India was in excess of fifty-seven per cent.*

Lancashire in exporting yarn to China and Japan is the great fall in Eastern exchange since 1873. The geographical advantage is admitted, but that, it is pointed out, has been constantly decreasing, while the power to compete with Lancashire has been increasing.

*" The truth is, that the Bombay cotton-spinners have by their energy and enterprise created a trade with China that had no existence before. India can not compete with Lancashire in the finer counts, and she can not come near us for spinning counts, for which our cotton is suitable. Lancashire is not, as Lancashire imagined, losing ground in China; only Bombay has, owing to the energy of her manufacturers, gained ground immensely. The cotton grows at her door, labor is cheap here, and freights to China have been reduced by one half since 1885."—*Speech of* Mr. Cotton, *before the Manchester Chamber of Commerce.*

In connection with this subject, the following extract from the record of the examination of Mr. H. Waterfield, Financial Secretary of the India Office, London, before the British Trade and Silver Commission (February, 1887), is important:

Question (Sir T. Farrer). " So that, while India has been doing much more, Lancashire has been doing more than she did before ? "

Answer. " Yes."

Q. " Then I will ask you, do the figures [submitted] justify the statement

Again, it is a popular idea that the steadily increasing supply to the markets of the world during recent years of Indian wheat, the product of low-priced labor—seriously affecting, through its competition, the prices and profits alike of the agriculturists of the United States and of Europe—has been in some way occasioned by the change in the relative values or purchasing powers of gold and silver, consequent on the "demonetization" of the latter metal. To all entertaining this idea the summary of evidence brought out by the British Gold and Silver Commission in the course of their investigations prosecuted and previously presented (see page 169) is worthy of attention.

Evidence was also submitted to the British Trade Depression Commission in 1866 to the effect that the increase of the acreage under wheat in India "exactly agrees with the development of the Indian railways," and that, "when more railways are made in India, a very much larger wheat production will immediately follow." *

---

that the present state of things—that is, the fall in exchange—is causing the gradual transfer of the yarn-trade of China to India ; that the exports from England have steadily declined since the fall of silver commenced, while those from India have enormously increased ? "

A. " The increase of the imports from India may, indeed, be termed enormous ; but it is not correct to say that the exports from England have steadily declined since the fall of silver commenced ; and I think that the fall in exchange is not the cause of the improvement in the Indian trade."

Q. " At any rate, you would not see in these figures any reason for protecting Lancashire against India by a radical alteration of our currency system ? "

A. " No ; I should think it as objectionable as allowing any protection of India against Lancashire."

* On this subject, the following testimony was submitted to the British Commission on the Depression of Trade, 1886 (" Third Report," pp. 82 and 83), by Mr. W. J. Harris, who is recognized as an authority in England on agricultural subjects :

" Our Indian Empire seems able to extend its corn-growing industry to almost any extent, and to produce more cheaply than any other country in the world. I am aware that Sir James Caird gave a somewhat different evidence on this question, but I think that neither Mr. Giffen nor Sir James Caird have taken sufficiently into account one or two things in their statistical computa-

Of late years the Government of India has published an annual record of the prices of food-grains and salt in about seventy districts, selected as typical of the different parts of each province. An analysis of the data thus supplied (although imperfect) has led the London "Economist" * to the following conclusions:

"That whereas in 1872 the rupee exchanged for 35¾ pounds of wheat, in 1885 it could command in exchange about 39 pounds of wheat. In the interval, therefore, the purchasing power of the rupee measured in wheat increased by about ten per cent. Since then, however, there has been a distinct change. In 1885 the rupee could purchase on an average no more than 35 pounds of wheat, and in 1886 it would exchange for no more than about 30 pounds. Since 1884, therefore, the value of the rupee in exchange for wheat in India appears to have fallen about twenty-five per cent, and it is obvious that such a decline invalidates much that has been written to prove that the fall in the price of silver has operated as a bounty upon the export of wheat

---

tion. They both maintain that the population of India is too large, or is getting too large, for the means of production. They do not seem to remember that every unit of population in India consumes about a fifth part of what the unit of population in the United States does. It is a comparison between India and the United States. Both Sir James Caird and Mr. Giffen admit that the capabilities of the United States are very enormous, but they think that the capabilities of India are comparatively very small. I differ from them, and I will give my reasons. If we follow (on the maps of India) the course of the railways which have been made for some time, you will find that the acreage under wheat exactly agrees with the development of those railways; and it appears to me that, when more railways are made in India, a very much larger wheat production will immediately follow. I have made several inquiries from the principal merchants who do business with India, and who have agents at many central points, and they all agree that the wheat production in India is not nearly developed yet. The population is not encroaching on the means of subsistence so much as the mere statistician would argue, because he does not take into account the habits of the people; and I believe that the United States population, in consequence of the habits of its people, is encroaching just as fast on their means of subsistence as are the people of India. There is a large acreage in India that is not fully cultivated with anything at the present time, and, where it is, it is very imperfectly cultivated, and the prices of produce are exceeding low in places remote from railway communication. Agriculture is very rude; they have very little machinery. The system might be greatly improved, and the produce thereby increased."

* London "Economist," June 30, 1888.

from India. The argument has been that, owing to the fall in silver, the gold which the seller of Indian wheat here gets for his produce is worth twenty-five per cent more rupees than before, and that, as the rupee commands in India the same amount of wheat it formerly did, the fall in silver is practically equivalent to a bounty of twenty-five per cent upon shipments hither. But if the purchasing power of the rupee, instead of remaining unchanged, has fallen twenty-five per cent, as the official record of prices would seem to show, then obviously this argument and the theories that have been based upon it fall to the ground."

A comparison of the price of wheat measured in gold with its price measured in silver, "which may be done in a rough way by comparing our (London) 'Gazette' average with the Indian average, shows that, while gold has slightly gained in purchasing power, the rupee has decidedly lost, and the inference is that it is to the diminished purchasing power of the rupee, and not to a change in the value of wheat, that the rise in the Indian price (from 2·6 rupees in 1885 to 3·7 rupees in 1887) was due. Neither in the price of rice nor of salt was there any movement corresponding to that in wheat. Of both of these products the rupee commanded on the average larger quantities than in 1885."

The evidence, therefore, warrants the belief that the fall in recent years in the price of Indian wheat, and its consequent appearance as an important element of supply in European markets, is to be accounted for mainly by changes in the conditions of its production and supply, and not by any changes in the relative values of gold and silver; and further, that if every measure for extending the monetary use of silver, which has been proposed, should be carried out to the fullest extent, it would produce no sensible influence in restraining the Indian ryot from competing with American and European agriculturists in the sale of wheat in the world's markets.

The whole subject of the disturbing influence of the decline in the value of silver on the trade between gold and silver using countries is complicated and difficult of analysis, and the opinions of persons practically interested in such trade are not harmonious; but it is difficult to see how one can investigate the subject, with the light of the experience which the years that have elapsed since 1873 has contributed, without coming to the conclusion that the seriousness of the disturbances has been greatly exaggerated, and that the expediency of attempting to provide remedies by legislation for such as may be acknowledged to exist—if legislation were practical—is very doubtful.

In forming an opinion in respect to this problem, it is important to steadily keep in mind the fact that international trade is trade in commodities, and not in money; and that the precious metals come in only for the settlement of balances. In fact, all such exchanges are, to within a very minute fraction, the result of an organized and elaborate system of barter, and the principle of barter prevails in them, and determines to a great extent the methods employed. The trade between England and India is an exchange of service for service. Its character would not be altered if India should adopt the gold standard to-morrow, or if she should, like Russia, adopt an irredeemable paper currency, or, like China, buy and sell by weight instead of tale. Will India give more wheat for a given amount of cloth because she uses silver instead of gold in her internal trade? Will England give less of cloth for a given amount of wheat because she keeps her accounts in pounds, shillings, and pence instead of in rupees? Unless all the postulates of political economy are false—unless we are entirely mistaken in supposing that men in their individual capacity, and hence in their aggregate capacity as nations, are seeking the most satisfaction with the least labor, we must assume that India, England, and America produce and sell their goods to one another for the most they can get in other goods, regardless of the kind of money that their neighbors use or that they themselves use. A silver currency does not give any additional strength to a Hindoo ryot, nor does it increase the fertility of his soil, or add to the number of inches of his rainfall. Nor does a gold currency detract in any way from the capability and resources of his rival, the

American farmer. Nor does the difference in their respective currencies affect the judgment of the buyer of wheat
in Liverpool. Is any single factor in the elements of production and transportation, by which alone the terms of
competition are settled, changed by the local currencies of
the several countries, or the mutations thereof? Surely no
mutations were ever more sudden or violent than those of
the currency of the United States during the late war.
They were not without their effects; but the effects were
not of a kind to change the terms of competition in international trade.*

---

* The fallacy of the assertion, so frequently made to the agriculturists of
England and the United States, that the fall in the gold price of silver has
acted as a bounty to the Indian wheat-producer, and unnaturally driven down
the price of wheat to the great injury of the English and American wheat-pro-
ducers, has also been admirably exposed by Mr. George W. Medley in one of
the recent "leaflets" published by the Cobden Club. The argument of those
who maintain the existence and influence of a bounty may be stated as follows: They say, and truly, that some fifteen years ago the pound sterling
could buy 10 silver rupees in India, which were worth 2s. each; whereas now
it can buy 14½ rupees, which are, consequently, worth now only about 1s.
4½d. They say further, and also truly, that prices in India in silver, being
about the same as at the former period, it follows that a pound sterling laid
out there in wheat now buys forty-five per cent more thereof than it did; and
hence it is argued that the Indian producer has been enabled to undersell the
English grower in the home market, and to bring about the fall in wheat from
40s. to 30s.; and this difference of 10s. per quarter, it is claimed, constitutes
a bounty on the export of Indian wheat to England.

To this Mr. Medley replies: "There never was a greater delusion. The
fallacy lies in reckoning the pound sterling in 1873 and in 1889 as the same
thing. Physically speaking, this is true, for the coin is of the same weight
and fineness in gold. Economically speaking, it is not the same thing, for a
pound sterling in 1889 represents a greater quantity of human effort than it
did in 1873. To obtain a pound sterling in 1873 a quantity in other commodities had to be given for it, which may be represented by the figure 100. In
1889, owing to the fall in prices, the quantity to be given in exchange is, say,
145. If the holder of the pound sterling can now get forty-five per cent more
wheat for it than he did in 1873, he at the same time has to give forty-five per
cent more of other commodities in order to get it, the same quantity of Indian
wheat exchanging for the same quantity of English commodities whatever year
be taken. There is no more bounty or bonus on the export of Indian wheat
to England than there is on the export of English commodities to India."

It may be that the Indian wheat-grower has been enabled by the decline in silver to get labor for less wages than before, and has thus gained an advantage over his competitors in America and Australia; but the evidence is all to the effect that wages generally in India in recent years have advanced and not declined.* But the terms of international competition are not altered by any division of the joint product of labor and capital in one of the competing countries. The person that has the most of a grievance growing out of the present state of the wheat-trade is the American farmer, who is restricted from buying in the same market in which he sells his surplus wheat to as good advantage as his competitors; but this is not due to any change in the value of silver, but to the fiscal policy of his own Government.

In Holland the disturbances assumed to have been occasioned by the decline in the value of silver have attracted public attention to an even greater degree than in England. But even here the disturbances have been mainly restricted to the commercial and financial relations of Holland with her East Indian colonies, Java, Sumatra, and other islands, and have been specially occasioned by the extraordinary fall in recent years in the prices of the principal exports of these islands, namely, sugar, and coffee. But no com-

---

* " It may be that prices of commodities in India have not risen to correspond with the fall in silver. If such is the case, then the producer in India of exported products will win until the equilibrium is restored—that is, he will win so long as the process is going on. On the other hand, however, the Indian consumer of imported commodities will lose, for he buys at a gold price, and has to pay with depreciated rupees. These two parties do not win and lose to each other; but they present the two opposite facets of the combined effect of the fall in silver on India. Therefore, whatever the Indian wheat-producer wins, he wins, not from his European customer nor from his American or Russian competitor, but at the expense of his Indian neighbor, and, if there was a desire to put an end to the existing state of things, the way to do it would be to hasten the movement of silver to the East, so as to complete the transition and raise the prices in India as soon as possible."—Prof. Sumner.

mercial fact is capable of more complete demonstration than that the fall in the price of these great staples has been in no way contingent upon any change in the value of silver.*

The idea of disturbance in connection with the decline in the value of silver has been and is pre-eminently connected with an annunciation of two propositions:—

First, that the almost universal decline in the prices of the world's staple commodities since 1873 has been occasioned by the fall in the price of silver; and, second, that a decline of prices is an evil. The first of these propositions rests upon an assumption which can not be verified by any conclusive evidence whatever; and, as for the second, if the fall of prices has been mainly due, as has been demonstrated, to natural and permanent causes, namely, the increased power of mankind in the work of production and distribution, then the result, by creating a greater abundance of all good things, and bringing a larger amount of the same within the reach of the masses for consumption and enjoyment, has been one of the greatest of blessings. All *permanent* reductions of the prices of the great staple products which are necessary for the world's existence and comfort, are furthermore indications that a greater abundance, with less and less toil or effort, has come to all those who depend upon each day's labor to meet each day's needs; and he who attempts to check or counteract such a reduction of prices is

---

* " During the last five years Java has been subject to the most fearful natural calamities. They have had a cattle-plague which destroyed almost the whole cattle in parts of the island; they have had cholera; they have had earthquakes of an unprecedented character; and they have had further an extraordinary fall in the values of their principal exports, which are sugar and coffee, owing, in the first place, to the competition of beet-root sugar in Europe, and, in the second place, to the fact that South America has been able to export coffee more favorably than Java; and to this extent we can trace a loss of £5,000,000 annually in these two articles. That has been the result in the last five years of natural causes, without any question of currency at all."—*Testimony of* MR. PAUL F. TIDMAN, *East India merchant. First Report of the British Gold and Silver Commission,* p. 142, 1886.

opposed to increasing civilization and an enemy of the poor. The question of true importance with every one is, not what amount of money, but what amount of useful things, can be obtained in exchange for what is sold.

Any discussion of the economic disturbances resulting from changes in the relative values of the precious metals would be incomplete that failed to point out how the events that originated the so-called " bimetallic " controversy were the natural outcome of the revolutionary changes in the methods of production and distribution that have occurred in recent years in all countries in proportion to their advance in civilization.

It is not easy to imagine that any person of ordinary intelligence can seriously believe that the enactment of laws looking to the recognition of gold as the single standard of value, thereby effecting what is called the demonetization of silver, could ever have resulted from mere whim or caprice, or with a view of occasioning either domestic or international economic disturbance. There was a time when nations, with the expectation of receiving benefit, did adopt policies and enact laws with the undisguised and sole intent of injuring the industry and commerce of neighbors with whom they were at peace ; but happily such days have long past. And the inference is, therefore, fully warranted that whatever steps have been taken, which have resulted in any territorial restriction of the use of silver as money, have been in consequence of a belief by the parties—nations— thus acting, that such a policy was called for by change in the economic condition of their affairs, and was likely to be to them productive of benefit. And the answer to the pertinent question as to what *benefit*, is simply, that which might be expected to accrue from the using of the best rather than an inferior tool ; or of a money instrumentality adapted to the new rather than to the old conditions of production and distribution.

One needs but to stand for a brief time at the marts of

trade in countries of varied degrees of civilization, to quickly
recognize and understand that the kind of money a country
will have and use, depends upon and will vary with the
extent and variety of its productions, the price of labor, and
the rapidity and magnitude of its exchanges; and investigation will further inform him that when mankind, savage,
semi-civilized, civilized, or enlightened, find out by experimentation what metal or other instrumentality is best adapted
to their wants as a medium of exchange, that metal or instrumentality they will employ; and that statute law can do
little more than recognize and confirm the fact.   In truth,
legislation in respect to money, as is the case in respect to
other things, never originates any new idea; "but merely
enacts that that which has been found beneficial or preju-
dicial in many cases, shall be used, limited, or prohibited in
all similar cases within its jurisdiction."   Thus, in all countries where prices are low, wages small, transactions limited,
and exchanges sluggish, nothing more valuable can be used
as money for effecting the great bulk of the exchanges than
copper; and in countries like Mexico and China, even the
copper coin corresponding to the American "cent," the
English "half-penny," and the French "sou," is often so
disproportionate in point of value to the wants of retail
trade, that in the former country it is made more useful by
being halved and quartered, and in the latter is replaced
with some even cheaper metal, as iron or spelter. The wages
in all such countries do not in general exceed twenty to
twenty-five cents a day, and the sum of such wages, when
represented in money, must be capable of division into as
many parts in order to be exchanged for the many daily
necessities of an individual or a family.   But with wages at
twenty-five cents per day, the use of coined gold would obviously be impracticable.   The equivalent of a day's labor in
gold would be too small to be conveniently handled ; the
equivalent of an hour's labor would be smaller than a pin's
head.   And in a lesser degree would be the inconvenience

of using coined silver for effecting the division of similar small wages.*

In countries of higher civilization, but still of comparatively low prices and limited exchanges (and these last mainly internal or domestic), silver naturally takes the place of copper as the coin medium of exchange and as the standard of value ; and as more than a thousand million people are the inhabitants of such countries, silver, reckoning transactions by number and probably also by amount, is to-day the principal money metal of the world.

On the other hand, in countries of high wages, rapid financial transactions, and extensive foreign commercial relations, the natural tendencies are altogether different, and

---

* In many of the sugar-producing islands of the West Indies, the greatest number of the separate retail purchases at the established stores do not exceed from two to three cents in value. In the island of Trinidad, probably seventy-five per cent of an annual importation of about 22,000,000 pounds of breadstuffs (110,000 barrels) pass into the ownership of the laboring-classes (whose average annual consumption is estimated at thirty-one pounds per head), through purchases for cash of quantities rarely exceeding a pound at any one time.

Corea, a country which until recently has been almost unknown to the civilized world, affords another striking illustration of the principle that the kind of money a people will have and use, if left free to choose, will be determined by the nature of their exchanges, through what may be termed a natural process of evolution, and not by artificial arrangements. Thus Corea has been proved to be a very poor country ; raising little more of any one product than will suffice for home consumption ; and with a very restricted internal trade, owing to small production and the lack of facilities for personal intercommunication and product distribution. To the majority of her people a monthly income equivalent to two or three dollars is represented to be sufficient to meet all their necessities. Yet even under these unfavorable and limited conditions of exchange, money has been found a necessity, and has come into use in Corea, in some unknown manner, in the shape of small metallic coinage—nominally copper, but really a sort of spelter-piece—500 to the dollar. With the opening of the ports of the country, a demand for certain foreign products has been created ; and these, when obtained in exchange for hides and gold-dust, are sold to the people in quantities so small, that only coins of the value and character mentioned can be conveniently used as media of exchange—kerosene, for example, being sold by the half-gill, and matches in bunches of a dozen.

favor the more extensive use of gold for money, without at the same time displacing from their legitimate monetary spheres either copper or silver.*

The metal coinage system of the world is not therefore " mono - metallic," nor " bimetallic," but trimetallic ; and the three metals in the form of coin have been used concurrently throughout the world ever since the historic period, and in all probability will always continue to be so used ; because by no other system that has yet been devised can the varying requirements of trade in respect to instrumentalities of exchange and measures of value be so perfectly satisfied. And the only change in this situation of monetary affairs has been, that gradually and by a process of evolution as natural and inevitable as any occurring in the animal or vegetable kingdom, gold has come to be recognized and demanded as never before in all countries of high civilization, as the best instrumentality for measuring values and effecting exchanges. It has become, in the first place, the money of account in the commercial world and of all international trade ; and any country that proposes to find a foreign market for the surplus products of its labor must employ the very best machinery of trade—railroads, steamships, telegraphs, or money—if it does not propose to place itself at a disadvantage.

In respect to portability, convenience for use, adaptation

---

* " When barter begins to yield place to a money system, gold is not much in request ; the payments are so small as to be best made in silver, or in some cheaper material, such as copper. At a later stage silver is used, and at a later stage still, gold. The saturation point of people's requirements for copper coin is soon reached ; in England, the poorest classes probably handle more copper coins than any other non-trading classes. The upper artisan and lower middle classes have already reached saturation point with regard to silver ; and a further increase in their incomes would lead them to handle more gold, but not more silver. In countries in which there is not much use of bank-notes, the amount of gold which a non-trading person handles increases rapidly with his income, until his payments become large enough to be made generally by checks. Then first is the saturation point for gold reached."—Prof. Alfred Marshall, *Journal of the Royal Statistical Society, December,* 1888.

to domestic and foreign business alike, the balance of advantage for all transactions, above $25 or £5, is also largely on the side of gold considered as a medium of exchange; as will be evident when it is remembered that it required, even before its depreciation, sixteen times more time to count silver in any considerable quantity than an equal value of gold; sixteen times more strength to handle it; sixteen times more packages, casks, or capacity to hold it, and sixteen times more expense to transport it. In other words, in this saving age, when the possibility of extensive business transactions is turning on profits reckoned not in cents but in fractions of cents per yard, per pound, or per bushel, to use silver for large transactions in the place of gold, is a misapplication of at least fifteen sixteenths of a given unit of effort, time, expense, and capacity, when one sixteenth would accomplish the same result.

The natural disinclination of a highly civilized commercial people requiring a large supply of currency to meet the wants of their domestic trade, to use silver directly as an instrumentality for effecting exchanges, is curiously illustrated by the recent monetary experience of the United States, which after having coined from 1878 to 1888, inclusive, 299,424,790 standard silver dollars, was only able at the close of the latter year to report 59,801,350 as in actual circulation; and 249,979,440 in the vaults of its treasury. As against this latter sum, certificates of deposit to the amount of $229,783,152 had been issued and passed into circulation as (paper) currency. During eleven months of the fiscal year 1888–'89, $30,000,000 of silver was coined, not one dollar of which was added in its metal form to the money circulation of the country.

Another factor which has without doubt powerfully influenced public opinion in countries of large and active domestic and foreign trade in favor of gold as the sole monetary standard in preference to silver, has been the advantage which gold seems to possess over silver in the element

of stability of cost of production. The amount of labor involved in the mining or washing for gold has remained
nearly constant for ages; while in the case of silver not only
are new deposits of great richness continually being discovered, but many old mines hitherto unworked and unprofitable by reason of inaccessibility, or by the character of their
ores, have been reopened and rendered profitable by improved facilities for transportation and cheaper processes of
reduction.

Now, it is not asserted that it was exactly these considerations, as thus specified, that influenced Germany in 1873 to
take advantage of the opportunity afforded by the payment
of the French war indemnity* to adopt gold as the standard
of her metallic coinage system — a policy which France
would probably have adopted in 1870, had not war intervened—and that subsequently induced other countries to
follow the example of Germany. But it can not be doubted
that the motive in general which prompted the action of
Germany in 1873, and which to-day enrolls so many of the
best of the world's thinkers, financiers, and merchants, on
the side of gold rather than that of silver in the pending
and so-called bimetallic controversy, has been and is a conviction that the movement in favor of a gold standard, by
highly civilized and great commercial nations, is in conso-
nance with the spirit of the age; that it was a necessity for
the fullest development of production and traffic, and the
same in kind which prompts to the substitution, regardless
of cost, of new machinery for old, if even the minimum of
gain can be thereby effected in the production and distribution of commodities. It may, however, be urged that granting all that may be claimed respecting the superiority of

* " It was from this source that Germany proposed to help herself before it
was too late, and thereby array herself in the rank of commercial states
which, having large transactions, chose gold, not merely as the most stable in
value of the two metals, but as the best medium of exchange for large payments."—PROF. LAUGHLIN, *History of Bimetallism in the United States*, p. 135.

gold over silver as a standard of value and a medium of exchange, there is not a sufficiency of gold to supply the wants of all who may desire to avail themselves of its use for such purposes; and, therefore, any attempt to effect innovations in former monetary conditions would be impolitic because likely to be generally injurious. But this would not be considered as an argument of any weight if pleaded in opposition to the whole or partial disuse of any other form of tool or machine in order that some better tool or machine might be substituted. That in such a case there would be an advantage to those who could afford to have and use the new, and a corresponding disadvantage to those who could not, may be admitted; but what would be the future of the world's progress, if the use of all improvements was to be delayed until all to whom such use would be advantageous could start on terms of equality?

If, therefore, the above premises are correct; if certain of the leading states of the world have given a preference to gold over silver in their trade, and have selected a single in place of a former double standard of value—not by reason of the adoption of any abstract theory or desire for experimentation, but rather through a determination to put themselves in accord with the new conditions of production and distribution that have been the outcome of inventions and discoveries during the last quarter of a century—then the inference is warranted that all attempts to enforce, through any international conference or agreement, any different policy or practice, would be as futile as to attempt to displace through legislation railroads by stage-coaches and steamships by sailing-vessels.

Finally, to comprehend the phenomenal reduction in the prices of the world's great staple commodities, which has taken place in recent years, it is essential to look for and consider more potent and extensive causes than any variation in the volume or relative values of the money metals, great as they may have been.

Mechanical and chemical appliances have been invented, developed, and applied for the production and distribution of commodities within the last quarter of a century, which, prior to that time, had hardly formed the subject of rational speculation. The prime object of all these inventions and discoveries, the great stimulus that led to their realization, was to cheapen cost, or, what is the same thing, reduce prices. And the measure of the value of any new industrial method—invention, discovery, appliance, or development— is the extent to which these results are effected by it. Thus, "the prices of cloth fell when the spinning-wheel and the hand-looms were superseded; the price of traveling, when steam superseded horses and the power of wind. The prices of all the world's great staple commodities fell when steam connected the chief sources of their supply with the market-places of all nations, and made possible the wide distribution of perishable products. The prices of all things, again, fell *pari passu* with the growth of financial institutions established to create credits and economize the supply and use of metallic money."

The investigations of Mr. Atkinson show that, " while one half the present effort to sustain life consists in the effort or cost of obtaining food, that effort, great as it still is, is so much less than it was prior to 1860, as to make it almost incapable of expression in specific terms. In 1860 the greater part of the wheat now consumed in Europe could not have been moved a hundred and fifty miles without exhausting its value; now wheat is moved half-way round the world at a fraction of its value." The preservation of food by artificial methods, which to an extent is equivalent to its increased supply, has also been to a very high degree perfected.

In the production of materials for clothing, vast areas of new territory have been added to areas formerly occupied for the production of cotton and wool; while, in the case of cotton, the change from slave labor to free labor alone has greatly reduced its cost of production in that country whose supply determines the price for the world. " In the conversion of cotton and wool into fabrics it can be proved that one factory operative can do four times the work which one corresponding operative could accomplish between the years 1840 and 1850; while the invention and application of the sewing-machine has reduced the time and labor cost necessary for the conversion of the cloth into clothing in vastly greater measure."

In the case of the useful metals—iron, steel, copper, lead, tin, and quicksilver—the revolution which has occurred in consequence of the discovery and opening of new mines, the application of new methods of smelting, and the facilities · for transportation at low cost, have unquestionably reduced the cost (price) of all these products to as great an extent as that of any other class of commodities.

To suppose, now, that a change in the relative value of the two precious metals, gold and silver—a change which has not in any degree restricted their natural supply or diminished their monetary or industrial uses—has exercised a concurrent superior and predominating influence in respect to the prices of all other commodities or services, would seem to be almost incompatible with the clear exercise of one's reasoning faculties.

VII.

AN important cause of economic disturbance in recent
years (i. e., since 1873), and one which, in the opinion of
the members of the British Commission " On the Depression
of Trade and Industry " (1886), and also of most European
writers, has been largely instrumental in occasioning universal depression of business, has been the increasing tendency among nations to favor and practically carry out the
policy that the prosperity of their respective people can be
best promoted by artificially stimulating domestic industries
on the one hand, and imposing restrictions on international
commerce or the free interchange of products with foreign
nations on the other.

After the repeal of the " Corn Laws " by Great Britain
in 1846, and the subsequent gradual adandonment by that

nation of its former illiberal commercial policy—followed, as were these measures, by a remarkable development of British trade and industry—the tendency of popular sentiment and the policy of governments throughout the civilized world was unquestionably in the direction of emancipating international trade from all arbitrary restrictions; and between 1854 and 1870 the leading nations negotiated numerous treaties for international commercial reciprocity for the achievement of this object, and at the same time materially reduced their duties on imports. This movement (as is now almost forgotten) first found expression in the form of positive legislation in the United States, which in 1854 negotiated a treaty which provided for a free exchange of nearly all crude materials, and mutually free fishery privileges with the British provinces of North America; and, in 1857 (by a vote of 33 to 12 in the Senate, and 124 to 71 in the House) reduced its average duty on all imports to less than fifteen per cent. In fact, had not civil war intervened in 1861, the United States, in a very few years more, would have undoubtedly rivaled Great Britain in freeing its foreign trade and commerce from all restrictions, save for revenue and sanitary purposes.* In 1860, England, under the lead of Mr. Cobden, negotiated with the Emperor Napoleon III, represented by M. Chevalier, the celebrated commercial treaty with France, which, while providing for large reciprocal reductions or entire removal of many duties on exports

---

* In 1860 a reduction of the national revenues, induced primarily by the commercial panic of 1857 and an increase of national expenditures, with threatened political troubles, led to the introduction of a bill, avowedly with the intent of restoring the tariff rates in force prior to 1857; and this bill, with amendments, increasing the rates considerably beyond that point, became a law in March, 1861. But, at that date, seven of the Southern States had seceded, and had withdrawn in great part their Senators and Representatives from the Federal Congress; so that the action of Congress, at the time of the passage of this bill, affords no indication of what the legislation of the United States on the subject of the tariff would have then been had domestic tranquillity not been interrupted.

as well as imports, also entirely abolished all absolute " prohibitions " on any branch of international commerce between the two nations; as, for example, in respect to coal, the exportation of which to France, England, under a fancied military necessity, had at one period prohibited.

Following the Anglo-French treaty, and as the result, doubtless, of its influence, twenty-seven other similar treaties, providing for what is called a system of " reciprocity," were negotiated ; in some one or more of which all the states of Europe, with the exception of Greece, participated ; Russia even breaking through her customary reserve, and entering into more liberal commercial agreements with more than one of her neighbors. And, as many of these different treaties successfully embodied new and special relaxations in respect to duties on imports—which, in virtue of the so-called " favored-nation clause " * existing in most previous treaties with other countries, became also and at once generally applicable—the area of commercial freedom and its accruing benefits extended very rapidly, and, as it were, without effort, over the greater part of Europe. So that, by the year 1870, " all the great trading nations of Europe—England, France, the states of the German Zollverein, Austria, Italy, Holland, and Belgium—had become one great international body, by all the members of which the principle of stipulating for exclusive advantages for their own commerce *seemed* to have been abandoned, and not one of whom could take off a duty without every other member at once enjoying increased commercial facilities; while within this body, the operation of the favored-nation clause was such as to make the arrival at almost unlimited freedom of exchange merely a question of time." †

---

* By the "favored-nation" clause is understood that provision which has been incorporated in most treaties in modern times, by which the contracting parties agree to give to each other as good treatment as each one, then or thereafter acting severally, may give to other and the most favored nations.

† Address of the President (Grant Duff, M. P.) of the Department of Econ-

Furthermore, not only were these same governments busy during this period in breaking down the artificial barriers which they had previously erected against international trade, but they also sought, as never before, to overcome the natural impediments that had hitherto limited the extension of their trade relations—internal as well as external—by improving their highways, constructing and combining railways, and undertaking such stupendous engineering operations as the St. Gothard and Arlberg Tunnels.

How wonderfully the trade of the states of Europe, that thus mainly co-operated for promoting the freedom of exchange, coincidently developed, with an undoubted corresponding increase in the wealth and prosperity of their people, is shown by the fact that the European trade of the six nations of Austria, Belgium, France, Holland, Italy, and Great Britain increased, during the years from 1860 to 1873, more than one hundred per cent, while their aggregate population during the same period increased but 7·8 per cent.* How much this remarkable increase of trade was due to the existence and influence of the commercial treaties noted, is demonstrated by the further fact that the increase of the trade of the above-named six nations during the same period with all other countries, in which the conditions of exchange had presumably not been liberalized, was at the rate of only sixty-six per cent. It is also interesting to note that the response made by the Chambers of Commerce and various industrial bodies throughout France to an inquiry addressed to them by the Government in 1875, not only testified to the great benefit which had accrued to French trade and

omy and Trade, at the annual meeting of the British Association for the Promotion of Social Science, October, 1875.

* The results of the Anglo-French treaty in the case of France, as shown by the subsequent rapid growth of French exports and imports, and of national savings, was akin to the marvelous. In fact, no higher evidence of the fiscal wisdom of the Emperor Napoleon III in agreeing to this treaty could be offered, than the ease with which the French people bore eleven years later the huge burdens of war indemnities imposed on them by Germany.

industries by reason of her commercial treaties, but also expressed an almost universal wish that they might be renewed upon their expiration upon even a more liberal basis; and it is altogether probable that a similar response would have been made in most of the other countries in Europe had like inquiries at the same time been instituted.

But, after the continuance for some years of the almost universal depression of trade and industry which commenced in 1873, or after the year 1876, the tendency of the governmental policy of the states of Continental Europe, and to a great extent also popular sentiment, turned in an opposite direction, or toward commercial illiberality; and now nearly all of the liberal commercial treaties above referred to have been terminated, or notice has been given of their non-renewal; and, with the exception of Great Britain, Holland, Denmark,* and possibly China, there is not a state in the world claiming civilization and maintaining commerce to any extent with foreign countries which has not within recent years materially advanced its import or export duties.

Russia commenced raising her duties on imports in 1877, and has continued to do so until the Russian tariff at the present time is in a great degree prohibitory, and one of the highest ever enacted in modern times by any nation. It is also to be noted that, whenever Russia extends its dominion, laws are at once promulgated with the undisguised purpose of greatly restricting or entirely destroying any commerce which the people of the newly-acquired territory may have previously possessed with other nations.

Italy and Austria-Hungary entered upon their reactionary tariff policy in 1878; Germany in 1879; France in

---

* Denmark must be regarded as a purely agricultural country, possessing no mineral resources or mining population, and very few manufactories, "and while one half of the population live exclusively by agriculture, the industries and various branches of general trade and commerce afford occupation to less than one fourth of the whole number."—*Testimony of the British Commission on the Depression of Trade and Industry.*

1881; Switzerland in 1885; the Dominion of Canada in 1879 and 1887; Roumania in 1886; Belgium and Brazil in 1887; while in the United States, owing to the decline in the prices of goods subject to specific duties, the average *ad valorem* rate of duty on dutiable merchandise has advanced from 41·61 per cent in 1884 to 47·10 per cent in 1887. In Spain, which quadrupled her foreign commerce under a very liberal commercial policy adopted in 1869, the restrictions on trade have since become so excessive that the only relief opened to the consumer is by alliance with the contrabandist, whose profession is becoming almost as well established in Spain, France, and Italy, as in the middle ages, when but for him, according to Blanqui, commerce would have well-nigh perished. In Holland, which has hitherto resisted all demands for increased restrictions on her foreign commerce, an association of manufacturers petitioned the Government in May, 1887, in favor of speedy legislation on the tariff, for the purpose of protection to home industries, and set forth the following as reasons for their request :

" The national industry lives in a most difficult time. It seems that the last period of the battle of life has appeared for many of its branches. Foreign competition, steeled by protection, equipped and encouraged to a decisive battle for the overpowering of a market for the world, even appears to drive aside the most natural protections of native industry. Now flour has its turn; next, cattle and meat. In other words, the aim of adjacent and more distant countries appears daily more openly. The industry of the Netherlands is menaced with a total ruin by their oppression."

And, as further illustrations of the degree to which a restrictive commercial policy is favored, and the extremes to which it is practically carried, it may be mentioned that some of the small British islands of the West Indies (Trinidad and St. Vincent, for example) maintain duties in a high degree restrictive of the interchange of their comparatively small products; while Venezuela, in 1886, when new and prospectively rich alluvial deposits of gold were discovered within her territory, at once imposed a duty on her exports of " raw gold."

During the past year (1888) the Manchester (England) Chamber of Commerce passed a resolution to the effect that—

" All goods of a nature and kind which we ourselves produce, offered in the markets of the United Kingdom, should pay that equal proportional share of the burden of imperial and local taxation which they would have paid if produced or manufactured in the United Kingdom."

Commenting upon the evidence thus afforded of a change in even British commercial sentiments—i. e., from liberality, foresight, and boldness, to illiberality, narrow-mindedness, and timidity—the London " Economist" has thus significantly written : " The time was when the men of Manchester were characterized by a spirit of sturdy self-reliance, and asked nothing better than that they should be left free to fight their own industrial battles ; but, if their Chamber of Commerce is to be regarded as a truly representative institution, they must have sadly deteriorated. Now they seem to live in perpetual fear of their foreign competitors, and a project has only to be presented to them in the guise of a blow to be struck against their dreaded rivals to insure its ready acceptance by them. The question with them is no longer ' *What can we do to help ourselves ?* ' but ' *What can we do to injure our competitors ?* ' and whether the injury is to be inflicted upon foreigners or upon our fellow-subjects in India appears to be a matter of perfect indifference." *

---

* The utter folly and disastrous consequences of the adoption by Great Britain, or other nations, of such a principle of fiscal policy as has been indorsed by the Manchester Chamber of Commerce is also thus demonstrated by the " Economist" : " Suppose," it says, " the men of Manchester to have their own way, and the people of the United Kingdom were to levy an import duty

To many, doubtless, these economic phenomena do not appear to admit of any ready and satisfactory explanation; while others will unhesitatingly ascribe them to the influence and acceptation of protectionist theories and teachings, inculcated under the advantageous but specious circumstance, that the almost universal depression of trade and industry that has prevailed since 1873 commenced at a time when the general commerce of the world was absolutely more free from artificial restrictions than at any former period of its history.

The factors that have been concerned in effecting these

---

upon cotton goods entering this country, we could not refuse to allow India to follow our example, and tax the cotton manufactures she receives from us, so that, to use the words of the Manchester fair-traders, they 'should pay that equal and proportional share of the burden of imperial and local taxation which they would have paid if produced or manufactured' in India. No doubt, if it be the wish of Manchester that India should act upon this principle, she will be only too pleased to comply with it. She parted reluctantly with her cotton duties, and is ready to reimpose them at once, should the home Government desire it. But what a sorry figure do the Manchester manufacturers present! They are apparently in an agony of apprehension because we import cotton manufactures of all kinds, to the value of less than £2,000,000 a year, and in order to put impediments in the way of those imports they are ready to indorse a system of protection which, in the case of India alone, would subject to taxation between £19,000,000 and £20,000,000 of their own manufactures, which now enter India every year free of duty. Is it possible to imagine any proposal more suicidal than this? And there is another point that the fair-traders have entirely overlooked. If there is to be a war of tariffs, it need not necessarily be a war of import tariffs alone. On the principle that a nation is bound to see that all who trade with it contribute as much to its taxation as its own inhabitants, India and the United States would obviously be justified in imposing an export duty upon all the raw cotton they send here. If that cotton were retained at home, and manufactured there, it would, in the process of manufacture, contribute to the revenue, since the manufacturers pay both State and local taxes. Why, then, if the new Manchester doctrine be sound, should not an export duty be levied upon it equal to the amount of taxation that would have been derived from it if it had been kept and worked up at home? It is no answer to this to say that export duties are restrictive trade. So are import duties; and if Manchester imagines that it can by means of fiscal arrangements strike at its foreign competitors without receiving tenfold heavier blows in return it is vastly mistaken."

economic changes and accompanying disturbances are not, however, simple, but somewhat numerous and complex. They, nevertheless, admit, it is believed, of clear recognition and statement. In the first place, the results of the Franco-German War—the radical changes in the character and construction of war-armaments since that period, and the continual augmentation of permanent military forces, have entailed upon all the states of Europe since 1873 continually increasing expenditures and indebtedness; and indirect taxation, by means of duties on imports, to meet these increasing financial burdens, has been found to be most in accord with the maxim attributed to Colbert, that the perfection of taxation consists in so plucking the goose—i. e., the people —as to procure the greatest amount of feathers with the least possible amount of squawking.

Again, with the introduction and use of new, more effective, and cheaper methods or instrumentalities of production, every nation of advanced civilization has experienced, in a greater or less degree, an increase in the product of nearly all its industries save those which are essentially handicraft in character, with not only no corresponding increase, but often an actual decrease in the number of laborers to whom regular and fairly remunerative employment constitutes the only means of obtaining an independent and comfortable livelihood. Every country with accumulating productions has accordingly felt the necessity of disposing of its surplus by exporting it to the markets most freely open to it; and, as a consequence, that has happened which might have been expected could the exact course of events have been anticipated, namely: increased competition in every home market, engendered by increasing domestic production and the efforts of foreign producers to export (introduce) their surplus; fiercer competition to effect sales of the excess of competitive products by the sellers of all nations in neutral markets; and an almost irresistible tendency toward a universal depression of prices and profits, and, to

a greater or less extent, a displacement of labor. It is also
to be noted that as the capacity for industrial production
increases, and competition to effect sales becomes fiercer,
the more feverish is the anxiety to meet competition—specially on the part of foreign rivals—by producing cheaper
goods; and that this policy in the states of Continental
Europe, and more particularly in Germany, is antagonizing
efforts to shorten the hours of labor and restrict the factory
employment of women and children; and is also tending in
a marked degree to do away with the heretofore general
practice of suspending labor on Sundays.*

---

* The results of an extensive inquiry, recently instituted by the British
Government, in respect to Sunday labor in Germany (and comprising with the
evidence taken three large volumes), shows that in Westphalia, Rhineland,
Würtemberg, Baden, Alsace, and Brunswick, Sunday work is only enforced
where necessary. Different reports come, however, from Saxony, one stating
that "Sunday labor has become usual in most factories and workshops solely
under the stress of competition, so that the hours of divine service are now
alone excluded, and these only from absolute necessity." Another report
says that Sunday labor has become "a principle with many employers,"
while in a number of cases the journeyman or operative seeking an engagement must bind himself to work on Sunday, and "if the workman refused to
work on Sunday, reprisals on the part of the employer would be the inevitable result, and this is so, even in spite of the legal restriction of work on Sundays and festivals." "On the whole," says the London "Economist," "the
evidence" (presented in the published report of the Government inquiry) "is
unfavorable to the principle of Sunday labor, though it is largely carried on—
in all probability more so than is admitted, for in innumerable cases it is admitted that it is hard to get at the real state of affairs. Nevertheless, there is
general disinclination against putting the principle of no Sunday work into
practice where the objectionable system has obtained a footing. On the part
of large industrial concerns, it is said that want of continuity would often be
a cause of serious loss, while without Sunday labor repairs could never be
carried out, even night-work being no adequate substitute. The number of
associations which recommend the absolute prohibition of Sunday labor is
small in proportion to those which advocate partial prohibition. The question of Sunday labor is one of considerable interest for England, for it is
unquestionable that, among the causes of Germany's ability to compete
with England as a mercantile and industrial country, the fact that here
more hours are worked for less money is not the least important. The
prohibition of Sunday labor would, of course, mean increased cost of production; and every increase in the cost of production will render it more difficult

To meet this condition or tendency of affairs, two lines of policy have commended themselves to the governments of many countries—especially in Continental Europe—as remedial and easy of execution, namely; to seek to diversify and increase the home demand for the products of domestic industry on the one hand, and to obtain new and larger markets in foreign countries for their surplus productions on the other. And the *first* of these results it has been sought to accomplish by restricting or prohibiting, through import (tariff) duties, the importation and competitive sale in their respective markets of the surplus products of other nations; and the *second*, by offering bounties on exports, or on the construction and multiplied use of vessels for employment in foreign commerce. In the pressing necessity for finding new and (if possible) exclusive markets for increasing machinery products, and for commodities whose production has been artificially stimulated, is undoubtedly also to be found the clew to the policy which within recent years has mainly prompted Germany, France, Belgium, Italy, and Spain to seek to obtain new territorial possessions in Eastern and Central Africa, Southeastern Asia, and in New Guinea and other islands of Polynesia.

The commercial policy of Russia under such circumstances must, however, be regarded as wholly exceptional, and that of the United States as partially so. In the case of the former, her recent increased restrictions on foreign commerce, through greatly increased duties on imports, have not, apparently, been due to the acceptance of any economic theory in respect to trade, or with any reasonable expectations that an extensive prohibition of imports could permanently add to her revenues from customs, but rather because such action is an essential part of what seems to be a larger and fully accepted national policy, which aims to

---

for Germany to outrival older manufacturing countries in the markets of the world."

banish and exclude from the empire everything foreign in its nature and origin *—persons, merchandisè, language, literature, immigration, and religion; while in the case of the latter the fiscal policy of the country for now more than a quarter of a century has been based upon the idea that foreign trade is injurious, and therefore importations, without which there can be no exportations, should be prevented.

Leaving Russia out of account, the nation that took the initiative in breaking in upon the system of comparatively free international exchanges that had gradually come to prevail among the commercial nations of Europe since 1860, was Austria-Hungary, which, feeling the necessity of securing larger markets for her manufactured products, increased her tariff in 1878, with the avowed expectation of obtaining, through new negotiations, greater commercial advantages or concessions, more especially from Germany, than were enjoyed under existing treaties. A similar policy also found favor at about the same time in France, and under its influence the "Anglo-French" and other commercial treaties were either allowed to lapse or were "denounced," and a new general tariff was constructed. The result was not what was probably anticipated. Increased restrictions on imports on the part of Austria, in place of inviting concessions, led at once to retaliatory tariffs by Italy and Germany, and the example thus set has been followed by one European Continental state after another, each raising barrier after barrier against the competition of other nations, until all stability of duties on the numerous frontiers has practically ended, baffling the calculations alike of exporters and importers, and making the development of almost every trade and industry dependent on bounties, subsidies, and restric-

---

* By a ukase issued in May, 1888, no foreigner thereafter is allowed to become or to remain a landed proprietor in Russia, a measure that was practically equivalent to the expulsion of a large number of Germans engaged in manufacturing or mining in Russia.

tions on exchanges, rather than on their own inherent strength and enterprise.

The following examples are illustrative of recent procedures in continuation of this policy: In 1885 Germany deliberately excluded Belgian linen from her markets. This act has not as yet been followed by reprisals by Belgium; but the action of Germany, in repeatedly augmenting in recent years her duties on breadstuffs has been promptly imitated by Austria-Hungary, whose export of cereals was seriously affected. But, notwithstanding these increased duties on the movements of grain between Germany and Austria, the prices of cereals in both of these countries have since continually receded, and the enactment of similar imposts in France has been followed by a like experience. Belgium, which for many years has been the typical free-trade state of the world, and which in 1885, by her Chamber of Deputies, refused to entertain a proposition to restrict the importation of cattle into the country, has since then, and mainly by a recognition of an inability to compete with the prices established for meats and grain by the United States and other foreign countries, felt compelled to impose high duties on the importation of all live-stock and dead meats—fresh, smoked, or salted. A new tariff, embodying the extreme protective principle recently adopted by Brazil, imposes high and almost prohibitory duties on the importations of rice and all other cereals produced in the country, and, as Brazil has heretofore imported annually some two hundred thousand sacks of rice from foreign countries, the disturbance of trade in this particular is likely to be serious.

The United States having imposed heavy duties on the importations of French wines and silks, France improves on the precedent thus established, and excludes by relatively higher duties the importation into her territories of American pork.*

* Under discriminating restrictive legislation on the part of France and

In Sweden and Norway, on the other hand, where, during the year 1887, an effort was made under similar circumstances to restrict by increased duties the entry of foreign flour and other breadstuffs, the proposition was signally defeated by the return of a large adverse majority to the lower house of the Swedish Riksdag.

On the 1st of January, 1888, a treaty of commercial reciprocity between France and Italy, negotiated in 1881, was terminated by original stipulation. So far from being renewed, a renewal was not only not seriously contemplated, but the expiration of the treaty was really regarded with feelings of unmixed satisfaction by many persons in both countries, by reason of the opportunity that would be afforded for mutually increasing the duties on their respective importations. And in this spirit each government has successively enacted special tariffs, all more or less retaliatory in spirit and destructive of international trade. For example, under the treaty the light, cheap wines of Italy were admitted into France at a mere nominal rate of duty, and were imported in large quantities to supply the deficit in the wine production of France occasioned by the ravages of the phylloxera, while the more valuable French wines were admitted on correspondingly favorable terms into Italy, and obtained an increased consumption. On the expiration of the treaty each government advanced its duties on wines to prohibitory rates, while on most other merchandise the respective increase in rates was from fifty to one hundred per cent. One of the first acts of the French Government after the expiration of the treaty was the promulgation of a decree absolutely prohibiting the future importation of " plants, flowers, cut or in pots, of fruits, fresh vegetables, and, in general, of all horticultural and market-garden produce of Italian origin " ; chestnuts without their shells excepted.

Germany, the export of American hog-products has diminished in value from $104,000,000 in 1881 to $59,000,000 in 1888.

How Italy retaliates for such proceedings is illustrated by the circumstance that the Italian custom-house recently levied fourteen pounds import duty on a dead body sent from France to Milan for cremation, and the same amount as export duty on the ashes as they were carried back into France. Again, the new customs duties and regulations of Italy having proved oppressive to French trade, France has retaliated by the withdrawal of all the privileges formerly granted to the Italians in respect to fishing, coasting-trade, and port dues on her Mediterranean coasts, including Algeria. The result of this war of tariffs has been exactly what might have been anticipated. Both countries have suffered severely from the restriction of trade thus artificially produced ; but it is a matter of comment that a certain satisfaction is manifested by the French that the Italians have suffered more than themselves, as it is conceded that the exports from Italy to France have fallen in a far greater proportion than the exports from France to Italy, entailing a very considerable reduction in the customs revenue of the latter country.* Smuggling from one country

---

* A comparison of the exports from Italy to France for the first five months of 1887 under the treaty, with the first five months of 1888 after its abrogation, showed the following diminutions of commodities : 24,000 casks and 695,000 bottles of wine ; cattle to the value of about 8,000,000 francs ; cereals to the value of 16,000,000 francs.

"Thus far the effects of the blockade seem to have fallen more severely upon Italy than France. In the former country there is a dearth of capital which paralyzes commercial enterprise, and the farmers are, in general, poorer and more dependent than the French upon the immediate sale of each year's vintage. In southern Italy the distress is already acute. Money is so scarce as to be almost unobtainable by people of moderate means, and many peasant proprietors with mortgages on their property have been forced to make ruinous sacrifices. The market values of ordinary wines have fallen as low as four, eight, and ten cents per gallon, and all collateral interests, including cooperage and the traffic in staves, are correspondingly depressed. The crisis was precipitated at a time when native ordinary wines were abundant and cheap in France, not so much by reason of a profuse vintage last year, as because the working-classes have learned to consume the 'piquettes,' or artificial wines made from dried grapes imported from the Levant. As the wine

to the other prevails to a large extent; but France feels the disturbance from this cause less than Italy, because French goods, being, as a rule, compact and of greater value in equal compass than the average of Italian products, are more easily passed through third countries or smuggled across the frontiers. At the same time it is certain that French trade with Italy has also suffered severely; the export of many articles of French produce, like silk-piece goods, silk-trimmings, cotton fabrics, paper-hangings, and the like, having declined from thirty to seventy-five per cent. And yet, notwithstanding these experiences, all negotiations for the renewal of a commercial treaty between the two nations have thus far led to no results, and political events and influences have constantly tended to make affairs worse, instead of better.

The purchase of horses by the Germans in the northeastern departments of France is regarded in France as an evil only to be met by enactments prohibiting the export of horses; and the cattle-dealers of Bordeaux and La Vendée accuse the British Government of underhand " protection " by orders in Council alleging cattle-plague to exist in the west of France, and putting restrictions upon the landing of French beasts.

In 1880, under a plea that French industry was burdened by high rates of inland transportation, and thus rendered less able to meet foreign competition, all taxation on the transportation of goods by the water-ways of France—

---

export to Italy had been previously confined mainly to champagne, Burgundy, and Bordeaux wines of high quality, the blockade has not sensibly affected the French wine growers or dealers. France has a steady and well-established export demand for her wines, which Italy has not; but if the present restrictions are to be permanently maintained, no one can doubt that the Italians, by perfecting their manufacture, will eventually produce large quantities of wines which will bear exportation, and seriously encroach upon a trade with Russia, England, the Netherlands, and the United States, over which France has hitherto held entire control."—*Report to the United States Department of State by Consul MASON, of Marseilles*, 1888.

rivers and canals—was abolished. But a movement has recently been started to re-establish this tax, on the ground that the facilities offered by the free use—so far as taxation is concerned—of the rivers and canals of France, favor foreign competition, by permitting English, German, and Belgian coal to reach the interior of France; the cheap transport destroying the effect of the import duty enacted for the protection of French coal.

With the establishment of French sovereignty over that large area of the earth's surface known as "Indo-China," the markets of that country have been practically closed to the manufactured products of all other countries except France. While the people of India under English rule may buy freely the cotton-stuffs, hardware, and other articles they require in France, Germany, Switzerland, and the United States, as well as in England, without being compelled to pay any tribute to the English manufacturers in the form of differential duties, the French still cling to the old colonial system of the sixteenth and seventeenth centuries, according to which it is the duty of the colonies to exclusively purchase and consume the products of the mother-country; and have endeavored to force, so far as possible, the Indo-Chinese to purchase in the French market, and pay, in addition to the Government taxes, an industrial tax, equal to the difference between the price and quality of the French-protected articles and those of competing countries. Thus, before the advent of the French, the wretchedly poor population of Indo-China were accustomed to clothe themselves mainly with a thin calico, made in China, called "étamine," which was brought into the country as an article for exchange, with little or no restrictions; but under the French rule a prohibitive duty of about fifty per cent of the value of étamine has been imposed on its importation; and as every tax is eventually paid by labor, the Indo-Chinese are thus obliged to work an hour or two longer every day to clothe themselves. It is also worthy of note that, since the application of this system, in September, 1887, the importations into Indo-China are reported as having diminished to the extent of forty-five per cent, and that the aggregate trade of the country has also been greatly impaired.*

The imposition for some time past of excessive discriminating duties by Roumania on importations from Austria— a duty, for example, of six hundred francs being levied on a double cwt. of shoes—has given rise to one of the most extraordinary proceedings in commercial history. To avoid these high duties, the Austrian manufacturers have adopted the plan of sending their goods, in the first instance, " to Switzerland or Holland, where in a frontier custom-house they pay a duty which naturalizes them, so that they become Swiss or Dutch products, and as such they are then forwarded to Roumania. The enormous cost of the long railway journey, the duty in Switzerland or Holland, and the duty at the Roumanian frontier, do not together amount to so much as the duty demanded of Austrian goods imported directly by the Roumanians." The Roumanian Government has, therefore, failed to a great extent in its plan of excluding Austrian products from its territory, and its people have had to pay the high duties imposed upon their importations. Roumania has, furthermore, found it impossible to protest against this scheme by which Austrian manufactures have been imported, because it is perfectly fair, and the arrangements for carrying it out are made in such correct form, that the countries whence the goods are imported could not suffer them to be rejected at the Roumanian frontier. Under such

---

* In a recent debate in the French Chamber of Deputies, a Rouen cotton-spinner defended the customs policy of France in respect to Cochin-China, and attributed the distress and decline of trade in that country to the failure of its rice-crop and the depreciation of silver. He argued that the effects of the policy adopted by France had been satisfactory, as the value of the exports of cotton goods from the Rouen district had risen, in the first six months of the year 1888, 346,000 francs.

experience the Roumanian Government has finally determined to reduce its customs on Austrian merchandise to
such an extent that they will not exceed in the aggregate
the cost of their transportation to Holland or Switzerland,
added to the duties laid by legitimate Swiss and Dutch
goods on their importation.

The policy of increasing taxes upon imports, and imposing further restrictions on trade, once entered upon with
a view of securing exceptional advantages, seems also to find
no limitations in respect to its exercise.   Thus, in France,
since her former liberal commercial policy was abandoned,
the duties upon the importation of wheat, rye, live-stock,
alcohol, and numerous other commodities, have been augmented to many times their former rates; and the intention
has been expressed to deal in the same way with all foreign
merchandise at the expiration of her few remaining treaties
of commerce, or "conventional tariffs." The duty on sheep
imported into France, which was formerly thirty centimes
per head, has been progressively raised in ten years to five
francs; that on horned cattle, from three francs sixty centimes to thirty-eight francs; on codfish, from twelve and a
half francs to forty-eight francs per one hundred kilo-
grammes; while on rye, a leading article of food with the
French peasantry, a former duty of ten francs per *tonne* has
been raised to thirty francs, with thirty francs additional if
the rye is grown in any country out of Europe and imported
from any country in Europe.

In the United States, notwithstanding the average *ad
valorem* rate of duty on dutiable merchandise has increased
from 41·6 per cent in 1884 to 47·10 per cent in 1888, a bill
largely advancing rates passed the Senate in January, 1889,
which has been characterized by the United States Secretary of the Treasury as embodying, in respect to many important commodities, "the very refinement of severity on
taxation, by making the rates either absolutely or practically prohibitive; thereby forbidding competition from

abroad and subjecting the consumer to inexorable exactions liable and likely to result from combinations of domestic producers." *

In July, 1887, Russia increased her duties—which were before very high—on the imports of all foreign iron and steel, to a point that is regarded as nearly or quite prohibitory of all imports; and Germany, which has heretofore had an important market for her iron and steel wares in Russia, and has also been a large purchaser of Russian grain, has since then further advanced her duties upon the import of all foreign cereals, her object being avowedly to shut out American as well as Russian competition.

A government commission, appointed to inquire into the condition of Russian agriculture, recently reported the lack of knowledge and use of modern tools and machinery as one of the prime causes that stand in the way of any improvement in the condition of the Russian peasantry; and yet the high duties which the Government imposes on the importations of such tools and machinery from foreign countries—more especially from England and the United States—militates more than any other one agency against their introduction and employment. It is not disputed that the only sound basis for the prosperity of Russia lies in her agricultural resources, and that there is not now, and neither is there likely to be, any important exportation of commodities other than agricultural produce. But the existing Russian tariff, enacted in the interests of Russian manufacturers, forces ships to arrive in her ports in ballast, thereby necessitating that the exported surplus grain of the country, which if not sold abroad will not be sold at all, shall be burdened with a double freight rate—i. e., for the voyage to Russia and the return to a foreign port and market. Russia has large areas of her territory underlaid by coal of the best quality; the coal-basin, for example,

* Letter of the United States Secretary of the Treasury, February 27, 1889.

which yields the famous Silesian coals, whose ashes are like the ashes of beech-wood, extending far across the Russian frontier, and attaining great development in Poland. With a view of promoting her domestic coal industries, and in accordance with her present general policy of excluding, as far as possible, all the products of other countries from the empire, very heavy duties have been imposed for some years on the imports of foreign coal. The result has been that coal has been rendered more expensive on the average in Russia than in any other of the leading countries of Europe; and yet so irregular and deficient is the supply of domestic coal, that the south Russian railways are often obliged to use foreign coal, notwithstanding the duty. Again, the policy by which so many German manufacturers have recently been driven from Russia, has, it is understood, almost arrested the exploration and working of the great coal formation in Poland above noticed.

It is further most interesting to note how, as the idea of the desirability of restricting trade and commerce is accepted and carried out, the larger and more logically consistent idea of the middle ages, that restrictions should be imposed, not merely on the freedom of commercial intercourse between country and country, but also between districts of the same country, and even between man and man, tends to reassert itself and demand recognition and acceptance,* as is demonstrated by a variety of incidents on both sides of the Atlantic. In this movement in Europe, France at present takes the lead. Thus, for example, French workmen and employers are apparently now in unison of opinion that all

---

* If foreign trade is something bad in itself, by a parity of reasoning, domestic trade must be also more or less injurious. If nations and states grow rich and prosperous by not trading with one another, the same principle ought to hold good in respect to neighboring cities and towns, and between man and man. These were indeed the views of the statesmen of the fifteenth, sixteenth, seventeenth, and eighteenth centuries, and they practically enforced them so far as the contrary natural instincts of man would permit.

foreigners shall be rigidly excluded from any kind of work done by or for the Government, and from furnishing any kind of supplies for the public service. Among the bills recently brought forward in the French Chamber of Deputies, and which have received the serious attention of the Government, one provides that only French coal shall be used in the navy, and only French oats in the army; and, in general, that nothing of foreign growth or production shall be bought for public use, except such articles as are not produced in France. Clauses in existing treaties with foreign nations and apprehensions of reprisals have, it is believed, alone prevented the project of imposing special and differential taxes on all foreign workmen. The committee in charge of the French International Exhibition of 1889, while invoking the co-operation and good feeling of other countries, restricted all bids for buildings to French firms exclusively, ruling out all foreign firms from participation in the work, even though established in France, and employing only French workmen. The ancient *guild* system of the middle ages, restricting craft-membership and the employment of apprentices, and claiming the right to exclusively regulate prices, hours of labor, and other conditions of service, is also everywhere re-establishing itself; the glaziers of Paris leading the advance in this direction, by formally petitioning the authorities for incorporation as a guild, to which no foreigner shall be admitted, and no one not a member, even if he be a Frenchman, shall be allowed to set glass or make repairs upon windows in French territory.

Paris carpenters and joiners having complained to the Municipal Council of the city, that joiner's work was sent from the provinces, where labor was cheaper, the Council have recently protected the Paris workmen against the competition of French workmen in the country by raising the *octroi* duty on all sawed and worked wood brought into the city. Taking advantage of this precedent, the Parisian

laundresses have also demanded protection against the competition of those in the suburbs, whose prices are lower than
those charged in the city, and have petitioned the Municipal Council to levy an *octroi* duty on all clean linen brought
into Paris.

In a discussion of the labor-problem at a recent Catholic
Congress in Belgium, the Bishop of Liége is reported as
saying that the old trade-guilds must be revived and placed
under the guardianship of Christian lay employers and of
the clergy.   Then each trade or calling must be placed
under the special protection of a saint; and brotherhoods
of those engaged in it, composed both of employers and
workmen, must be formed for the celebration of the saint's
féte and for participation in religious processions and fu-
nerals, and the rendering of mutual assistance in times of
need.   But it was also remarked that while labor was pretty
sure to indorse the recommendation of the revival of the
guild, it would be equally sure to wholly disregard the ideas
of the bishop as to the use that should be made of it.   It
should also not be overlooked, in this connection, how closely,
and yet perhaps unintentionally, the modern labor organizations—"Trades-Unions," "Knights of Labor," and the
like—have come to resemble and be assimilated to the
ancient "*guilds*"; with this marked difference, that in the
old craft-guilds the masters or employers of labor remained
in and participated in the organization ; but, in the modern
organizations of labor, the masters or employers are especially excluded.

In Germany the extensive intervention of the state in
industrial and social matters has come to be, in recent years,
a fundamental policy of the Government; and is resulting
in a series of experiments for controlling or even entirely
absorbing great industries—as sugar and distilled spirits—
and for promoting the economical and moral prosperity of
the people by schemes for compulsory insurance of life and
against accidents, which have hitherto had no precedents in

the legislation of any country; and which will require a long time before final judgment can be pronounced on their expediency and practicability. At the same time, in all these movements the Government makes no secret of its desire, in fostering the interests of the people, to concurrently augment their ability to pay taxes.

In the United States, notwithstanding the provisions in the Federal Constitution to the contrary, an attempt has been made during the present year (1889) to enlarge the sphere of the " protective " (restrictive) policy, and make it applicable, not merely to the competitive products of foreign countries, but also to the competitive products of the different States comprised in the Federal Union; bills having been introduced in the Legislatures of several States, and enacted into law in two, prohibiting, through indirect methods, the importation of dressed meat, the product of other States. It seems hardly necessary to say that such propositions and enactments are antagonistic to the fundamental idea upon which the Federal Union of States, known as the " United States," is based—namely, the idea of equality of rights in all the States to the citizens of each and every State—and involve the recognition of a principle which needs only a wider application to effect the dismemberment of the republic.

The recent action of the French Government, in providing that nothing shall be bought for public use which is not of domestic production, and which the outside world has regarded as a policy unworthy of an enlightened nation, has also had its counterpart and precedent in the previous legislation of quite a number of the States of the Federal Union; with this exception, that in France the discrimination is made against foreigners only, while in the United States the discrimination is made against their own countrymen living in different political divisions of the country.

Nothing, furthermore, in the way of intervention with the domestic pursuits and social practices of the people can

be found in Germany or Europe to parallel the recent legislation of one of the leading States of the Northwest (Minnesota), a large part of which was the work of a single legislative session (limited to sixty days) in 1885, and which has
thus been described by a recent writer : *

Prominent in importance were statutes providing for the
weighing, handling, and inspection of grain; the construction and location of grain-warehouses, the providing of cars
and side-tracks by railroads, and the regulation of rates of
transportation. Next, was legislation respecting State loans
of " seed-grain " to farmers whose crops had been ruined by
grasshoppers; for the subsidizing of State fairs from the
State treasury; for enabling farmers to avoid the payment
of a portion of their debts; for protecting butter-makers
from the competition of artificial products, such as " butterine "; for regulating the details of the cattle industry, to
the extent of registering and giving State protection to
brands and other modes of identification, and of stamping
out contagious diseases with small courtesy to the rights
and wishes of individual owners; and for regulating the
lumber business to such an extent, that not a log can float
down a stream to the saw-mill for which it is destined without official cognizance. One State board regulates the practice of medicine and the admission of new practitioners; a
second, the examination of druggists and compounding
clerks, as precedent to entering into business; while a third
regulates the practice of dentistry. Various enactments pre-
scribe the toll to be exacted for grinding wheat; when one
man may slay his neighbor's dog with impunity; how railway companies must maintain their waiting-rooms at their
stopping-places for passengers; the hours of labor, and the
employment of women and children; the maximum time
for which locomotive engineers and firemen may be con-

---

* " The American State and the American Man," Albert Shaw, " Contemporary Review," May, 1887.

tinuously employed ; what books shall be used in the public schools ; forbidding " raffles " at church fairs under " frightful penalties," and making it a crime to give away a lottery-ticket, and a misdemeanor " to even publish an account of a lottery, no matter when or where it has been conducted." Among bills introduced, and which found considerable support, but were not enacted, was one forbidding persons of different sexes to skate together, or even be present at the same hour on the rink floor ; and another to license drinkers, which provided that no person should be permitted to use intoxicants or purchase liquors of any kind without having first obtained a public license.

Concurrently with the increasing restrictions in recent years on the commercial intercourse of nations, and as an undoubted sequence or phase of such policy, has come also a revival of the idea which, since the successful revolt of the British American colonies and the abandonment of the old-time European colonial policy, has been regarded as alike antagonistic to civilization and the Christian precept of national brotherhood and the interdependence of mankind, namely, that it is advantageous for the people of the separate nationalities to forbid immigration and residence, with a view of participating in their industries and developing their natural resources, to the people of other countries. In initiating this retrogression in the comity of nations, Russia took the lead by adopting measures looking first to the expulsion of her Jewish subjects, then of all resident foreigners engaged in manufacturing or mining, and, finally, by forbidding any foreigner from becoming or continuing a landed proprietor within her empire. Germany followed, by expelling great numbers of Poles from her northeastern provinces, under the pretext that they were Catholics (or non-Lutherans) and Slavs, but, in truth, because the more civilized and more Christian (?) German laborers disliked their industrial competition. The United States, in like manner, has forbidden the emigration and residence within

her territory of the Chinese, ostensibly because they are
" heathen," immoral, and not capable of political assimila-
tion, but really because they have labor to sell in competition
with other like vendors ; and a bill has been reported in the
Federal House of Representatives—but not passed—which
imposes conditions on the landing in the United States of
any immigrant whatever, which are capable of a very stringent restrictive application. Australia, also, is expelling the
Chinese bodily from her colonies ; and intimations are made
that China, in retaliation, will fall back upon her old-time
policy of commercial seclusion, at least to the extent of expelling from her empire the citizens of those states that
have discriminated against her own people. France, by a
decree in 1888, orders that all foreigners settling permanently in France must be registered and obtain permission
to do so ; the main and avowed object of the same being to
restrict or prevent the further immigration and settlement of
the Belgians and Italians, who are the only foreigners who
participate to any extent in the domestic trade and industry
of the country ; and it is understood that this registration
is only a preliminary step to the imposition of heavy differential taxes upon all immigrants into France who receive
wages. It is not alleged that these classes of foreign immigrants disobey the laws of France or resist her officials ; but,
on the contrary, it is conceded that they pay their taxes as
regularly as French citizens, and do not, like the Chinese in
the United States or the Jews in Southeastern Europe, perceptibly lower the standard of general civilization. As foreigners, they are, however, exempt from the burden of con-
scription for military service, which is now more severe in
France than in any other country except Russia. The Italians, on the other hand, in the absence of law, are endeavoring
to drive away French workmen from northern Italy ; resorting even, in some instances, to physical force to effect their
object. The Swiss, also, by their communal laws, heavily
handicap the foreigner, who shares in none of the communal

distributions; and even in England there is a loud demand for interference with the Polish Jews, who in some quarters of London underbid certain descriptions of artisans, and are becoming an objectionable feature in the population. In truth, it would seem as if the people of the different nationalities are beginning to dislike each other as they used to do in the middle ages, though for entirely different reasons; the old-time feeling of antagonism having been mainly due to mutual ignorance of each other; while in these latter days it is undoubtedly referable to an increased acquaintance, due to the greatly increased facilities for personal intercommunication. "National brotherhood for the future seems therefore likely to be made more cordial by non-intercourse." One further sequence of this condition of affairs—apart from the economic disturbances and contingent losses it has occasioned—which may be regarded as certain is, that the amity between nations, which has grown so much during the last half-century, and which it has been fondly hoped would put an end to war and enormous anticipatory war expenditures, has experienced a marked decrease within a recent period.

The outlook for the future has, however, one encouraging feature; and that is, that the result of such a conflict of tariffs as has prevailed in Europe since 1877–'78 has entailed so much of commercial friction, such a series of retaliatory measures, and such an arrest of material development, that there are now many signs that the continuation of this state of affairs will not be much longer endurable. In this conflict, Austria, which was the first country that broke in upon the International Commercial Union that prevailed among the Continental states prior to 1878, has suffered most severely; her exports and imports having notably decreased, while her customs taxes have risen in recent years from 1s. 8d. to 3s. 7d. per head of her population, and her internal taxes on consumption from 3s. 7d. to 6s. 8d. Between 1877 and 1888 Austria's exports of cereals to Germany decreased from 131,000,000 florins to 101,000,000. In 1878 her exports of wheat were 6,000,000 cwts., but in 1886, when there was by no means a bad harvest in Austria-Hungary, they were reduced to 1,570,000 cwts. During the same time her exports of cattle have been reduced to one fourth and of pigs to one half of their former proportions. There has been a marked decline in banking profits, an increase in the mortgages on real property, and a decline in the consumption both of meat and of farinaceous articles of food. To such an extent has her fiscal policy invited reprisals that she is described as " standing alone commercially," and reduced to the position of consuming her own products through necessity. On the other hand, the export trade of Germany with Austria-Hungary has suffered even more. In the five years ending in 1887, its aggregate decrease is reported as 70,000,000 florins. In 1881, 248,000,000 florins' worth of manufactured goods were exported by Germany to Austria and Hungary; in 1886, the sum amounted to 204,-000,000 only. In 1882, the quantity of twist exported was 18,000,000 florins; in 1886, it was $12\frac{8}{10}$ millions. The exports of iron and iron articles also decreased in these same years from $17\frac{4}{10}$ to $\frac{9}{10}$ million florins. The recent prohibitory duties decreed by Russia on the importation of iron and steel have closed numerous iron-furnaces in Silesia, and some of the frontier towns of north Germany, which are extensively interested in flour-milling, have also suffered severely by the all but prohibitory duties imposed by Germany on the imports of Russian grain. In Königsberg, for example, business is mainly dependent on the Russian grain-trade; but German grain is now so well protected that only 20,000 tons of Russian wheat came into Königsberg in 1887, as compared with 60,000 tons in 1884. The same place used also to do a good business with Russia in tea, but the Russian tariff has killed this, so that the city appears almost in a state of decay. Dantsic is suffering in the same way, from the same causes, aggravated by the expulsion of the Poles and Jews from Russia, who played an important part in the local trade of the frontiers. While one of the main objects of the present German tariff was to effectually protect her iron and steel industries, experience is showing that these same industries are less able than formerly to compete in foreign markets for the sale of their products. The price of steel rails was much higher in 1888 in Germany than in either England or Belgium ; and German manufacturers complain that, by reason of the high prices they have to pay for their crude materials, they are not only unable to obtain foreign contracts, but are put upon the defensive as regards English and Belgian makers. Comparing 1888 with 1887, the German exports of pig-iron, rails and manufactures of iron decreased 2,095,820 tons, or over sixteen per cent; while her imports of the same increased to the extent of 538,301 tons, or nineteen per cent. And of this increase of imports Great Britain furnished the greater part.

The returns of the foreign trade of France—imports and exports—show a continuous decline since 1880. Notwithstanding her high protective duties, the importation by France in 1888 of articles of food increased by more than 80,000,000 francs, while her exports of the same decreased to the extent of 17,000,000. France purchased in 1888 44,500,000 francs less in raw material and partly manufactured goods, and exported less than in the previous year. Of manufactures, her exports were notably less in 1888 than in 1887. The production of iron and steel in France declined between the years 1883 and 1886 to the extent of 850,000 tons, or twenty-four per cent. There was some recovery in production in 1887—estimated at 95,000 tons—mainly of pig-iron.

The statistics of the foreign trade of Italy for 1888 are particularly striking and instructive. During the year 1887 a general increase in her tariff rates on imports took effect, and the tariff-war between Italy and France broke out.

The immediate result was a great decrease in the exports and imports, and in the customs revenue of the country. Comparing 1888 with 1887, the decrease in the value of imports was twenty-six per cent; in exports, eleven per cent; and in revenue, 24·8 per cent. For the fiscal year 1889–'90 the revenue of the kingdom is estimated at £61,820,000 ($290,355,000), and the deficit of receipts to expenditures at about £9,000,000 ($43,740,000). The condition of the country under the combined influences of increased war expenditures and restrictions in trade has been recently described by Count Guisso, ex-Mayor of Naples, and a member of the Italian Parliament, as most critical. From one end of the peninsula to the other the cry is, he says, " Give us the means of selling our products, and we will pay the taxes." *

Russia having sought to close her doors against the produce of other countries, they in their turn have curtailed their purchases of Russian products; and the shrinkage in the foreign trade of Russia in recent years, and during a period of peace, has accordingly been almost without precedent in commercial history. Comparing 1883 with 1887, the decline in her imports was from £51,371,000 to £29,-160,000 (the depreciation of the value of the ruble being taken into account), or forty-three per cent; while in the case of her exports the decline, although not so marked (owing to large shipments of cereals contingent on good harvests), was still very significant—namely, from £60,788,-000 in 1883 to £43,651,000 in 1886, or twenty-six per cent.†

---

* See also page 178.

† The restricted character of the foreign commerce of Russia, as measured by the value of her imports, is well illustrated by comparing their aggregate (estimated at £29,160,000, or $141,717,600 for 1887) with the aggregates of other leading nations during recent periods. Thus, in the case of Great Britain, the aggregate net value of her imports for 1888 was £321,968,579 ($1,503,-757,000); for the United States, 1887–'88, $723,957,000; Holland, 1887, $457,-072,000; France, 1888, $810,000,000. While excluding foreign products by almost prohibitory duties, Russia at the same time continues to supply West-

On the other hand, and in striking contrast, the returns of the foreign commerce of Great Britain for 1888 show a gain in the aggregate net value of her exports and imports of £20,632,000 ($100,271,000) as compared with the aggregates of 1887. In fact, the idea that a few years ago found great acceptance in Europe, and undoubtedly influenced the commercial policy of the different states—namely, that increased restrictions on the importation and competitive sales of foreign products and the resort of bounties on exports would conjointly stimulate industries, relieve their markets from anything like over-production, and inaugurate a period of general prosperity — has utterly failed of realization when subjected to the test of long and actual experience; and for the following reasons : The stimulus being artificial, was unnatural. Production rapidly increased, and soon created an additional supply of articles, which were already produced in the localities best fitted for their production, in quantities sufficient, or more than sufficient, to meet any existing market demand at remunerative prices, thus occasioning an augmentation of the very evils which it was expected the restrictive commercial policy would prevent, and which may be enumerated in their sequential order somewhat as follows : 1. Over-production in the natural seats of production. 2. Domestic competition to effect sales destructive of all profits. 3. Special concessions of prices to effect sales in foreign countries which have been disturbing to the legitimate industries of such countries. 4. A general depression of prices, and the reduction of business profits to a mini-

---

ern Europe with grain; and having been favored with three good harvests in succession, the balance of trade in her favor has been attained as completely as any one could desire ; and for the first ten months of 1888 amounted to no less than 327,000,000 rubles. All this, however, has not brought favorable results to the country, and especially to the grain-producers ; the tenor of official reports being that the peasantry are so borne down by the burden of their taxation, and lack of facilities for selling their produce, that even in the past years of abundant harvests their condition has not experienced any sensible improvement.

mum—all resulting in a condition of affairs which two years ago is said to have drawn out from Count Karolyi, the Prime Minister of Austria, the assertion that " the European States, by their present retaliatory tariffs, are doing themselves more injury than the most unrestricted international competition could possibly inflict."

It seems to be also now generally conceded in Germany and other states of Europe that the depression of business and the disturbances occasioned by the fall of prices, which were most influential in inducing the general reaction in favor of protective duties in 1878, were due to causes that were not to be reached by such remedies, and that the same continue operative to-day in spite of all the customs barriers against international trade that have been erected. Hard experience is also forcing conviction into the minds of men everywhere, that the tendency to impose restrictions on exchanges by high protective taxes is directly antagonistic to the progress of modern methods of transportation ; and that it is clearly irrational to expend large sums in constructing and perfecting railways and steamships, and then place difficulties in the way of marketing the merchandise they carry. All the indications, therefore, seem to favor a reactionary commercial policy in Europe, and a termination of, at least, the severity and intolerance of the existing trade restrictions between the Continental states, Russia excepted. The following are additional evidences in favor of such a conclusion : The German Chambers of Commerce, in their recent reports, have, with very few exceptions, declared against the present tariff policy as most injurious to the industry and commerce of the empire. A recent report, especially, of the Stuttgart Chamber of Commerce, earnestly urges the Government to improve trade by a return to its former reciprocal conditions.*

---

* " The result of the intensive and extensive development of the protective system," observes the Stuttgart Chamber of Commerce, " notwithstanding its

With a view of promoting navigation, Austria has recently decreed that materials and machines for the building of ships may be imported free of duty. Roumania, after having enacted almost prohibitive tariff duties, is beginning to modify them by granting special favors; a manufacturer of wooden articles, for example, having been granted fifteen years' free import of wood under the condition that eighty per cent of the goods manufactured are again exported. New commercial treaties, involving limited reciprocities, have been made during the past year (1888) between Austria and Switzerland, and Germany and Switzerland. In the *former*, Austria reduces her duties on Swiss cotton fabrics, silks and laces, condensed milk, and a few other articles, and Switzerland on her imports of Austrian cattle and mineral waters. In the *latter*, which is shared by other countries to whom Germany has accorded the position of the most favored nations, Germany considerably recedes from the extravagantly high duties imposed in 1885 on watches, cotton embroideries, and silk fabrications, and Switzerland makes concessions on certain German manufactures, as linens, ready-made clothing, etc. A treaty of commerce between Austria and Italy, negotiated in 1878, expires during the year 1889, and the Austrian Government has the question of its renewal under consideration. If the existing restrictive commercial policy of the empire is to prevail, it

---

beneficial influences on many branches of industry, has been to doubly increase the international uncertainty which now burdens trade and commerce. Every movement in favor of protective duties results in efforts on the part of each country interested in the matter to outbid its neighbor; and the very duty which is expected to protect a nation produces a reaction on home prices, and causes them to become assimilated to those of international commerce." This Chamber believes that the prospect of a lasting improvement in trade would " be better grounded could only further exactions in international customs tariffs be avoided, and the uncertainty of market-price, which is the outcome of the protective system, be removed by an equitable establishment of mutual customs and commercial relations, by an increased stability and certainty of the duration of tariffs, and by a reciprocal return to former conditions."

will not be renewed; but a circular issued by M. Bacque-
hem, Minister of Commerce, to the Austrian Chambers of
Commerce, has much significance. For in it he says:

"It is important to maintain intact the outlets offered to the commerce, agriculture, and manufactures of the country. Nay, it is desirable to increase these outlets in various directions. But the only way
to do this is to have with the other powers treaties of commerce based
on stipulated tariffs. The conclusion of such treaties is now the work
before the Government."

Nevertheless, there are great difficulties to be overcome,
as the Italians think that the Austrian treaty of 1878 has
been disadvantageous to them, because under it Austrian
exports to Italy have risen by 13·3 per cent, while those of
Italy to Austria have decreased by forty-five per cent.

In Germany, when the era of tariff protection was inaugurated, it was maintained that its effect would be a more
equal distribution of wealth; but the German people are
now fast recognizing that the result has been to increase the
strength of the great bankers and manufacturers, who, having nothing to fear from foreign competition, now exercise
complete control over the home market, and, through the
creation of a great number of "trusts" or "syndicates,"
have been especially successful in enforcing higher prices on
consumers.*

---

* In Germany, which leads all other countries in the number, variety, and
power of its trusts, it is admitted that their formation began immediately after
the passage of the high tariff law of 1879. A recent writer in the "Économiste
Français" (M. Raffalovich), as the result of a study of the trade combinations
of all countries—indeed contends—that any trade or manufacturing syndicate
not having "the advantage of fiscal protection, and which operates on any
article of which the production is not extremely restricted and for more than
a very brief period, is absolutely certain to end in disaster." There are instances of so-called trusts in articles unprotected by tariffs that appear to con-
tradict this theory; but M. Raffalovich believes they are all capable of explanation consistent with his conclusion. The most striking instance in the
United States is the Standard Oil Company; but in this case the absence of
foreign competition until recently and its comparative disadvantages has had
the same effect on the domestic market as a prohibitive tariff. Evidently no

One project, originally proposed by Prof. Kaufmann, of the University of Tübingen, with a view of improving the condition of trade of Germany, which has been much discussed, and the adoption of which, in the opinion of not a few, is not improbable, is the formation of a Zollverein, or commercial union, among the nations of Central Europe, with a view, as the " Kölnische Zeitung " (which is regarded to some extent as an official organ of the German Government) has expressed it, " of expanding their markets by means of treaties, so that the surpluses at any one place within their dominions may serve to make up for the deficiencies in another," and which, more especially, would " find its account in collectively fighting against economical commonwealths, like the United States, Russia, China, and Great Britain, which embrace whole continents." †

THE EXPERIENCE OF THE BEET-ROOT SUGAR BOUNTIES.—The attempt to artificially stimulate the manufacture of beet-sugar in the states of Continental Europe, and at the same time to obviate the evils from the production of this commodity in excess of local or domestic demand by the payment of bounties on its exportation, has constituted such an extraordinary factor of disturbances in the world's

---

syndicate can maintain abnormal prices in any country for any commodity which is extensively produced in other countries, unless it is itself protected by a tariff on competitive imports, or is able to effect the improbable achievement of inducing the producers in all other countries to enter into its combination.

† Such a formation of the " United States of Europe "—this phrase being borrowed from the " Kölnische Zeitung "—coupled with the avowed objects to be prospectively attained by it, would have a peculiar significance for the United States of America, as the feeling in Europe in respect to the export trade of the United States, especially of food-products, has not been and is not now friendly. " The prohibition of her hog-products, the successive additions to the duties on grain and cattle, and the readiness with which any complaint against an American staple is taken up and widely circulated, often in a grossly exaggerated form, are indications of what would be the position of such a customs union toward the United States, could it become an accomplished fact."

recent economic history as to be worthy of special narration and attention.

Although the practice of stimulating through high protective duties and export bounties the production of beetroot sugar in Europe in competition with the cane-sugar product of the tropics dates back to the first quarter of the century, the present complicated and curious state of affairs is really due to an unexpected result of the German method of taxing beet-sugar, which was adopted in 1869. The idea involved in this method was, in brief, to collect an excise or internal-revenue tax on all sugar produced; in the first instance by taxing the raw beets, and subsequently to give a drawback on whatever sugar was exported equivalent to the tax paid on the beets from which the sugar was made. At the outset it was assumed that about twelve pounds of beets were required to make a pound of sugar, and on this basis the drawback was calculated; or for every hundred-weight of sugar exported, there was granted a drawback of nearly twelve times the tax paid on each hundred-weight of beets. For a number of years after 1869 this arrangement worked well, the drawback being about equivalent and no more than the tax. But nothing stimulates human ingenuity in a greater degree than the prospect of gain through the avoidance of a tax; and gradually a change in the condition of affairs took place. By careful and scientific cultivation the saccharine element in the beet was so much increased and the mechanical and chemical methods of extracting it so greatly perfected, that while in 1869 twelve pounds of beets were needed in the average German factories to make one pound of sugar, in 1878 the requisite quantity was 10·78 pounds; in 1882, 10·08 pounds; in 1884, 9·28 pounds; and in 1886, 8·80 pounds. Sugar was also extracted from the beet-root molasses, which was not taxed at all; a result at the outset not anticipated, and even considered impracticable. The effect of this was to make the drawback on the exports of sugar no longer equivalent to the tax, and convert it into a bounty; or the exporter received a drawback as if he had paid an excise-tax on twelve pounds of beets, when in reality he had paid on a much smaller quantity—less than nine pounds after 1885. The fact that this bounty was accruing was not unknown to the German Government; but as it became especially manifest during the years 1876–'79, when the great depression of industry had developed a strong protectionist feeling, nothing was done to stop it; but, on the contrary, it was popularly regarded with satisfaction. Under such favorable circumstances, the beet-root sugar product of Germany increased with great rapidity; and as the amount soon far exceeded any requirements for domestic consumption, and as a net profit of from six to seven per cent was guaranteed to the manufactories by the export bounties, the exportations soon assumed gigantic proportions, rising from about 500,000 cwt. in 1876 to over 6,000,000 cwt. in 1885. The other states of Continental Europe, finding the markets for their own product of beet-root sugar everywhere supplanted by the German sugars and their domestic manufacturers being even thereby brought to the verge of ruin, made haste to follow the example of Germany, and improve upon it, by offering larger bounties for the domestic production and export of sugars than were offered elsewhere; until the policy of Germany, France, Belgium, Holland, Austria, and Russia during recent years, seems to have been to stimulate their domestic product of sugar to the greatest extent, and then enter into competition with each other to see which of them could sell cheapest to foreigners at the expense of their own people; the home-grown sugars of France and Germany, for example, selling, it is reported, in England for about one half the prices paid for the same article by the French and German people.*

---

* In 1883–'84, Germany, at an estimated cost of about $8,000,000 in the way of export bounties, exported more than three fifths of her annual product

The Russians determined nearly forty years ago to make their own sugar out of the beet-root, and at first encouraged their manufacturers with a specific bounty. Subsequently they substituted for the bounty an almost prohibitory duty on imports, and under this system the production of beets and sugar increased rapidly for many years, with large resulting profits to producers. In 1881 the Russian manufacturers produced just enough to satisfy the demands of the home market. In 1882 there was an excess of production. Prices then began to fall and manufacturers to fail. They could not export their surplus at a profit, because they could not compete in foreign markets. More protection at home was not wanted, because the protection existing was complete. Under these circumstances application was made to the Government to pay them for exporting their surplus, and this the Government agreed to do, to the extent of giving a bounty of one ruble per pood * on an exportation that was to be limited to two million poods, with a remission also of all internal taxes on the same. This arrangement continued until January, 1886, when, the Russian market being overstocked with sugar, an extension of the bounty on an unlimited exportation was demanded, and granted by the Government for a period of about six months, or until July, 1886. The result was that the Russian exporters poured upon the English and Italian markets (the only ones readily available to them) during this brief time, and to the great disturbance of the world's markets, sugar to the amount of seven and a half million poods (227,000,000 pounds), leaving still three million poods surplus at home unsold and unsalable.

---

of beet-sugar. Of this exportation a large part went to the United Kingdom, where the average consumption of sugar for that year was in excess of seventy pounds per capita, as compared with an average of seventeen pounds for the population of Germany.

* The Russian pood equals thirty-five English pounds, and the single silver Russian ruble may be reckoned at sixty cents.

The sugar experience of France has been similar to that of Germany, but characterized by some features of special interest. Previous to 1884 the excise tax was levied on the manufactured sugar, but since that year it has been assessed against the raw material, or the beet-root. The average yield had previously been 5·50 per cent, or five and a half kilos to one hundred kilos of root, and under the new system the yield was fixed for the three years ending on the 31st of August, 1885, 1886, and 1887, for the purpose of taxation, at five or six per cent of refined sugar, according to the process of manufacture employed, pressure or diffusion. All the surplus yield escaped duty and formed the bounty. Manufacturers consequently applied themselves to obtain beet-root rich in saccharine, and the result was that the yield was increased from five and a half per cent in 1884 to 7·27 in 1885; 8·12 in 1886; 8·87 in 1887; and 9·50 per cent in 1888. The surplus of home-made sugar that thus escaped taxation amounted to 22·56 per cent of the total production in 1885; 31·21 per cent in 1886; and 36·44 per cent in 1887. In order not to place French colonial sugar at a disadvantage, a rebate, first of twelve per cent, and afterward of twenty-four per cent, of the duty was made. This further increased the quantity of French sugar free of taxation, which rose from 50,728 tons in 1885 to 87,910 in 1886, and 184,154 tons in 1887, representing in money a loss to the treasury and a bounty to the manufacturer of 25,364,-177 francs in 1885; 43,955,072 francs in 1886; and 92,077,-278 francs in 1887. French sugar-manufacturers, to stimulate the growers of beet in producing a root rich in sugar, pay a premium above a certain density; but it has been found that improvements in quality can be obtained only through a considerable sacrifice of quantity. By a law enacted in 1887, the yield of sugar liable to duty was raised to seven per cent for 1888, to increase one quarter per cent yearly for four years, but, with an effective yield of over nine per cent, a good margin now remains for the manufacturer's bounty.

The present (1889) export bounty in Germany, and the annual treasury expenditure in order that foreigners may have cheap sugar, owing to recent changes in the law, will not probably exceed $4,000,000 (£800,000).

In Austria, it was estimated that the sacrifice imposed by the sugar bounties cost her population five million florins in 1887, and that the increase in the price of sugar to domestic consumers, in consequence of the prohibitory import duties on foreign sugars, amounted to over four and a half million additional; so that the country paid nine and a half million florins ($3,277,000) in 1887 for its participation in the business of sugar production. For the year 1885–'86 Belgium is reported to have paid about $4,000,000, and Holland $1,500,000, on account of sugar-export bounties. The United States, in this business of selling sugar cheap to foreigners at the expense of their own people, has also played a not undistinguished part, the exports of refined sugars having risen from 22,227,000 pounds in 1881 to 252,579,000 pounds in 1885, or 26,000,000 pounds in excess of the entire cane-sugar product of the country for the latter year. The secret of this probably was, that a bounty was paid under the guise of a drawback, which the English sugar-refiners estimated at thirty-nine cents per one hundred pounds. This drawback having been reduced by the Treasury Department to seventeen cents, the exports for the succeeding year, 1885–'86, at once fell off to 164,339,000 pounds, and in 1888 to only 34,449,000 pounds. The bounty practically paid by the United States to the producers of sugar in the Sandwich Islands, by the relinquishment of duties on all sugars imported therefrom, while duties are maintained on the import of sugars from all other countries, also amounts at present to at least $6,000,000 per annum.

The experiences that have followed this attempt, on the part of practical statesmen, to interfere with the natural progress and development of a great industry, constitute one of the most instructive chapters in all economic history.

Judged from certain standpoints, the bounty system, as applied to beet-root sugar, has been unquestionably most successful. It has increased the aggregate product of this variety of sugar so rapidly that, in place of constituting twenty per cent of the whole sugar-product of the world, as it did in 1860, it now represents at least fifty-six per cent of such aggregate. Its artificially increased product has so far exceeded the current demands of the world for consumption that sugar in 1886–'87 ranked in point of retail value with such articles as oatmeal, barley, and flour, and was used to some extent in England as food for cattle; while its use as a fertilizer, in competition with artificial manures, was even also advocated. The average price of the raw sugars imported into England from 1884 to 1888, as officially reported, was 13·63s. per cwt., in comparison with an average of 24·47s. for the period from 1869 to 1875, and 20·97s. from 1879 to 1883.

Such a reduction in the price of a prime necessity of life has been of immense advantage to consumers. In Great Britain, whose policy since 1874 has been to give her people sugar free of taxation, the per capita consumption has risen from fifty-six pounds in that year to seventy-four pounds in 1886 (as compared with a per capita of about fifty-four pounds in the United States in 1885), while the saving to the British people, from the reduction of the cost of this one item of their living, in the single year of 1884, was estimated by a committee representing West India producers, as at least £5,000,000 ($25,000,000), or more than the entire value of the annual sugar product of the West Indies (estimated at £4,500,000) ; and at twice the fixed capital invested in sugar-refining in the United Kingdom.

Again, the bounty policy developed a large local industry in many of the states of Continental Europe, and for a time paid enormous profits to manufacturers and refiners producing for export. During the year 1886 the profits of the two leading sugar-refiners of France from export bounties, exclusive of their domestic trade, were reported as about £450,000 ($2,225,000) each; but how much of this they were required to part with in order to force, through reduced prices, the sales of their product in other countries, is, of course, not known. It is claimed to have greatly injured the sugar-refining industry of Great Britain; but, on the other hand, it is certain to have given a great impetus to the business of manufacturing confectionery, preserved fruits, jams, etc., in that country; industries which have given employment to many more persons than were ever occupied in refining sugar.*

But there is another side to this picture. Under the influence of an extraordinary and artificial stimulus more sugar has been produced than the world was ready to absorb, even at the reduced prices which the bounties made possible. The price of beet-root, and therefore of all sugar, has continued to decline, until the sugar-industry of Continental Europe (with the possible exception of France) has experienced the severest depression. Many establishments have closed or passed into bankruptcy, and it is now well understood that the only profit available to the manufactories is that derivable from so much of their product as is exported, which in the case of Germany represents more than half of the annual production. In a recent discussion in the Ger-

---

* With the advantage of cheaper sugar than any other commercial nation, the "jam" industry has developed in Great Britain to a great extent; and this, too, notwithstanding that Great Britain is a country not especially adapted to the growing of fruits, and in which domestic fruits are, as a rule, costly. According to Sir Thomas Farrer, about 100,000 tons (200,000,000 pounds) of refined sugar was used in this industry in the United Kingdom in 1884; employing 12,000 men, or more than double the number employed in the British sugar-refineries; and for 1888 the estimate was 150,000 tons. With the reduction in the price of jam, consequent on the low cost of sugar, the consumption of jam throughout the world has received an enormous impulse; and preserves of every kind—more especially orange marmalade—which were formerly regarded as luxuries, are reported as becoming articles of daily use in England among the very poorest families, supplanting to a certain extent the use of butter.

man Reichstag, Deputy Heine opposed the continuance of
the present bounty system in that country, upon the ground
that it was disastrous to the agricultural laborer, who had
been compelled to sacrifice all his land to the beet-cultiva-
tors. These cultivators, who farmed upon a large scale, he
maintained, had effected many improvements in labor-saving machinery, and thus reduced the laborer's wages to a
minimum; so that in some districts the laborers were little
better off than serfs. At the same time the people of the
sugar-producing states of Europe uniformly pay more for
what proportion of their own sugars they consume than is
paid by foreigners on the proportion exported. Deputy
Gelhert, continuing the discussion, is reported as saying:

"I can not discern the smallest gain to our country. The profits
of the system have only been reaped by England. It is German sugar
that has enabled England to give sugar to her cattle; it is German
capital that has so developed the English manufacture of sweets, that
it successfully competes with the German manufacturer in the markets
of the world and in Germany itself. We pay one and a half to two
millions sterling to enable England to consume what would probably
be worked up by our German industry. Gentlemen, I fear that this
system has made us the laughing-stock of our English cousins!"

In Russia, where the depression is extreme, the manufacturers have petitioned the Government, but thus far un-
successfully, to restrict production by law to whatever extent
would be necessary to keep the price up to the point at
which it stood when the domestic product was just sufficient
to supply the home market; or, in other words, to permit
production to continue at the producer's discretion, but not
to allow him to sell anything over the regulation amount in
the home market.

The disaster which the extreme artificial reduction in
recent years in the price of sugars has brought to other
great business interests and to the material prosperity and
even civilization of large areas of the earth's surface, can
not also well be overstated. In Barbadoes (British West

Indies), in February, 1887, it was estimated * that the loss at that time on every ton of sugar produced and exported to London was £1 15s. ; and in the absence of all profit on what is almost the sole industry of the West Indies, it would seem as if civilization would disappear from many of the islands, as indeed it already has in a great degree from some of them—the island of Tortola, for example, which was, comparatively a few years ago, the seat of a profitable sugar-industry. In the Spanish islands of Cuba and Porto Rico poverty is reported to be almost universal, save among the large planters and merchants in the cities; and brigandage has so greatly increased as to be devoid of novelty. Taxes on the sugar product of these islands (mainly through export duties) have hitherto constituted an important source of revenue to the Spanish treasury; but latterly the home Government, as a condition for saving the planters from ruin, has felt obliged to relinquish most of them. The suggestion has even been seriously made that, as the tobacco-crop commands good and increasing prices, the cultivation of sugar should be abandoned altogether, and the islands converted into tobacco-farms. In Java the situation of the sugar-industry has been so deplorable that, in order to save it from destruction, with the consequent throwing of half a million of Javanese laborers out of employment, and thereby increasing the already large number of Malay pirates, the Dutch ministry, in 1886, decided, besides making advances to planters on their crops, to purchase from their colonial planters five eighths of their production at a price that would entail a sacrifice on the Dutch treasury of about 40,000,000 francs, or $8,000,000.† And since then it seems to have been

---

* " Barbadoes Agricultural Reporter," February, 1887.

† " Journal des Fabricants de Sucre," October, 1886.

A further idea of the depression of the sugar-trade in Java may be gained from the fact that the imports of raw sugar from the island by Holland have declined—comparing the results of the year 1870 with those of 1885—about ninety per cent.

well established that German beet-root sugar has been and
is now exported half round the globe, and largely sold in
Singapore, the center of the great sugar-producing countries of Asia, at a price which makes its use to the manufacturers of preserved fruits more advantageous than the
sugars of Java and the other islands of the Indian Archi-
pelago.

In British India, owing to the competition of European
beet-sugar, the exports of sugar, comparing 1884 with
1887, experienced a decline of 632,439 cwts.; and a similar
competition as respects Australia has threatened with ruin
the developing sugar-industry of these countries. In the
island of Madagascar, also, the manufacture of sugar, which
was formerly the staple industry, has become so unprofitable, that the people have largely abandoned the cultivation
of the cane, and are devoting their labor to the production
of tea, tobacco, tapioca, and other tropical products.

Finally, the states of Continental Europe, in which the
burden of taxation is already most grievous, and in most of
which there is a regular and increasing annual deficit, are
beginning to feel that they can no longer endure the strain
upon their finances which the bounty-paying system to their
sugar-industries entails, and which has not brought prosperity to them or the state. In this reaction, Russia has
taken the lead, and with the exception of bounties granted
for a period of five years on the export of sugars to Persia,
has abolished her former general system of bounties; and
all the other states of Continental Europe exhibit unmistakable evidences of a desire to follow her example. It is generally agreed in Europe that not only have the fiscal results
of the bounty system been wholly unsatisfactory to the
several sugar-producing states, but also that the bounties
have enabled foreign consumers to obtain sugar at less than
its actual cost of production. Competition among the refiners has compelled them to share their bounties with
their customers, and their own have been compelled to pay

prices abnormally high, in order that foreigners might buy at prices abnormally low.

Recent investigations have also developed this curious feature of this sugar-bounty question, and that is, that the country paying the heaviest export bounty does not export the greatest quantity. Thus France, with a reported annual production of 550,000 tons, and paying a much higher bounty than Germany, exports twenty-nine per cent of her product; while Germany, with an annual production of about a million tons, and paying a much smaller bounty, exports sixty-one per cent of her product.

It is furthermore recognized that, while a bounty unnaturally stimulates the production of sugar, it also operates to a like extent in discouraging production where no bounty is given; and that, if the bounty system is continued long enough, it will in a great measure destroy natural production.

The great difficulty of the situation, however, is that much of the sugar-industry that has been called into existence artificially would be immediately ruined, with great loss and suffering to a large number of people, if the bounties were at once discontinued; and the same result would follow by the putting an end to any possibility of exporting, if one, or all but one, of the states should cease paying bounties, and one, like France, should continue to do so.

An invitation extended by the British Government, in 1887, to the various sugar-producing nations, to meet in conference through their representatives, " with a view of arriving at a common understanding for the suppression of (export) duties," was therefore promptly accepted; and in November of that year such a conference assembled in London, at which officially appointed delegates from Germany, Austria, Belgium, Sweden, France, Denmark, Spain, Great Britain, Italy, the Netherlands, Russia, and Brazil were present and participated.* The results of the first

---

* The United States was invited to send delegates, but no action was taken

meeting were a unanimous condemnation of the system of bounties; and the adoption of a convention for submission, with a view of ratification, to the respective governments, of which the following was the first article:

" The high contracting parties engage to take such measures as shall constitute an absolute and complete guarantee that no open or disguised bounty shall be granted on the manufacture or exportation of sugar."

The conference reassembled in August, 1888, at which meeting a further convention was drafted, embodying methods for practically enforcing the object of the conference; the main features of which were that the contracting powers should exclude from their territories all sugar and sugar products that have been benefited by either open or disguised bounties; such exclusion to be effected, either by direct prohibition, or by the levying of duties in excess of the bounties; and that beet-root sugars intended for exportation should be manufactured in bond. To this proposition the representatives of England, Germany, Spain, Italy, and Russia agreed. Of other countries, the United States did not participate; Belgium was not satisfied with the idea of manufacturing in bond for exportation; Austria and France reserved their concurrence until all other sugar producing and consuming countries agreed to adhere; Denmark and Sweden refused to sign absolutely; Brazil reserved her freedom of action.

As unanimity of action is clearly essential to the successful working of any international agreement for the suppression of the sugar-bounty system, and as no such agreement has thus far been attained, or seems possible—public opinion in Great Britain, for example, being apparently very adverse to the indorsement of the recommendations of the British representatives at the conference—the efforts of the

in response further than the authorization of the secretary of the legation at London to attend the convention, without participation in the proceedings.

conference to effect a result which it had unanimously declared was most desirable, appear at present to have been wholly ineffectual. But as final action on the part of the states represented in the conference is deferred until September, 1891, further experiences may remove obstacles that now appear insurmountable.* The fact that the people of Great Britain—which neither imposes taxes nor pays bounties on sugar—consume more sugar per capita than the people of any other country in the world—namely, 74 pounds—while the people of those countries which have endeavored to artificially encourage the production and consumption of sugar, consume comparatively small amounts per capita—namely, in the case of France, 28 pounds; Germany, 20¾ pounds; Austria, 14½ pounds; Russia, 9 pounds; Italy, 8 pounds; Holland, 28½ pounds; and Spain, 9¼ pounds—would seem furthermore to amount to a demonstration, that the most certain way of providing for the greatest consumption of sugar, and of speedily relieving the world's markets of any over-production of this most desirable commodity, would be for governments to refrain to the greatest possible extent from all interferences with its production and distribution.

---

* The clause of the treaty adopting stringent provisions against the violation of its provisions " is a new departure in international agreements, and its exact terms will be fully scrutinized in all countries. The expediency of some compulsion of this nature seems to have been admitted by all the delegates, including those of France ; but it would seem a question how far the exclusion by us of the sugar, say, of France, would be compatible with our existing treaty engagement to extend to her the most-favored-nation treatment, and it is difficult to see how our Government, which has always declined to impose differential duties upon sugar, can now go to such a far greater length in differentiating as wholly to exclude the products of some countries while opening our ports freely to sugar from all other quarters. We might as well exclude from our ports all foreign ships which receive bounties from their governments, and all the goods which such ships carry. In fact, if once we admit the principle that it is right to fight bounties by customs duties or regulations, we commit ourselves to a policy of commercial reprisals, and upon such a policy it would, in our opinion, be the height of folly for us to enter."—*London Economist.*

To bring up the narrative of this curious chapter in the world's economic experience to the present date (1889), it is to be added that, owing to a reduction in the production of sugar through the discouragement of the low prices which the bounty system has occasioned, conjoined with an unfavorable season, and an increasing consumption consequent on an increasing population, the world finds itself threatened for a time (1889) with a temporary scarcity of sugar. Prices, accordingly, have greatly advanced, with a prospective outlook for another year of increased production, and a repetition of price disturbances in the not-distant future.

It is also interesting to note that, notwithstanding the experience of the sugar bounties, the Government of the Argentine Republic, while the sugar convention was pending, determined to appropriate an annual sum of $550,000 for three years, in order to stimulate the export trade of that country in beef and mutton for the European market.

BOUNTIES FOR SHIPPING.—The recent experience of France in attempting to stimulate ship-building and ship-using, through a carefully-devised system of subsidies and bounties, furnishes another illustration of the effect of governmental interference with the natural course of industries, second in importance only to that afforded by the experience of sugar.

Thus, to accomplish the purpose above noted, the French Government offered in 1881 to give a bounty of twelve dollars a ton on all ships built in French yards of iron and steel; and a subsidy of three dollars per ten tons for every thousand miles sailed by French vessels; and as they did not desire to put any inhibition on the citizens of France buying vessels in foreign countries and making them French property, in case they desired to do so, they proposed to give one half the latter subsidy to vessels of foreign construction bought by citizens of France and transferred to the French flag.

At the outset, as was the case with the sugar bounties, the scheme worked admirably. New and extensive steam-ship lines were organized with almost feverish haste, and the construction of many new and large steamers was promptly commenced and rapidly pushed forward in various French ports, and also in the ship-yards of Great Britain and other countries. The Government paid out a large amount of money, and it got the ships. In two years their tonnage increased from a little over 300,000 to nearly 700,000 tons for steamers alone; while the tonnage engaged on long voyages increased in a single year from 3,600,000 to over 4,700,000 tons.

It was probably a little galling to the French to find out after two years' experience that most of the subsidies paid by the Government were earned by some two hundred iron steamers and sailers, and that over six tenths of these were built and probably owned in large part in Great Britain; so that the ship-yards on the Clyde got the lion's share of the money. But as all the vessels were transferred to and sailed under the French flag, and were regarded as belonging to the French mercantile marine, everything seemed to indicate that the new scheme was working very well, and that the Government had really succeeded in building up the shipping of France. But the trouble was that the scheme did not continue to work. The French soon learned by experience the truth of the economic maxim that ships are the children and not the parents of commerce; and that while it was easy to buy ships out of money raised by taxation, the mere fact of the ownership of two or three hundred more ships did no more to increase trade than the purchase and ownership of two or three hundred more plows necessarily increased to a farmer the amount of arable land to plow; or, in other words, the French found that they had gone to large expense to buy a new and costly set of tools, and then had no use for them.

And, what was worse, they found, furthermore, that

while they had not increased trade to any material extent, they had increased the competition for transacting what trade they already possessed.   The result has been that many French shipping companies that before the subsidy system were able to pay dividends were no longer able; fortunes that had been derived from the previous artificial prosperity have melted away, and the French mercantile marine ceased to grow—only $584,288 being paid out for construction bounties in 1886, as compared with a disbursement of $982,673 in 1882.*   In fact, the whole scheme proved so disastrous a failure that the late Paul Bert, the eminent French legislator and orator, in a speech in the French Assembly, seriously undertook to defend the French war of invasion in Tonquin on the ground that its continuance would afford employment for the new French mercantile marine, which otherwise, we have a right to infer, in his opinion would have remained idle.   A recent writer—M. Raffalovich—in the "Journal des Économistes," has also thus summed up the situation.   "It may be asserted," he says, that

"the bounty system in France, which was intended to bridge over a temporary depression, has aggravated the situation, and has proved itself to be a source of mischief, not of cure."

The experience of the mercantile marines of Europe during recent years affords the following curious results: It shows, *first*, that the payment of bounties has practically availed nothing in arresting the continued decrease in sailing-tonnage; *second*, that in the eight years prior to 1880, French shipping, in its most valuable branch-steamers, increased faster than the shipping of any of its Continental competitors; but after 1880, the increase in the steam marine of Germany, where no bounties were paid, was relatively greater both in number and tonnage of vessels than in

---

* The total amount paid by France for the construction and running of ships is estimated to have been 10,583,965 francs in 1887, and 9,000,000 in 1888.

France where large bounties were given after 1881; and was also greater as respects the aggregate tonnage of all vessels—sail and steam. The obvious expectation of the French Government in resorting to the bounty system for shipping was that ships built and navigated with the aid of the bounties would carry French manufactures into foreign countries, and thus open new markets for domestic products. But experience, thus far, has shown that all that has been effected is a transfer, to some extent, of the carriage of goods formerly brought in foreign vessels to French vessels. But, on the other hand, the increase of tonnage, under the stimulus of the bounties, beyond the requirements of traffic, and the consequent reduction of freights, has entailed " a loss, and not a gain to the French nation; by throwing upon it the burden of a shipping interest that, but for the Government aid, would have been unprofitable, and which, because of such aid, can not conform itself to the demands of trade." * The experience of Austria-Hungary in attempting to find new outlets for their produce, or fresh employ-

---

* " Report on the Mercantile Marines of Foreign Countries," by Worthington C. Ford, U. S. Department of State, Executive Documents, 1886.

A report (1889) to the British House of Commons affords the latest information respecting the payment of bounties in European countries with a view to favoring the construction and running of ships. It appears that such payments are made in France, Italy, and Spain. In France the annual outlay on bounties for construction is officially reported to have been £181,620 ($982,673) in 1882, and £120,224 ($584,288) in 1886. The sums allowed by France for navigation depend upon the age of the vessel and the materials used in construction. The amount of bounties for navigation paid in 1886 was 7,578,347 francs. In Italy, for 1887, the following amounts were paid by the Government: namely, for construction of vessels, £4,587; for repairs, £7,210; for importing coal, £6,931; for navigation—steamers, £44,956; sailing-vessels, £96,289; total, £159,973. In Spain the bounty is 32s. per ton paid to Spanish ship-builders on vessels constructed by them. In Spain, and also in Austria and Belgium, materials used in ship-building are exempted from payment of customs duties. No statement, however, is supplied as to the actual or estimated amount of the aid thus afforded to the construction of vessels in the three countries last named. Postal subsidies are granted in almost all European states; but these payments can not be reckoned as bounties.

ment for their shipping by the payment of subsidies, has been analogous to that of France, and equally unfortunate. The steamers of the Austrian Lloyd Company have made more voyages to the " Far East " than when unsubsidized ; but the exports of Austrian products have not materially increased, while the mercantile marine generally of Austria is rapidly declining.

The experience of Great Britain, occcupying, as she has, the position of being the only country in the world of *large* production and commerce which has not within recent years imposed restrictions on the competitive sale of foreign prod-ducts in her markets, is also exceedingly interesting and instructive. That British trade and production have been injured by attempts in the nature of forced sales on the part of competitors in protected countries to dispose of their surplus products in the English duty-free markets—while the tariffs of their own countries have shielded them from reprisals—and that from like causes Great Britain has experienced severe foreign competition in neutral markets, where British trade had formerly almost exclusive possession, can not be doubted.   Thus, the report of the British Commission " On the Depression of Trade and Industry " (1886) shows that the importation of foreign manufactured or partially manufactured goods into Great Britain has increased since 1870, at " a slightly more rapid rate " than the increase of its population, having been £1.97 per head in the period 1870–'74, and £2.35 per head in the period 1880–'84. The extent of the injury to British interests from these changes in the conditions of the world's trade does not, however, appear to have been as great as might have been anticipated, or as is popularly supposed, and very curiously has manifested itself in a reduction of profits, rather than in any reduction of the volume of British trade ; the value of British exports to the six protectionist countries of the world—the United States, France, Germany, Russia, Spain, and Italy—having been larger during the years 1880–'84 than in any quinquennial period of British history, with the exception of the period from 1870–'74, when British trade is known to have been abnormally inflated.   Thus the average annual value of British and Irish produce exported to France, Germany, Spain, Italy, Russia, and the United States was £2 26 per head of her population in 1880–'84, as compared with $2 06 in 1875–'79, and £2 18 for 1865–'69. Of the total increase in the shipping trade of the principal maritime nations from 1878 to 1887, one third occurred in British tonnage; while of the increase in the merchant steam tonnage of different countries, during the same period, nearly two thirds is to be credited to Great Britain.   In the year 1887 the mercantile navy of Great Britain, while carrying three fourths of the whole of her own immense commerce, carried at the same time one half of that of the United States, Portugal, and Holland ; nearly one half of that of Italy and Russia; and more than one third of that of France and Germany.   As the ocean mercantile tonnage of the United States declined between the years 1878 and 1887 in a greater degree than that of any other country, it is very clear at whose expense the increase in the shipping of other nations was made during this same period.   It is also not a little interesting to note that the countries of the world in which, according to the most recent and accepted statistics, the ratio of wealth and the ratio of foreign commerce to the population are the greatest, are Holland and Great Britain, the two states that have emancipated themselves in the greatest degree from all restrictions on the interchange of products with foreign nations—the customs revenue of the former amounting to about one per cent on her imports, and that of the latter to about five and a half per cent.*   In India, also, where there

---

* It is popularly believed that the per capita wealth of the people of the United States, which the census of 1880 fixed at $860—but which, allowing for duplications, is probably not over $500—is greater than that of any other people. This, however, is not the fact ; the ratio of wealth to each inhabitant

are few artificial restrictions on the freedom of exchange,
internal trade, manufactures, and foreign commerce have
increased in an extraordinary degree within recent years,
and the wages of skilled labor have also, at the same time,
notably advanced.

An analysis of the comparative values of the export
trade of the nations of Europe during the five years from
1880–'85—a period of intense struggle for the domination of
the world's markets—affords the following significant results: In cotton and woolen yarns and dry-goods, England
strengthened her position; in iron and steel goods, her
share of the world's trade increased from 64·2 to 66·5 per
cent; while in machinery her exports were pushed up from
66·7 to 69·1 per cent.   In glass and glass goods England's
percentage remained constant, while that of France and
Belgium declined.   Germany increased her exports of glass
and glassware, and also very largely of paper and slightly
of machinery, losing ground in respect to the exportation
of iron and steel goods, in common with France and Austria.   In leather and leather goods Germany leads, while
France appears to be rapidly losing her former supremacy.

Apart, however, from their bearing on any particular
country, a review of all the circumstances connected with
the multiplication of restrictions on international commerce,
which the majority of civilized nations have united in creating in recent years, fully justifies the British Commission
and other European authorities in regarding it as a most
influential agency in occasioning almost universal economic
disturbance.   It has been progress backward—progress in
the direction of that sentiment of the middle ages, which

---

in Great Britain being $1,245, and in Holland, $1,200. The wealth of Holland, moreover, doubled in the twenty years next prior to 1880, while the
gain in population of the country during the same period was comparatively
insignificant.   In respect to commerce, the ratio to each inhabitant, in 1880,
was $150 in Holland, as compared with $91 for Great Britain, and $32 for
the United States.

held that, as commerce benefited one country only as it injured some other, it was the duty of every country to impose the most harassing restrictions on its commercial intercourse. The evidence, furthermore, is overwhelming that, as civilization grows more complex, and the use and perfection of machinery increases, all obstacles placed in the way of the freest interchange of commodities have an increasingly disastrous effect in deranging and destroying industry everywhere. Or, in other words, increased knowledge respecting the forces of Nature, and a wonderful subordination and use of the same having greatly increased and cheapened the abundance of all useful and desirable things, the majority of the world's legislators and statesmen have seemed to have considered it incumbent upon them to neutralize and defeat the beneficent results of such abundance. And the most comforting assurance that progress will not continue to be made in this same direction, is to be found not so much in the intelligence of the masses or their rulers, as in the circumstance that existing restrictions on commerce can not be much further augmented without such an impairment of international trade as would be destructive of civilization.

As the existing restrictions on commercial intercourse within recent years have not been all imposed at one time, but progressively, and as their influence has accordingly been gradual, the world does not, however, seem to have as yet fully appreciated the extent to which the exchange of products between nations has been thereby interrupted or destroyed. But, as the case now stands, Russia practically prohibits her people from any foreign purchases of iron and steel, and in fact seems to desire to limit exchanges of her products for the products of all other nations to the greatest extent possible. Germany, by repeated enactments since 1879, has imposed almost prohibitory duties on the importation of wheat; a measure directed, in the first instance, against Russia, as a means of retaliation for the persecution of German landed proprietors in Poland, but which has severely damaged the German steam flour industry, and benefited no one.   Austria imposes heavy tariff rates on the import of almost all German manufactures.   Belgium prevents the importations of cattle and meats; Austria, Russia, Germany, France, Belgium, and Holland, of sugar; France, of pork and pork products; Brazil, of rice; while trade between Italy and France has been interrupted to almost as great a degree as mutual governmental action will admit.

The imports of Russia, as before pointed out, decreased forty-three per cent in the four years from 1883 to 1887; and in the case of no one of the Continental states of Europe has the condition of their foreign trade in recent years been regarded as satisfactory.   For the year 1888 there was a decline in the exchanges of every such state with foreign countries; or, what is the same thing, there was a greater restriction to each one of them of markets for the industrial products of their own people.   The avowed policy of the United States has for years been to prohibit or obstruct trade on the part of her citizens, in respect to many articles, with the citizens of all foreign countries; and with this example, and in part from a spirit of retaliation, there can be no doubt that the objective of much of the restrictive commercial legislation of other countries in recent years has been the United States—à policy which has notably affected the agricultural supremacy of the latter country in the world's markets; the exports from the United States, comparing 1888 with 1881, of cattle, having declined 24·5 in quantity and nineteen per cent in value; of hog-products, 43·3 in value; and, of dairy products, over fifty per cent in value.   The decline in the value of the exports of the United States to France has been especially noteworthy, namely, from a value of $99,000,000 in 1880 to $40,000,000 in 1886, and $37,780,000 in 1888.

Great Britain alone of all the nations, in increasing her territorial possessions, does not take to herself any commercial privileges which she does not readily and equally share with the people of all other countries.

In all discussions as to the expediency of imposing taxes on imports with a view of protecting domestic industries, the question as to the amout of indirect taxation thereby actually entailed through augmentation of prices on the consumers of protected products constitutes a most important and interesting feature. Many estimates of the incidence and extent of such taxes—which consumers pay, but which the Government does not receive—have from time to time been made, especially in the United States; but in the absence of sufficiently precise and unquestionable data they have not been generally regarded as satisfactory, and as a reality are often even unqualifiedly denied. The publication during the year 1888, under the auspices of the American Iron and Steel Association, of a complete collection of the statistics of the iron and steel industries of the United States, for many years down to the close of 1887, embracing both production and prices, with the concurrent prices of British iron and steel from 1830 to 1887,* affords, however, data so exact, as to permit the relative prices or cost of iron and steel to the consumers of these metals in the United States and Great Britain for the years from 1878 to 1887 inclusive, to be clearly exhibited ; and the amount of indirect taxation paid by the people of the former country in the form of increased prices contingent on the duties levied on their importations of iron and steel, to be computed with undoubted accuracy.

The average annual consumption of iron and steel in the United States, in one form or another, during the ten years 1878 to 1887 inclusive, was 6,000,000 tons of 2,000

---

* " A Collection of Statistics to the Close of 1887, relating to the Iron and Steel Industries of the United States ; to which is added much Valuable Statistical Information relating to the Iron and Steel Industries of Great Britain, etc.," by JAMES M. SWANK, *General Manager of the American Iron and Steel Association, Philadelphia,* 1888, 8vo pp. 24.

pounds each, or a fraction less than thirty per cent of the world's entire product of iron. For the year 1887 the consumption was more extraordinary—about 9,270,000 tons, or a fraction less than forty per cent of the world's product; the domestic product of pig-iron amounting to 7,187,000 tons. The average product of pig-iron in Great Britain for the same period, 1878 to 1887, was a little less than 8,400,000 net tons; and her product for 1887 corresponded very closely to the average of the whole period. It therefore appears that the consumption of iron and steel in the United States for the ten years in question, was equal to seventy-five per cent of the average product of Great Britain in that period; and at the present time is nearly equal to her entire product. As no other country than Great Britain exports any quantity of iron and steel that bears any important proportion of the present total consumption of the United States, nearly every other country importing more iron than it exports, it would be obviously impossible, therefore, for the United States to procure their necessary supply of these metals, except from their own mines.

From 1878 to 1887 inclusive, the average price of anthracite foundry pig in Philadelphia was $21.87 per ton. For the same period, the average (home) price of "Scotch" pig was $12.94; or, making an ample allowance for freights, a fraction under $15 per ton when landed in the United States. Deducting this from the price of anthracite foundry iron, as above stated, there was a disparity in price on all the pig-iron consumed in the United States during the ten years named, of seven dollars per ton in excess of the average concurrent market price of pig-iron in Great Britain.

If objection is made to the quality of iron above selected for examination, a comparison of the relative prices of the higher grades will afford results even more significant. Thus, from 1878 to 1887, the average price of the best rolled bar-iron in Philadelphia was $50.30 per ton of 2,240 pounds. The average price in England of the best Staffordshire marked bars was $35.48—a difference of $14 per ton. And here it may be noted that the disparity in the prices of iron in the United States and Great Britain becomes greater, the higher we rise in the qualities considered. But taking the *minimum*, or only the average difference between the price of anthracite foundry and Scotch pig, namely, seven dollars, and applying it to the aggregate consumption of the United States from 1878 to 1887—60,000,000 tons—it follows that the American consumers of iron in these ten years paid $420,000,000 in excess of the cost of like quantity to the consumers of Great Britain.

Again, the aggregate consumption of steel in the United States—domestic and foreign—during the ten years from 1878 to 1887, was over 20,000,000 tons ; or at an average of 2,000,000 tons per annum. Taking here, again, the lowest form of steel—namely, steel rails—for the purpose of exhibiting the difference in the average price or cost of the American and the British product of steel, it will be found that the average price of steel rails in the United States, during the period named, was forty-four dollars per ton, and in Great Britain thirty dollars. With this difference in price, the increased cost of the ten years' consumption of steel by American consumers was $280,000,000. But, as a difference of seven dollars per ton in the comparative price of the iron used for making steel has been already allowed in these computations, the consumption of steel in the United States can only be properly charged with half the disparity in the price of rails above noted, or $140,000,000.

Taking, therefore, the lowest grades of iron and steel as the basis for estimating the disparity in the cost of these products in the United States and Great Britain respectively, the conclusion is warranted that the excess of cost of iron and steel to the consumers in the United States, in the ten years from 1878 to 1887, was $560,000,000, or at an average of $56,000,000 per annum.

On a separate computation, made in the same way for

the year 1887, the data being derived from the source before mentioned, the disparity of the cost or price of the iron and steel consumption in the United States for that year, in comparison with the prices paid in Great Britain, rises to $80,000,000.

The total aggregate revenue derived by the Federal Government during the fiscal year ending June 30, 1887, from the duties levied on the importation of iron-ores, pig-iron, and all manufactures of iron and steel, was $20,713,000. In collecting this amount of revenue, which constituted less than one fifth per cent of the excess or surplus revenue of that year, the United States was, therefore, subjected to an additional tax of $60,000,000, which was ultimately paid by the consumers of iron and steel. Doubtless the difference was largely absorbed in the cost of assembling the material, and by charges contingent on the making of iron and steel in furnaces and rolling-mills which are either out of date or out of place, and was therefore not in the nature of a bounty.

Finally, the entire capital invested in the iron industry of the United States in 1880—including iron and coal mines and the manufacture of coke—according to the census data of that year, could not have been in excess of $341,000,000. The price paid, therefore, by the consumers of iron and steel in the United States, in order to sustain the iron-furnaces and rolling-mills of the country for ten years (which industries, as before observed, can not be displaced or destroyed by any possible foreign competition), paying wages somewhat less on the average than those paid to outside labor, has been about sixty-five per cent in excess of the entire capital invested. The magnitude of the economic disturbances, in the way of arresting local development and changing the course of the world's exchanges, occasioned by the continuous imposition of such a burden of taxation on an industry which may be regarded as the foundation of all industries, has passed into history. What economic disturbances will be contingent on the discontinuance of such taxation, pertain to the future.*

THE ECONOMIC DISTURBANCES SINCE 1873 CONTINGENT ON WAR EXPENDITURES are not different in kind from those of former periods, but much greater in degree. This subject has been so thoroughly investigated and is so well understood, that nothing more need be said in this connection than to point out that the men in actual service at the present time in the armies and navies of Europe are in excess of 4,000,000, or about one to every fifteen of all the men of arms-bearing age—all consumers and no producers. The number of men in reserve, who are armed, subject to drill, and held ready for service at any moment, is about 14,250,000 in addition. Including the reserves, the present standing armies and navies of Europe require the services of one in every five of the men of arms-bearing age, or one in every twenty-four of the whole population. It is also estimated that it requires the constant product of one peasant engaged in agriculture, or of one operative engaged in manufacturing in the commercial and manufacturing states of Europe, to equip and sustain one soldier ; that it requires the labor of one man to be diverted from every two hundred acres ; and that a sum equivalent to $1.10 shall be deducted from the annual product of every acre. The present aggregate annual expenditure of Europe for military and naval purposes is probably in excess of a thousand million dollars. We express this expenditure in terms of money, but it means work performed : not that abundance of useful and desirable things may be increased, but decreased ; not that toil may be lightened, but augmented.

As to the ultimate outcome of this state of affairs—ostensibly kept up for the propagation or promotion of civili-

---

* For a more detailed exhibit of the relative production and prices of iron and steel in the United States and Great Britain, and of the extent to which the duties on imports augment the price of these metals in the former country, reference is made to the Appendix.

zation—there is an almost perfect agreement of opinion among those who have studied it; and that is, that the existence and continuance of the present military system of Continental Europe is impoverishing its people, impairing their industrial strength, effectually hindering progress, driving the most promising men out of the several states to seek peaceful homes in foreign countries, and ultimately threatening the destruction of the whole fabric of society.

The contrast between ancient and modern war, limiting the comparison of results to human suffering, is very great; but in respect to the destruction of values it is not great. Carthage is not now destroyed ; but taxation, debt, interest, national reputation, and private losses represent a vast and perhaps greater amount of devastation. Recent authorities estimate the debt of Europe in 1865–'66 to have been £2,640,000,000; and that it had been increased in 1887— mainly by reason of war expenditures—to £4,684,000,000 ($22,264,000,000), entailing an annual burden of interest of £213,640,000 ($1,038,000,000).* It is a somewhat popular idea that, as the perfection of machinery for taking away human life makes war, or the preparation for war, every year more costly, the burden on the different nations will eventually become too heavy to be borne, and thus compel a general disarmament. Experience, unfortunately, does not favor any such conclusion. Nations seem always to be able to raise money for war, when they can not for other purposes ; and the classes upon whom the burdens of war rest are not the ones who initiate it. The result of increasing war burdens may not, therefore, presage disarmament and peace, but an ultimate terrible social struggle " between the classes and the masses."

---

* " Les Debtes publiques Européenes," M. Neymarck, Paris.

VIII.

THE predominant feeling induced by a review and consideration of the numerous and complex economic changes
and disturbances that have occurred since 1873 (as has been
detailed in the foregoing chapters), is undoubtedly, in the
case of very many persons, discouraging and pessimistic.
The questions which naturally suggest themselves, and in
fact are being continually asked, are: Is mankind being
made happier or better by this increased knowledge and
application of the forces of nature, and a consequent increased power of production and distribution? Or, on the
contrary, is not the tendency of this new condition of things,
as Dr. Siemens, of Berlin, has expressed it, "to the destruction of all of our ideals and to coarse sensualism; to aggra-
vate injustice in the distribution of wealth; diminish to

individual laborers the opportunities for independent work, and thereby bring them into a more dependent position; and, finally, is not the supremacy of birth and the sword about to be superseded by the still more oppressive reign of inherited or acquired property?"

What many think, but hesitate to say, finds forcible expression in the following extract from a letter addressed to the author by a large-hearted, sympathetic man, who is at the same time one of the best known of American journalists and leaders of public opinion. After referring to his great interest in the exhibit that has been made of the extraordinary economic disturbances since 1873 and their effect on persons, production, distribution, and prices, he says:

"But what a deplorable and quite awful picture you suggest of the future! The wheel of progress is to be run over the whole human race and smash us all, or nearly all, to a monstrous flatness! I get up from the reading of what you have written scared, and more satisfied than ever before that the true and wise course of every man is to get somewhere a piece of land, raise and make what he can for himself, and try thus to get out of the crushing process. It seems to me that what we call civilization is to degrade and incapacitate the mass of men and women; and how strange and incongruous a state it is! At the same time these masses of men are thrown out of their accustomed employments by the introduction or perfection of machinery—at that very time the number of women and children employed in factories rapidly increases; an unprecedented cheapness of all necessaries of life is coincident with an intensification of the bitter struggle for bread and shelter. It is a new form of slavery which, it seems to me, projects itself into view —universal slavery—not patriarchal, but mercantile. I get yearly more tired of what we call civilization. It seems to me a preposterous fraud. It does not give us leisure; it does not enable us to be clean except at a monstrous cost; it affects us with horrible diseases—like diphtheria and typhoid fever—poisoning our water and the air we breathe; it fosters the vicious classes—the politicians and the liquor-sellers—so that these grow continually more formidable; and it compels mankind to a strife for bread, which makes us all meaner than God intended us to be. Do you really think the 'game pays for the candle'?"

. From another, occupying high position as an economic thinker and writer, come also these questions :

" What are the social and political results to follow the sweeping reconstruction of our material prices and our labor system? Are we not unconsciously, and from the sheer force of these new elements, drifting fast into a form of actual socialism—if not exactly such as the *doctrinaire* reformers preach, yet a form which in respect to material interests swallows up individualism in huge combinations? Does not the economizing of the new methods of production necessitate this tendency? And, if so, to what sort of social reconstruction is it likely to lead? Does it mean a future of industrial kings and industrial slaves? How far does the new situation harmonize with current aspirations of labor? Are these aspirations a reflex effect of the new conditions of industry?"

To form now any rational opinion concerning the present and future influences of the causes of the recent and existing economic disturbances, and to be able to return any intelligent answers to the questions and impressions which they have prompted or created, there is clearly but one practical, common-sense method to adopt, and that is to review and analyze the sociological sequences of these disturbances so far as they have been developed and determined. A review in which sympathetic sentiments are allowed to predominate is not, however, what is needed; but rather one which will array and consider the facts and the conclusions which can fairly be deduced from them, apart, if possible, from the slightest humanitarian predisposition. The surgeon's probe that trembles in sympathy with the quivering flesh into which it penetrates, is not the instrumentality best adapted for making a correct diagnosis.

Such a review it is now proposed to attempt, and in entering upon it the first point worthy of attention is, that with the exception of a change unprecedented in modern times —in the relative values of the precious metals—all that has occurred differs from the world's past experience simply in *degree* and not in *kind*. We have, therefore, no absolutely unknown factors to deal with; and if the record of the past is not as perfect as could be desired—for it is only within a comparatively recent period that those exact statistics which constitute the foundations and absolute essentials of all correct economic reasoning have been gathered—it is, nevertheless, sufficiently so to insure against the commission of any serious errors in forecasting the future, of what in respect to industry and society is clearly a process of evolution.   This evolution exists in virtue of a law of constant acceleration of knowledge among men of the forces of nature, and in acquiring a capacity to use them for increasing or supplementing human effort, for the purpose of increasing and cheapening the work of production and distribution.   There is, furthermore, no reason for doubting that this evolution is to continue, although no one at any one time can foretell what are to be the next phases of development, or even so much as imagine the ultimate goal to which such progress tends.   The ignorance, prejudice, and selfishness of man may operate in the future, as in the past and at present, in obstructing this progress; but to entirely arrest it, or even effect a brief retrogression, would seem to be utterly impossible.*

That many of the features of the situation are, when considered by themselves, disagreeable and even appalling, can not be denied.   When one recalls, for example, through what seemingly weird power of genius, machinery has been summoned into existence—machinery which does not sleep, does not need rest, is not the recipient of wages; is most profitable when most unremittingly employed —and how no one agency has so stimulated its invention and use as the opposition of those whose toil it has supplemented or lightened —the first remedial idea of every employer whose labor is discontented being to devise and use a tool in place of a

---

* Those persons whose business renders them most conversant with patents are the ones most sanguine that nothing is likely to occur to interrupt or even check, in the immediate future, the progress of invention and discovery.

man; * and how in the place of being a bond-slave it seems
to be passing beyond control and assuming the mastery;
when one recalls all these incidents of progress, the following story of Eastern magic might be almost regarded in the
light of a purposely obscured old-time prophecy : A certain
man, having great learning, obtained knowledge of an incantation whereby he could compel inanimate objects to
work for him, commanded a stick to bring him water. The
stick at once obeyed. But when water sufficient for the
man's necessities had been brought, and there was threatened danger of an oversupply, he desired the stick to stop
working. Having, however, omitted to learn the words
for revoking the incantation, the stick refused to obey.
Thereupon, the magician in anger caught up an axe,
and, with a view to diminish or destroy the power of the
stick to perform work, chopped it into several pièces;
whereupon, each piece immediately began to bring as much
water as one had formerly done; and in the end not only
the magician but the whole world was deluged and destroyed.

---

* The following is one striking illustration in proof of this statement:
After the reaping-machine had been perfected to a high degree, and had come
into general use in the great wheat-growing States of the Northwest, the
farmer found himself for ten or fifteen days during the harvest period at the
mercy of a set of men who made his necessity for binding the wheat concurrently with its reaping, their opportunity. They began their work in the
southern section of the wheat-producing States, and moved northward with
the progress of the harvesting : demanding and obtaining $2, $3, and even
$4 and upward, per day, besides their board and lodging, for binding;
making themselves, moreover, at times very disagreeable in the farmers'
families, and materially reducing through their extravagant wages the profits
of the crop. An urgent demand was thus created for a machine that would
bind as well as reap; and after a time it came, and now wheat is bound as it
is harvested, without the intervention of any manual labor. When the sheafs
were first mechanically bound, iron wire was used as the binding material ;
but when a monopoly manufacturer, protected by patents and tariffs, charged
what was regarded an undue price for wire, cheap and coarse twine was substituted ; and latterly a machine has been invented and introduced, which
binds with a wisp of the same straw that is being harvested.

The proposition that all transitions in the life of society, even those to a better stage, are inevitably accompanied by human suffering, is undoubtedly correct. It is impossible, as an old-time writer (Sir James Stewart, 1767) has remarked, to even sweep a room without raising a dust and occasioning temporary discomfort. But those who are inclined to take discouraging and pessimistic views of recent economic movements, seem not only to forget this, but also to content themselves with looking mainly at the bad results of such movements, in place of the good and bad together. So it is not difficult to understand how a person like the Russian novelist Tolstoi, a man of genius, but whose life and writings show him to be eccentric almost to the verge of insanity, should, after familiarizing himself with peasant-life in Russia, come to the conclusion that " the edifice of civil society, erected by the toil and energy of countless generations, is a crumbling ruin." But the trials and vicissitudes of life as Tolstoi finds them among the masses of Russia are the result of an original barbarism and savagery from which the composite races of that country have not yet been able to emancipate themselves ; coupled with the existence of a typically despotic government, which throttles every movement for increased freedom in respect to both person and thought. But these are results for which the higher civilization of other countries is in no way responsible and can not at present help, but the indirect influence of which will, without doubt, in time powerfully affect and even entirely change. No one, furthermore, can familiarize himself with life as it exists in the slums and tenement-houses of all great cities in countries of the highest civilization ; or in sterile Newfoundland, where all Nature is harsh and niggardly ; or in sunny Mexico and the islands of the West Indies, where she is all bountiful and attractive, without finding much to sicken him with the aspects under which average humanity presents itself. But even here the evidence is absolutely conclusive that matters are not worse,

but almost immeasurably better, than formerly; and that
the possibilities for melioration, through what may be termed
the general drift of affairs, is, beyond all comparison, greater
than at any former period.

The first and signal result of the recent remarkable
changes in the conditions of production and distribution,
which in turn have been so conducive of industrial and societary disturbances, has been to greatly increase the abundance and reduce the price of most useful and desirable
commodities. If some may say, " What of that, so long
as distribution is impeded and has not been correspondingly perfected?" it may be answered, that production
and distribution in virtue of a natural law are correlative
or reciprocal. We produce to consume, and we consume
to produce, and the one will not go on independently
of the other; and although there may be, and actually
is, and mainly through the influence of bad laws, more
or less extensive maladjustment of these two great processes, the tendency is, and by methods to be hereafter
pointed out, for the two to come into closer and closer
harmony.

Next in order, it is important to recognize and keep
clearly in view in reasoning upon this subject, what of good
these same agencies, whose influence in respect to the future
is now regarded by so many with alarm or suspicion, have
already accomplished.

A hundred years ago the maintenance of the existing
population of Great Britain, of the United States, and of all
other highly-civilized countries, could not have been possible under the then imperfect and limited conditions of production and distribution. Malthus, who in 1798 was led by
his investigations to the conclusion that the population of
the world, and particularly of England, was rapidly pressing
upon the limits of subsistence, and could not go on increasing because there would not be food for its support, was entirely right from his standpoint on the then existing economic

conditions; * and no society at the present time, no matter how favorable may be its environments in respect to fertility of land, geniality of climate, and sparseness of population, is making any progress except through methods that in Malthus's day were practically unknown. The Malthusian theory is, moreover, completely exemplifying itself to-day in India, which is densely populated, destitute in great degree of roads, and of the knowledge and use of machinery. For here the conditions of peace established under British rule are proving so effective in removing the many obstacles to the growth of population that formerly existed, that its increase from year to year is pressing so rapidly on the means of subsistence, that periodical famines, over large areas, and accompanied with great destruction of life, are regarded as so inevitable that the creation of a national famine fund by the Government has been deemed necessary.†

---

* " Malthus made no prediction in the strict sense of the word. He had drawn out from experience that the human race tended to increase faster than the means of subsistence ; its natural increase being in geometrical ratio, and the increase of its means of subsistence an arithmetical one ; so that population had been kept down only in past times by war and famine, and by disease as the consequence of famine. He was bound to anticipate that a continuance of the process would expose the race once more to the operation of these natural checks, or to a descent of the masses in the scale of living, or to both of these evils. That the new experience has been different from the former one, and that owing to various causes the means of subsistence have increased faster than the population, even when increasing at a Malthusian rate, is no disproof surely of the teaching of Malthus. His statistical inquiries into the past remain as valuable as ever."—" *Some General Uses of Statistical Knowledge,*" ROBERT GIFFEN, *Royal Statistical Society of England*, 1885.

† The present condition of India constitutes one of the most curious and interesting economic and social problems of the last quarter of the nineteenth century. While the general average of the population for the whole country is 184 to the square mile, there are districts in India in which a population, to be counted by tens of millions, averages from 300 to 400 to the square mile, and others in which a population, to be counted by some millions, rises to 800 and even 900 to the square mile. These latter probably constitute the most densely-populated districts of the world, the population of the most densely-peopled country of Europe—namely, Belgium—averaging 480 to the square mile. The total population of India is estimated at 268,174,000. Under the old-time system of native rulers, frequent wars, consequent on for-

Under different circumstances the correctness of the ideas of Malthus are also being demonstrated in Japan. Recent investigations by Prof. Rein, of the University of Bonn, Germany, show " that with an area about the same as the State of California (157,000 square miles), and with only one tenth of such area practically available for cultivation, Japan supports a population of 36,000,000 almost entirely from her own product. Making due allowance for what may be eked out of the nine tenths taken up by forest, desert, and mountain, it appears that the incredible number of 2,560 inhabitants are supported from each square mile of cultivated land, or four to the acre. It is well known

---

eign invasions and internal race antagonisms, with accompanying famines and epidemic diseases, materially restricted the growth of population. But under the conditions of peace, with protection for life and property, which have been attendant in late years on British rule, the population of India is increasing so rapidly—nearly one per cent per annum—and so disproportionately to the amount of new and fertile soil that can be appropriated, as to leave but little margin, under existing methods of cultivation, for increasing the means of subsistence for the people. Much new soil has been put under cultivation during the last century of British rule, and a quarter of a million of square miles of cultivable waste yet remains to be occupied ; but the fact that the national revenues from the taxation of land have not increased to any extent in recent years is regarded as proof that land cultivation is not increasing in proportion to the growth of population, and that the limits of agricultural production are approaching exhaustion. An annual increase of one per cent on the present population of India means at least 20,000,000 more people to feed in ten years, and upward of 40,000,000 in twenty years ; and the problem to which the British Government in India has now before it, and to which it is devoting itself with great energy and intelligence, is, in what way, and by what means, can the character and habits of the people—especially in respect to their methods of agriculture—be so developed and changed that " their industry can become more efficient on practically the same soil ?" Much has been already done in the way of increasing and cheapening, through roads, canals, and railroads, the means of transportation, and in promoting irrigation and education, and especially the use of new tools and methods for cultivating the soil. But so many are the obstacles, and so great is the moral inertia of the people, that, although remarkable progress has been made, the prospect seems to be that, " from decade to decade, larger and larger masses of the semi-pauperized, or wholly pauperized, will grow up in India, requiring state intervention to feed them, and threatening social and financial difficulties of the most dangerous character."

that this can be done on a small scale, but its application to a nation is marvelous." Nothing is wasted in Japan; everything is utilized, and all arable land has been brought to the highest state of cultivation. But as the existing population is disproportionate to the maximum product that can be obtained from the land under the most favorable circumstances, there is already no margin left above the cost of a very frugal living; and no further large increment of population under present agricultural conditions is considered possible.

France, also, at the present time, according to Yves Guyot—one of the leading French economists and statesmen—" is Malthusian in practice though not in doctrine," and he thus illustrates it :

"The virtue of frugality has been preached to the Frenchman, and the *bourgeois* has put this virtue in practice. He has labored, only to be able the sooner to rest. The man who is honored has long been the man who 'does nothing.' In order to attain this dignity, the *bourgeois* lived scantily, and sought in economy a security for the future. Stinginess was the *bourgeois's* virtue. Logically enough he stinted himself or children as in everything else. Little by little the peasant proprietors and large farmers perceived and adopted the *bourgeois* system. They began with scraping together a few crowns to buy a morsel of land. Then, foreseeing the partition of this land, and dreading its attendant expenses, which would have swallowed up at a single gulp all the fruits of their toil, they effected a further saving—in children—and contemptuously left it to the poorest classes to burden themselves with large families. We give the proof of this assertion ! The increase of population is slower in France than anywhere else. The birth-rate of France is eighty per cent lower than in England and Prussia. For every one hundred persons in England and France respectively in 1801, there were in 1878 two hundred and twelve in England, and in France only one hundred and forty-two !"—" *Principles of Social Economy,*" by YVES GUYOT (*English translation by C. H. Leppington, London, 1884*).

Illustrations confirmatory of the assertion that the food resources of half a century ago would be inadequate for the support of the existing population of the leading civilized

countries are familiar, but the following are so striking as
to warrant renewed presentation :

All the resources of the population of the United States,
as they existed in 1880, would have been wholly inadequate
to sow or harvest the present average annual corn or wheat
crops of the country; and, even if these two results had
been accomplished, the greater proportion of such a cereal
product would have been of no value to the cultivator, and
must have rotted on the ground for lack of any means of
adequate distribution; the cost of the transportation of a
ton of wheat, worth twenty-five dollars at a market, for a
distance of a hundred and twenty miles over good roads,
and with good teams and vehicles, entirely exhausting its
initial value.

Forty years ago corn (maize) was shelled in the United
States by scraping the ears against the sharp edge of a
frying-pan or shovel, or by using the cob of one ear to
shell the corn from another. In this way about five bushels in ten hours could be shelled, and the laborer would
have received about one fifth of the product. The six great
corn States are Illinois, Indiana, Missouri, Iowa, Ohio, and
Kansas. They produce more than one half the corn raised
in the country. These States, by the census of 1880, had
2,056,770 persons engaged in agriculture, and it would have
been necessary for this entire community to sit astride of
shovels and frying-pans for one hundred and ten days out
of three hundred and sixty-five to shell their corn-crop for
the year 1880 by the old processes.

In 1790, before the grain-" cradle " was invented, an
able-bodied farm - laborer in Great Britain could with a
sickle reap only about a quarter of an acre of wheat in a
day; at the present time a man with two horses can cut,
rake, and bind in a day the wheat-product of twenty acres.

Forty years ago a deficient harvest in any one of the
countries of Europe entailed a vast amount of suffering and
starvation on their population. To-day the deficiency of

any local crop of wheat is comparatively of little consequence, for the prices of cereals in every country readily accessible by railroad and steamships are now regulated, not by any local conditions, but by the combined production and consumption of the world ; and the day of famines for the people of all such countries has passed forever.* The extent to which all local advantages in respect to the supply and prices of food have been equalized in recent years through the railway service of the United States, is demonstrated by the fact that a full year's requirement of meat and bread for an adult person can now be moved from the points of their most abundant and cheapest production, a thousand miles, for a cost not in excess of the single day's wages of an average American mechanic or artisan.

The same conditions that one hundred, or even fifty,

---

* It is not a little difficult to realize that the causes which were operative to occasion famines a hundred years ago in Western Europe, and which have now apparently passed away forever, are still operative over large portions of the Eastern world. The details of the last great famine in China, which occurred a few years ago, indicate that over five million people died of starvation in the famine district, while in other portions of the empire the crops were more abundant than usual. The trouble was, that there were no means of transporting the food to where it was needed. The distance of the famine area to the port of Tientsin, a point to which food could be and was readily transported by water, was not over two hundred miles ; and yet when the foreign residents of Shanghai sent through the missionaries an important contribution of relief, it required fifteen days, with the employment of all the men, beasts, and vehicles that could be procured, to effect the transportation of the contribution in question over this comparatively short distance. Relief to any appreciable extent to the starving people from the outside and prosperous districts was, therefore, impracticable. Consul H. M. Jewett, in writing to the United States Department of State, in June, 1887, on the great distress by reason of deficiency of food and threatened famine at that time in Asia Minor states, that while certain districts were greatly suffering for want of grain, an oversupply in other districts was wholly unavailable for lack of facilities for railroad transportation ; a condition of affairs identical with what prevailed in France during the last half of the eighteenth century. Contrast these experiences with the fact that when Chicago burned up in 1871 a train loaded with relief contributions from the city of New York, over the Erie Railroad, traversed nearly a thousand miles and reached its destination in twenty-one hours after the time of departure.

years ago limited the supply of food, and made it confessedly inadequate to meet the demands of a population increasing in a greatly disproportionate ratio, also limited the
opportunities for employment to such increasing numbers
apart from agriculture. Nearly and probably fully one half
of all those who now earn their living in industrial pursuits,
do so in occupations that not only had no existence, but
which had not even been conceived of, a hundred years ago.
The business of railroad construction, equipment, and operation, which now furnishes employment, directly or indi-
rectly, to about one tenth of all the population of the United
States engaged in gainful occupations, was wholly unknown
in 1830. Apart from domestic or farm service little opportunity existed for women to earn a livelihood by labor at
the commencement of the present century; but at the present time more than three million women in the United
States are engaged in nearly every kind of labor pursued by
men, from tilling the prairies of the West to preaching—a
vast multitude that every year grows greater.

The existence of the present populations of Europe and
the United States—nay, more, the continuance and progress
of civilization itself — has therefore been made possible
solely through the invention and use of the same labor-saving machinery which not a few are inclined to regard as
likely to work permanent injury to the masses in the future.
It is still easy to avoid all trouble arising out of the use of
labor-saving machinery by going to the numerous countries
—many of which are rich in the bounties of Nature—which
do not possess it. But these are the very countries to which
no person of average intelligence desires to go.

Restless and progressive humanity generally believes also
that the continued betterment of the race is largely conditioned on the extension of free government based on popular representation and constitutional safeguards; and also
on the successful continuation of the experiment under such
conditions which was entered upon by the people of the

United States just a hundred years ago. But the Government of the United States, under its existing Constitution, has been made possible only through the progress which man has made in recent years in his knowledge and control of the forces of nature. Without the perfected railroad and telegraph systems, the war for the maintenance of the Federal Union under the existing Constitution could not probably have been prosecuted to a successful conclusion ; and even if no domestic strife had intervened, it is more than doubtful whether a federation of numerous States, sovereign in many particulars—floating down the stream of time like an elongated series of separate rafts, linked together—could have been indefinitely perpetuated, when the time necessary to overcome the distance between its extremities for the mere transmission of intelligence amounted to from twenty to thirty days.*

In every highly civilized country, where accurate investigations have been instituted, the consumption of all the substantial articles of food, as well as of luxuries, has, within recent years, been largely and progressively increasing ; and as the consumption of rich and well-to-do people in such countries remains almost stationary, inasmuch as they have always been able to have all they desired of such articles, it is reasonable to infer that this result has been mainly due to the annually increasing ability of the masses to consume. In Great Britain, where this matter has been more thoroughly investigated than in any other country, the facts revealed (as will be presently shown) are most extraordinary. In the case of the population of Paris, M. Leroy-Beaulieu also reports a wonderful increase in the consumption of food-products since 1866, and states that, if the ravages of the phylloxera (vine-pest) could be checked, and the price

---

* When the battle of New Orleans was fought, in 1815, more than twenty-two days elapsed before the Government at Washington received any information of its occurrence.

of wine reduced, the cost of living for the whole of France would be less than it has ever been during the last half-century.   In the United States the increase in the consumption of such pure luxuries as spirits and tobacco is increasing in a greater ratio than population.   In 1888, the consumption of distilled spirits was 1·23 gallons per capita. The consumption of beer has increased from 6·68 gallons per capita in 1878 to 8·26 gallons in 1880, 10·18 gallons in 1883, and 12·48 in 1888.   The increase in the consumption of tobacco in recent years has also been enormous.   In 1868 the recorded consumption was about 1·30 pounds per capita of manufactured tobacco and 16·7 cigars per capita each year, with no consumption of cigarettes.   In the ten years ending with 1878, notwithstanding the general depression in business in the later year, the consumption on the whole more than doubled, rising to 2·31 pounds per capita of manufactured tobacco and 40·5 cigars per capita, besides 3·5 cigarettes for each inhabitant.   In the ten years ending in 1888, the consumption of manufactured tobacco increased about fifty per cent, or to 3·23 pounds per capita; of cigars, more than fifty per cent, or 61·4 for each inhabitant; and of cigarattes, from 3·5 to 29·7 for each person.   In these figures, therefore, is to be found a demonstration that the ability of the masses in the United States in recent years to satisfy their desires has materially increased, and that the condition of the working-people has at all events been far removed from privation.

Great improvements have been made during the last ten or twenty years in the breeding of live-stock and its economical management, whereby a greatly increased product of animal food can be obtained from a given number with comparatively little increased labor or expense.   In the matter of dairy produce, recognized authorities in England estimate that the average increase in the yield of milk per cow in that country has been at least forty gallons per annum since 1878; and this for the 3,500,000 cows in milk, owned by British farmers, " means 140,000,000 extra gallons of milk over and above what the same animals yielded in 1878; and at 6*d.* per gallon would amount to an extra return of no less than £3,500,000 for the United Kingdom, or £1 per cow. If made into cheese, it would mean an increase of 62,500 tons." In the case of both cattle and sheep, it is entirely practicable to get the same weight of meat in an animal at two or three years of age as was formerly obtained at four or five years; and improvement in this early maturity in turn means that the quantity of meat made by the same number of animals is very much greater than formerly.

Furthermore, not only has the supply of food increased, but the variety of food available to the masses has become greater. Nearly all tropical fruits that will bear transportation have become as cheap in non-tropical countries as the domestic fruits of the latter, and even cheaper; and the increased consumption thus induced has built up new and extensive branches of business, and brought prosperity to the people of many localities that heretofore have had no markets for any products of their industry.*

The knowledge gained in recent years respecting the wonderful fecundity of fish, and the conditions for their favorable breeding and preservation, is so complete, that the claim has been made that the world might be fed from the ocean alone, and that an acre of the sea properly cultivated is capable of yielding more food than ten acres of arable land. Thirty or forty years ago fish in its most acceptable form—namely, fresh—was only available to consumers living in close proximity to the ocean; but now, fish caught on the waters of the North Pacific, and transported more than

---

* In the seven years from 1880 to 1887 the importation of bananas into the United States increased forty-fold. In that same year twenty-six steamers per month, together with a large number of sailing-vessels, were engaged in this business; and in the city of New Orleans more than five hundred people found employment in the mere handling of this single article of fruit.

two thousand miles, are daily supplied fresh to the markets of the Atlantic slope of the United States, and sea-products of the coast of the latter, transported two thousand miles, are regularly furnished in a fresh condition to British markets.

During the whole period from 1870 to 1888 the world's consumption of luxuries—of tea, coffee, and fermented liquors—has gone on increasing, and shows only a certain retardation of the rate of progress, and not a positive decline, even in the specially bad years.

One point of immense and novel importance in helping to a conclusion as to whether the race under the conditions of high civilization is tending toward increased comfort and prosperity, or toward greater poverty and degradation, is to be found in the fact which recent investigators have determined, namely: that in the United States the daily wages paid, or the daily earning capacity of a healthy adult worker, in even the most poorly remunerated employments, is more than sufficient, if properly expended, to far remove the individual recipient from anything like absolute want, suffering, or starvation. Thus, in the case of fifty-nine adult female operatives in a well-managed cotton-mill in Maryland, the per capita cost of subsistence, with a bill of fare embracing meats, all ordinary groceries and vegetables, milk, eggs, butter, fish, and fruit, has been found to be not in excess of twenty cents per day, including the cost of the preparation of the food and its serving. In Massachusetts, where the results were derived from the six months' boarding of seventeen men and eight women (three servants), the men being engaged in arduous mechanical employments, and consuming comparatively large quantities of meat, the daily cost of the subsistence of each individual was twenty-eight cents per day. In the jails of Massachusetts the average daily cost of the food of the prisoners and of the employés of the prisons for the year 1883—bread of the best quality, good meats, vegetables, tea, rye-coffee, being furnished liberally—was a trifle over fifteen cents per day for each person.*

In the State of Maine the average cost of the food (raw material) of the convicts in the State-prison, for the seven years next preceding November, 1887, was 11·63 cents per day; the quality of the food being very good (including meat or fish, milk, coffee, and molasses every day), and the quantity supplied to each person being limited only to his or her eating capacity.

In one of the best conducted almshouses of Connecticut, the condition of which was carefully investigated by the writer in 1887, the sum of $7,000 per annum, exclusive of interest on the plant and extraordinary repairs, was found to be sufficient to maintain an average of sixty-five inmates, mainly adults, in a building of modern construction, scrupulously clean, thoroughly warmed and ventilated, with an abundance of good and varied food, clothing and medical attendance, or at an average daily expenditure of about thirty cents per capita. The average weekly cost of the patients in the six establishments for the care of the insane in Massachusetts for the year 1887 was $3.50 for each patient.

The evidence, therefore, is conclusive that "an ample and varied supply of attractive and nutritious food can be furnished in the Eastern portions of the United States—and probably in Great Britain also—at a cost not exceeding twenty cents per day, and for a less sum in the Western sections of the country, provided that it is judiciously purchased and economically served"; and the legitimate inference from these results is, that the problem of greatest

---

* These results are due to the laborious and careful investigations of Mr. Edward Atkinson, of Massachusetts, and were first published in 1884, under the title of "The Distribution of Products." Together with the results of similar investigations conducted by Mr. Robert Giffen, of England, they rank among the most important and valuable contributions ever made to economic and social science.

importance to be solved in the United States and in Great Britain, in the work of ameliorating the condition of the honest and industrious poor is (as Mr. Atkinson has expressed it), to find out how to furnish them with ample and excellent food as cheaply as it is supplied to the inmates of our prisons and almshouses.

The facts in regard to the general increase in the deposits of savings-banks, and the decrease in pauperism, are also entitled to the highest consideration in this discussion. In the United States the aggregate deposits in such banks were probably about $1,500,000,000 in 1888 as compared with $759,946,000 in 1873–'74 ; an increase of nearly one hundred per cent in fourteen years, while the increase of population during the same period was probably not in excess of thirty-six per cent.*   A rapid increase in recent years in the savings-bank deposits of most of the countries of Europe is also reported.   In Great Britain the increase between 1875 and 1885, as regards deposits, was forty per cent, and in the number of depositors over fifty per cent. ; while the increase in population during the same period was about ten per cent.   The capital of all the " trustee " and " postal " savings-banks in Great Britain in May, 1889, was £106,502,-200 ($517,659,892).   But, besides these savings-banks, there are in Great Britain a number of institutions for the pro-

---

* The development of the savings-bank system in the United States up to the year 1888 has been confined almost entirely to the Eastern and Middle States ; and in that year such banks were in full operation in only ten States, and only partially so in three other States. These thirteen States were Maine, New Hampshire, Vermont, Massachusetts, Rhode Island, Connecticut, New York, New Jersey, Pennsylvania, Maryland, Ohio, Wisconsin, and Minnesota. The deposits in these banks, furthermore, by no means represent the entire result of the provident savings of the people of the United States. Life-insurance takes a not unimportant share of the savings of the people, building and loan associations attract some, and cheap and easy investments in real estate doubtless take their share of savings. Still, the fact remains that, as shown by the territorial distribution of the savings-banks, a very considerable field for the extension of the system in the United States still continues open.

motion of thrift, which have no exact counterpart in the United States, and which also hold large amounts of the savings of the people ; as railway savings-banks, incorporated provident building societies (with £53,000,000 of funds in 1887), friendly societies, etc., and in all of which the deposits are rapidly increasing. Savings-banks, it may also be mentioned, have been established in connection with the schools of Great Britain; and the number of schools having such arrangements in 1887 was reported at 2,225. The statistics of the " postal savings-banks" of Great Britain, institutions not known in the United States, but which seem to find special favor with the British people, are especially worthy of notice. Their increase from 1878 to 1887 has been from 5,831 to 8,720 in number, from 1,892,756 to 3,951,761 in depositors, and from £30,411,563 to £53,974,000 in credits to accounts. " Despite all fluctuations in trade, the deposits in these banks have gone on steadily increasing year by year ; and that this has been due to greater thrift among the working-classes, and not to the growth of a larger class of accounts, is proved by the fact that the average amount to the credit of each depositor was decidedly less in 1888 than in 1878. Or, to put it in another way, the depositors have increased in number nearly one hundred and nine per cent, while the deposits have increased by only seventy-seven per cent."

The aggregate capital of all the savings-banks and provident institutions of Great Britain in 1888 was probably about £215,000,000, or considerably in excess of one thousand millions of dollars.

Switzerland and Sweden and Norway lead all the nations of Europe in the ratio of savings-deposits to the population —the increase, comparing 1860 with 1881, having been from the ratio of 4·2 to 35·5 in the former, and in the case of the latter from 6·8 to 18·1. In Prussia, where the savings-banks are used almost exclusively by the poorer classes, the deposits are regularly increasing, and for 1887–'88 were larger than in any previous year.

The percentage increase in deposits and depositors in France and Italy in recent years has also been large, and far in excess of any percentage increase in their population. The aggregate savings-deposits in various institutions and societies for the Continent of Europe, in 1885, was estimated at £338,000,000; or, including Great Britain, £538,000,000 ($2,614,000,000). It is clear, therefore, from these data, that the habit and the power of saving have greatly increased in recent years in all highly civilized countries and are still increasing.

There are no statistics of national pauperism in the United States, and general conclusions are based mainly on the returns made in the eight States of New York, Pennsylvania, Ohio, Illinois, Massachusetts, Wisconsin, and Michigan. A report made by the standing committee of the various State boards of charities to the National Conference of Charities in 1887 was, that " except for the insane, who are everywhere constantly accumulating beyond their due ratio to the whole population, there has never been for a period of five years any increase in the proportion of paupers to the population; while for longer periods there has generally been a decrease in the number of the poor as compared with the whole population "; and this, too, notwithstanding the very great obstacles which stand in the way of all public and private effort for the checking of pauperism in a country like the United States, " which annually receives such armies of poor from European countries, and at home permits intemperance to breed so much of pauperism, especially in cities."

In England, where the population, between 1875 and 1885, increased in a larger proportion than in any previous decade, there was no increase but a very steady decrease of pauperism; or, from an annual average number of 952,000, or 4·2 per cent of the whole population in 1870–'77 to 787,000, or three per cent of the population for 1880–'84. For the year 1888 the number relieved in England and

Wales was 2·7 per cent of the population. For Scotland, the corresponding figures are much the same; although the Scotch administration of the poor is totally independent of that of the English. In short, there is no evidence that pauperism is increasing in England and Scotland with their recent marked increase in population, or that the people are less fully employed than formerly; but the evidence is all to the contrary. In Ireland, the experience has been different. " Here, there has been an increase in pauperism, accompanied by a decline in population," the number of paupers in receipt of relief, on the 1st of January, 1887, being returned as 113,241, as compared with 106,717 in 1885.*

Prussia, with a marked increase in population, returned a decrease in the number of paupers receiving relief from cities and towns from 3·87 per cent of the whole number in 1884, to 3·65 per cent in 1885.

Crime in Great Britain is diminishing in a remarkable manner. A diminution is also reported in Italy. In the United States, while crime has diminished in a few States, for the whole country it has, within recent years, greatly increased. In 1850 the proportion of prison inmates was reported as one to every 3,448 of the entire population of the country; but in 1880 this proportion had risen to one for every 855. These results are believed to be attributable in the Northern States mainly to the great foreign immigration, and, in the Southern, to the emancipation of the negroes.

Finally, an absolute demonstration that the progress of mankind, in countries where the new economic conditions have been most influential in producing those disturbances and transitions in industry and society which to many seem fraught with disaster, has been for the better and not for

---

* " The Material Progress of Great Britain " ; address before the Economic Section of the British Association, 1887, by Robert Giffen.

the worse, is to be found in the marked prolongation of human life, or decline in the average death-rate, which has occurred within comparatively recent years in these same countries. Thus, the average annual death-rate in England and Wales, during the period from 1838 to 1875, was 22·3 per thousand. From 1876 to 1880, it was 20·08. But, for the six years from 1880 to 1887, the average has not exceeded 19·3; which means that about 500,000 persons in England and Wales were alive at the close of the year 1886 who would have been dead if the rate of mortality which prevailed between 1838 and 1875 had been maintained.* The average annual death-rate of the city of London for the decade beginning in 1860 was 24·4 per thousand. In the following ten years it declined to 22·5. But for the year 1888 it was only 18·5 per thousand; a rate lower than any previously recorded within the metropolitan area, and which entitles London to the claim of being the healthiest of all the world's great cities. In Vienna, Austria, the death-rate has decreased since 1870 from 41 to 21 per thousand; a result that has been sequential to the introduction into the city of an improved supply of good water, and to the extensive construction of new and improved houses—fifty-eight per cent of all the houses of Vienna having been built since 1848. The average death-rate for the whole United States, for the census year 1880, was between 17 and 18 per thousand; which is believed to be a less mean rate than that of any European country except Sweden.

The results of the most recent and elaborate investigations on this subject, communicated, with data, by M. Vachee, to the " Bulletin de l'Institut International Statistique," Rome, 1887, are, that the mortality of Europe has diminished from twenty-five to thirty-three per cent, and

---

* It is also to be noted that by far the larger proportion of the increased duration of human life in England is lived at useful ages, and not at the dependent ages of either childhood or old age.

that the mean duration of life has increased from seven to twelve years, since the beginning of this century.   This estimate of the rate of improvement for all Europe is higher than the English data would alone warrant, but may be correct.   At the same time it is well recognized that through the absence of reliable data it is impossible to speak *with certainty* as to the decrease in mortality, or as to the expectation of life in any country, except in respect to the last forty or fifty years.

Now, while improved sanitary knowledge and regulations have contributed to these results, they have been mainly due to the increase in the abundance and cheapness of food-products, which in turn are almost wholly attributable to recent improvements in the methods of production and distribution.   But, whatever may have been the causes of these changes, they could not have occurred without an increase of vitality among the masses.

Again, if civilization is responsible for many new diseases, civilization should be credited with having stamped out, or greatly mitigated, not a few that a century ago were extremely formidable.   Plague and leprosy have practically long disappeared from countries of high civilization.   For the five years from 1795 to 1800 the average annual number of deaths from small-pox in the city of London was 10,180 ; but for the five years from 1875 to 1880 it was only 1,408. Typhus and typhoid fevers are now known to be capable of prevention, and cholera and yellow fever of complete territorial restriction.   Typhus fever, once the scourge of London, and especially of its prisons, is said to have now entirely disappeared from that city.   Anæsthetics have removed the pain attendant upon surgical operations; and the use of antiseptics has reduced the mortality contingent upon the same in the larger hospitals; or, taking the experience of Germany as the basis of comparison, from 41·6 in 1868 to 4·35 per cent in 1880.   According to Mr. Edwin Chadwick, " in the larger schools of the districts of the poor-law union of Great Britain . . . the chief diseases of children are now practically abolished. These institutions may be said to be children's hospitals, in which children, orphans of the lowest type from the slums, are taken in large proportions with developed diseases upon them, often only to die from constitutional failure alone. Yet in a number of these separate schools there are now no deaths from measles, whooping-cough, typhus, scarlatina, or diphtheria, . . . while the general death-rate of the children in these schools is now less than one third of the death-rates prevalent among the children of the general population of the same ages."

The science and practice of medicine and surgery are, furthermore, "undergoing a revolution of such magnitude and importance that its limits can hardly be conceived. Looking into the future in the light of recent discoveries, it does not seem impossible that a time may come when the cause of every infectious disease will be known; when all such diseases will be preventable or easily curable; when protection can be afforded against all diseases, such as scarlet fever, measles, yellow fever, whooping-cough, etc., in which one attack secures immunity from subsequent contagion; when, in short, no constitutional disease will be incurable, and such scourges as epidemics will be unknown. These results, indeed, may be but a small part of what will follow discoveries in bacteriology. The higher the plane of actual knowledge the more extended is the horizon. What has been accomplished within the past ten years as regards knowledge of the causes, prevention, and treatment of disease far transcends what would have been regarded a quarter of a century ago as the wildest and most impossible speculation."—PROF. AUSTIN FLINT, M. D., *The Forum, December*, 1888.

Dealers in ready-made clothing in the United States assert that they have been obliged to adopt a larger scale of sizes, in width as well as in length, to meet the demands of the average American man, than were required ten years ago; and that in the case of clothing manufactured for the special supply of the whole population of the Southern sections of the country, this increase in size since the war, attributable almost entirely to the increased physical activity of the average individual, has been fully one inch around the chest and waist. Varieties of coarse clothing, as the brogan shoe and cotton drills, which before the war were sold in immense quantities in this same section of the country, have now almost passed out of demand, and been superseded by better and more expensive products. The American is, therefore, apparently gaining in size and weight, which could not have happened had there been anything like retrogression, or progress toward poverty on the part of the masses.

On the other hand, there are certain sequences of the new conditions of civilization pertaining to individual and societary life which are less flattering and promising. In the same ratio as the facilities for the production and distribution of commodities have been expanded and quickened, the necessity of untiring attention to business, as a prerequisite for success, has been increased, and the intensity of competition stimulated. The forces of business life are no longer subject to the control of the man of business. Having subordinated the lightning to the demands of business, business must go at lightning speed. "The electric message is superseding the leisurely letter. There is now no quiet waiting for foreign correspondence. The cable announces a bargain struck on another continent, and the same day, before the goods have been even shipped, the cargo is sold and the transaction ended." If one trader keeps himself in instantaneous contact through the telegraph with markets and customers, all must do the same, or be left behind in the struggle for success. Thus dominated by new conditions, the merchant and financier of to-day has been rendered almost as much of a machine as the worker in the factories, whose every movement has been automatic, or subordinate to the physical forces acting through machinery; and one result of the continuous mental and nervous activity which modern high-tension methods of business have necessitated, coupled with the high living and the frequent use of alcoholic stimulants to which such activity leads, has been to increase (if not create) a class of diseases which may be regarded as diseases of civilization, and which have in turn entailed a rapidly increasing mortality. Thus, the statistics of the Health Department of the city of New York show that, comparing 1870 and 1887, the death-rate from " Bright's disease " increased from 890 to 2,375 per annum, or nearly threefold; and in the case of " heart-disease," from about 700 to 2,020 per annum—an increase again of nearly threefold; and an increase in both cases in far greater ratio than any increase of the population of the city.*   Besides the causes of death above enumerated, there is also a very serious mortality arising from what is commonly but vaguely denominated " nervous exhaustion," directly referable to the same influences under consideration. The accepted statistics for the European nations also show that the rate of suicide is increasing.   In France and Germany it has gone on increasing steadily through good years and bad years indifferently, until it is now more than fifty per cent greater than it was in 1870.   In England the rate reached a maximum in 1879, but was, nevertheless, higher in 1888 than in 1870–'75.   The marriage-rate during recent years is also reported as declining in all the countries of Europe except Italy, but not to a very notable extent.   The statistics of divorce in the United States, recently collected by the order of the Federal Government, show an increase largely in excess of the percentage growth of population. Thus, the increase in the population from 1867 to 1886 is estimated at about sixty per cent, while the number of di-

---

* The population of the city of New York was, in 1866, about 750,000; in 1870, 942,000; in 1880, 1,206,000; and in 1887, about 1,460,000.

vorces for the last year of the period exceeded that for the first year by 156·9 per cent. There has also been an increase in the proportion of divorces to the number of married couples.

One curious commercial or societary phenomenon, and one which, in view of the statement before submitted, may seem paradoxical, should not be overlooked in this connection—and that is, that notwithstanding the tendency of existing conditions to concentrate trade and manufactures in the hands of a few, with large capital and special facilities, and to crowd out the smaller and weaker establishments, the number of persons engaging in trade—taking the experience of the United States as a guide—increases every year in a more rapid rate than population.   This in turn is counteracted in part, but not wholly, by an increase in the number of failures, and the annual retirement of a much greater number of persons or firms with the losses of a part or the whole of their invested capital—240,000 firms registered at one of the leading mercantile agencies having ceased to exist in 1888, as against 10,679 that failed.   But for the frequency of disasters, therefore, the proportion of the population of the United States seeking to get a living by trading rather than by direct production would be soon so great as to actually endanger the public welfare.   The explanation of this phenomenon undoubtedly is, that the temptations to a commercial life, without adequate training or capital, are of constantly increasing strength, while the amount of capital and of trained skill required to insure success also tends to increase.   The number of those who try such a life and fail each year consequently enlarges.*

---

* There has long been a substantial agreement among those competent to form an opinion that ninety per cent of all the men who try to do business on their own account fail of success. Investigations recently instituted by Mr. Joseph H. Walker in a comparatively old city (Worcester), in the long-settled State of Massachusetts, have led to the following interesting conclusions: Of every hundred men in business in that place in 1845, twenty-five were out of

The steady drift of population, not only in the United States but in all countries in which railroads are numerous and the art of reading widely diffused, from the country to towns and cities, is undoubtedly one of the sequences of the recent changes in economic conditions, and, as suggestive of the impoverishment of rural sections, and discontent with agricultural pursuits, is popularly regarded as an unhealthy social phenomenon; although, as will be hereafter pointed out (see page 433), such a conclusion may not be wholly warranted. In the State of Massachusetts, the proportion of all the people gathered in cities and towns of more than eight thousand inhabitants has risen from less than one twentieth a hundred years ago, and but little over a third in 1850, to quite two thirds (66·4 per cent) when the last State census was taken in 1885. In the State of New York, with a population in 1880 of 5,082,000, one third of the whole number is massed in two cities—New York and Brooklyn—while, as in Massachusetts, two thirds of the whole is gathered in places with over eight thousand inhabitants. In England not only are farms lying vacant in great numbers,

---

business in five years, fifty in ten years, and sixty-seven in fifteen years ; and most of these disappearances mean simply failures. That wealth does not, as a rule, in the United States long remain in the families of those who acquire it would also seem to be shown by these investigations. Out of seventy-five manufacturers in 1850, only thirty died or retired with property ; and only six of the sons of the seventy-five now have any property, or died leaving any. There were one hundred and seven manufacturers in 1860, of whom sixty died or retired with property, but only eight of the sons of the one hundred and seven now have any property, or died leaving any. In 1878 there were one hundred and seventy-six individuals engaged in ten of the leading manufacturing industries of the city in question, but only fifteen of this number were themselves the sons of manufacturers. Going back to an earlier generation, the above proportion was found to be essentially maintained ; but the fact was not so striking when so many branches of manufacturing industry were new, as they now appear. Of the one hundred and seventy-six manufacturers of 1878, moreover, no less than one hundred and sixty-one commenced their career as journeymen ; a fact illustrative of what seems to be almost in the nature of an economic axiom, namely, that the capitalists of to-day are themselves the workingmen of twenty-five years ago, as the workingmen of to-day will be the capitalists of twenty-five years hence.

owing to the fall in agricultural prices, but the supply of
farm-labor is rapidly diminishing, in the face of a marked
and steady advance in wages and greatly increased inducements in the shape of improved cottages.   There is, in fact,
an exodus from the soil throughout the whole of Great
Britain.   In France, the same movement of the agricultural
population toward the towns exists, and is regarded with a
feeling akin to alarm.   According to M. Baudrillard, there
is a positive diminution of population in fifteen of the richest and most prosperous agricultural departments of France,
but an increase in the population of their towns.   The
young men, and especially the young women, will not live
on the farms if they can help it.   Agriculture offers greater
inducements than ever in the shape of higher wages and
better food and lodging, but these have little or no effect on
the rising generation.   This disinclination for farm-life is,
he thinks, to be accounted for in the same way as the small
number of children to a marriage.   " Moral progress," he
says, " has not marched abreast with material progress."
Everywhere the aspirations of the rural classes are out of
proportion to their intelligence and resources.   The rise of
wages has created a crowd of more or less factitious wants,
which are difficult to meet and which keep alive a constant
sense of privation.   Education has created in the farming
man an intellectual curiosity, which it is hard to satisfy, and
which keeps him constantly in mind of his isolation, of the
loneliness and dullness of his life.   One effect of this state
of things in France is the influx from Italy and Belgium of
a very low grade of laborers, whom the farmers are only too
glad to hire to prevent their fields lying waste, but who are
anything but a wholesome addition to the French population.   In fact, in every country, wherever we find the natives abandoning in disgust the cultivation of the soil, we
find a lower grade of labor, a less civilized man, who asks
for less and is content with less, taking their places.
     Evidently, the contribution of greatest value that could

be made to the discussion of this subject, would be to spread before us an exhibit of the exact results of the experience of a country and a people where, under average, or not too favorable conditions, the recent changes in industrial and social life, consequent upon the new methods of production and distribution, have operated most influentially. Such an exact exhibit can not be made; but the experience of Great Britain, where economic data have been gathered and recorded during the last fifty years with an exactness and completeness not approached in any other country, furnishes a most gratifying and instructive approximation. To the record of this experience, attention is next requested.

During the last twenty-five or thirty years, the aggregate wealth of Great Britain, as also that of the United States and France, has increased in an extraordinary degree. In Great Britain the increase from 1843 to 1885 in the amount of property assessable to the income-tax is believed to have been one hundred and forty per cent, and from 1855 to 1885 about one hundred per cent. The capital subject to death duties (legacy and succession taxes) which was £41,-000,000 in 1835, was £183,930,000 in 1885; an increase in fifty years of nearly three hundred and fifty per cent. An estimate of the total income of the country for 1886 was £1,270,000,000; and of its aggregate wealth, about £9,000,-000,000, or $45,000,000,000.* Have now the working-classes

* In France, notwithstanding the indemnity of over a thousand millions of dollars paid to Germany in 1872–'73, and a total governmental expenditure, in addition to all ordinary but most heavy annual expenses since then, of 7,710,000,000 francs ($1,540,000,000), with enormous losses in recent years contingent on the vine-disease, bad crops of cereals, and disastrous speculations, like the Panama Canal, copper syndicate, and the like, the savings of the French people are still so large that the supply of new capital for every enterprise that promises security or profit continually tends to exceed demand. Conclusive evidence of the rapid and enormous increase in the wealth of the United States is claimed to be afforded by the rapid increase in the amount of property annually made subject to fire-insurance. Thus, the amount of fire risks outstanding in 1888 was reported as more than $900,000,-000 in excess of the aggregate for the previous year; and, as there is no reason

of Great Britain gained in proportion with others in this enormous development of material wealth ? Thanks to the labors of such men as the late Dudley Baxter and Leone Levi, David Chadwick, and Robert Giffen, this question can be answered (comparatively speaking for the first time) with undoubted accuracy.

Fifty years ago, one third of the working masses of the United Kingdom were agricultural laborers; at present less than one eighth of the whole number are so employed. Fifty years ago the artisans represented about one third of the whole population; to-day they represent three fourths. This change in the composition of the masses of itself implies improvement, even if there had been no increase in the wages of the different classes. But, during this same period, the "money" wages of all classes of labor in Great Britain have advanced about one hundred per cent, while the purchasing power of the wages in respect to most commodities, especially in recent years, has been also very great. Among the few things that have not declined, house-rent is the most notable, a fact noticed equally in Great Britain and France, although in both countries the increase in the number of inhabited houses is very large; the increase in the item of houses in the income-tax assessments of the United Kingdom between 1875 and 1885 having been about thirty-six per cent.* But high rents, in the face of considerable building, are in themselves proof that other things are cheap, and that the competition for comfortable dwellings is great.

---

for supposing that property in 1888 was better insured than in 1887, the only means of accounting for this great increase in the volume of insurance business is, that there was substantially that amount of new wealth added to the country on which insurance was desired. It would seem to be further obvious that this gain could not be in the value of land (for land, as it can not be destroyed by fire, is not insured), but must have consisted in new buildings and personal property of a perishable nature.

* The houses built in Great Britain since 1840 have been estimated in value at double the amount of the British national debt.

The Government of Great Britain keeps and publishes an annual record of the quantities of the principal articles imported, or subject to an excise (internal revenue) tax, which are retained for home consumption per head, by the total population of the kingdom. From these records the following table has been compiled. From a humanitarian point of view, it is one of the most wonderful things in the history of the latter half of the nineteenth century:

Per capita consumption of different commodities (imported or sub-
ject to excise taxes) by the population of Great Britain.

ARTICLES.	1840.	1886.	1887.
Bacon and hams ....lbs.	0·01	11·95	11·29
Butter................. ... "	1·05	7·17	8·14
Cheese...................... "	0·92	5·14	5·39
Currants and raisins........... "	1·45	4·02	4·34
Eggs........................No.	3·63	28·12	29·37
Rice... ....lbs.	0·90	10·75	7·69
Cocoa...................... "	0·08	0·41	0·43
Coffee.................. ...... "	1·08	0·86	0·79
Wheat and wheat-flour........ "	42·47	185·76	220·75
Raw sugar................... "	15·20	47·21	52·95
Refined sugar .... "	None.	18·75	20·25
Tea........................ . "	1·22	4·87	4·95
Tobacco.................... "	0·86	1·42	1·44
Wine.......................gals.	0·25	0·36	0·37
Spirits (foreign)............. "	0·14	0·24	0·23
Spirits (British) .... "	0·83	0·73	0·72
Malt ....bush.	1·59	1·64*	....
Beer (1881)..................gals.	27·78	26·61	26·90

During all the period of years covered by the statistics of this table, the purchasing power of the British people in respect to the necessities and luxuries of life has therefore been progressively increasing, and has been especially rapid since 1873–'76. Converting this increase in the purchasing power of wages into terms of money, the British workman can now purchase an amount of the necessaries of life for 28s. 5d., which in 1839 would have cost him 34s. 0½d.† But

---

* 1879.   † David Chadwick, British Association, 1887.

this statement falls very far short of the advantages that have accrued to him, for wages in Great Britain, as before stated, are fully one hundred per cent higher at the present time than they were in 1839.

The impression probably prevails very generally in all countries that the capitalist classes are continually getting richer and richer, while the masses remain poor, or become poorer. But in Great Britain, where alone of all countries the material (i. e., through long-continued and systematized returns of incomes and estates [probate] for taxation) exists for scientific inquiry, the results of investigations demonstrate that this is not the case.

In the case of estates, the number subjected to legacy and succession duties within the last fifty years has increased in a ratio double that of the population, but the average amount of property per estate has not sensibly augmented. If, therefore, wealth among the capitalist classes has greatly increased, as it has, there are more owners of it than ever before; or, in other words, wealth, to a certain extent, is more diffused than it was. Of the whole number of estates that were assessed for probate duty in Great Britain in 1886, 77·5 per cent were for estates representing property under £1,000 ($5,000).

In the matter of national income, a study of its increase and apportionment among the different classes in Great Britain has led to the following conclusions: Since 1843, when the income-tax figures begin, the increase in national income is believed to have been £755,000,000. Of this amount, the *income* from the capitalist classes increased about one hundred per cent, or from £190,000,000 to £400,-000,000. But, at the same time, the number of the capitalist classes increased so largely that the average amount of capital possessed among them per head increased only fifteen per cent, although the increase in capital itself was in excess of one hundred and fifty per cent. In the case of the " upper " and " middle " classes, the income from their " working " increased from £154,000,000 to £320,000,000, or about one hundred per cent ; while, in the case of the masses (i. e., the manual labor classes), which have increased in population only thirty per cent since 1843, the increase of their incomes has gone up from £171,000,000 to £550,000,000, or over two hundred per cent. Between 1877 and 1886 the number of assessments in Great Britain for incomes between £150 ($750) and £1,000 ($5,000) increased 19·26 per cent, while the number of assessments for incomes of £1,000 and upward decreased 2·4 per cent.* What has happened to all that large class whose annual income does not reach the taxable limit (£150) is sufficiently indicated by the fact that while population increases pauperism diminishes.

Thus, in the United Kingdom, during the last fifty years, the general result of all industrial and societary movement, according to Mr. Giffen, has been, that " the rich have become more numerous, but not richer individually; the ' poor ' are, to some smaller extent, fewer ; and those who remain ' poor ' are, individually, twice as well off on the average as they were fifty years ago. The poor have thus had almost all the benefit of the great material advance of the last fifty years."

---

* The following table shows how wealth is distributed in the different classes of income-tax-payers in Great Britain under Schedule D, which comprises incomes from profits on trades and employments :

"In 1887 the number of assessments of incomes from £150 to £500 was 285,754, and in 1886 it was 347,031, showing an increase of 21·4 per cent ; of incomes between £500 and £1,000, the numbers were, in 1877, 32,085, and in 1886, 32,033, no increase at all ; of incomes between £1,000 and £5,000, the numbers were, in 1877, 19,726, and in 1886, 19,250, a decrease of 2·4 per cent ; and of the incomes over £5,000, the numbers were, in 1877, 3,122, and in 1886, 3,048, a decrease of 2·3 per cent. It results that from these figures the increase of the income-tax during times of depression and during ordinary times, during the times which we have been going through and which have not been times of great prosperity, there has been a most satisfactory increase in the incomes below £500, while no similar increase is seen in the incomes between £500 and £1,000, and upward."—Mr Goschen, " On the Distribution of Wealth," Royal Statistical Society of England, 1887.

The following further citations from the record of the recent economic experiences of Great Britain are also strongly confirmatory of the above conclusions :

The amount of life-assurance in the United Kingdom exceeds that of any other country; having risen from £179,-900,000 ($872,214,000) in 1856 to £426,600,000 ($2,073,-376,000) in 1885. The record further shows a very rapid increase in the number of policies issued, while the average amount of the policies continues small; the meaning of which clearly is, that a larger number of people are not only continually becoming provident, but able to insure themselves for small amounts.

The amount of savings invested in the co-operative stores of Great Britain, in which her working-classes are especially interested, was estimated in 1888 to be adequate for the handling of a retail business exceeding a hundred million dollars per annum.

The changes in the relations of crime and of educational facilities during the last fifty years of the history of the British people, which have occurred and are still in progress, are in the highest degree encouraging. In 1839 the number of criminal offenders committed for trial was 54,000 ; in England alone, 24,000. Now the corresponding figures (1887) were, United Kingdom, 18,305 ; England, 13,292. In 1840 one person for every 500 of the population of the British Islands was a convict ; in 1885 the proportion was as one to every 4,100.

As late as 1842 there was no national school system in England, and there were towns with populations in excess of 100,000 in which there was not a single public day-school and not a single medical charity. Now education has become one of the principal cares of the nation. In 1884 the number of attendants upon schools in the United Kingdom was reported at 5,250,000. In 1887 the number in attendance upon schools, for the support of which grants of money are made by Parliament (and which correspond to the pub-

lic schools of the United States) was 4,019,116, an increase
over the preceding year of 103,801. The amount of such
parliamentary grants for 1887 was—including Ireland—
$24,617,965 ; increase over 1886 of $1,431,005. If we gauge
the efficiency of the British educational system in 1887 with
what it was in 1870 by the number of teachers employed,
the results are equally remarkable. In 1870 there were only
12,467 certificated and 1,262 assistant-masters, while in 1887
there were 43,628 certificated and 18,070 assistant-masters
engaged in teaching in the elementary schools. The amount
of money expended in erecting, enlarging, and improving
" voluntary " schools in Great Britain, which came under
the inspection of the Government since 1870, amounts to
£6,000,000 ($29,160,000). One illustration of the effect of
this greater attention to education upon the masses of the
people of Great Britain is found in the fact that, while in
1855, 35·4 per cent of the persons contracting marriage
signed the register with their mark, in 1885 only 12·9 per
cent did so.

The change which has taken place in the relations of
the Government of Great Britain to the national life of its
people is also very remarkable. Thus, at the commencement
of the present century the British Government annually
appropriated and spent about one third of the national income ; now it expends annually about one twelfth. But for
this greatly diminished expenditure the masses of the people
now receive an immensely greater return than ever before :
in the shape of increased postal and educational facilities,
safer navigation, greater expenditures for the maintenance
of the public health and public security, greater effort for
preventing abuses of labor, etc. Another notable thing is
the extent to which the poorer classes of Great Britain have
been relieved from immediate burdens of taxation. The
taxes which they have to bear, as is the case in the United
States, fall primarily on commodities, and are included in
national accounts under the heads of customs and excise.

In 1836 the receipts per head of population from these sources were 30s. 6d., and in 1886 24s. 6d. But of these revenues the largest proportion is derived from the taxes on liquors and tobacco, which are pure luxuries; and if such taxes be deducted and allowed for, the taxation of Great Britain through her excise and customs, which was 15s. 6d. per head on the necessaries or semi-necessaries of life in 1836, was not more than 5s. per head in 1886. Again, with an increase in population from 27,800,000 in 1855 to 36,300,000 in 1885, or thirty per cent, and without a single additional acre of land to place them upon, the physical, intellectual, and moral condition of the British people has steadily improved; the consumption of spirits, in illustration, having declined in Great Britain, during the last decade, to an extent sufficient to materially affect the national income.* Between 1881 and 1888 the national debt of Great Britain was reduced by the sum of $302,846,940; or from $3,830,722,305 to $3,527,-875,365.

The general conclusion from all these facts, as Mr. Giffen has expressed it, is, that what " has happened to the working-classes in Great Britain during the last fifty years is not so much what may properly be called an improvement, as a revolution of the most remarkable description." And this progress for the better has not been restricted to Great Britain, but has been simultaneously participated in to a greater or less extent by most if not all other countries claiming to be civilized. So far as similar investigations have been instituted in the United States, the results are even more favorable than in Great Britain. If they have not been equally favorable in other than these two countries, we have a right to infer that it has been because the people of the

---

* The decline in the British revenues from taxes on "home" and "foreign" spirits, from 1876 to 1887, was £4,140,000 ($21,000,000); whereas, if consumption had kept pace with the growth of population, there would have been an increase during this same period of over £2,000,000.

former have not only started in their career of progress from a lower level of civilization and race basis than the latter, but have had more disadvantages—natural and artificial— than the people of either Great Britain or the United States. The average earnings per head of the people of countries founded by the Anglo-Saxon race are confessedly larger than those of all other countries.*

But some may say: This is all very interesting and not to be disputed. But how does it help us to understand better, and solve the industrial and social problems of to-day, when the cry of discontent on the part of the masses is certainly louder, and the inequality of condition, want, and suffering is *claimed* to be greater than ever before? In this way:

The record of progress in Great Britain above described is indisputably a record that has been made under circumstances that, if not wholly discouraging, were certainly unfavorable. It is the record of a country densely populated and of limited area, with the ownership, or free use of land, restricted to the comparatively few; with (until recent years) the largest national debt known in history; with a heavy burden of taxation apportioned on consumption rather than on accumulated property, and the reduction of which, a participation in constant wars and enormous military and naval expenditures have always obstructed or prevented; with a burden of pauperism at the outset, and, indeed, for the first half of the period under consideration, which almost threatened the whole fabric of society; and, finally, with a long-continued indisposition on the part of the governing classes to make any concessions looking to the betterment

---

* A recent British authority makes the highest average earnings per head in any country to be in Australia, namely, £43 4s. Next in order, he places the United Kingdom, with an average per capita earning capacity of £35 4s. ; then the United States, with an average capacity of £27 4s. ; and next, Canada, with an average of £26 18s. For the Continent of Europe the average is estimated at £18 1s.—Sir Richard Temple, " *Journal of the Royal Statistical Society*," September, 1884, p. 476.

of the masses, except under the pressure of influences which they had little or no share in creating. And yet, without any "violent specifics," or radical societary changes, and apart from any force of statute law, except so far as statute law has been an instrumentality for making previously existing changes in public sentiment effective; but rather through the steady working of economic laws under continually increasing industrial and commercial freedom, the working masses of Great Britain, "in place of being a dependent class, without future and without hope, have come into a position from which they may reasonably expect to advance to any degree of comfort and civilization."

Now, with humanity occupying a higher vantage-ground in every respect than ever before; with a remarkable increase in recent years in its knowledge and control of the forces of nature—the direct and constant outcome of which is to increase the abundance of all useful and desirable commodities in a greater degree than the world has ever before experienced, and to mitigate the asperities and diminish the hours of toil—is it reasonable to expect that further progress in this direction is to be arrested? Is the present generation to be less successful in solving the difficult social problems that confront it than were a former generation in solving like problems which for their time were more difficult and embarrassing? If the answer is in the negative, then there is certainly small basis for pessimistic views respecting the effect of the recent industrial and social transitions in the future.

But, in view of these conclusions, what are the reasons for the almost universal discontent of labor?

IX.

THE causes of the almost universal discontent of labor, which has characterized the recent transitions in the world's methods of production and distribution, and which, intensified by such transitions, have been more productive of disturbances than at any former period (for, as previously shown, there are really no new factors concerned in the experiences under consideration), would seem to be mainly these:

1. *The displacement or supplanting of labor through more economical and effective methods of production and distribution.*

2. *Changes in the character or nature of employments consequent upon the introduction of new methods—machinery or processes—which in turn have tended to lower the grade of labor, and impair the independence and restrict the mental development of the laborer.*

3. *The increase in intelligence, or general information, on the part of the masses, in all civilized countries.*

To a review of the character and influence of these several causes, separately and in detail, attention is next invited.

And, *first*, as to the extent and influence of the displacement of labor through more economical and effective methods of production and distribution. Of the injury thus occasioned, and of the suffering attendant, no more pitiful and instructive example of recent date could be given than the following account, furnished to the United States Department of State,* of the effect of the displacement of hand-loom weaving in the city of Chemnitz, Saxony, by the introduction and use of the power-loom:

> In 1875 there were no less than 4,519 of the so-called "*master-weavers*" in Chemnitz, each of whom employed from one to ten journeymen at hand-loom weaving in his own house. The introduction of machinery, however, imposed conditions upon these weavers which they found the more difficult to meet the more the machinery was improved. The plainer goods were made on power-looms, and work in the factories was found to be more remunerative. Instead of giving work to others, they were gradually compelled to seek work for themselves. The independent "master" soon fell into ranks with the dependent factory-hand, but as he grew older and his eye-sight failed him he was replaced by younger and more active hands, and what once promised to become a well-to-do citizen in his old age now bids fair to become a burden upon the community. Those who had means of procuring the newer Jacquard contrivance, or even the improved "leaf" or "shaft-looms," managed to eke out a subsistence; but the prospects of the weavers who have learned to work only with the hand-looms are becoming more hopeless every day.

Now, while such cases of displacement of labor appeal most strongly to human sympathy, and pre-eminently constitute a field for individual or societary action for the purpose of relief, it should be at the same time remembered

---

* Report of United States Consul George C. Tanner, Chemnitz, December,. 1886.

that the world, especially during the last century, has had a large experience in such matters, and that the following points may be regarded as established beyond the possibility of contradiction : 1. That such phases of human suffering are now, always have been, and undoubtedly always will be, the inevitable concomitants of the progress of civilization, or the transitions of the life of society to a higher and better stage. They seem to be in the nature of " growing-pains," or of penalty which Nature exacts at the outset, but for once only, whenever mankind subordinates her forces in greater degree to its own will and uses. 2. That it is not within the power of statute enactment to arrest such transitions, even when a large and immediate amount of human suffering can certainly be predicated as their consequent, except so far as it initiates and favors a return of society toward barbarism ; for the whole progress in civilization consists in accomplishing greater or better results with the same or lesser effort, physical or mental. 3. All experience shows that, whatever disadvantage or detriment the introduction and use of new and improved instrumentalities or methods of production and distribution may temporarily entail on individuals or classes, the ultimate result is always an almost immeasurable degree of increased good to mankind in general. In illustration and proof of this, attention is asked to the following selection from the record of a great number of well-ascertained and pertinent experiences:

The invention of the various machines which culminated in the knitting or weaving of stockings by machinery in place of by hand, occasioned great disturbances about the commencement of the present century among a large body of operatives in the counties of Leicester and Nottingham, in England, who had been educated to old methods of stocking-making and were dependent upon the continued prosecution of them for their immediate livelihood. The new stocking-frames as they were introduced were accordingly destroyed by the handicraft workmen as opportunity favored (over one thousand in a single burst of popular fury), houses were burned, the inventors were threatened and obliged to fly for their lives, and order was not finally restored until the military had been called out and the leading rioters had been arrested and either hanged or transported. Looking back over the many years that have elapsed since this special labor disturbance (one of the most notable in history), the first impulse is to wonder at and condemn what now seems to have been extraordinary folly and wrong on the part of the masses, in attempting to prevent by acts of violence the supersedure of manual labor engaged in making stockings through the introduction and use of ingenious stocking-making machinery. But, on the other hand, when one remembers the number of persons who, with very limited opportunity for any diversity of their industry, and with the low social and mental development incident to the period, found themselves all at once and through no fault of their own deprived of the means of subsistence for themselves and their families, and are further told by the historian of the period * that, from the hunger and misery entailed by this whole series of events, the larger portion of fifty thousand English stocking-knitters and their families did not fully emerge during the next forty years, there is a good deal to be set down to and pardoned on account of average human nature. The ultimate result of the change in the method of making stockings and its accompanying suffering has, however, unquestionably been that for every one person poorly fed, poorly paid, badly clothed, and miserably housed, who at the commencement of the present century was engaged in making stockings on hand-looms or in preparing the materials out of which stockings could be made, one hundred at least are probably now so employed for a third less number of hours per week, at from three to seven times greater

---

* " History of the Machine-wrought Hosiery Manufactures," by Willia₁.
Felkin, Cambridge, England, 1867.

average wages, and living under conditions of comfort that their predecessors could hardly have even anticipated.*

The following positive statistical data, derived from another department of textile industry, will also show that in these statements there is nothing of assumption and over-estimate, but rather a failure to present the magnitude of the actual results. Thus, Arkwright invented his cotton-spinning machinery in 1760. At that time it was estimated that there were in England 5,200 spinners using the spin-ning-wheel, and 2,700 weavers; in all, 7,900 persons engaged in the production of cotton textiles. The introduction of this invention was opposed, on the ground that it threatened the ruin of these work-people; but the opposition was put down (in some instances by force), and the machine brought into practical use. Note next what followed. In 1787—or twenty-seven years subsequent to the invention—a parlia-mentary inquiry showed that the number of persons actually engaged in the spinning and weaving of cotton had risen from 7,900 to 320,000, an increase of 4,400 per cent. In 1833, including the workmen engaged in subsidiary in-dustries, such as calico-printing, this number had increased to 800,000; and at the present time the number who di-rectly find employment in Great Britain in manufacturing cotton is at least 2,500,000.

In strong contrast also with the report of the pitiful dis-tress of the displaced hand-loom weavers of Saxony comes this other statement from many sources: That in all the great manufacturing centers of Germany, and especially in

---

* The wages of the stocking-knitters in Leicestershire in the early years of this century were among the very lowest paid in any branch of industry in Great Britain, and did not exceed on an average six shillings a week. In 1880 the wages paid first-class operatives (men) in the hosiery-factory of the late A. T. Stewart, at Nottingham, England, were 44s. 5d. per week, and for girls of similar capabilities 16s. 6d. Within more recent years further improve-ments in machinery, by creating a disproportion between the supply of the labor of framework-knitters and the demand for it, has again greatly disturbed the condition of the work-people in this branch of industry in England.

the cities of Chemnitz (where the hand-looms are being rapidly displaced), in Crefeld, Essen, and in Düsseldorf, the standard of living and of comfort among the masses is far higher than at any former period. Writing from Mayence under date of January, 1887, United States Commercial Agent J. H. Smith reports that, "although business is in an unsatisfactory state, it does not seem to affect the working-man greatly. Wages remain pretty much the same, and few discharges of hands take place. The stagnant state of the market only serves to make the necessaries of life cheaper, and to enhance the purchasing power of the laborer's money." United States Consul-General Raine, at Berlin, during the same month, also reported that " wages in Germany show a rising tendency"; that workingmen with permanent work, and wages unchanged, are deriving marked advantages from the low prices of provisions; and that, although the population of Germany has experienced an increase of three millions since 1879, "no lack of work was noticeable."

The readiness with which society comprehends the suffering contingent on the relentless displacement of labor by more economical and effective methods of production and distribution, and the overmastering feelings of sympathy for individual distress thereby occasioned, cause it to generally overlook another exceedingly interesting and important involved factor, and that is the relentless impartiality with which the destructive influences of material progress coincidently affect capital (property) as well as labor. It seems to be in the nature of a natural law that no advanced stage of civilization can be attained, except at the expense of destroying in a greater or less degree the value of the instrumentalities by which all previous attainments have been effected. Society proffers its highest honors and rewards to its inventors and discoverers; but, as a matter of fact, what each inventor or discoverer is unconsciously trying to do is to destroy property, and his measure of success

and reward is always proportioned to the degree to which
he effects such destruction.   If to-morrow it should be
announced that some one had so improved the machinery of
cotton-manufacture that ten per cent more of fiber could be
spun and woven in a given time with no greater or a less
expenditure of labor and capital than heretofore, all the
existing machinery in all the cotton-mills of the world,
representing an investment of millions upon millions of
dollars, would be worth little more than so much old iron,
steel, and copper; and the man who should endeavor to
resist that change would, in face of the fierce competition of
the world, soon find himself bankrupt and without capital.
In short, all material progress is effected by a displacement
of capital equally with that of labor; and nothing marks the
rate of such progress more clearly than the rapidity with
which such displacements occur.   There is, however, this
difference between the two factors involved : Labor displaced,
as a condition of progress, will be eventually absorbed in
other occupations; but capital displaced, when new machinery is substituted for old, is practically destroyed.

It has previously been pointed out that the great and
signal result of the recent extraordinary material progress
has been to increase the abundance and reduce the price of
most useful and desirable commodities.   But this statement
applies to capital, as a commodity, in common with other
commodities; and here comes in another very significant
and, from a humanitarian point of view, a most important
result, or perhaps rather a " law " (pointed out years ago by
Bastiat, and in proof of which evidence will be presently
submitted), that, " in proportion to the increase of capital,
the relative share of the total product falling to the capitalist
is diminished, while, on the contrary, the laborer's share is
relatively increased.   At the same time all progress, from
scarcity to abundance, tends to increase also the absolute
share of product to both capitalist and laborer, inasmuch as
there is more to divide."

Again, it is a singular anomaly that, while an increasing cost of labor has been the greatest stimulant to the invention and introduction of labor-saving machinery, labor employed in connection with such machinery generally commands a better price than it was able to do when similar results were effected by more imperfect and less economical methods.   Perhaps the most remarkable illustration of this is to be found in the experience of the American manufacture of flint-glass, in which a reduction, since 1870, of from seventy to eighty per cent in the market price of such articles of glass table-ware as goblets, tumblers, wine-glasses, bowls, lamps, and the like, consequent upon the adoption of methods greatly economizing labor and improving quality, has been accompanied by an increase of from seventy to one hundred per cent in wages, with a considerable reduction in the hours of labor.*   M. Poulin, a leading French manufacturer at Rheims, has recently stated that the results of investigations in France show that during this century the progress of wages and machinery has been similar—the wages in French wool-manufactories, which were one franc and a half per day in 1816, being (in 1883) five francs; while the cost of weaving a meter of merino cloth, which was then sixteen francs, is now $1f.$ $45c.$ "In Nottingham," says Mr. Edwin Chadwick, the distinguished English economist,† "the introduction of more complex and more costly machinery for the manufacture of lace, while economizing labor, augmented wages to the extent of over one hundred per cent.   I asked a manufacturer of lace whether the large machine could not be worked at the common lower wages by any of the workers of the old machine.   'Yes, it might,' was the answer, 'but the capital invested in the new machinery is very large, and if from drunkenness or misconduct

---

* "Report on the Statistics of Wages," by Joseph D. Weeks, "Tenth Census of the United States," vol. xx.

† "Employers' Liability for Accidents to Work-people," by Edwin Chadwick.

anything happened to the machine, the consequences would be very serious.' Instead of taking a man out of the streets, as might be done with the low-priced machine, he (the employer) found it necessary to go abroad and look for one of better condition, and for such a one high wages must be given." All factory investigations in Great Britain further show that the lowest rates of wages, as a rule, are paid in establishments using old and imperfect machinery, where the output is necessarily comparatively small and inferior.

A remarkable exhibit made in a recent report of the Illinois Central Railroad, showing the cost of the locomotive service for each year for the past thirty years, is also especially worthy of attention in connection with this subject. From this it appears that the cost per mile run has fallen from 26·52 cents in 1857 to 13·93 cents in 1886; a reduction which has been effected wholly by inventions and improvements in machinery. But a further point of greater interest is, that during this same period the wages of the engineers and firemen have risen from 4·51 cents to 5·52 cents per mile run; or, in other words, the engineers and firemen on the Illinois Central, who in 1857 received seventeen per cent of the entire cost of its locomotive service, received in 1886 nearly forty per cent (39·6) of the total cost.

A comparison of the accepted statistics of the cotton-manufacturing industry of the United States for the years 1831 and 1880 warrants conclusions which might properly be designated as extraordinary if they were at all exceptional. Thus, the number of spindles operated by each laborer was nearly three times greater in 1880 than in 1831; the product per spindle one fourth greater; the product per laborer employed nearly four times as great; the price of cotton cloth sixty per cent less; wages eighty per cent higher; and the consumption of cotton cloth per capita of the population over one hundred per cent greater.

The introduction of machinery in many branches of industry—and more especially in agriculture—while increasing, perhaps, the monotony of employment, has also greatly lightened the severity of toil, and in not a few instances has done away with certain forms of labor which were unquestionably brutalizing and degrading, or physically injurious.* In fact, one of the special, if not the special characteristic of machinery is, that it always saves the lowest and crudest forms of labor; and every invention or machine which releases manual labor from inferior kinds of work, or from occupations which can be better supplied by a machine, is a positive gain to society.

Another paradox which should not be overlooked in this discussion is, that those countries in which labor-saving machinery has been most extensively adopted, and where it might naturally be inferred that population through the displacement and economizing of labor would diminish, or at least not increase, are the very ones in which population has at the same time increased most rapidly. On the other hand, the reports of U. S. Consul Schöenhof to the State Department (1888) show, that the woolen industry of Ireland, which by reason of the abundance and cheapness of capable labor-supply ought almost to defy competition, is most unprosperous; and, in great part, through want of enterprise in the use of machinery; few mills being thoroughly equipped in this respect, while in whole districts the weaving of woolen cloth is yet done in cabins upon hand-looms. As a result, the number of people employed in this industry in Ireland is comparatively very small, and at wages only sufficient for the insuring of a most miserable subsistence.

Taking all the machinery-using countries into account,

---

* Mowing, reaping, raking machinery, winnowing, shelling, and weighing machines, hay-tedders, horse-forks, wheel-harrows, improved plows, better cultivators, and so on through almost the entire list of farm-tools, have combined to make the change in farm-work almost a revolution; and those only who have spent years in farming by old methods can fully realize the extent to which the severity of toil has been lightened to the farmer by the introduction and use of machinery.

the number of persons who have been displaced during recent years by new and more effective methods of production
and distribution, and have thereby been deprived of occupation and have suffered, does not appear to have been so great
as is popularly supposed; a conclusion that finds support in
the fact that, notwithstanding trade generally throughout
the world has been notably depressed since 1873, through a
continued decline in prices, reduction of profits, and depreciation of property, the volume of trade—or the number of
things produced, moved, sold, and consumed—on which the
majority of those who are the recipients of wages and salaries depend for occupation, has all this time continually increased, and in the aggregate has probably been little if any
less than it would have been if the times had been considered prosperous. In the United States there is little evidence thus far that labor has been disturbed or depressed to
any great extent from this cause. But there is undoubtedly
a feeling of apprehension among the masses that the opportunities for employment through various causes—continued
large immigration, absorption of the public lands, as well as
machinery improvements—are less favorable than formerly,
and tend to be still further restricted; and this apprehension finds expression in opposition to Chinese immigration,
to the importation of foreign labor on contract, to the increase in the number of apprentices, and in the endeavor to
restrict the participation in various employments to mem-
bership of certain societies. The reports from many of the
large industrial centers of the United States during the year
1887 were to the effect that, while specific results are now
attained at much less cost and with the employment of
much less labor, the increased demand, owing to a reduction
in the price and improvement in the quality of the articles
manufactured under the new conditions, has operated not
merely to prevent any material reduction in the rates of
wages, or in the number of employés, but to largely increase
both rates and numbers. The annual investigation made

by the managers of "Bradstreet's Journal" into the condition of the industries of the country for 1887, indicated that in March of that year 400,000 more industrial employés were at work than in 1885. In thirty-three cities the number of employés at work was 992,000 by the census of 1880, 1,146,000 in January, 1885, and 1,450,000 in March, 1887. The change in the average wages received between 1885–'87 as compared with 1882–'85, shows a very general increase: from ten to fifteen per cent in woolen goods and clothing; fifteen in cotton goods, silk goods, and iron-mills; twelve per cent in the wages of three fourths of the employés of beef- and pork-packing establishments; twenty per cent in anthracite-coal mining, and the like. In the case of the boot and shoe industry, an opinion expressed by those competent to judge is, that while "there has been a reduction in cost and in the number of employés per one hundred cases produced of from fifteen to twenty per cent, the actual number of persons employed has been increased; and in cases where the wages of old classes of workmen are affected they have been raised."

In the United States, notwithstanding the large supplementation in recent years of manual labor engaged in agriculture by machinery, and the further fact that certain branches of agriculture have been regarded as unprofitable, no large number of agricultural laborers have been reported as unemployed; the continually increasing diversity of occupations concurrently opening up to them, in common with all laborers, new avenues for employment.

On the Continent of Europe, the grievances of labor, attributable to new conditions of production and distribution, seem to be mainly confined to the agriculturists and to those bred to handicraft employments; and for both of these classes the outlook is not promising.

In Great Britain the number of persons who are in want, for lack of employment, appears to have largely increased in recent years.* But as there has been no cessation in the growth of the mechanical industries of the United Kingdom, or in her transportation service by land or sea, or in her production of coal and iron, or in the consumption of her staple food commodities—such growth, although not increasing as it were by "leaps and bounds," as in some former periods (as during the decade from 1865 to 1875), being always in a greater ratio than her increase in population,† it would seem that any increase in the number of her necessarily unemployed must have been mainly derived from the one branch of her industry that has not been prosperous, namely, agriculture, in which the losses in recent years on the part alike of landlords, tenants, and farm-laborers, from decline in land and rental values, in the prices of farm products, and through reduction of wages, has been very great.‡

---

* " The one thing which I, and those associated with me, always at once peremptorily refuse to do," said recently an English (London) clergyman whose life is among the poor, " is to try and get men, women, and children work to do. I say at once : ' That is impossible. To get you work would be to deprive some other one of work, and that I can not do,' " the meaning of which was that every occupation in London, in the opinion of the speaker, was full.

† The ratio of increase in the population of the United Kingdom between 1875 and 1885 was about ten per cent. During the same period the increase in the production of coal was twenty per cent ; in pig-iron, sixteen per cent ; in railway receipts from goods-traffic per head of population, eighteen per cent ; in shipping engaged in foreign trade, thirty-three per cent ; in consumption of tea per head, thirteen and a half per cent ; in sugar per head, nineteen per cent.

‡ " The agricultural returns for Great Britain tell us that, from 1873 to 1884, the quantity of arable land in the country has decreased considerably more than a million acres. The reason of this is chiefly that landlords having farms thrown on their hands, and being unable to obtain fresh tenants, find it the most economical method to lay down the land in permanent pasture, which requires the minimum of labor, superintendence, and expenditure to work. This in part explains the forced exodus of the agricultural laborers no longer required to cultivate the land thus laid down. About twenty-five laborers are required on an arable farm of one thousand acres, while probably five would be ample on the same quantity of pasture ; and we should have a diminution of twenty thousand laborers from the change of cultivation which has taken place, or, with their families, a population of sixty or eighty thou-

Mr. Alfred Russel Wallace inclines to the opinion that twenty thousand English farm-laborers, involving, with their families, a population of from sixty to eighty thousand, were, between 1873 and 1887, obliged to quit their homes, and mostly drifted to the larger cities, in consequence merely of substituting, through the increasing unprofitableness of grain-culture, pasture for arable land.

We have in these facts, furthermore, a clew to the cause of the increased discontent in recent years in Ireland. If the Irish tenantry could pay the rent demanded by the landlords, and at the same time achieve for themselves a comfortable subsistence, there would be no necessity for extraordinary governmental interference on their behalf; and this was what, prior to the years 1873-'75, the prices of farm products—especially of all dairy products—enabled the better class of Irish tenants to achieve. But, since then, the fall of prices has entirely changed the condition of affairs, and made a reduction and perhaps an entire abolition of the rents of arable land in Ireland an essential, if the Irish tenant is to receive anything in return for his labor. A French economist—M. de Grancey—who has recently published the results of a study of Ireland, founded on a personal investigation of the country, is of the opinion that, although the population of the island has been reduced by emigration from 8,025,000 in 1847 to 4,852,000 in 1887, it is not now capable of supporting in decency and comfort more than from two to three million inhabitants. The same authority tells us that agricultural distress, occasioned by the same agencies, exists to-day in France in as great a degree as in Great Britain. The peasant proprietors have ceased to buy land and are anxious to sell it; and in the department of Aisne,

---

sand, which, from this cause alone, have been obliged to quit their homes, and have mostly drifted hopelessly to the great towns." In addition, a large number of farms " are now, and have been for some years, lying absolutely waste and uncultivated."—" *Bad Times*," ALFRED RUSSEL WALLACE, *London*, 1885.

one of the richest in France, one tenth of the land is abandoned, because it is found that, at present prices, the sale of
produce does not cover the expenses of cultivation.*

Now, if it were desirable to search out and determine
the primary responsibility for the recent large increase in
the number of the English unemployed, or for the distress
and revolt of the Irish tenantry, or the growing impoverishment of the French and German peasant proprietors, it
would be found that it was not so much the land and rent
policy of these different countries that should be called to
account, as the farmers on the cheap and fertile lands of the
American Northwest, the inventors of their cost-reducing
agricultural machinery, of the steel rail, and of the compound marine engine, which, collectively, have made it both
possible and profitable " to send the produce of five acres of
wheat from Chicago to Liverpool for less than the cost of
manuring one acre in England." France, in addition, might
regard as a special grievance the invention of analine dyes,
which have abolished the cultivation of madder, and deprived
whole districts in the valley of the Rhône of what was formerly a most profitable agricultural industry. But, looking
into this matter from a cosmopolitan point of view, and
balancing the aggregate of good and bad results, how small
are the evils which have been entailed upon the agricultural laborers in England, Ireland, France, or elsewhere,
in consequence of changes in the condition of their labor,
in comparison with the almost incalculable benefits that
have come, in recent years, to the masses of all civilized countries, through the increased abundance and cheap-

---

* M. de Grancey is of the opinion that one of the most fertile sources of
Irish misery and degradation is the unauthorized and illegal subletting of
farms. He states that he met with cases where from forty-five to fifty persons lived in a state of semi-starvation on a farm calculated to yield a comfortable subsistence to a family of five or six. In each generation, the farm,
in despite of special prohibitory clauses in the lease, is divided among the
sons. Where there are no sons, subtenants are found willing to take small
parcels of land at the most exorbitant prices.

ness of food, and a consequent increase in their comfort and vitality !

Another matter vital to this discussion may here and next be properly taken into consideration. As the evidence is conclusive that the direct effect of material progress is to greatly increase and cheapen production and to economize labor; and as there is no reason to suppose that the maximum of progress in this direction has been attained, and every reason to expect that the future will be characterized by like and even greater results progressively occurring, the question arises, Is labor to be continually, and in a degree ultimately, displaced from occupation by progressive economy of production? Is continual and fiercer competition to effect sales, both of product and labor, in excess of current demands, likely to produce continued disturbance and unhealthy fall of prices, extensive reductions in wages, and the more extensive employment of the cheaper labor of women and children? Is society working through all this movement toward what has been called an " anarchy of production "?

Experience thus far, under what may be termed the new *régime* of production and distribution, does not, however, fairly warrant any such anticipations. Wages, speaking generally, have not fallen, but have increased ; and, except in Germany, there is little indication of a tendency to increase the hours of labor, or encroach upon the reservation of Sunday. Everywhere else, even in Russia, the tendency is in the opposite direction.

The extent and rapidity of the increase in the consumption of all useful and desirable commodities and services which follows every increase in the ability of the masses to consume, is one of the most wonderful of modern economic phenomena ; and the one thing which, more than any other, augments their *ability* to consume, is the reduction in the price of commodities, or rather the reduction in the amount of human effort or toil requisite to obtain them, which the recent improvements in the work of production and distribution have effected.   Better living, contingent on a reduction of effort necessary to insure a comfortable subsistence, induces familiarity with better things ; constitutes the surest foundation for the elevation of the standard of popular intelligence and culture, and creates an increasing desire for not only more, but for a higher grade, of commodities and services.   There are, therefore, two lines upon which the consumption of the products of labor is advancing : the one, in which the stimulant is animal in its nature, and demands food, clothing, shelter, and fuel, for its satisfaction; and the other intellectual, which will only be satisfied by an increased supply of those things which will minister to a higher standard of comfort and education.   Thus far the world's manual laborers have not kept up in culture with the improved and quickened methods of production ; and therefore in certain departments there is not yet that opportunity for work that there undoubtedly will be in the future.

"There is no good reason why a workingman earning one thousand or fifteen hundred dollars a year, as many do, should not desire as many comforts in the shape of furniture, books, clothing, pictures, and the like for himself and his family, and desire them as intelligently, as the minister, or lawyer, or doctor, who is earning a similar amount."

But as abstract conclusions in economic as well as in all other matters are best substantiated and comprehended through practical examples, to examples let us turn.   And first as to certain notable instances derived from recent experiences, showing how remarkably and rapidly increase of consumption has followed reduction of prices, even in cases where the reduction has been comparatively slight, and a marked increase of consumption could not have been reasonably anticipated.

Among the staple food articles that have greatly declined in price during recent years is sugar, and this decline has been attended with a large increase in consumption; the decline in the average price of fair refining sugar in the United States (in bond) having been from 4·75 cents per pound in 1882 to 2·92 cents in 1886; while the average consumption per capita, which was thirty-nine pounds for the five years from 1877 to 1882, was 49·8 pounds for the five years from 1882 to 1887, and 52·6 pounds in 1888. Comparing 1885 with 1887, the consumption of sugar in the United States increased over eleven per cent, or largely in excess of any concurrent growth of population. Converting, now, so much of this larger consumption as was due to diminished price (probably more than one hundred million pounds) into terms of acres and labor employed in its production; into the ships and men required for its transportation; into the products, agricultural and manufactured, and the labor they represent, that were given in exchange for it, and we can form some idea of the greater opportunities for labor through larger volume of exchanges, and the increased comfort for those who labor, that follows every reduction in the cost necessary to procure desirable things.

In 1887, with an import price of about sixteen cents per pound, the importation of coffee into the United States was 331,000,000 pounds. In 1885, with an average import price of eight cents, the importation was 572,000,000 pounds. Between 1873 and 1885 the coffee product of the world that went to market, concurrently with this large decline in its price, increased to the extent of fifty-two per cent. Subsequent to 1885, the price of coffee, by reason primarily of a deficient crop in Brazil, greatly advanced, and consumption declined in the year 1887 to the estimated extent of a million bags for Europe, and an average of two pounds per head in the United States. With the decline in the volume of exchanges consequent on such a decline in the production and consumption of this commodity, the opportunities for the employment and remuneration of labor must obviously also have been correspondingly restricted.

Previous to the closing months of the year 1887, there was (as has been before shown) a great reduction in the price of copper, contingent upon an increased product and a surplus offering upon the world's markets. The result was such a general extension of the uses of this metal that the United States Geological Survey estimated that, for the year 1886, the increase in the consumption of copper by the leading American manufactories of copper and brass was in excess of twenty-four per cent; and that a very nearly equal increase was experienced in the preceding year (1885); all of which indicated a large if not a fully proportional increase for the periods mentioned in the opportunity for labor, at comparatively high wages, in these departments of industry. On the other hand, with a large advance in the price of copper during the latter months of 1887, the operations of the manufacturers of copper and brass all over the world were very greatly restricted.

Every reduction in the price of gas has been attended with greatly increased consumption, entailing greater demand for labor in the mining and transporting of coal and other materials, and in service of distribution; and it is very doubtful whether the apprehensions of impairment of the value of the capital of the gas companies, which are always excited by such reductions, are ever, to any disastrous extent, realized; while it is the general experience that the profits on the increased demand created by cheaper supply continue to afford to the gas companies reasonable and often equal returns on their invested capital. It seems to be also well established that the extensive introduction and use of the electric light has in no way impaired the aggregate consumption of gas.

In 1831 the average price of cotton cloth in the United States was about seventeen cents per yard; in 1880 it was seven cents. This reduction of price has been accompanied by an increase in the annual per capita consumption of the people from 5·90 pounds of cloth to 13·91 pounds; which in turn represents a great increase in all the occupations connected with cotton, from its growth to its transformation into cloth and cloth fabrications; and the evidence is conclusive that in all these occupations the share of labor in the progressing augmentations of values and quantities has continually increased; the advance in the wages of the cotton-mill operatives, during the period under consideration, having been fully eighty per cent.

When, through competition, the companies controlling the submarine telegraph lines between the United States and Europe reduced in 1886 their rates from forty to twelve cents per word, two hundred and twelve words, it was reported, were regularly transmitted in place of every one hundred previously sent. Assuming this report to be correct, a comparison of receipts under the new and old rates would give the following results: Two hundred and ten words at twelve cents each, $25.20; one hundred words at forty cents each, $40; or a reduction in rates of seventy per cent impaired the revenues of the lines to an extent of only thirty-seven per cent.

A reduction in 1886 in the postal system of the United States of *three* cents in the fee for domestic money-orders not exceeding $5 (or from eight to five cents) has operated to increase the use of this service to the remitters of small sums in a very noticeable degree, the average amount of each order issued in 1887 being but $12.72 as against an average of $14.33 in 1866, and larger sums in previous years; while the increase in the number of money-orders issued in 1887 was 16·27 per cent greater than in 1886.

The following have been the economic changes within a decade in the business of manufacturing American watches, and the manner in which such changes have affected the welfare alike of owners and employés: "A great reduction in price from which there has been no recovery. Business has invariably, and with scarcely notable friction, adjusted itself to new conditions; and save only in exceptional cases

—new companies struggling for a place—the capital invested has been fairly remunerative. Best of all, the wages of operatives have been maintained; for one reason among others, that reductions in rates paid for piece-work have operated to stimulate the intelligence of the workman, so that he devises for his special works methods and appliances which not only increase his speed but his product also, and improve its quality. The great decline in recent years in the price of American watches has not been caused by the importation of foreign watches, but has sprung wholly out of an intense competition between American manufacturers; and from this and other causes the industry has experienced all the vicissitudes incident to the occurrence of what are generally denominated 'hard times.'"

The following examples of the increase in the consumption of commodities, consequent on reductions of price through abatements of taxation, also indicate how largely the opportunities for labor and of the sphere of exchanges or business can be increased in the future by an extension of this policy:

Reductions in the price of tea in Great Britain, following a progressive reduction in the duties on the imports of this commodity, from 2s. 2½d. in 1852 to 6d. (the present rate), have been accompanied by an increase in its annual consumption from 58,000,000 pounds in 1851 to 183,000,000 pounds in 1886, or from 1·9 pound per head of the population to five pounds.

A removal in 1883 of the comparatively small tax of one cent on every hundred matches imposed by the United States, is reported to have reduced the price about one half, and to have increased the domestic consumption to the extent of nearly one third.

In 1883 a few additions were made to the free list under the tariff of the United States, and among them were included unground spices, which had been previously subjected to duties, which, although heavy as *ad valorem*, were in themselves so small specifically (as five cents per pound each on pepper, cloves, and pimento) that their influence on the consumption of the American people, with their acknowledged tendency to extravagance, would not have been generally regarded as likely to be considerable; and yet the removal of the duties on these commodities, which pass almost directly into consumption, carried up their importations in the following remarkable manner: In the case of pepper, from 6,973,000 pounds in 1883 to 12,712,000 pounds in 1888; pimento, from 1,283,000 pounds to 2,000,000 pounds; cassia-buds, from 27,739 pounds to 248,000 pounds; cloves, from 989,000 pounds to 1,854,000 pounds; nutmegs, from 661,132 to 1,246,806 pounds; while the importation and consumption of mace in the country more than doubled and that of cayenne pepper more than trebled during the same period. It is evident, therefore, that the masses of the United States during the continuance of these taxes did not have all the spices they would like, to make their food more palatable and savory; that trade between the spice-producing countries and the United States was restricted; and, as all trade is essentially an exchange of product for product, that the labor of the United States gained under the new conditions, either by sharing in the greater abundance of useful things, or through an increased opportunity for labor in producing the increase of commodities that the increase of exchanges demanded.

The original cost of the suspension-bridge between the cities of New York and Brooklyn was $15,000,000, entailing an annual burden of interest at five per cent of $750,000. When first opened to public use in September, 1883, the rates of fare were fixed at five cents per ticket for the cars, and one cent per ticket for foot-passengers, no ticket being sold at any less price by packages. The total receipts for the first year (1883–'84) from all traffic sources were $402,-938, and the total number of car and foot passenger was 11,503,440; 5,324,140 of the former and 6,179,300 of the latter.   The results of the first year's operations were not, therefore, encouraging as to the ability of the bridge to earn the interest on the cost of its construction.   During the second year (1884–'85), the rates of fare remaining the same, the increase in the aggregate number of passengers was comparatively small, or from 11,503,440 to 14,051,630; but in February, 1885, the rates of fare were greatly reduced—i. e., tickets for the cars (when sold in packages of ten) from five cents to two and a half, and tickets for promenade (when bought in packages of twenty-five) from one cent to one fifth of a cent.   The results of this reduction immediately showed themselves in a remarkable increase for the year of seventy-one per cent in the number of car and foot passengers, or from an aggregate of 14,051,630 in 1884–'85 to 25,082,587 in 1885–'86, and this aggregate has gone on increasing to 33,116,810 for the year ending December 1, 1887.   Concurrently also the bridge receipts from traffic tolls have increased from $565,544.45 in 1884–'85 (the last year of high fares) to $917,961 for the year ending December 1, 1888, with a net profit on the operations of the year sufficient to pay two thirds of the interest on the original investment; or, the result of the bridge operations since the reductions of the rates for its use has been accompanied by an increased passenger movement—car and foot—of one hundred and thirty-five per cent, and a gain in receipts of sixty-two per cent.

A further analysis of the experiences of the New York and Brooklyn Bridge since its construction also reveals some curious tendencies of the American people in respect to consumption and expenditures.   During the first year the bridge was open to the public, the number of foot-passengers paying one cent was 6,179,300, and the number of car-passengers paying five cents was 5,324,140.   The next year, fares remaining unchanged, the number of foot-passengers declined to 3,679,733, and the number of car-passengers increased to 11,951,630.   In the third year, with a reduction of foot-fares to one fifth of a cent, the number of foot-passengers declined 440,395, or to an aggregate of 3,239,337; while the number of car-passengers (with a reduction of fare from five to two and a half cents) increased 10,130,957, or to 21,843,250. For the year ending December 1, 1887, the number of foot-passengers further declined 574,929, or to 2,664,413, while the number of car-passengers further increased 8,097,063, or to 27,940,313; or to a total aggregate of 30,604,313. In the year ending December 1, 1888, the number of foot-passengers increased 121,125, while the increase in the number of car-passengers was 2,390,970, making the total of the latter 30,331,000. A correct explanation of these curious results may not be possible, but one inference from them that would seem to be warranted is, that when the American people find their pecuniary ability is abundantly sufficient to enable them to satisfy their desire for certain commodities or services, they will disdain to economize; and this idea may find illustration and confirmation in another incident of recent American experience. Thus, when the great decline in the price of sugars occurred in 1883, the American refiners expected that, whatever of increase of consumption might be attendant, would occur mainly in the lower grades of sugar; but, to their surprise, the actual increase was largely in respect to the higher grades. A leading refiner, who, somewhat puzzled at this result, asked one of his workmen for an explanation of it, received the following answer: "I give my wife fifty cents every Monday morning with which to buy sugar for the week for my family, and, as she finds that fifty cents will now buy as many pounds of the white as we once could get of the yellow sugars, she buys the white." A European workman (certainly a Frenchman) would probably have acted differently. He would have taken the same grade as before and got two pounds of additional sweetening for his money; or, more likely, he would have bought the same quantity and quality as before, and saved up the measure of the decline of price in the form of money.

Another explanation of the bridge phenomenon may be that the average American, who is always in a hurry, may think that, with the privilege of riding for two and a half cents, he can not afford the time to avail himself of the privilege of walking for a payment of one fifth of a cent.

Mr. Robert Giffen, in a review of the "Recent Rate of Material Progress in England" (British Association, 1887), recognizes an evident tendency, as that country increases in wealth, for the numbers employed in miscellaneous industries, and in what may be called "incorporeal functions"— that is, as artists, teachers, and others, who minister to taste and comfort in a way that can hardly be called material—to increase disproportionately to those engaged in the production of the great staples; and that, therefore, the production of these latter is not likely to increase as rapidly as heretofore. All of which is equivalent to affirming that, in virtue of natural law, the evils resulting from the displacement of labor, through more economic methods of production by machinery, are being gradually and to a large extent counteracted. No one can doubt that this is the tendency in the United States equally as in England, and it finds one striking illustration in the large number of new products that are demanded, and in the number of occupations that have been greatly enlarged or absolutely created in recent years, in consequence of the change in popular taste, conjoined with popular ability, to incur greater expense. Especially is this true in respect to house-building and house-decoration. Ten or fifteen years ago the amount of fine outside work in building constructions—in brick, terra-cotta, stone, and metal—and on interiors, in the way of painting, paper-hangings, wall-coverings with other materials, fine wood-work, carving, furniture-making, carpet-weaving, draperies for doors and windows, stained glass and mirrors, and improved and elaborate sanitary heating and ventilating apparatus, was but a very small fraction of what is now required.

A few years ago plain buttons, both as respects form and color, represented the bulk of the demand on the part of the public. Gradually, however, the old style of these goods failed to suit the tastes of the multitude and the requirements of fashion; and the button-manufacturers now report that four times as many buttons—differing widely in form, material, color, ornamentation, and cost—are manufactured and sold than the market ten years ago demanded. Nothing, furthermore, is more certain than that all these new departments of industry are to continue progressively enlarging; for all achievements in this direction increase taste and culture, and these in turn create new and enlarged spheres for industrial occupation.

How these same influences exert themselves for the extension of the intercommunication of intelligence, with the attendant increased demand for service and materials which represent opportunities for labor, is exemplified in the following postal statistics, the result of recent German investigation: Thus, for the year 1865 it is estimated that the inhabitants of the world exchanged about 2,300,000,000 letters; in 1873, the aggregate was 3,300,000,000; in 1885, including postal-cards, it was 6,257,000,000; in 1886, 6,926,000,000, with a larger ratio of increase in the transmission of printed matter, patterns, and other articles; the whole business giving employment to about 500,000 persons, for more than one half of which number there was probably no requirement for service under conditions existing in 1873. And to this aggregate should be added the increased number required to meet the greater requirements for the machinery and service of larger transportation, and vastly larger consumption of all the material and service incident to correspondence. The experience of the postal service of the United States also shows that, at all those points where a free delivery of letters has been established, the postal revenues have quickly and greatly augmented—another illustration that every increased and cheapened facility for consumption brings with it greater demands for service or production.

A comparatively few years ago the highly specialized profession of journalism did not exist at all, even in its simplest form; and, even more recently, the specialties of making and attending to telephones have come into existence without anything in the nature of an antecedent foundation. In fact, no small proportion of the many new applications of science that are constantly made have in view the creation of new wants, rather than the satisfying of old ones.

In view, then, of the undoubted tendency, as abundance or wealth increases, for labor to transfer itself, in no small proportions, from lower to higher grades—from the production of the great staples to occupations that minister to comfort and culture, rather than to subsistence—how impolitic, from the standpoint of labor's interests, seems to be the imposition of high taxes (as in the United States) on the importation of works of art of a high character and large cost, under the assumption that it is desirable to tax all such articles as luxuries, and that it is for the interest of the masses to adopt such a policy! In illustration, let us suppose a man of wealth to purchase and import a costly and beautiful art product. Having obtained it, he rarely finds a compensating return for his expenditure in an exclusive and selfish inspection, but rather in exhibiting it to the public; and the public go away from these exhibitions with such higher tastes and culture as impel them to desire to have in their life-surroundings, as much that is artistic and beautiful—not the work of one, but of many—as their means will allow; even if it be no more than a cheerful chromolithograph, a photograph, a carpet or a curtain of novel and attractive design, a piece of elegant furniture, or of bronze, porcelain, or pottery. And to supply the new and miscellaneous industries that are created or enlarged by such desires and demands, labor will be, as it were, constantly drained off from occupations in which improved machinery tends to supplant it, into other spheres of employment in which the conditions and environments are every way elevating, because in them the worker is less of a machine, and the rewards of labor are very much greater.

The phenomena of the over-production, or unremunerative supply at current market prices, of certain staple commodities, although for the time being often a matter of difficulty and the occasion of serious industrial and commercial disturbances, are also certain, in each specific instance, to sooner or later disappear in virtue of the influence of what may be regarded as economic axioms, namely: that we produce to consume, and that, unless there is perfect reciprocity in consumption, production will not long continue in a disproportionate ratio to consumption; and also that, under continued and marked reduction of prices, consumption will quickly tend to increase and equalize, or accommodate itself to production. Illustrations of the *actua* and *possible* under this head, and of the rapidity with which conditions are reversed and "over-production" disappears, are most curious and instructive. For example, all authorities in 1885 were agreed that the then existing capacity for manufacturing cotton was greatly in excess of the world's capacity for consumption; the season of 1885–'86 closing with a surplus of nearly 400,000,000 yards on the British market, for which the manufacturers found no demand. Since that date, however, and with no extraordinary development of business activity in any country, the world's consumption of cotton fabrics has reached a larger total than ever before, and there are probably at the present time (1889) no more spindles in existence than are necessary to supply the current and immediately prospective demand for their products. In the case of sugar, also, an increase in consumption occasioned by low prices, and a notable restriction of production through the same price influences, reduced an estimated actual surplus of sugar on the world's markets in October, 1885, of 1,042,956 tons, to 568,188 tons in October, 1887, and to practically nothing in January, 1889.

The production of very few articles has increased in recent years in a ratio so disproportionate to any increase of the world's population as that of iron, and prices of some standard varieties have accordingly touched a lower range than were ever before known. Gloomy apprehensions have accordingly been entertained respecting continued over-production, and its disastrous influence in the future on the involved capital and labor. To comprehend, however, the possibilities for this industry in the future, it is only necessary to have in mind, that in 1882 (and the proportions have not probably since varied) the population of the United States and of Europe (398,333,750), comprising about one fourth of the total population of the world (1,424,686,000), consumed nineteen twentieths of the whole annual production of iron and steel, and that if the population of the world outside of Europe and the United States should increase their annual per capita consumption of iron (which is not now probably in excess of two pounds) to only one half of the average annual per capita consumption of the people of a country as low down in civilization as Russia, the annual demand upon the existing producing capacity of iron would be at once increased to the extent of over six million tons. And, when it is further remembered that civilization is rapidly advancing in many countries, like India, where the present annual consumption of iron per capita is very small (2·4 pounds), and that civilization can not progress to any great extent without the extensive use of iron, the possibilities for the enormous extension of the iron industry in the future, and the enlarged sphere of employment of capital and labor in connection therewith, make themselves evident.*

---

* According to a table presented to the British Iron Trade Association by Mr. Jeans in 1882, and subsequently incorporated in a report submitted by

As constituting a further contribution to the study of the so-called industrial phenomenon of "over-production," and as illustrating how a greater abundance and cheaper price of desirable commodities, work for the equalization and betterment of the conditions of life among the masses, the recent experience of the article of quinine should not be overlooked. Owing to greatly increased and cheaper supplies of the cinchona-bark, from which quinine is extracted, and to the employment of new and more economical processes, by which more quinine can be made in from three to five days than could be in twenty under the old system, the markets of the world in recent years have been overwhelmed with supplies of this article, and its price has declined in a most rapid and extraordinary manner, namely: from 16s. 6d. ($4.10) the ounce in the English market in 1877, to 12s. ($3) in 1880; 3s. 6d. (84 cents) in 1883; and to 1s. 3d. (30 cents), or less, in 1887. As quinine is a medicine, and as the increase in the consumption of medicines is dependent upon the real or fancied increase of ill-health among the masses, rather than on any reduced cost of supply (although, in the case of this specific article, decreased cost has undoubtedly somewhat increased its legitimate con-

Sir Lowthian Bell to the British Commission "On the Depression of Trade" in 1885 (and from which the above data have been derived), the total consumption of iron in the above year was 20,567,746 tons. Of this aggregate, the United States and the several countries of Europe, with a population at that time of 398,333,750, consumed 19,057,963 tons, the following five countries, namely, the United States, the United Kingdom of Great Britain, France, Germany, and Belgium, with a population of 174,500,935, consuming 16,259,- 514 tons. The aggregate consumption of iron by the population of all the other countries of the world at that time (assumed to be 1,424,686,570) was estimated at 1,509,783 tons, or, deducting the consumption of the population of the British possessions other than in India (as Australia, etc.), at only 888,298 tons, or 1·96 pound per head per annum. The annual per capita consumption of different countries in 1882 was reported as follows: The United Kingdom, 287 pounds; the United States, 270 pounds; Belgium, 238 pounds; France, 149 pounds; Germany, 123 pounds; Sweden and Norway, 77 pounds; Austrian territories, 37 pounds; Russia, 24·06 pounds; South America and the islands, 13·5 pounds; Egypt, 7·5 pounds; India, 2·4 pounds.

sumption), the problem of determining how a present and apparently future over-production was to be remedied has been somewhat difficult of solution. But recently the large manufacturers of Europe have made an arrangement to put up quinine (pills), protected by gelatine, and introduce and offer it so cheaply in the East Indies and other tropical countries, as to induce its extensive consumption on the part of a vast population inhabiting malarious districts which have hitherto been deprived of the use of this valuable specific by reason of its costliness. And it is anticipated that by reason of its cheapness it may, to a considerable extent, supersede the use of opium among the poorer classes living along the Chinese rivers, who it is believed extensively consume this latter pernicious and costly drug, not so much for its mere narcotic or sensual properties, as for the relief it affords to the fever depression occasioned by malaria.*

All this evidence, therefore, seems to lead to the conclusion that there is little foundation for the belief largely entertained by the masses, and which has been inculcated by many sincere and humane persons, who have undertaken to counsel and direct them, that the amount of remunerative work to be done in the world is a fixed quantity, and that the fewer there are to do it the more each one will get; when the real truth is, that work as it were breeds work; that the amount to be done is not limited; that the more there is done the more there will be to do; and that the continued increasing material abundance which follows all new methods for effecting greater production and distribu-

---

* One curious result of the change in the basis of the world's supply of cinchona-bark from South America to the British East Indies has been the almost complete collapse of a formerly large item of the export trade of Colombia, South America. Thus, the annual value of cinchona-bark exported by Colombia as recently as the year 1880 was returned at £1,024,763 ($4,979,-358); but for 1887 the maximum value of its export was not in excess of £8,000 ($38,880).

tion is the true and permanent foundation for increasing general prosperity.

Again : Some pessimists, looking forward to the occupation and highest possible tillage of all the land on the earth's surface, or to the exhaustion of the coal-supply, will perhaps urge that this sanguine view has necessarily its limitations. So, too, geologists tell us that all the water on the earth is being gradually absorbed into the mass of the planet, and that ultimate universal aridity is certain ; and some astronomers say that the earth's axis is swinging round so as to bring on another glacial epoch. But we are not dealing with remote cycles and millenniums, of which we know nothing ; and it is sufficient for the present to alone consider what is now going on in the world, and what we have every reason to believe will continue under substantially the same conditions as now exist.

X.

ATTENTION is next asked to the *second* (assumed) cause for the prevailing discontent of labor, namely :

Changes in the character or nature of employments consequent upon the introduction of new methods—machinery or processes—which it is claimed have tended to lower the grade of labor, impair the independence, and restrict the mental development of the laborer.

That such changes have been in the nature of evil, can not be questioned ; but they are not new in character, nor as extensive in number and effect as is popularly supposed. Subordination to routine and method is an essential element in all systematized occupations ; and in not a few employments and professions—as in all military and naval life, and in navigation and railroad work—an almost complete surrender of the independence of the individual, and an unreasoning mechanical compliance with rules or orders, are the indispensable conditions for the attainment of any degree of successful effort. In very many cases also the individual finds compensation for subordination and the surrender of independence in the recognition that such conditions may be but temporary, and are the necessary antecedents for promotion; and routine and monotony are doubtless in a greater or less degree alleviated when the operative can discern the plan of his work as an entirety, and note its result in the form of finished products. But in manufacturing operations, where the division of labor has been carried to an extreme, where the product of the worker is never more than a fraction of any finished "whole," and where no greater demand is made upon the brain than it shall see to it that the muscles of the arm, the hand, or the finger execute movements at specific times and continuously in connection with machinery, there are few such compensations or alleviations; and the general result to the individual working under such conditions can not, to say the least, be in the line of either healthy mental or physical development.

Happily, however, the number of industries, in which the division of labor and its subordination to machinery has been productive of such extreme results, is not very large; the manufacture of boots and shoes by modern machine methods, in which every finished shoe is said to represent sixty-two distinct mechanical employments or products, being perhaps the most notable. And yet even here there is not a little in way of compensating benefit to be credited to such a system. Thus, for example, it is stated that "the use of machinery has compelled employés to apply themselves more closely to their work; and, being paid by the piece, has enabled them to make better wages." When shoemaking was a handicraft, "the hours of labor were very irregular; the workmen, who decided their own hours of labor, working some days only a few hours, and then working far into the night for a few days to make up for lost time. It was once customary for shoemakers (in New England) to work on an average fifteen hours a day "; now the hours of labor in the shoe-factories are not in excess of ten hours. It is also claimed that the introduction of the sewing-machine into the manufacture of boots and shoes has greatly increased the opportunities for the employment of women, at better rates of wages. In the manufacture clothing, which, in routine and monotony, is analogous to the manufacture of boots and shoes, it is generally conceded that the influence of the sewing-machine has been to increase wages, and that, " notwithstanding the constantly growing use of these machines, the number of employés is greater than formerly, owing to the enlargement of the business."* Furthermore, the " collective work which admits of being carried on by the factory principle of great subdivision of labor and by the bringing together of large numbers of people under one roof and one control " does not at present, in the United States, give occupation to more than one in ten of all who follow gainful occupations in the whole country; while for the other nine the essential elements of industrial success continue, as of old, to be found in individual independence and personal mental capacity; and this experience of the United States will probably find a parallel in all other manufacturing countries.

The supersedure of men by women and young persons in textile manufactories, which (as previously noticed) has occurred to such an extent in New England that certain factory towns have come to be popularly designated as " she-towns," at first thought seems deplorable. But, on the other hand, it is certain that such supersedure has been mainly the result of such a diminution of the severity of toil through the improvements in machinery, or such a greater division of labor consequent upon new methods of produc-

---

* " Report on the Statistics of Wages," J. D. Weeks, United States census, vol. xx.

tion, as have opened up new opportunities for employment to women by making it possible for them to easily do work which, under old systems, required the greater strength and endurance of men ; children, for example, being able to spin yarn on a "ring-frame," which men alone were able to do on a "spinning-mule." And, however such changes may be regarded from the standpoint of the men operatives, the greater opportunity afforded for continuous work at greater wages than could be readily obtained in other occupations, is probably not regarded by the women operatives in the light of a misfortune. Experience also shows that the larger the scale on which capitalistic production and distribution is carried on, "the less it can countenance the petty devices for swindling and pilfering," and the neglect and disregard of the health, safety, and comfort of operatives, which so generally characterize industrial enterprises on a small scale ; or, in other words, the maintenance of a high standard of industrial and commercial morality is coming to be recognized by the managers of all great enterprises as a means of saving time and avoiding trouble, and therefore as an undoubted and important element of profit. And it is to these facts—the natural and necessary growth of what has been termed the "capitalistic system "—that a recent English writer on the condition of the working-classes largely attributes the suppression of the truck (store) system, the enactment of laws limiting the hours of labor, the acquiescence in the existence and power of trade-unions, and the increasing attention to sanitary regulations ; reforms that have reformed away the worst features of the condition of labor as it existed thirty or forty years ago in Great Britain.* The larger the concern, the greater usually the steadiness of employment, and the more influential the public opinion of the employed.

---

* "The Condition of the Working Class in England in 1844," by Frederick Engles.

Dr. Werner Siemens, the celebrated German scientist and inventor, in a recent address at Berlin on "Science and the Labor Question," claimed that the necessity for extensive factories and workshops—involving large capital and an almost "slavish" discipline for labor—to secure the maximum cheapness in production, "was due, to a great extent, to the yet imperfect development of the art of practical mechanics"; and that mechanical skill will ultimately effect "a return to the system (now almost extinct) of independent, self-sustaining domiciliary labor" by the introduction of cheap, compact, easily set up and operated labor-saving machinery into the smaller workshops and the homes of the workingmen. Should the difficulties now attendant upon the transmission of electricity from points where it can be cheaply generated, and its safe and effective subdivision and distribution as a motive force be overcome (as it is not improbable they ultimately will be), thus doing away with the necessity of multiplying expensive and cumbersome machinery — steam-engines, boilers, dams, reservoirs, and water-wheels—for the local generation and application of mechanical power, there can be no doubt that most radical changes in the use of power for manufacturing purposes will speedily follow, and that the anticipations of Dr. Siemens, as to the change in the relations of machinery to its operatives, may at no distant day be realized.

The third cause which has especially operated in recent years to occasion discontent on the part of labor has been undoubtedly *the increase in intelligence or general information on the part of the masses in all civilized countries.*

The best definition, or rather statement, of the essential difference between a man and an animal, that has ever been given is, that a man has progressive wants, and an animal has not. Under the guidance of what is termed instinct, the animal wants the same habitat and quantity and quality of food as its progenitors, and nothing more. And the more nearly man approaches in condition to the animal, the more limited is the sphere of his wants, and the greater his contentment. A greater supply of blubber and skins to the Eskimo, more "pulque" to the native Mexican, to the West Indian negro a constant supply of yams and plantains without labor, and the ability to buy five salt herrings for the same price that he has now to give for three, would, in each case, temporarily fill the cup of individual happiness nearly to repletion. And, among civilized men, the contentment and also sluggishness of those neighborhoods in which the population come little in contact with the outer world and have little of diversity of employment open to them, are proverbial.

Now the wonderful material progress which has been made within the last quarter of a century has probably done more to overcome the inertia, and quicken the energy of the masses, than all that has been hitherto achieved in this direction in all preceding centuries. The railroad, the steamship, and the telegraph have broken down the barriers of space and time that formerly constituted almost insuperable obstacles in the way of frequent intercourse between people of different races, countries, and communities, and have made the civilized world, as it were, one great neighborhood. Every increased facility that is afforded for the dissemination of intelligence, or for personal movement, finds a marvelously quick response in an extended use. The written correspondence—letters and cards—exchanged through the world's postal service, more than doubled between the years 1873 and 1885; while in the United States the number of people annually transported on railroads alone exceeds every year many times the total population of the country, the annual number for the New England States being more than sixteen times greater than their population. Under these powerful but natural educating influences, there has been a great advance in the intelligence of the masses. They have come to know more of what others are doing; know better what they themselves are capable of doing;

and their wants have correspondingly increased, not merely in respect to quantities of the things to which they have always been accustomed, but very many articles and services which within a comparatively recent period were regarded as luxuries, are now almost universally considered and demanded as necessaries. At the same time, the increased power of production and distribution, and the consequent reduction in the cost of most commodities and services, have also worked for the satisfaction of these wants in such a degree that a complete revolution has been effected during recent years in the every-day life of all classes of the people of the great industrial and commercial countries. Let any any one compare the condition of even the abject poor of London, as described in recent publications, with the condition of English laborers as described by writers of acknowledged authority not more than forty years ago,* and he can not resist the conclusion that the very outcasts of England are now better provided for than were multitudes of her common laboring-men at the period mentioned.†

---

* The condition of agricultural laborers in general, and large classes of artisans, in the United Kingdom, forty or fifty years ago, as described by Carlyle in his "Past and Present" and "Sartor Resartus," and by another most reliable English authority, Mr. W. T. Thornton, in his "Over-population and its Remedy," was so deplorable that it is now difficult to realize that it ever existed.

† What an enormous stride has been made in the amelioration of the condition of the masses of the people of England, taking a more lengthened period into consideration, is strikingly illustrated by the following description, based on authentic data, by Rev. Augustus Jessop, of the condition of the people of the parish of Rougham, in the time of Henry III (1216–1272):

"The people who lived in this village six hundred years ago were living a life hugely below the level of yours. They were more wretched in their poverty; they were incomparably less prosperous in their prosperity; they were worse clad, worse fed, worse housed, worse taught, worse tended, worse governed; they were sufferers from loathsome diseases which you know nothing of; the very beasts in the field were dwarfed and stunted in their growth, and I do not believe there were any giants on the earth in those days. The death-rate among the children must have been tremendous. The disregard of human life was so callous that we can hardly conceive it. There was everything to harden, nothing to soften; everywhere oppression, greed, and fierce-

The widening of the sphere of one's surroundings, and a larger acquaintance with other men and pursuits, have long been recognized as not productive of content.* Writing to his nephew more than one hundred years ago, Thomas Jefferson thus concisely expressed the results of his own observation: "Traveling," he says, "makes men wiser, but less happy. When men of sober age travel they gather knowledge, but they are, after all, subject to recollections mixed with regret; their affections are weakened by being extended over more objects, and they learn new habits which can not be gratified when they return home." Again, as the former few and simple requirements of the masses have become more varied and costly, the individual effort necessary for the satisfaction of the latter is not relatively less, even under the new conditions of production, than before, and in many instances is possibly greater. Hence, notwithstanding the large advance in recent years in the average rates of wages, and a greatly increased purchasing power of wages, there is

---

ness. The law of the land was hideously cruel and merciless, and the gallows and the pillory—never far from any man's door—were seldom allowed to remain long out of use. The ghastly frequency of the punishment of death tended to make people savage and bloodthirsty. It tended, too, to make men absolutely reckless of consequences when once their passions were roused. 'As well be hung for a sheep as a lamb,' was a saying that had a grim truth in it. The laborer's dwelling had no windows; the hole in the roof which let out the smoke rendered windows unnecessary. The laborer's fire was in the middle of his house; he and his wife and children huddled around it, sometimes groveling in the ashes; and going to bed meant flinging themselves down upon straw. The laborer's only light at night was the smoldering fire. Why should he burn a rush-light when there was nothing to look at?

"Should we like to change with these forefathers of ours, whose lives were passed in the way described, six hundred years ago? Were the former times better than these? Has the world grown worse as it has grown older? Has there been no progress, but only decline?"

* Increased facility for communication between Great Britain and the United States has without doubt been a large factor in occasioning the present profound discontent of Ireland; and political subjugation and their existing land system have been more intolerable to the Irish peasant and artisan, since they have been enabled to compare the institutions under which they live with those which their expatriated fellow-countrymen enjoy elsewhere.

no less complaint than ever of the cost of living; when (as M. Leroy-Beaulieu has pointed out in the case of France *) the foundation for the complaint is for the most part to be found in the circumstance that a totally different style of living has been adopted, and that society makes conformity with such different style a standard of family respectability. The change in the character of the people of Germany in respect to content since the Franco-German War in 1871, is especially noticeable. Before the war the unpretending, stationary habits of the people tended to make every one contented with his lot and averse to social changes. The war, with its excitements and triumphs, and the establishment of the empire, which was conditioned upon and accompanied by the enactment of a multitude of laws freeing the social life of the people from a multitude of restrictions by which it was formerly bound, effected a complete metamorphosis, and this, coinciding with a brief period of great commercial activity and wild speculation (see pages 4, 5), created a profound impression upon the masses of the people, and seems to have changed permanently and in a great degree their former character. Germany before the war was a country of comparatively cheap living and production. To-day it is not.

There is, therefore, unquestionably in these facts an explanation in no small part of what to many has seemed one of the greatest puzzles of the times—namely, that with undoubtedly greater and increasing abundance and cheapness of most desirable things, popular discontent with the existing economic condition of affairs does not seem to diminish, but rather to greatly increase. And out of such discontent, which is not based on anything akin to actual and unavoidable poverty, has originated a feeling that the new conditions of abundance should be further equalized by some other meth-

---

* "The Fall in the Price of Commodities; its Cause and Effect." By Leroy-Beaulieu.—*Economiste Française, April*, 1887.

ods than intelligent individual effort, self-denial, and a natural, progressive material and social development (the actuality of which is proved by all experience); and that the state could, if it would, make all men prosperous; and therefore should, in some way not yet clearly defined by anybody, arbitrarily intervene and effect it. And this feeling, so far as it assumes definiteness of idea and purpose, constitutes what is called "socialism." *

As it is important to make clear the full force and meaning of the term "self-denial" and "natural progressive material and social development," as above used, attention is asked to the following considerations: The investigations of Mr. Atkinson show that an increase of five cents' worth of material comfort per day, for every day in the year, to each inhabitant of the United States, would require the annual production and equitable distribution of more than $1,000,000,000 worth of commodities! In the last analysis, therefore, national prosperity and adversity are measurable by a difference which is not in excess of the price of a daily glass of beer; or, if five cents' worth of product for each inhabitant could be added to the capital of the country in excess of the average for each day in the year, such a year, by reason of its increased exchanges and sum of individual satisfactions, could not be other than most prosperous.

---

* On this point the Commissioner of the Bureau of Labor Statistics of the State of Connecticut, in his report for 1887, speaks as follows : "Necessary wants have multiplied, and society demands so much in the style of living that the laboring-man finds it almost impossible to live as respectably now on his wages as his father did thirty years since upon his. That is, wages have not kept pace with the increasing wants and style of living demanded by society. The laborer thinks he sees a wider difference between the style in which his employer lives and the way he is compelled to live, than existed between employer and employés thirty years ago. He thinks that this difference is growing greater with the years. Now, as a man's income is, in general, measured by his style of living, he can not resist the conclusion that a larger share of the profits of business goes to his employer than employers received in former years; that the incomes of employers have increased more rapidly than the wages of employés. The laboring people are fully alive to the fact that modern inventions and the like make larger incomes possible and right. They do not complain of these larger incomes, but they do believe most profoundly that they are not receiving their fair share of the benefits conferred upon society by these inventions and labor-saving machines. In this belief lies the principal source of their unrest."

Again, the extraordinary and comparatively recent reductions in the cost of transportation of commodities by land and water (in the case of the New York Central and Hudson River Railroad, for example, from an average of 3·45 cents per ton per mile in 1865 to 0·68 of a cent in 1885), which have reduced the prices of the common articles of food to the masses to the extent of substantially one half, did not involve in their conception and carrying out any idea of benefiting humanity; but on the contrary those immediately concerned in effecting the improvements that have led to such results never would have abated the rates to the public, but would have controlled and maintained them to their own profit, had they been able. But, by the force of agencies that have been above human control, they have not only not been able to do so, but have been constrained to promptly accept business at continually decreasing rates, as a condition of making any profit for themselves whatever. And what is true of the results of improvements in the transportation of products is equally true of all methods for economizing and facilitating their production. They are all factors in one great natural movement for continually increasing and equalizing abundance.

With this analysis of the causes of the prevailing and almost universal discontent of labor, the following other results—industrial and social—which have been attendant upon the world's recent material progress are worthy of consideration by all desirous of fully comprehending the present economic situation, and the outlook for the future.

ADVANCE IN WAGES.—The average rate of wages, or the share which the laborer receives of product, has within a comparatively recent period, and in almost all countries— certainly in all civilized countries—greatly increased. The extent of this increase since 1850, and even since 1860, has undoubtedly exceeded that of any previous period of equal duration in the world's history.

Mr. Giffen claims, as the result of his investigations for Great Britain, that " the average money-wages of the working-classes of the community, looking at them in the mass, and comparing the mass of *fifty* years ago with the mass at the present time, have increased very nearly one hundred per cent.* It is also conceded of this increase in Great Britain that by far the largest proportion has occurred within the later years of this period, and has been concurrent with the larger introduction and use of machinery. Thus the investigations of Mr. James Caird show, that the advance in the average rate of wages for agricultural labor in England in the twenty-eight years between 1850 and 1878 was forty-five per cent greater than the entire advance that took place in the eighty years next preceding 1850.

Mr. Giffen has also called attention to an exceedingly interesting and encouraging feature which has attended the recent improvement in money-wages in Great Britain—and which probably finds correspondence in other countries; and that is, that the tendency of the economic changes of the last fifty years has been not merely to augment the wages of the lowest class of labor, but also to reduce in a marked degree the proportion of this description of labor to the total mass—" its numbers having diminished on account of openings for labor in other directions. But this diminution has at the same time gone along with a steady improvement in the condition of the most unskilled laborers themselves." So that, if there had been no increase whatever in the average money-wages of Great Britain in recent years, the improvement in the general condition of the masses in that country "must have been enormous, for the simple reason that the population at the higher rate of wages has increased disproportionately to the others." One of the most interesting and unquestionably one of the most accurate investigations respecting the range of wages since 1850,

---

* This statement was first made by Mr. Giffen in 1883, in his inaugural address as President of the Royal Statistical Society of England, and was received with something of popular incredulity. But recurring to the same subject in another communication to the same society in 1886, Mr. Giffen asserts that further investigations show that there is no justification whatever for any doubts that may have been entertained as to the correctness of his assertions.

in the leading industries of Great Britain, was prepared in 1883 by Mr. George Lord, President of the Manchester (England) Chamber of Commerce, which showed that the percentage increase in the average wages paid in eleven of the leading industries of that city between 1850 and 1883 was forty per cent; the increase ranging from 10·30 per cent in mechanical engineering (fitters and turners) to 74·72 per cent in the case of other mechanics and in medium cotton spinning and weaving.

At the meeting of the "Industrial Remuneration Conference" at London, in 1885, Sir Lowthian Bell stated that in the chemical manufacturing industries on the Tyne, England, employing nineteen thousand workmen directly, wages had been increased within his own knowledge in the last twenty-five years thirty-seven and a half per cent, while during the same period the average value of the products had declined forty per cent. He also added that all the evidence received from France, Germany, Belgium, and Austria goes to prove that while during the last forty years the cost of living in all these countries had been notably augmented (with an accompanying rise of wages) in the United Kingdom under free-trade measures, with a large average rise in wages, the cost of living has sensibly diminished.

In the United States, according to the data afforded by the census returns for 1850 and 1880, the average wages paid for the whole country increased during the interval of these years by 39·9 per cent; or in a slightly smaller ratio of increase than was experienced during the same period in the industries of that district of England of which its city of Manchester is the center. The figures of the United States census of 1850 can not, however, be accepted with confidence.*

---

* It is at the same time not a little significant that the Commissioner of the Massachusetts Bureau of Labor Statistics should have reported in 1884, as the

As respects agricultural labor in the United States, the assertion is probably warranted that, taking into account the hours of work, rates of wages, and the prices of commodities, the average farm-laborer is one hundred per cent better off at the present time than he was thirty or forty years ago. In Massachusetts the average advance in the money-wages of this description of labor between 1850 and 1880 was fifty-six per cent, with board in addition. Between 1842 and 1846 the wages of agricultural labor in the United States sank to almost the lowest points of the century. According to the investigations of the Massachusetts Bureau of Labor Statistics, the average advance in general wages in that State from 1860 to 1883 was 28·36 per cent, while the conclusions of Mr. Atkinson are that the wages of mechanics in Massachusetts were twenty-five per cent more in 1885 than they were in 1860.

A careful investigation instituted by the Bureau of Labor Statistics for Connecticut of the comparative wages paid in the brass, carpet, clock, silk, and woolen industries of that State in 1860 and 1887, and the comparative cost of the necessaries of life to the operatives at the same periods (see report for 1888), gave the following results: average advance in the wages of males about forty-three per cent, and of females fifty-seven per cent; decline in the price of staple dry goods, thirty-nine per cent; of carpets, thirty-six per cent; increase in the average price of groceries and provisions, ten and a half per cent. "There was an average advance in the retail price of such kinds and cuts of meat as are common to the market reports of both dates of thirty-three per cent."

Taking the experience of the cities of St. Paul and Minneapolis as a basis, recent investigations also show a

result of his investigations, that while from 1872 to 1883 wages advanced on an average 9·74 per cent in Great Britain, they declined on the average in Massachusetts during the same period 5·41 per cent.

marked increase in the average wages of all descriptions of
labor in the Northwestern sections of the United States,
comparing 1886 with 1875, of at least ten per cent.   In all
railroad-work, the fact to which Mr. Giffen has called attention as a gratifying result of recent English experience also
here reappears—namely, that the proportion of men earning
the highest rates of wages is much greater than it was ten
years ago, or more skilled workmen and fewer common
workmen are relatively employed.

A series of official statistics, published in the " Annuaire
Statistique de la France," respecting the rates of wages paid
in Paris and in the provinces of France in twenty-three
leading industries, during the years 1853 and 1883 respectively, show that, during the period referred to, the advance
in average wages in Paris was fifty-three per cent and in the
provinces sixty-eight per cent, the figures being applicable
to 1,497,000 workmen out of a total of 1,554,000 ascertained
to be occupied in these industries by the French census of
1876.*   More recent returns show that for the whole of
France, exclusive of Paris, the increase of wages from 1853
to 1884, " pour la petite industrie," was about sixty-six per
cent.

Accepting the wage statistics of France (and they are
official), it would, therefore, appear that the rise of wages
in that country during the years above reviewed was greater
than was experienced in either England or the United
States.

M. Yves Guyot, the eminent French economist, is also
the authority for the statement that the average daily wages
of work-women in France engaged in the manufacture of
clothing, lace, embroideries, laundry-work, and the like,
increased ninety-four per cent between the years 1844 and

---

* " On the Comparative Efficiency and Earnings of Labor at Home and
Abroad," by J. S. Jeans, " Journal of the Royal Statistical Society " (G. B.),
December, 1884.

1872. In both France and England there has been in recent years a very marked tendency in men to abandon trades in which they formerly competed with women, because better channels have been opened to the women for their activities, and consequently the demand for women's labor has become more and more considerable.

In the cotton-mills at Mülhausen, Germany, the rates of increase in wages between 1835 and 1880 range between sixty and two hundred and fifty-six per cent, the increase in the later years, as in other countries, having been particularly noticeable. M. Charles Grad, a French economist, has called attention to the fact that in the textile and metallurgic industries of France it is the lowest class of workmen whose wages have risen most in the last fifty years.

One factor which has undoubtedly contributed somewhat to the almost universal rise of wages during the last quarter of the century has been the immense progress that has been made in the abolition of human slavery—direct, as well as in its modified forms of serfdom and peonage—which thirty years ago existed unimpaired over no inconsiderable areas of the earth's surface, and exerted a powerful influence for the degradation of labor and reduction of average wages to a minimum.

RELATION OF WAGES TO THE COST OF LIVING.—All conclusions as to the effect of changes in the rates of wages in any country are, however, incomplete, unless accompanied by data which permit of a conversion of wages into living; for, even the places where an advance in money-wages can not be found (if there are any such), the decline in recent years in the price of commodities is equivalent to an advance in wages. In the case of the United States, and for the period from 1860 to 1885, such data have been furnished by Mr. William M. Grosvenor, through a careful tabulation of the prices of two hundred commodities, embracing nearly every commodity in common use. From these comparisons, that have thus been made available, it appears that, if the purchasing power of one dollar in gold coin in May, 1860, be taken as the standard—or as one hundred cents' worth—the corresponding purchasing power of a like dollar in the year 1885 was 26·44 times greater. The artisan in Massachusetts in this latter year, therefore, could either "have largely raised the standard of his living, or, on the same standard, could have saved one fourth of his wages." Similar investigations instituted in Great Britain (and which had been before made) indicate corresponding results.

Another conclusion by Mr. Atkinson would also seem to be incapable of contravention, namely : That the greatly increased product of the fields, forests, factories, and mines of the United States which has occurred during the period from 1860 to 1885 "must have been mostly consumed by those who performed the actual work, because they constitute so large a proportion—substantially about ninety per cent—of the whole number of persons by whom such products are consumed," and that "no other evidence is needed to prove that the working man and woman of the United States, in the strictest meaning of these words, are, decade by decade, securing to their own use and enjoyment an increasing share in a steadily increasing product."*

The report of the Bureau of Industrial Statistics of the State of Maine, for the year 1887, also present some notable evidence of the continued increase in the purchasing power of wages, and show that, taking the experience of a typical American family in that State, deriving their living from manufacturing employments as a basis, as much of food could be bought in 1887 for one dollar as would have cost $1.20 in 1882 and $1.30 in 1877 ; the difference being mainly due to reductions in the prices of flour, sugar, molasses, fresh meats, lard, oil, and soap.

In a paper presented to the British Association in 1886 by Mr. M. G. Mulhall, the increase in the purchasing power

---

* " Century Magazine," 1887.

of money as respects commodities, and its decrease in purchasing power as respects labor in England during the period from 1880–'83 as compared with the period from 1821 to 1848, was thus illustrated by being reduced to figures and quantities: Thus in 1880–'83, 117 units of money would have bought as much of grain as 142 units could have done in 1821–'48; but, in respect to labor, it would have required 285 units of money to have bought as much in 1820–'23 as 201 units did in 1821–'48. In respect to cattle, the purchasing power of money had increased in the ratio of 312 in the latter to 218 in the former period; but since 1879 the carcass price of dressed meats has notably declined in England: inferior beef upon the London market (in 1885–'86) to the extent of forty-three per cent; prime beef, eighteen per cent; pork, twenty-two per cent; middling mutton, twenty-seven per cent. It is also undoubtedly true, as Mr. John Bright some years since pointed out,[*] that meat, in common with milk and butter, commands comparatively high prices in England, " because our people, by thousands of families, now eat meat who formerly rarely tasted it, and because our imports of these articles are not sufficient to keep prices at a more moderate rate."

One point of interest pertinent to this discussion, which has for some time attracted the attention of students of social science in England and France, has also been made a matter of comment in the cities of the Northwestern United States, especially in St. Paul and Minneapolis, and is probably applicable to all other sections of the country; and that is, that expenditures for rent form at present a much larger item in the living expenses of families than ever before, and for the reason that people are no longer content to live in the same classes of houses as formerly; but demand houses with all the so-called modern improvements—gas and water

---

[*] Letter to the London " Times," November, 1884.

and better warming, ventilating, and sanitary arrangements
—which must be paid for.

One of the most striking illustrations or rather demon-
strations of the improvement of the condition of the masses
in respect to subsistence is afforded by a comparison of the
statistics of pauperism in London for the years 1815 and
1875. In the former year the number of paupers in London
was about 100,000. In 1875, although the population of
the city in the intervening period had increased threefold,
the number of paupers was smaller; but the cost of maintaining 100,000 paupers in London in 1875 was five times
what it was in 1815. At the same time the cost of almost
all the essentials for a simple livelihood—bread, sugar, tea,
fuel, and clothing—were much cheaper in 1875 than in 1815,
and numerous small comforts and conveniences which materially smooth and civilize life, and which sixty years ago
were not obtainable by the working-classes, can now be procured at a trifling cost. The pauper, furthermore, does
not fix for himself the style of his living, but it is fixed for
him by others; "and the common rule is, that he shall not
live materially better, nor much worse, than he would do if
he worked for his living, as a laborer of the lowest class."
An examination of the accounts furnishes, however, an explanation of this curious societary phenomenon. Thus, "the
ideas of what is absolutely or primarily necessary for the
decent maintenance of paupers have risen in recent years.
The laborers have reached a much higher standard of existence. A much more elevated minimum of wages has been
secured. Their numbers have greatly increased, but their
welfare has grown in a much higher ratio." And through
the agencies which have effected these results the very lowest stratum of society has been gradually and without any
direct effort lifted to higher and better conditions—a fact,
from a social and humanitarian point of view, of the greatest importance.

REDUCTION IN THE HOURS OF LABOR.—Concurrently

with the general increase in recent years in the amount and purchasing power of money-wages throughout the civilized world, the hours of labor have also generally diminished. In the case of Great Britain Mr. Giffen is of the opinion that the reduction during the last fifty years in the textile, house-building, and engineering trades has been at least twenty per cent, and that the British workman now gets from fifty to one hundred per cent more money for twenty per cent less work.

In the United States, the data afforded by the census returns of 1880 indicate that in 1830 81·1 per cent of the recipients of regular wages worked in excess of ten hours per day; for 1880, the number so working was about 26·5 per cent. In 1830, 13·5 per cent worked in excess of thirteen hours. In 1880 this ratio had been reduced to 2·5. For the entire country the most common number of hours constituting a day's labor in 1880 was ten.

For Germany, the reports are much less favorable. In Bavaria, according to the German factory reports for 1886, the hours of labor in 24·4 per cent of all industries ranged from eleven hours and a quarter to sixteen hours daily; in 56·6 per cent from ten to eleven hours, and for the remainder from eleven hours down to five. The extremely short limit was, however, reached only in the exceedingly dangerous and almost fatal trade of quicksilvering the backs of looking-glasses. In breweries the hours of labor seem to be the longest, being never less and often more than sixteen hours.

In Prussia, recent official investigations show that in a very large proportion—more than one half—of the factories, and establishments for trade and transportation in the kingdom, there is no cessation of labor on Sunday.* In Russia,

---

* The results of an investigation recently instituted by the Prussian Government in consequence of a demand made for an absolute prohibition of Sunday labor in business occupations in that country, have revealed a curious and apparently an unexpected condition of public sentiment on the subject: Thus from returns obtained from thirty out of thirty-five provinces or departments,

an average of twelve hours daily is reported as the normal working hours of most industrial establishments.

That the conclusions of Mr. Giffen respecting the general effect in Great Britain of the increase in wages and reduction in the hours of labor, as above stated, find a correspondence in the United States, might, if space permitted, be shown by a great amount and variety of testimony. A single example—drawn from the experience of the lowest class of labor—is, however, especially worthy of record. In 1860, before the war, the average amount of work expected of spade-laborers on the western divisions of the Erie Canal, in the State of New York, was five cubic yards of earth excavation for each man per day; and for this work the average wages were seventy-five cents per day. At the present time the average daily excavation of each man employed on precisely the same kind of work, and on the same canal, is reported as three and a half cubic yards, at a compensation of from $1.50 to $2 per day.

Any review of the recent experiences, in respect to wages

---

containing 500,156 manufacturing establishments and 1,582,591 workmen, it was found that 57·75 per cent of the factories kept at work on Sunday. On the other hand, the larger number of the workmen, or 919,564, rested on Sunday. As regards trade and transportation, it was found that in twenty-nine provinces (out of thirty-five), of 147,318 establishments of one sort or another, employing 245,061 persons, seventy-seven per cent were open on Sunday, and fifty-seven per cent of the employés worked on that day. A canvass of the persons naturally most interested in the matter—i. e., the workmen—showed, however, that only a comparatively small number were in favor of the proposed measure. Thus, for example, of those who were consulted iu the great factories or stores, only thirteen per cent of the employers and eighteen per cent of the employed were in favor of total prohibition. In the smaller industries the proportion was eighteen per cent of the employers and twenty-one per cent of the employed. In trade only forty-one per cent of the employers and thirty-nine per cent of the employed, and in transportation only twelve per cent of the employers and sixteen per cent of the employed, were in favor of total prohibition. (See also page 269.)

A "factory bill," introduced as a government measure in the French Chamber of Deputies, in 1888, contained the curious provision that one day of rest should be given weekly to all operatives; but that the choice of the day should be left discretionary with the employers.

and hours of labor, would be imperfect that failed to call
attention to the fact that the benefits from advances in the
one case, and reductions in the other, have accrued mainly
to operatives in factories and to artisans and skilled mechanics, and have been enjoyed in the least degree, and
largely not at all, by employés, clerks, book-keepers, copy-
ists, etc., engaged in mercantile and commercial operations
and establishments. The reason of this is manifestly, that
the supply of this latter class of labor has been disproportionately greater than that of the former, and continually
tends to be in excess of demand; and under such circumstances, although the amount of discontent may be, and undoubtedly is, very great and well warranted, the organized
and aggressive expression of it finds little sympathy on the
part of the public.

The question has been asked, Why is it that wages of
manual labor have been constantly rising in recent years,
while all other prices have been concurrently falling? or, to
put it differently, why is it that over-production, while cheapening the product, should not also cheapen the work that
produces it? The answer is, that the price of the products
of labor is not governed by the price of labor, or wages, but
that wages, or earnings, are results of production, and not
conditions precedent. Wages, as a rule, are paid out of
product. If production is small, no employer can afford to
pay high wages; but if, on the contrary, it is large, and
measured in terms of labor is of low cost—which conditions
are eminently characteristic of the modern methods of production — the employer is not only enabled to pay high
wages, but will, in fact, be obliged to do so, in order to obtain what is really the cheapest (in the sense of the most
efficient) labor. The world has not yet come to recognize
it, but it is nevertheless an economic axiom, that the invariable concomitant of high wages and the skilled use of machinery is a low cost of production and a large consumption.
In the first of the results is to be found the explanation for

the continually increasing tendency of wages to advance; in the second, an explanation why the supplantation of labor by machinery has not been generally more disastrous. If, however, it be rejoined that " the *comparative* poverty of cotton- and woolen-mill operatives, and of women who run sewing-machines," and the like, does not sustain the above explanations, the question is pertinent, Comparative with what ? For low and insufficient as may be the wages of all this class of operatives, they were never, in comparison with other times, so high as at present.*

IMPAIRMENT OF THE VALUE OF CAPITAL RELATIVELY TO LABOR.—While the remuneration of labor has enormously increased during recent years, the return to capital has not been in any way proportionate, and is apparently growing smaller and smaller. For this economic phenomenon there can be but one general explanation; and that is, that regarding labor and capital as commodities, or better, as instrumentalities employed in the work of production and distribution, capital has become relatively more abundant than labor, and has accumulated faster than it can be profitably invested; and, in accordance with the law of sup-

---

* The not infrequent assertion that " the rich are growing richer and the poor poorer," and that the rewards of labor are growing less, has been thus recently answered, as far as the labor of machinists in the United States are concerned, by James Bartlett, a Massachusetts machinist, in a recent public address. Speaking from his own memory of the condition of things in 1842, he said :

" The wages of a machinist in shop were $1 to $1.25 a day ; one nabob of a pattern-maker received the great sum of $1.50. They went to work at five o'clock in the morning, and worked till 7.30 at night, with an hour for breakfast and three quarters for dinner. It was several years before we obtained eleven hours a day. It has now been ten hours a day for twenty-five years or more, and we grumble at that, though we get more than twice the wages we did forty years ago ; and we are hoping to get the same or higher pay for working eight hours. I know the condition of the machinist is better than it was when I first joined the guild ; he has better pay, better houses, better education, better living. For my part, I don't want any more of the good old times. The present time is the best we have ever had, though I hope not the best we shall ever see."

ply and demand, the compensation for its use—interest or profits—has necessarily declined as compared with the compensation paid for labor.

The position taken by some investigators and writers of ability is, that the great decline in the value of capital—by reason of an impairment of the ability of its owners, i. e., through loss of dividends on investments and of profits in business, to purchase and consume the products of labor, and a diversion of capital, from lack of remunerative income-yielding investments, into enterprises not needed and so occasioning over-production—has been a prime and perhaps the main cause of all the economic disturbances in recent years. That such a factor, in common with many others, has been instrumental in occasioning serious disturbances, may not be questioned; but that its influence has not been in any sense primary would seem evident, when it is considered that the reason why capital has increased and cheapened in these latter years is, that mankind, through a larger knowledge and better use of the forces of Nature, has been enabled to produce, and actually has produced, a far greater abundance of almost all material things (or, in other words, a greater abundance of capital) with the same effort than at any former period of its history. Capital, at the outset, greatly contributed to such a development, or, like the wizard in the Eastern fable, it pronounced the incantation which set the natural forces at work; but the wonderful increase and consequent impairment in the value of capital was an after-result, something not anticipated, and the continued progress of which the owners of capital, like the enchanter, now find themselves powerless to check. The saving in the cost of the freight moved on the railroads of every country, comparing 1887 with 1850, and assuming like quantities to have been transported at the different periods, would represent every year more than the original cost of the railroads and their equipment.

One efficient cause of this greater abundance of capital

is, that every new invention or discovery produces always as much as, and often a much greater amount, of product on a less amount of capital than was previously invested. The result of material progress is, therefore, to both supplement the need or economize the use of capital, and at the same time increase it. For example, a first-class iron freighting screw-steamer cost in Great Britain, in 1872–'74, $87.48 (£18) per ton. In 1887 a better steamer, constructed of steel, fitted with triple compound engines, with largely increased carrying capacity, and consequent earning power, and capable of being worked at much less expense, could have been contracted for $34 (£7) per ton. How rapidly capital has accumulated in recent years under the new conditions of production is indicated by the circumstance that, although most of the great loans which have been negotiated within the last twenty-five years have been for the replacement of capital unproductively used up, or absolutely destroyed in war or military operations, and notwithstanding the immense amount of capital that has also been destroyed during the same period by the replacement of machinery contingent on new inventions, the vacuum thus created has not only been promptly filled, but the competition for the privilege of furnishing further supplies of capital for similar purposes was never greater.

Again, as capital increases and competition between its owners for its profitable investment becomes more intense, and as modern methods can bring all the unemployed capital of the world within a few hours of the world's great centers for financial supply, the rate of profit, or interest to be obtained by the investor or lender, from this cause, also necessarily tends to shrink toward a minimum. Such a minimum will be reached when the returns for the use of capital become insufficient to induce individuals to save it, especially in the form of its representative, money, and thus add to the available reserves by which expanding industries can be supported. And to such a minimum the financial world seems to be always moving by the force of laws which no combination of capitalists can resist.

To those who are the possessors of large properties, a gradually diminishing rate of return for the use of capital makes but little difference so far as personal comforts are concerned; but to the small capitalists the steady reduction in income which has been experienced in recent years means always discomfort, and often misery. A striking illustration of this, derived from actual experience, and contingent on a reduction by the Prussian Government of the interest on its debt to three and a half and three per cent, is thus given by a recent correspondent (1887) of the London "Economist":

"This reduction," he says, "struck a heavy blow at the existence of what may be called the 'middle classes' in Germany—that is, the great number of people who own a small capital invested in funds, besides carrying on some business or having some other profession. The combined income from both enabled them to live in fair style, making both ends meet by way of carefully regulated expenditure. These classes have formed for over half a century the 'back-bone' of Germany. They are now gradually disappearing, making room for great wealth on one side and great poverty on the other."

The following are other illustrations to the same effect, derived from the recent experience of the United States: In 1877 the average rate of interest received by the Massachusetts savings-banks was 6·8 per cent., but from that rate it has descended by an almost regular progression to 4·8 per cent in 1887. In 1877 these institutions had $55,881,882 loaned at seven per cent, $48,387,908 loaned at six per cent, $13,758,476 loaned at five per cent, and $2,905,000 loaned at four per cent. In 1887 the amount of seven-per-cent loans was $1,717,827, six-per-cent loans $38,277,441, five-per-cent loans $77,474,331, four-per-cent loans $16,091,983. Such a shrinkage of interest obviously represents an enormous reduction in the income of the depositors.

The average interest paid on the aggregate funded debts

of railroads of the United States for the year 1886 was only 4·77 per cent, while the percentage of dividends on their whole share capital was only 2·04 per cent.

An investigation in 1887 by the Bureau of Labor Statistics of Connecticut into the details of business establishments in that State, having a capital of $48,665,000, employing 28,256 hands, and covering twenty-two distinct lines of industry, showed the aggregate profit over and above all expenditures, on an annual production of $45,500,000, to have been $2,800,000, or 6·15 per cent. In certain classes of manufactures—as bakeries, forging, knit goods, and corset-making—the profits were much larger; but on the great industries of woolen, general hardware, and cotton-duck manufacturing, the profits of the year were less than three per cent on the capital invested.*

---

* Those not familiar with financial experiences can hardly realize the great decline within the last few years in the price and profits of capital. Thus, the average rate of interest in the cities of Boston, New York, Philadelphia, Cincinnati, St. Louis, and Chicago, as computed from the record of public transactions, from 1844 to 1858, was 10·5 per cent. In 1871 the London " Economist " estimated that the average rate of interest on a majority of the foreign and colonial stocks and bonds at that time held in Great Britain, amounting to not less than twenty-eight hundred and fifty million dollars, was equal to six or seven per cent as a minimum. Up to 1871 the United States had not been able to sell any portion of its funded debt, bearing six per cent gold interest in European markets, on terms as favorable as par in gold, United States five-twenty 6s being quoted on the London market in 1870 as low as 87½. The following is a transcript of the prices of various securities as quoted on the London market in 1871: German Confederation obligations, five per cents, 87 ; French national defense 6s, 87 ; Massachusetts 5s, 91 ; Georgia 7s, 78 ; Spanish five per cents, secured by a mortgage on the celebrated quicksilver-mines of New Almaden, in addition to the faith of the Government, 76 and 77 ; Italian six per cents, secured by a pledge of the state revenues from tobacco, 87¾ ; Japanese nine per cents, 89 ; Panama Railroad seven per cent general mortgage, 93 ; Michigan Central Railroad, first-mortgage sinking-fund, eight per cent, 85 ; Pennsylvania Railroad six per cent general mortgage (sterling), 91.   To-day the Governments of Great Britain and the United States can readily borrow money at 2½ per cent; all first-class railroad corporations at four per cent ; while millions of money have been loaned in recent years on real-estate security in the United States for four per cent, and in Great Britain for three per cent. In Germany the market rate of discount for

DECLINE IN LAND-VALUES.—Another interesting and curious feature of the existing economic condition—the direct outcome of the recent radical changes in the methods of production and distribution—has been the decline in the value of land over large areas of the earth's surface.

Thus, in the case of Great Britain, while every other item of national wealth has shown an increase—often most extraordinary—since 1840, the estimated value of land in the United. Kingdom since that date, notwithstanding a large increase in population, has heavily decreased.* Formerly Paris obtained its fruit and vegetable supply entirely from lands in its own neighborhood; and the difference in the cost of transportation gave such lands a marked advantage over more distant places. But now the railways bring

a considerable period in 1887 was as low as from 1½ to 1⅝ per cent. Not many years ago the customary rate of interest allowed by the savings-banks and trust companies of the United States was six per cent; now the former for the most part pay but four, and the trust companies but two to three per cent. British consols in November, 1887, paid to the investor 2¹⁵/₁₆ per cent, while of the best (debenture) railroad stocks of Great Britain none now return as much as four per cent on their current market prices. The dividends of the Imperial (Reichbank) Bank of Germany, in the four years from 1883 to 1886 inclusive, declined 0·96 per cent, and the average of the private banks of Germany during the same period, 1·60 per cent; all of which clearly indicates that the banking business of Germany is becoming less and less profitable.

* According to Mr. Mulhall, the English statistician, the following table exhibits the changes in the leading items of wealth in Great Britain since 1840:

[Omitting 6 ciphers.]

	1840.	1860.	1887.
Railways..........................	£21	£348	£831
Houses.........	770	1,164	2,640
Furniture	385	582	1,320
Lands.............................	1,680	1,840	1,542
Cattle, etc........................	380	460	414
Shipping...........	23	44	130
Merchandise......................	70	190	321
Bullion...........................	61	105	143
Sundries	710	827	1,869
Total	£4,100	£5,560	£9,210

the same commodities from very distant places for the same or a less price, and the value of land in the environs of Paris has naturally declined.   Fresh grapes are even now brought in large quantities, in casks or baskets, from Algeria—the climate of which favors the growth of the produce of the vine, but is not favorable to wine-making—to the cooler regions of central and eastern France, where they are manufactured into wine.   In certain of the departments of France the peasant proprietors of land have ceased to buy land and are anxious to sell it; and in some instances large tracts have been practically abandoned because the sale of the products of the soil, under the competition to which they are exposed by reason of new conditions, does not return the expenses of their cultivation.   In Austria and Germany the competitive supply of agricultural produce from the United States has been so influential, that it is claimed that if the state should wholly discontinue its encouragement of the beet-root sugar-industry by bounties, immense tracts of land would become comparatively valueless.

In Portugal, the owners and cultivators of the soil seem to be in a remarkably unfortunate condition.   The Portuguese farmer, despite heavy protective duties, finds himself unable to successfully contend against the increased import of cereals, mainly from the United States.   The industry in olive-oil, formerly flourishing, is languishing, through the alleged extensive use of American cotton-seed oil as a substitute; while the demand for Portuguese wines, which for a time was increased by the bad vintages of France, is being impaired, and possibly threatened with destruction, by the continually increasing supply in the French markets of cheaper and more suitable wines for mixing purposes from California, the Cape of Good Hope, and Australia.   In the Canary Islands, where the soil is most cheap and fertile, and the vegetation of both the tropic and temperate zones flourishes in great luxuriance, the land question has also become of as much importance and embarrassment as in less

favored countries. The former great remunerative industry of these islands was wine, " canary "; but this, by the impairment of the vines, has become of little account. These
islands also formerly constituted a large source of supply to
the world of cochineal, for the production of which they
have special advantages; but since the discovery and use of
the aniline dyes, this industry has been almost destroyed.
Curiously, also, a comparatively extensive export of potatoes
from the islands to the Spanish West Indies is diminishing
through a competitive exportation of the same vegetable
from the United States. So that there seems to be nothing
left for the land proprietors and cultivators in this locality
to do, except to resort to the method, so much in favor at
the present time, of mutually taxing each other for their
mutual benefit! Over large portions of the West India
Islands, great quantities of excellent land, advantageously
situated as regards facility of communication with other
countries, under exceptionally healthy climatic conditions,
and much of which had been formerly under a high state
of cultivation, have been absolutely abandoned, or are in
the rapid process of abandonment. In the United States,
the decline in the value of land has, in many instances, been
also very notable. In the New England States, agricultural
land, not remote from large centers of population, can often
be bought at the present time for a smaller price than what
fifty years ago would have been regarded as a fair appraisal,
and even less than the cost of the buildings and walls at
present upon it.* Since the last decennial appraisal of real

---

* In 1887 a house and barn, in good repair, and forty acres of good farming
land in the town of Killingsworth, Conn., seventeen miles from the Connecticut River, were bought for a church rectory, for $350. " In many places in
the very heart of the State of Massachusetts it is as it was in Eden when we
read that ' there was not a man to till the ground.' Thirty miles inward from
Worcester, the ' heart of the Commonwealth,' there are whole acres which, sixty
years ago, sold for twenty-two dollars an acre, that are now selling for eleven
dollars an acre, although railroads and telegraphs skirt the fields, and the
fields themselves are excellent farm-land."—*Springfield Republican.*

estate in Ohio (in 1880) "there has been a heavy decline; farm property is from 25 to 50 per cent cheaper to-day than it then was." * In Illinois, according to the Report of the Bureau of Labor Statistics for 1888, there has been an increase in land-values in that State since 1880 in twenty-five counties, a decrease in twenty counties, while in sixteen counties values have remained unchanged. In one county —Madison—the value of farm-lands is thought to have depreciated 33 per cent since 1880. The increase in the value of all the lands in the State, for the decade 1870–'80, according to the United States census for the latter year —the valuation of 1870 being reduced to a gold basis—was 27 per cent; but, for the eight years from 1880 to 1888, the net gain in land-values for the whole State is now estimated at 6·2 per cent. "In the ten cotton States, the value of agricultural land was in 1860, $1,478,000,000 ; in 1880, $1,019,000,000, a decrease of $459,000,000. It would require an addition of 45 per cent of its value in 1880 to raise it to its value in 1860." Meanwhile, the population of these same States has increased 53 per cent. "In 1860, the value per acre of improved land in Georgia was $6; in 1886, below $3.50; decrease, $2.50. Were the agricultural land divided out among the people, the value per head would have been : in 1860, $150; in 1886, $63; decrease, $87.†

* "Inaugural Address of Governor Foraker," January, 1887.

† Report of a committee of citizens of the ten cotton-growing States ("Sam" Barnett, of Georgia, chairman), "On the Causes of the Depressed Condition of Agriculture, and the Remedies," 1887.

XI.

The economic outlook, present and prospective—Necessity of studying the situation as an entirety—Compensation for economic disturbances—Inequality in the distribution of wealth a less evil than equality of wealth—The problem of poverty as affected by time—Tendency of the poor toward the centers of population—Relation of machinery to the poverty problem—Reduction of the hours of labor by legislation—Fallacy of eight-hour arguments—The greatest of gains from recent material progress—Increase of comfort to the masses from decline of prices—Oleomargarine legislation—Difference between wholesale and retail prices—Relation between prices and poverty—Individual differences in respect to the value-perceiving faculty—Characteristics of the Jews—Relative material progress of different countries—Material development of Australia and the Argentine Republic—Great economic changes in India—Great material progress in Great Britain—The economic changes of the future—Further cheapening of transportation—Future of agriculture—Position of the last third of the nineteenth century in history.

IN the preceding chapters an attempt has been made to trace out and exhibit in something like regular order the causes and the extent of the industrial and social changes and accompanying disturbances, which have especially characterized the last fifteen or twenty-five years of the world's history. The questions which connect themselves with, and are prompted by, such an inquiry and exhibit, are numerous and relate to widely different subjects. But, of all these, the one of greatest interest and importance is, What has been, and what is likely to be, the effect of these complex economic changes—of this recent and unquestionably great material progress—on the mass of mankind ? Has it been, and is it to be in the future, for the better or the worse ? To not a few, as experience abundantly and also unfortunately proves, a ready and sufficient answer may seem pos-

sible; but most of those who through continued study and
reflection have endeavored to qualify themselves for answer-
ing, will probably agree that, upon no other one subject,
apart from theology, does the line of investigation run so
rapidly into deep waters. The more difficult, however, it is
to emerge from such depths, the more important is it to lay
hold of and put in place whatever may serve as stepping-
stones to attain more definite conclusions than are now possible—conclusions which, while helping continually to more
comprehensive views of the situation, will also make all remedial action on the part of society for acknowledged societary evils, more intelligent, and consequently more effective; and it is in this direction that the line of most desirable
work, and the movement for solving the difficult involved
problems, would for the present seem to lie. Entertaining
these views, the following deductions, in addition to those
which have been incorporated into the preceding pages—
which from the outset have been designed to be historical
and not controversial — are finally and deferentially submitted.

It seems clear that the first and most essential thing for
all those who are desirous of determining the extent of the
evils which the recent economic disturbances have occasioned, and what course of procedure on the part of society
and individuals is likely to prove most remedial of them, is
to endeavor to understand the situation as an *entirety ;* and
that effort is likely to be ineffectual and disturbance intensified by all discussions and actions that start from any other
basis. In fact, one of the remarkable features of the situation has been the tendency of many of the best men in all
countries to rush, as it were, to the front, and, appalled by
some of the revelations which economic investigators everywhere reveal, and with the emotional largely predominating
over their perceptive and reasoning faculties, to proclaim
that civilization is a failure, or that something ought immediately to be done, and more especially by the state, with-

out any very clear or definite idea of what can be done, or
with any well-considered and practical method of doing.
How human society is ever to be at any time anything but
the product of human character and culture, they never tell
us; but they intimate that if the industrious do not promptly
divide more freely with the idle, the frugal with the im-
provident, the workers with the drones, there will be trouble
—mysterious in its nature, but unknown in amount. The
position of the Russian novelist Tolstoi, before noticed, is a
case in point. The distressing picture of what the world
has come to during the fifty years of the reign of Queen
Victoria, as drawn by the poet Tennyson in his new " Locks-
ley Hall," and which Mr. Gladstone has so impressively reviewed and effectually disapproved, is another. To what a
doleful condition mankind is certainly tending, as the result
of the unprecedented accumulation of knowledge in the
present age, is foretold by Mr. W. H. Mallock, in the following assemblage of words, in which mysticism rather than
sense is predominant :

" For the first time," he says, " man's wide and varied history has
become a coherent whole to him. Partly a cause and partly a result
of this, a new sense has sprung up in him—an intense self-conscious-
ness as to his own position ; and his entire view of himself is undergoing a vague change. It is impossible to conceive that this awakening, this discovery by man of himself, will not be the beginning of his
decadence ; that it will not be the discovery on his part that he is a
lesser and a lower thing than he thought he was, and that his condition will not sink till it tallies with his own opinion of it."

On the other hand, it may be confidently asserted that a
comprehensive view of the situation will show that not an
evil referable to recent economic changes or disturbances
can be cited which has not been attended with much in the
way of alleviation or compensation, the comparison being
between individuals and classes and society as a whole.
Thus, the facts in relation to the wages earned by the poor
men and women who work for the sellers of cheap clothing,

and who seem to be unable to find any more remunerative
occupations, are indeed pitiful; but, if clothes were not thus
made cheap, many would be clothed far more poorly than
they now are, or possibly not at all. It is not the rich man
who buys "slop" coats and shirts, but the man who, if he
could not be thus supplied, would go ragged or without
them. If the decline in the price of cereals and in the
value of arable land has forced many who follow agricultural pursuits out of employment, there never was a time in
the history of the world when the mass of mankind were fed
so abundantly and so cheaply as at present. If the decline
in the rates of interest on capital has been a sore grievance
to the small capitalists, a reduction in the rate of income
from invested property "means in the final analysis that
the world pays less than it has before for the use of its
machinery, and that labor is obtaining a 'larger' and capital
a 'smaller' share of the compensation paid for production."

Inequality in the distribution of wealth seems to many
to constitute the greatest of all social evils. But, great as
may be the evils that are attendant on such a condition of
things, the evils resulting from an equality of wealth would
undoubtedly be much greater. Dissatisfaction with one's
condition is the motive power of all human progress,* and
there is no such incentive for individual exertion as the apprehension of prospective want. If everybody was content
with his situation, or if everybody believed that no improvement of his condition was possible, the state of the world
would be that of torpor, or even worse, for society is so constituted that it can not for any length of time remain stationary, and, if, it does not continually advance, it is sure to
retrograde.†

---

* "The incentives of progress are the desires inherent in human nature—
the *desire* to gratify the *wants* of the animal nature, the *wants* of the intellectual
nature, and the *wants* of the sympathetic nature—*desires* that, short of infinity,
can never be satisfied, as they grow by what they feed on."—HENRY GEORGE.

† The conditions which are naturally imbedded, as it were, in human na-

It is a matter of regret that those who declaim most loudly against the inequalities in the distribution of wealth, and are ready with schemes for the more " equal division of unequal earnings " as remedies against suffering, are the ones who seem to have the least appreciation of the positive fact, that most of the suffering which the human race endures is the result of causes which are entirely within the province of individual human nature to prevent; and that, therefore, reformation of the individual is something more important than the reformation of society. Furthermore, " the accumulation of wealth and the centralization of production and trade in great combinations have never, as a rule, in the United States, been a source of oppression, or of poverty to the non-capitalist or wage-worker "; and, very curiously, almost every investigation into the wages and employments of the poorer classes shows that their greatest

---

ture, and which war against the realization of the idea of an ultimate equality in the distribution or possession of capital, have been thus clearly and forcibly pointed out by Mr. George Baden Powell, in his " New Homes for the Old Country," published in 1872 after a visit to Australia and New Zealand: " Since the arrival of man in the world there have been perpetual questionings as to why all men are not well off. Why should the good things of this life be so unequally distributed ? The two great causes, one as powerful as the other, are *circumstances* and *talents*. But these two opposite causes all through man's life influence each other greatly. Circumstances call forth peculiar talents which might otherwise be uselessly dormant, and talents often take advantage of peculiar circumstances which might otherwise be overlooked and missed. It is by no means improbable that as the world grows wiser some means will be found of considerably raising the lowest stage of existence, but *it is entirely against the nature of things that all should be equal in every way.* Innate pride continually urges men to seek that which is above them, and to many happiness in life is the mere gaining of such successive steps. The essential rule is to work one's own circumstances to the highest point attainable by means of the talents possessed. These talents may be said to resolve themselves into various capitals, and a man may have capital for the improvement of his condition in the form of money, brains, or health and strength— in fact, he may thrive by the possession of ' talents,' whether of gold, of the mind, or of the body. With this fully recognized fact of the diversities of capital, it would seem obviously *impossible for a people to continue long in the humanly imposed possession of equal personal shares in any capital.*"

oppressors are very frequently the comparatively poor themselves.

To understand the problem of poverty, especially with reference to remedial effects, as it at present exhibits itself, it is necessary to look at it comprehensively from two different standpoints. Viewed from the standpoint of twenty or twenty-five years ago, or before what may be termed the advent of the " machinery epoch," there is no evidence that the aggregate of poverty in the world is increasing, but much that proves to the contrary. The marked prolongation of human life, or the decline in the average death-rate, in all countries of high civilization; the recognized large increase in such countries in the per capita consumption of all food products; and the further fact that fluctuations in trade and industry, calamitous as they still are, are less in recent times than they used to be, and less disastrous on the whole in their effects on the masses, are absolutely conclusive on this point. Great as has been the depression of business since 1873, there is no evidence that it has yet made any impression on the " stored wealth " of the people of the great commercial countries; and that, slow as is the accumulation of capital, a year probably now never passes in which some addition is not made to the previous sum of the world's material resources. The recognized tendency of the poor to crowd more and more into the great centers of population—drawn thither, undoubtedly, in no small part by the charities which are there especially to be found, and also by the fact that town labor is better paid than country labor—and the contrasts of social conditions, which exhibit themselves more strikingly at such centers than elsewhere,*

---

* " It might sound paradoxical, but it was nevertheless true, that while those who had means were perpetually trying to get out from London, those who were destitute were always trying to find their way in. There were tens of thousands of men who preferred to live or starve in the streets of London rather than work in comparative comfort in the fields."—FREDERIC HARRISON.

Recent investigations have also shown that London, in particular, is

naturally cause popular observation of poverty to continually center, as it were, at its focus of greatest intensity, and create impressions and induce conclusions that broader and more systematized inspections often fail to substantiate.*

No proposition, for example, finds a more general acceptance among the unthinking masses than that a sparse population always commands higher wages and a higher standard of comfort than a dense one; and yet there is hardly a proposition in economics which can command so little evidence in its favor from the results of experience.

" Even in the middle ages it was only the places where population was dense that wages were high, and in modern times the thinner the people on the land the lower is their standard of comfort; the laborer, for example, in some parts of Austria and Hungary, where labor is scarce, being worse fed than the average of English paupers. The

---

swollen mainly by its births, and that the total increase from immigration into that city, after deducting the emigration from it, is only about 10,000 a year. " London is, in fact, a nation of five millions, and that a nation of five millions should increase by one and a half per cent a year, or 75,000, is nothing in the present condition of human affairs, when we have neither wars nor famines nor pestilences to create the least surprise among the well-informed. An addition of 7,500 a year to a city of half a million would, indeed, cause scarcely a remark."

* A chapter from the recent experience of the city of Brooklyn, New York, in respect to pauperism, affords a very striking illustration of this statement. In the five years from 1874 to 1878 inclusive, the number of persons who asked and received outside poor relief from the city authorities increased more than fifty per cent, while the increase in the population of the city during the same period was less than fourteen per cent. The evidence would, therefore, almost seem conclusive that the masses of this city were rapidly becoming poorer and poorer. In the latter year, however, the system of giving outside poor relief was wholly discontinued. It was feared by many that this action would lead to great distress and suffering, and many charitable persons made preparations to meet the demands they expected would be made upon them. Nothing of the kind occurred. Not only was the whole number (46,093) drawing aid from the county wholly stopped, but it was also accompanied by a decreased demand on the public institutions and private relief societies of the city, and a reduction in the number of inmates in the almshouse. The teaching of this experience, which has since been elsewhere substantiated, is, therefore, to the effect that what seem to be unmistakable proofs of increasing poverty were merely methods to supplement wages on the gains from mendicancy.

great increase in the population of England during the last half-century has been accompanied by an extraordinary rise in wages; and it is in London, where the population is most dense, and not in any decaying towns in Great Britain or on the Continent, that wages are the highest. The concentration of energy caused by a thick population more than pays for the extra food consumed, and the fluctuations of wages are caused by the rise and fall in the demand for the article made, not by the rise and fall in the number of those who make it. The absolute and final proof of that is, that in any manufacturing town a time of low wages and a time of complaint about want of employment always go together. It is when a trade becomes brisk and hands crowd in from all less employed places, and the population increases every year, that wages are at their highest. In the popular mind the immense importance of a great supply of labor is overlooked, and it is assumed unconsciously that this labor is given without adequate return. That is not so, wages being always highest in the fullest centers of industry. There are districts of England where two masters are seeking one man, and where wages, nevertheless, are under twelve shillings a week, the cause being not any thickness or thinness of population, but the unprofitableness of growing cereals at present prices. There is, of course, danger of a kind in any great aggregation of population, because any trade may be suspended, as the cotton industry was, by an unexpected misfortune; but the danger is political, not economic. If the bulk of the workers of Lancashire had moved away in that famine, the wages of the remainder would not, when prosperity returned, have been perceptibly higher. Population is in one way a cause of trade, just as much as steam-power is; and, if England had fifty millions, we should probably find her trade proportionately increased and wages as high as ever. She would, in fact, have attracted business which without her free command of labor in masses would never have reached her shores. That is the secret, to take a single instance, of the great and growing prosperity of Bombay as a city of manufactures—a prosperity which, though it has brought population, has raised and not lowered the average of wages." *

One thing which those interested in the discussion of these societary problems need especially to recognize more fully than is generally done is, that, in most of the leading nations, systematic and rigid investigations, in respect to most economic subjects and questions, have now been prose-

* London " Economist."

cuted for a considerable period by governments and individuals; that the broad general conclusions deducible therefrom in respect to mortality, health, wages, prices, pauperism, population, and the like, are not open to anything like reasonable doubt or suspicion; and also that the pessimistic views which many entertain as to the future of humanity are often directly due to the exposure of bad social conditions which have been made in course of these investigations with the purpose of amending them.

During the last quarter of a century, however, the problem of poverty has been complicated by a new factor; namely, the displacement of common labor by machinery, which has been greater than ever before in one generation or in one country. To what extent the numbers of the helpless poor have been increased from this cause is not definitely known; but the popular idea is doubtless a greatly exaggerated one. In fact, considering the number and extent of the agencies that have been operative, it is a matter of wonderment that these influences in this direction have not been greater. In the United States little or no evidence has yet been presented that there has been any increase in poverty from this cause.* In London, where the cry of dis-

---

* According to the Report of the Bureau of Statistics of Labor for Massachusetts for 1887, the whole number of persons of both sexes in that State, who were unemployed at their principal occupation during some part of the year preceding the date of the census enumeration (May 1, 1885), was 241,589, of whom 178,168 were males and 69,961 were females. Comparing these figures with those of the population in 1885, viz., 1,941,465, it is found that for every 8·04 persons there was one person unemployed for some part of the year at his or her principal occupation, the percentage of unemployed being greater in the case of males and less in the case of females. These conclusions, however, throw no light on the number of persons who were unemployed by reason of displacement by machinery; and are also likely to mislead, unless sufficient consideration is given to the fact that the number of industrial occupations which only admit of being prosecuted during a portion of the year is in every community very considerable. And, as a matter of fact, the investigations in question show that there were only 882 persons, representing hardly more than one third of one per cent of the whole number of the unemployed in this State, who were returned as having been unemployed during the entire twelve months.

tress is at present especially loud and deep, it is "noteworthy that no measures have yet been taken to ascertain whether that distress is normal or abnormal, and whether it is increasing or decreasing."* But even here the opinion, based on what is claimed to be an exhaustive inquiry, has been expressed that, "although the number of those who are both capable and willing to give fair work for fair pay and are at the same time destitute, is in the aggregate considerable, they yet form but a very small proportion of the unemployed"; and "that probably not over two per cent of the destitute are persons of good character as well as of average ability in their trades."† "It is by no means settled that we have too much labor; indeed, the evidence is rather the other way. In many agricultural districts there are not hands enough left to do the work, and from almost all trades the report comes in that no skilled hand who will do work need now lack employment."‡

The following additional facts, of a more general nature, are also pertinent to this subject: That wages everywhere have not fallen but advanced, as a sequence to the introduction and use of cheaper and better machinery and processes, proves that labor, through various causes, probably in the main by reason of increased consumption—has not yet been supplanted or economized by such changes to an extent sufficient to reduce wages through any competition of the unemployed. The multiplicity and continuance of strikes, and the difficulty experienced in filling the places of strikers with a desirable quality of labor, are also evidence that the supply of skilled labor in almost every department of industry is rather scarce than abundant.

---

* "The Distress in London," "Fortnightly Review," London, January, 1888.

† "The Workless, the Thriftless, and the Worthless," "Contemporary Review," London, January, 1888.

‡ London "Economist," January 26, 1889.

Again, it is a matter of general experience, that when in recent years, wages, by reason of a depression of prices, have been reduced in any specialty of production, such reductions have been mainly temporary, and are rarely, if ever, equal to the fall in the prices of the articles produced; which in turn signifies that the loss contingent on such reductions has been mainly borne by capital in the shape of diminished profits.

Notwithstanding all this, it will have to be admitted that the immense changes in recent years in the conditions of production and distribution have considerably augmented— especially from the ranks of unskilled labor and from agricultural occupations—the number of those who have a rightful claim on the world's help and sympathy.   That this increase is temporary in its nature, and not permanent, and that relief will ultimately come, and mainly through an adjustment of affairs to the new conditions, by a process of industrial evolution, there is much reason to believe.   But, pending the interval or necessary period for adjustment, the problem of what to do to prevent a mass of adults, whose previous education has not qualified them for taking advantage of the new opportunities which material progress offers to them, from sinking into wretchedness and perhaps permanent poverty, is a serious one, and one not easy to answer.

A comprehensive review of the relations of machinery to wages, by those who by reason of special investigations are competent to judge, has led to the following conclusions: When machinery is first introduced it is imperfect, and requires a high grade of workmen to successfully operate it; and these for a time earn exceptionally high wages.   As time goes on, and the machinery is made more perfect and automatic, the previous skill called for goes up to better work and better pay.   Then those who could not at the outset have operated the machinery at all, are now called in; and at higher wages than they had earned before (although less than was paid to their predecessors), they do the work. Capital in developing and applying machinery may, therefore, be fairly regarded as in the nature of a force; unintentionally, but of necessity, continually operating to raise all industrial effort to higher and better conditions: and herein we have an explanation of the economic phenomenon, that while the introduction of improved machinery economizes and supplements labor, it rarely or never reduces wages.

One of the most curious features of the existing economic situation is the advocacy of the idea, and the degree of popular favor which has been extended to it, that a reduction of the hours of labor, enforced, if needs be, by statute, is a "natural means for increasing wages and promoting progress." * This movement in favor of a shorter day of work is not, however, of recent origin, inasmuch as it has greatly commended itself to public sentiment in Great Britain and in the United States for many years, and more recently in a smaller degree in the states of Continental Europe. But it is desirable to recognize that the early agitation in furtherance of this object, and the success which has attended it, were based on reasons very different from those which underlie the arguments of to-day. Thus, in England and on the Continent, the various factory acts by which the day's labor has been shortened, were secured by appealing to the moral sense of the community to check the overworking of women and children; or, in other words, most of such legislation has thus far been influenced by moral considerations, and has so commended itself by its results that there is probably no difference of opinion in civilized countries as to its desirability. But the form which this movement has of late assumed is entirely different. It is now economic, and not moral, and its final analysis is based on the assumption

---

* "Wealth and Progress," by George Gunton. D. Appleton & Co., New York.

that the laborer can obtain more of wealth or comfort by working less.

It would seem to need no elaborate argument to demonstrate the absurdity of this position. Production must precede consumption and enjoyment, and the only way in which the ability of everybody to consume and enjoy can be increased is by increasing, so to speak, the output of the whole human family. If production be increased, the worker will necessarily receive a larger return; if diminished, he will necessarily get a smaller return. And it makes no difference whether the diminution be effected by reduction in the hours of work, or by less effective work, or by disuse of labor-saving machinery, or by other obstructive agencies. The result will inevitably be the same : there will be less to divide among the producers after the constantly diminishing returns of capital have been withdrawn.

It will doubtless be urged that man's knowledge and control of the forces of Nature have increased to such an extent in recent years that almost any given industrial result can be effected with much less of physical effort than at any former period; and therefore a general and arbitrary reduction of the hours of labor, independent of what has already occurred and is further likely to occur through the quiet influence of natural agencies, is not only justifiable, but every way practicable. This would undoubtedly be true if mankind were content to live as their fathers did. But they are not so content. They want more, and this want is so progressive that the satisfactions of to-day almost cease to be satisfactions on the morrow. But what "more" of abundance, comfort, and even luxury to the masses has been achieved—and its aggregate has not been small—has not been brought about by any diminution of labor, but has been due mainly to the fact that the labor set free by the utilization of natural forces has been re-employed, as it were, to produce them; or, in other words, recent material progress is more correctly defined by saying that it consists in the attainment of greater results with a given expenditure of labor, rather than the attainment of former results with a diminished expenditure.

Whether the present relation of production to consumption which it now seems necessary should be maintained, if the present status of abundance, wages, and prices is to be continued and further progress made, can be maintained with a diminished amount of labor, may not at present admit of a satisfactory answer. Production in excess of current demand, or over-production, which has been and still is a feature of certain departments of industry, and which may seem to favor an affirmative answer, is certain to be a temporary factor, for nothing will long continue to be produced unless there is a demand for it at remunerative prices from those possessed of means to purchase and consume, and therefore can not be legitimately taken into account in forming an opinion on this subject; but, other than this, all available evidence indicates that the answer must be yet in the negative.

Thus, for example, the latest results of investigation by the Massachusetts Bureau of Labor Statistics show that during the year 1885 all the products of manufacture in that State could have been secured by steady work for three hundred and seven *working* days of 9·04 hours each, if this steady work could have been distributed equally among all the persons engaged in manufactures. But, to effect such an equitable distribution is at present almost impossible; and if it could be brought about, a reduction of the hours of labor to eight per day in such industries, as has been advocated by not a few, would reduce the present annual product of Massachusetts to the extent of more than one ninth. Apart, therefore, from the disastrous competition which would be invited from other States and countries where labor was more productive, to expect that under such a reduction of product the share at present apportioned to the workers, or, what is the same thing, the existing rates of wages could be maintained, seems utterly preposterous.   It is not even too much to say that the very existence of multitudes would be endangered, if the present energy of production were diminished twenty per cent.   And in this connection how full of meaning is the following deduction which Mr. Atkinson finds warranted by investigation, namely: " That over a thousand millions' worth of product must be added every year and prices be maintained where they now are, in order that each person in the United States may have five cents more than he now does, or in order that each person engaged in any kind of gainful occupation may be able to obtain an increase in the rate of wages of fifteen cents a day.   Great and undoubted, therefore, as have been the benefits accruing from machinery and labor-saving inventions, the margin that would needs be traversed in order to completely neutralize them by rendering human labor less efficient, is obviously a very narrow one."   To which may be added that there is probably no country at the present time where the entire accumulated property would sell for enough to subsist its population on the most economic terms for a longer space than three years.

One argument now frequently advanced in favor of the establishment by legislation of eight hours as the uniform standard of a day's labor is worthy of notice, from the curious lack of foresight which it displays.   An hour off the day of every workman now employed would, it is said, create a demand, and give room for many additional laborers.   A recent writer * estimates that, assuming eleven hours as the average length of the working day in the United States, an eight-hour system, or a uniform reduction of three hours labor a day, " would withdraw the product of 28,416,477 hours' labor a day from the market without discharging a single laborer."   What would then happen is thus described :

---

* George Gunton.

"The commercial vacuum thus produced would, in its effect upon labor and business, be equal to increasing the present demand over one fourth, and create a demand for 3,500,000 additional laborers. To meet this demand, about one sixth more factories and workshops would be needed, besides setting our present machinery in operation; and a further demand for labor would be created in the mines, forges, furnaces, iron-works, and the various industries that contribute to the building and equipment of the requisite new factories and workshops. . . . Nor is this all. The new demand for labor thus created would necessarily increase the number of consumers, and thereby still further enlarge the demand for commodities; and, according to the popular doctrine of supply and demand, the increased demand for labor, by reducing competition among laborers, must tend to increase wages.

"The mass of laborers throughout the country, having three hours a day extra time for leisure and opportunity, and being less exhausted, mentally and physically, will be forced into more varied social relations—a new environment, the unconscious influence of which will naturally awaken and develop new desires and tastes that will slowly and surely crystallize into urgent wants and fixed habits, making a higher standard of living inevitable. . . . This increased consumption necessarily implies a corresponding increase in production, and consequently an increased demand for labor and higher wages. . . . It is therefore manifest that the general and permanent economic effect of an eight-hour system would be to naturally increase the aggregate consumption and production of wealth."

Such reasoning naturally prompts to the asking of a few pertinent questions. If the beneficial results named are certain to follow a uniform reduction of the hours of labor from eleven to eight in the United States, why arbitrarily limit the application of this principle? Why not fix upon four hours as the day's standard? This would create employment for over 7,000,000 in place of 3,500,000 laborers, and render necessary the erection of more than one sixth more new factories and workshops? Why, in short, if by a reduction of the hours of labor by statute we can infallibly increase the production of wealth or abundance, will not the condition of the race be infinitely improved by a general cessation of all tiresome exertion? Furthermore, those who advance the above argument in favor of a reduction of the hours of labor by arbitrary legislative enactment, ignore completely the fact, that if each man does an hour's less work a day, he must lose an hour's pay, and that therefore the purchasing power of the men now employed would be reduced by exactly the amount by which that of the now unemployed men would be increased by employment. If it is proposed to overcome this difficulty by incorporating in the statute reducing the hours of labor a further provision, that employers shall pay the same amount for eight hours' service that they formerly had for nine or ten, or what is the same thing, shall pay for " idle time," it may be rejoined that no special legislation can invalidate the economic axiom, " Less work, less pay," without destroying the rights of property, and with it civilization itself. Another point in connection with this subject is worthy of attention. That the efficiency of labor is largely increased by the use of machinery and new inventions can not be questioned. The world would not be what it is but for these improvements. In default of them the present population of the world could not exist, even in a state of savagery. But machinery can not work alone. It is made useful and effective only through the co-operation of human labor—labor of hand and of brain. But if men are to work only four fifths, one half, or one third less number of hours than at present, then the working hours of machinery will be reduced in the same proportion, and the productiveness of labor will be diminished not in proportion to the reduction in the number of hours that are given by hand and brain, but in a much greater proportion. It is possible to even completely neutralize the benefits of all machinery and labor-saving inventions by making human effort less efficient.

But it may be said that the productive work of machinery will be so increased by new inventions and discoveries as to compensate for any reduction in productive effect likely to follow from any reduction in the hours of labor at present contemplated. This may be in the future, but there is no evidence that such a result has been yet attained. Some years ago the State of Massachusetts enacted that the labor of women and children should not exceed ten hours per day. The practical effect of this in textile factories was to cut down the labor of the men operatives to an equal extent. The limit of working-time in such establishments being thus shortened, the speed of the machinery was generally increased, and thus, within a few months, in connection with the benefit accruing to the operatives by fewer hours of labor, unquestionably restored the former level of production. But manufacturers now agree that to increase the speed of machinery to an extent sufficient to compensate for any further reduction of working-time is at present impossible.*

The course of events, nevertheless, warrants mankind in expecting that the progress which has been made in recent years in diminishing the necessity for long hours of labor will be continued; but such progress will be permanent and productive of the highest good only so far as it is determined by natural agencies. If the attempt is made to save the time of the masses by radical and artificial methods, leisure will become license; but, if they can be taught to save their own time, leisure, as already pointed out, will be opportunity.

Finally, in all discussions of this subject, it is of the highest importance to keep steadily in view the one great fact taught us by experience in respect to this subject, which is, *that, thus far in the history of industry, all that has been achieved in the way of diminishing the hours of labor has been the result of conditions rather than of legislation.*

The greatest of the gains that have accrued to the masses through recent material progress has been in the saving of

---

* At the recent meeting of the International Labor Congress, in England, the delegates agreed that, in order to have an eight-hour rule work successfully, it must be adopted simultaneously by all the countries of Europe, for, in the absence of this general acceptance, the country that maintained the ten-hour system would obtain the work which the others would necessarily lose.

their time ; not so much in the sense of diminishing their hours of labor, as in affording them a greater opportunity for individual self-advancement than has ever before been possible. To clearly comprehend this proposition, it is necessary to keep in view the fact that all men, with the exception of the comparatively few who inherit a competence, are born, as it were, into a condition of natural bondage or servitude. Bondage and servitude to what? To the necessity of earning their living by hard and continuous toil. " In the sweat of thy brow shalt thou eat bread " has been recorded as a divine injunction, and experience shows that a great majority of mankind, as the result of long years of toil, have never hitherto been able to compass much more than a bare subsistence. In countries of even the highest civilization, where the accumulation of wealth is greatest and most equably divided, investigation has also led to the conclusion, that ninety per cent at least of the population are never possessed of sufficient property at the time of their demise to require the services of an administrator.

If now, in the course of events, it has become possible, through a greater knowledge and control of the forces of Nature, to gain an average subsistence with much less of physical effort than ever before, what is the prospect thereby held out to the multitude, who, to compass as much, have heretofore been compelled to toil as long as physical strength and years would permit? The answer is, the certain prospect of emancipation from such unfavorable conditions. Thus if eight hours' labor will now give to an individual the subsistence or living, for the attainment of which ten, twelve, fourteen, or even more hours of labor were formerly (but not remotely) necessary, intelligent self-interest would seem to dictate to him to work eight hours on account of subsistence, and then as many more hours as opportunity or strength would permit; and, out of the gain for all such work not required by necessity, purchase his emancipation from toil before age has crippled his energies ; or, if he prefers, let him surround himself as he lives, in a continually increasing proportion, with all those additional elements—material and intellectual—that make life better worth living. And, through the rapid withdrawals from the ranks of competitive labor, or the increased demand for the products of labor that would be thus occasioned, the number of the unemployed, by reason of lack of opportunity to labor, would be reduced to a minimum.

That these possibilities are already recognized and accepted by not a few of the great body of workers, is proved by the fact that the greater the opportunity to work by the piece, and the greater the latitude afforded to workmen to control their own time in connection with earnings, the greater the disinclination to diminish the hours of labor.*
" No man," says a distinguished American, who from small beginnings has risen to high position, " ever achieved eminence who commenced by reducing his hours of labor to the smallest number per day, and no man ever worked very hard and attained fortune who did not look back on his working days as the happiest of his life." †

---

* A recent writer, in describing certain factories in New England, where the work is mainly of this character, says: " The days are long for ' piece-work,' and the busy employés are indifferent to eight-hour rules. They reserve only light enough to find their way home, and at twilight they take up their line of march. At present they are earning from three to five dollars per day, according to their capacity." But, as illustrating further how labor treats labor, it is added: " The employés are union men, and they will not allow a single non-unionist to work; neither will they permit any boy under sixteen or any man over twenty-one years of age to learn the trade."

† Another, whose life-experience has been similar, also thus aptly states the case: " I have often wondered how workers expect to get on upon eight hours a day. I can not do it. I have worked year after year twelve hours a day, and I know men in my vocation who have done so fourteen hours—not for eight hours' pay, but for fourteen hours' pay. Let a man who is getting day wages for day's work consider how many hours there are in the day. Suppose the day's work is even ten; allow two for meals—that makes twelve; allow nine for sleep and dressing, that makes twenty-one. There are three hours a day for getting on. That is clear profit. There is room for more profit to himself in those three hours than the profit to the employer on the

Probably the most signal feature of the recent economic transitions has been the extensive decline in the prices of most commodities ; and as great material interests have been for a time thereby injuriously affected—commodities at reduced valuation not paying the same amount of debt as before—the drift of popular sentiment seems to be to the effect that such a result has been in the nature of a calamity. Accordingly, a great variety of propositions and devices have been brought forward in recent years, and have largely occupied the attention of the public in all civilized countries, which, in reality, had for their object not merely the arrest of this decline, but even the restoration of prices to something like their former level ; and in such a category the attempt to artificially regulate the relative values of the precious metals, the increasing restrictions on the freedom of exchanges, the stimulation of trade by bounties, the formation of " trusts," " syndicates," trade and labor organizations, and the like, may all be properly classed. But all such attempts, as Dr. Barth, of Berlin, has expressed it, " are nothing more than designs to lengthen the cloth by shortening the yard-stick." Decline and instability in prices, if occasioned by temporary and artificial agencies, are to be deprecated ; but a decline in prices caused by greater economy and effectiveness in manufacture, and greater skill and economy in distribution, in place of being a calamity is a benefit to all, and a certain proof of an advance in civilization. The mere fact, that the general fall of prices which has occurred, has been attended with an almost simultaneous and universal increase in the consumption of the necessaries of life and other commodities, is conclusive not only of a great improvement in the condition of the masses, but also that all attempts to retard or reverse this movement by governmental interference or individual organizations is the

ten hours of his working day. Three hours a day is eighteen in the week— nearly the equivalent of two clear days in the week, a hundred days in the year."

worst possible economic policy. In Great Britain alone the decline in the price of meats and cereals between 1872 and 1886 has been estimated to have resulted in producing an annual saving to each artisan consumer of $1.95 per head in meat and $3.75 per head in wheat, or an aggregate on 25,-000,000 consumers of $142,500,000 per annum. At the same time, and very curiously, investigations seem to prove that the aggregate consumption of wheat and meats in Great Britain has not in recent years increased; but such an unexpected result will probably find an explanation in the circumstance that the increased earnings of the masses have been used for the satisfaction of a desire for many commodities which heretofore they could not gratify, rather than for an increased consumption of breadstuffs and meat products.

Judged by their fiscal policies, most governments would also seem to regard a decline in prices, especially in respect to food products, as in the nature of a calamity to their people. With the exception of Great Britain and Holland, nearly every nation—pretending to any degree of civilization —has within recent years greatly increased its taxes on its supply of food from without, and more especially on meats and cereals. A comparison of the prices of wheat in England and France for 1886 shows that French consumers paid during that year alone 6s. 3d. ($1.50) per quarter more than they would needs have done for all the wheat used by them as food in the country, had the free importation of wheat into France been permitted, or about $37,000,000 on their minimum aggregate consumption for twelve months. In March, 1887, an increase in the French duties on the importation of wheat further increased its price in France to an average of 9s. 8d. ($2.19) per quarter over the corresponding average rates in England; which difference, for the ensuing twelve months, must have increased the aggregate cost of bread to French consumers by the large sum of $50,000,000. France also practically prohibits the importation of meats into her territory.

In 1885 the registered sales of horse-flesh for human consumption in Paris were 7,662,412 pounds. In 1886 the sales were officially reported as having increased to 9,001,300 pounds, with an accompanying marked diminution in the consumption of pork. Whether there is any necessary connection between the two experiences may not be affirmed, but the facts are suggestive.

The attempt to crush out of use, by legislation, one of the most brilliant discoveries of the age, namely, the manufacture of butter from the fat of the ox, equally as wholesome as that made from the fat (cream) of the cow, is a libel on civilization ; and, as depriving the masses of a better article of desirable food at cheaper rates, than very many of them have been accustomed to have, or can now procure, would be fiercely resented by them, if once properly and popularly understood.*

As it is, the experience of the United States in attempting to enforce its so-called " oleomargarine laws " well illustrates the futility of all attempts to permanently benefit one rival commercial interest at the expense of another through the agency of discriminating class legislation. Thus, notwithstanding the enactment of a great amount of legislation restricting or prohibiting the manufacture and sale of oleomargarine by many of the States and the Federal Government, the report of the United States Bureau of Internal Revenue for 1888 shows that the manufacture and consump-

* A report on the subject of " Oleomargarine," by the Royal Health Department at Munich, submitted March, 1887, says : " This product is made in great part from such proper ingredients as are useful in nourishment, namely, the fats or greases ; and therefore it is of importance, as it furnishes to the poorer classes a substitute for butter which is cheaper and at the same time nourishing. We think that this want has been supplied in a most satisfactory manner by the manufacture of artificial butter. And it is offered in the markets in a condition superior to natural butter as far as cleanliness and careful preparation are concerned." The conclusions of the chemists employed by the United States Internal Revenue Bureau, as the result of their investigations of this product, are also to the same effect, namely, that it is a wholesome and unobjectionable product.

tion of this article in response to popular demand is steadily increasing. While the inspection laws of the United States were sufficient to enable its officials to recognize and tax the production during that same year of the great amount of 69,000,000 pounds of oleo-oil—" an article produced for the sole purpose of being used in the manufacture of a butter substitute "—they were not sufficiently potent to allow these same officials to determine the use which was made of more than 27,000,000 pounds of this same product; it having been neither exported nor used in the manufacture of oleo-margarine. No doubt, however, was entertained that it was secretly used for the manufacture of some other food product—such, for example, as cheese.

The fact that in no country do the masses ever experience as much of benefit from a fall of prices as they would seem to be fairly entitled to have, owing to the great difference between wholesale and retail rates, and that this difference is always greatly intensified in the case of the poor who purchase in small quantities, clearly indicates one of the greatest and as yet least occupied fields for economic and social reform. Flour, in the form of bread, costs usually three times more, when distributed to the poorer consumers in cities of the United States, than the total aggregate cost of growing the wheat out of which it is made, milling it into flour, barreling, and transporting it to the bakeries. The retail prices of meats are enhanced in like manner ; and investigation some years ago showed that, when anthracite coal was being sold and delivered in New York city for $4.50 per ton, it cost people on the East and North Rivers, who bought it by the bucketful, from $10 to $14 per ton.

While in recent years the cost of nearly all food products in the United States has (as has been already shown) been so greatly cheapened that their competitive supply has reduced the value of land in Europe and impoverished its agriculturists, the results of the investigations of the Labor Bureau of Connecticut prove that the retail cost to the wage-earners of that State of most of these articles of food-supply—which on the average represents one half of their wages—has, comparing the prices of 1887 with those of 1860, greatly increased; corn-meal by the barrel, for example, having advanced forty per cent, and butter from thirty-five to fifty per cent.

Similar results are noticed in all other countries. Out of every £100 paid by the consumers of milk in London, Sir James Caird estimates that not more than £30 finds its way into the hands of the English dairy farmers who in the first instance supply it. In the case of some varieties of fish—mackerel—the cost of inland distribution in England has been reported to be as high as four hundred per cent in excess of the price paid to the fishermen. Eggs collected from the farmers in Normandy are sold according to size to Parisian consumers, at an advance in price of from eighty-two to two hundred per cent.

The experience of different countries in respect to the difference in the retail and wholesale prices of staple commodities is not, however, uniform; the most notable exception perhaps being that American beef, flour, bread, butter, and cheese are, as a rule, sold more cheaply at retail in London than in New York.

The payment of rent is believed by not a few to be the chief cause of social distress, and a continual draught on the resources of the poor, for which no adequate equivalent is returned. And yet investigations similar to those (before noticed) which have demonstrated how small needs be the first cost of the food essentials of a good living, have also led to the opinion that "not much more than half the money that men usually pay for rent would, if expended in the right direction and under easily prepared guarantees, give them possession of good homes, protected in all the rights given by a title in fee simple, and which they could transmit unencumbered to their families."

Co-operative associations have done something in the

way of remedying the evils resulting from unfair and unnecessary enhancements of prices to consumers buying at
retail or in small quantities; but as yet the success that has
attended their efforts in this direction, although promising,
has been partial and incomplete. Associations of this character appear to find much more of popular favor and support in England than in the United States; and, probably,
for the reason that the great establishments which have
sprung up in recent years at almost all the considerable centers of population in the United States for the sale of non-
perishable commodities, and which are systematically conducted on the economic basis that large sales with relatively
small profits ultimately assure the largest aggregate of profits,
sell goods of the character indicated at relatively lower retail
prices than generally prevail in England, and so limit the
sphere of beneficial operation of the American co-operative
societies.*

---

* " Co-operation is an excellent thing, but society will not be regenerated
because thousands of decent men have the sense to see that if they combine
to buy leather wholesale, and to purchase boots for themselves, they will get
their boots good and cheap. Even if the principle were applicable to everything, society would only be a little more comfortable, and it is not applicable
to everything. Every man is not the stronger, as all co-operators affirm, because he is one of a crowd, and there are some operations, swimming, for example, in which to be untouched by others is a condition of success. As to
extinguishing that evil spirit, competition, it is not extinguished or threatened
by co-operation, for if the societies became numerous they would compete
with one another, and the competition of corporations is the severest of all.
Indeed, if they did not, the world would be much injured. Some co-operators
dream a dream of a co-operative society growing so large as to monopolize
business, but, supposing that dream realized, business would be badly done.
Everybody would grow lazy, the goods would deteriorate in quality, prices
would become larger, and by-and-by some philanthropic co-operators, purely
in the public interest, would be compelled to revolt and set up competition
again. Human nature can conquer the temptation to dishonesty, but it never
can conquer the disposition to take its ease, and, if it is to strain itself and
always do its best in business or anything else, it needs a heavy whip. No
whip has ever been discovered so effective as competition, and if it were dispensed with, the human race, even if happier, would be less vigorous and less
prone to make steady advance toward more perfect work its rule of life."—
London Economist.

The relation between prices and poverty has long attracted attention, and nothing new in the way of theory remains to be offered. Three thousand or more years ago, a certain wise man, who had sat at the marts of trade, and made himself conversant with the nature of wholesale and retail transactions, embodied in the following short and simple sentence as much in the way of explanation of their involved phenomena as the best results of modern science will probably ever be able to offer, namely—" *The destruction of the poor is their poverty.*"—*Proverbs, 10th chapter, 15th verse.* Something in the way of a real contribution to our general understanding of this subject would, however, seem to be found in the recent observation that the value-perceiving sense or faculty is not implanted by Nature in every person, but differs widely in different races and families; and that " he who has it will accumulate wealth with comparatively slight exertion, while he who has it not will not gain it, no matter how energetically he labors." * Illustrations of this are familiar to every student and investigator of social science; but the following one seems especially worthy of record : On the ferries between New York and Brooklyn, the rates of toll were some years ago reduced nearly one half to all who would buy at one time (or at wholesale) fifty cents' worth of tickets. But it was soon noticed that the working-classes, who at morning and evening constituted the bulk of the travel, rarely bought tickets, while they were bought as a rule by those who belonged to banking and mercantile establishments." †

---

* " The Labor-Value Fallacy," by M. L. Scudder. Chicago, 1886.

† " No one familiar with business life would question the special ability of German Jews in all business which requires a comprehension of finance, as well as in all mercantile pursuits. They do, no doubt, outstrip Englishmen very frequently, almost as frequently as they outstrip Germans in Berlin or Vienna. In the race for wealth, as a result of trade, they have probably distanced all mankind, and the English bankers can no more contend with the Rothschilds in London or Paris than the Parsee traders can compete in Bombay with the great Jew house of Sassoon. But then, not to mention the spe-

The countries of the world which within the last third of the century have made the greatest material progress are the United States, Australia, and the States of the Argentine Republic. This has been due largely in all these cases to the vast abundance of cheap and fertile land, which has occasioned and made possible a great increase in population. Like conditions have been similarly influential in increasing the population of Russia in a more rapid ratio than in most of the other countries of Europe. The United States, by reason of its great natural resources, and extensive use of machinery and consequent ability to control the supply and the price of many of the great staple articles of the world's consumption—cotton, cereals, meats, tobacco, petroleum, and silver—is at present the great disturbing factor in the world's economic condition.

In Australia, the recent increase in population and wealth is extraordinary, and finds a parallel only in the past experience of the United States. During the year 1887 the increase of the population of all the colonies, including New Zealand, was three and a half per cent over that of 1886. At the present rate of increase, the inhabitants of Australia at or before the close of the next century will number about 190,000,000; and constitute no inconsiderable part of the population of the world. That the increase of wealth in these colonies is also increasing even faster than the increase

---

cial aptitudes of Jews for trading, the result of the unjust persecution of centuries which has closed all other careers to them, the Jews are for the most part taught business very early as a method of making money, but are not required to put any intellectuality into it. Though often intellectual men, their intellect usually manifests itself outside their business, which they conduct with skill indeed, but without any special display of mind. Some of the most successful among them have been very ignorant men, and almost all have succeeded rather by virtue of a sort of faculty of accumulation and attention to the uses of money than by any display of what would be deemed intellectual power in business. They know, as we once heard it described, the 'smell of the markets'—that is, their tendency toward rising or falling, and they seek carefully for profit; but it is by business aptitude rather than culture that they achieve their highest results."—*London Economist*.

of population, is claimed to be shown by comparing the average amount left by each person dying in Victoria in the years 1872–1876 with similar bequeathed possessions during the years 1877–1881 and 1882–1886, it being assumed that the average amount left by each person dying is equivalent to the average amount possessed by each person living. On this basis, the national wealth amounted to £185 ($899) per head in the five years, 1872 to 1876; to £223 ($1,083) in the five years, 1877 to 1881; and to £305 ($1,482) in the five years, 1882 to 1886. This wealth, however, is not accumulated in the hands of the few, but is tolerably wide-spread; nineteen and a half per cent of the population having savings-banks deposits. The average rate of wages is also higher in Australia than in any other country.

In the Argentine Republic, during the twenty-five years next preceding 1888, the population increased in a ratio nearly double that of the United States; while the increase in the value of its landed property since 1882 is estimated at fifty per cent. About forty-five hundred miles of rail-roads were in operation within the territory of the republic on the 1st of January, 1889, with a large number of additional miles under contract. Sleeping-cars now run regularly from the Atlantic Ocean to the foot-hills of the Andes; and the completion of a through line from ocean to ocean, saving five thousand miles of ocean navigation around the extremity of the continent, is a near certainty. In 1878 the exports of wheat, maize, and linseed from the republic were reported as aggregating only 213 tons; in 1887 the aggregate was 632,700 tons. Patagonia, which is in great part included in the territory of the republic, and which only a few years since appeared in our geographies as a dreary and uninhabitable waste, has developed into the richest of pastures, with immense possibilities for supplying the world with meat and other desirable animal products—wool, hides, and skins.

The immense change which has taken place in the economic condition of India in recent years is also a matter of profound interest and importance. The India of antiquity, so far as its relations to Europe were concerned, has been not unfitly described as a " dealer in curiosities," and, under the rule and administration of the East India Company, "as a retail trader in luxuries." But India under British dominion has become a wholesale exporter of food products, seeds, and fibers, and is becoming a manufacturer on a large scale on its own account. In 1834 the value of the aggregate exports of India was reported at £9,500,000 ($46,170,-000); in 1887 this aggregate had increased to £92,000,000 ($447,000,000).* In 1865 the manufacture—spinning and weaving—of cotton by machinery was very inconsiderable. In 1878-'79 the India mill consumption of cotton was only 268,000 bales (of 392 pounds each); in 1887-'88 it was 815,-000 bales, an increase in a decade of two hundred and four per cent. The history of commerce can also show no parallel to the recent growth of the export trade of India in the item of cotton yarns of her own manufacture; and the period may therefore be not far distant when India, if this department of her trade and industry continues to expand, will be under the necessity of importing raw cotton, in place of exporting it, as she has done for centuries. Another interesting feature of this change in economic conditions is, that whereas India, down to a comparatively recent period, insisted upon being paid for her commodities in the precious metals—largely silver—her foreign trade to-day, as is the case with other great commercial nations, consists mainly in the interchange of commodities exclusive of the precious metals, and with the minimum use of money.

But of all old countries, England, considered as the representative of the United Kingdom, leads in all that per-

---

* "Statistical Abstract for the Colonial Possessions of the United Kingdom," 1888.

tains to civilization; and, making allowance for the exceptional advantages enjoyed by the United States and Australia, her relative progress has probably been as great as that of any country. In no one of the countries of Europe has the increase of population been greater, and in Italy, Germany, and Russia only has there been an approximate increase; and this result has been especially remarkable, inasmuch as for many years England has not had an acre of virgin soil to expand upon. In no country of Europe, furthermore, has the increase of population been probably so largely accompanied by an increase in comfort as in England. Forty years ago the United Kingdom owned only about one third of the world's shipping. Now it probably owns about seven twelfths, and of the existing steam-tonnage it owned seventy-two per cent (in 1887). In respect to exports and imports—comparisons being made per capita—no other nation approximates Great Britain in its results to an extent sufficient to fairly justify a claim in its behalf to the holding of a second place.*

In every movement in recent years toward a material betterment of the masses through reduction of the hours of labor, compulsory education of children, advancing wages, acts regulating the payment of wages, factory and mine inspection, extermination of diseases and reduction of the death-rate, cheap postage, diminishing the risks of ocean navigation as to both life and property, establishing co-operative institutions, and the like, England has led the way. In no other of the leading industrial nations are the deposits of savings-banks and provident associations increas-

---

* " At the present moment the foreign trade of England—imports and exports together, including the transit trade—is in round figures £750,000,000 per annum, about £20 per head of the population. In France the corresponding figures are £429,000,000, and £12 per head; in the United States, £306,-000,000, and £6 per head; in Germany, £488,000,000, and £11 per head; in Russia, £160,000,000, and £1 10s. per head; in Austria-Hungary, £143,000,-000, and £3 10s. per head; in Italy, £100,000,000, and £3 10s. per head; and so of other nations."—ROBERT GIFFEN, *Letter to the London Times,* 1884.

ing more rapidly, or the benefits of life and health insurance so widely extended, or more attention given or greater comparative expenditures made in behalf of education, or so small an amount of crime in proportion to population, or in which pauperism is so rapidly diminishing,* or where greater progress is acknowledged in respect to the equal distribution of wealth. In 1837 the national debt of England amounted to 19·5 per cent of the national wealth; in 1880 it amounted to only 8·8 per cent. With the exception of the United States, England is the only other great nation that is reducing its national debt; and notwithstanding the continuance of an antiquated and unequal system of land tenure, and rigidly defined lines of social organization, England is the one highly civilized country in which the doctrines of socialism have made the least progress. Wherever and whenever England now acquires new territory she establishes commercial liberty, and neither claims nor exercises any privilege of trade which she does not equally share with the people of all other countries. Under her recent rule India is experiencing an industrial awakening which finds no parallel in her previous history—threatening the supremacy of China in respect to the world's supply of tea, the United States in respect to the supply of wheat, and Lancashire (England) in the manufacture and exports of cotton fabrics.† In 1884 Great Britain virtually took possession of Egypt, and from that moment there was initiated, under the management of a body of skilled engineers and practical

---

* " We are prone (in the United States) to bewail the condition of the English laborer and lament the existence of pauperism in England, but the official figures certainly do not warrant much self-gratulation. It may be that English private benefactions far exceed our own in amount, but the fact remains that the English Government aids fewer paupers, proportionately to population, than our own."—CARROLL D. WRIGHT.

† No country in the world can point to such remarkable figures as India can in her export trade in cotton yarns. In eleven years—i. e., from 1877 to to 1888—the shipments rose from about 7,000,000 pounds to over 113,000,000 pounds.

men, a renovation of the water-supply and irrigation system of the country upon which the life and prosperity of its people depend, and which has already been attended with results of extraordinary beneficence. In Lower Egypt land reclamation is going on at the rate of fifty thousand acres per annum, and in other sections of the Nile Valley at double that amount; giving to a down-trodden and impoverished race better opportunities than they have had for centuries of supporting themselves by their own labor. Formerly one or two hundred thousand of the wretched fellaheen were annually torn from their homes and forced to labor for months in clearing out the canals of mud and ooze, without pay and with an insufficient supply of the poorest food. Under English management this system of slavery has been practically abolished, and the laborers are now paid wages or allowed to buy their exemption from work for a very small sum.

Something of inference respecting the economic changes of the future may be warranted from a study of the past. It may, for example, be anticipated that whatever of economic disturbance has been due to a change in the relative value of silver to gold, will ultimately be terminated by a restoration of the bullion price of the former metal to the rates (sixty to sixty-one pence per ounce) that prevailed for many years prior to the year 1873. The reasons which warrant such an opinion are briefly as follows :

Silver is the only suitable coin medium for countries of comparatively low prices, low wages, and limited exchanges, like India, China, Central and South America, which represent about three fifths of the population of the world, or about a thousand millions of people. Civilization in most of these countries, through the advent of better means of production and exchange, is rapidly advancing—necessitating a continually increasing demand for silver as money, as well as of iron for tools and machinery. Generations also will pass before the people of such countries will begin to economize

money by the use to any extent of its representatives—paper
and credit. Under such circumstances a scarcity, rather
than a superabundant supply of silver, in the world's market,
is the outlook for the future, inasmuch as a comparatively
small per capita increase in the use of silver by such vast
numbers would not only rapidly absorb any existing surplus,
but possibly augment demand in excess of any current supply.* The true economic policy of a country like the
United States, which is a large producer and seller of silver,
would therefore seem to be, to seek to facilitate such a result,
by removing all obstacles in the way of commerce between
itself and silver-using countries, in order that, through increased traffic and consequent prosperity, the demand for
silver on the part of the latter may be promoted.

The great reduction in the cost of transportation of commodities has been one of the most striking features of recent
economic history; and how essential this reduction has
been, and is, to the achievement and maintenance of the
present conditions of civilization, may be inferred from the
circumstance that "it takes an annual movement of about
a thousand tons one mile to keep alive each inhabitant of
the United States." Produce is now carried from Australia
to England, a distance of eleven thousand miles, in less time
and at less cost than was required a hundred years ago to
convey goods from one extremity of the British Islands to

---

* According to statements submitted to the Royal (English) Commission
on Trade Depression, " The quantity of pure silver used for coinage purposes,
during the fourteen years ending 1884, was about eighteen per cent greater
than the total production during that period ; and there are other estimates
which place the consumption at a still higher figure. It is to be remembered
that the coinage demand is fed from other sources than the annual output of
the mines. It is supplied to some extent by the melting down of old coinage.
Allowing for this, however, the evidence of statistics goes to show that the
coinage demand for the metal is, and has been, sufficient to absorb the whole
of the annual supply that is left free after the consumption in the arts and
manufactures has been supplied ; and this conclusion is supported by the fact
that nowhere throughout the world has there been any accumulation of un-
coined stocks of the metal."—*London Economist.*

the other. The average cost of transporting each ton of freight one mile on the Pennsylvania Railroad during the year 1887 was $\frac{426}{1000}$ of a cent. At first thought it would seem as if improvement in this sphere of human effort had certainly found a limit; but there are reasons for believing that even greater reductions are possible. Apart from improvements in machinery, and greater economies in operating, very few of the great lines of transportation, especially the railways, have as yet sufficient of business to continuously exhaust their carrying capacity;* but, when this is effected, and the present ratio of a large class of fixed expenditures to business is thereby diminished, lower rates for freight, from this cause alone, will be permissible; all of which, however, is simply equivalent to reaffirming the old trade maxim, that it costs proportionately less to do a large than a small business.

An anticipation of an immense increase in the near future, in the commerce between the countries of the western and eastern hemispheres, owing especially to the introduction into the latter of better methods for effecting exchanges and transmitting information, is certainly warranted by recent experiences. Thus, if the trade between the United Kingdom alone and the leading countries of the East, exclusive of India, continues to increase in the next quarter of a century in the same ratio as it has during the last quarter, when commercial facilities were much less than at present, its aggregate value of $190,000,000 in 1860, and $427,000,000 in 1885, will swell to over $1,000,000,000 in the year 1910; and, beyond that date, to an amount that must be left to the imagination.

That the only possible future for agriculture, prosecuted for the sake of producing the great staples of food, is to be found in large farms, worked with ample capital, especially

---

* During the year 1887 the mileage of empty freight-cars on the Chicago, Milwaukee and St. Paul Railroad was reported at 61,210,749, or more than one third of the total mileage run by loaded freight-cars.

in the form of machinery, and with labor organized somewhat after the factory system, is coming to be the opinion
of many of the best authorities, both in the United States
and Europe. As a further part of such a system, it is
claimed that the farm must be devoted to a specialty or a
few specialties, on the ground that it would be almost as
fatal to success to admit mixed farming as it would be to
attempt the production of several kinds of diverse manufactures under one roof and establishment.

Machinery is already largely employed in connection
with the drying and canning of fruit and vegetables, and in
the manufacture of wine. In the sowing, harvesting, transporting, and milling of wheat, its utilization has reached a
point where further improvement would seem to be almost
impossible. In the business of slaughtering cattle and hogs,
and rendering their resulting products available for food
and other useful purposes, the various processes, involving
large expenditure and great diversity of labor, especially in
" curing," succeed each other with startling rapidity, and
are, or can be, all carried on under one roof, and on such a
scale of magnitude and with such a degree of economy that
it is said that, if the entire profits of the great slaughtering
establishments were limited to the gross receipts from the
sale of the beef-tongues in the one case and the pigs' feet in
the other, the returns on the capital invested and the business transacted would be eminently satisfactory. It is not,
however, so well known that the business of fattening cattle
by the so-called " factory system," on a most extensive
scale, has also been successfully introduced in the Northwestern and trans-Mississippi States and Territories, and
that great firms have at present thousands of cattle gathered
under one roof, and undergoing the operation of fattening
by the most continuous, effective, and economic processes.
The results show that one laborer can take care of two hundred steers undergoing the process of grain-feeding for the
shambles, in a systematic, thorough manner, with the ex-

penditure of much less time and labor per day than the ordinary farmer spends in tending fifteen or twenty head of fattening steers under the disadvantages common upon the ordinary farms. In these mammoth establishments " a steam-engine moves the hay from one large barn to another, as needed, by means of an endless belt, and carries it to a powerful machine where it is cut into lengths suitable for feeding, and afterward carries the cut hay by other belts to the mixing-room where by means of another machine it is mixed with corn-meal, the corn having been previously shelled and then ground on the premises by power from the same engine. Again, the mixed feed is carried automatically to the feed-boxes in the stalls. The same engine pumps the water for drinking, which runs in a long, shallow trough within reach of the steers ; and even the stalls are cleaned by water discharged through a hose, the supply being raised by the engine and stored for use. The steers are not removed from the stalls in which they are placed from the time the fattening process is begun until they are ready for transportation to the big establishments above mentioned for systematic slaughtering. The advantages of such establishments are not, moreover, confined to labor-saving expedients merely. The uniformity of temperature secured through all kinds of weather is equivalent to a notable saving of feed ; for where fluctuations of temperature are extreme and rapid, and not guarded against, " a great deal of the grain which the farmer feeds is ' blown away ' after having been consumed by his stock," in form of vital heat, strength, and growth, which are the products of the conversion of the grain on digestion.*

---

* It has been found that the present usual method adopted on Western farms of feeding grain, especially corn, without previous grinding, is most costly, as the grain in its natural condition is imperfectly digested. Another serious objection to the imperfect methods of the ordinary farm in grain-feeding is, that the grain is fed in a too concentrated form ; the fact being unknown, or disregarded, that the thrift of the fattening animal depends

How great a revolution in the business of agriculture is yet to be effected by the cultivation of land in large tracts, with the full use of machinery and under the factory-system, is matter for the future to reveal; but it can not be doubted that the shiftless, wasteful methods of agriculture, now in practice over enormous areas of the earth's surface,

---

largely on the intimate admixture of ground grain with coarse forage; and that hay, also, must be chopped, and more thoroughly intermingled with it, for the attainment of the best results. But the chopping of the hay and straw and the mixing with meal and water are laborious operations, and hence the economy of applying the steam-engine, and thus saving labor in the business of feeding. Another saving is in building materials: the larger the structure in which the machinery, the hay and grain, and the animals are kept, the less the proportionate quantity of lumber needed; and then, again, in such an establishment, temperature and ventilation, which in ordinary farming are matters that receive little attention, are economically and effectively regulated. An American practical farmer, the owner and manager of seven thousand acres (Mr. H. H——, of Nebraska), to whom the writer is indebted for many items of information, communicates the following additional review of this subject from the American (Western) standpoint: " The average Western farm is now recklessly managed, but capital will come in greater volume and set up processes which will displace these wasteful methods. The revolution is certain, even if the exact steps can not now be precisely indicated. At present the hay, and much of the grain, and nearly all of the tools and implements, are unsheltered; and more than fifty per cent of the hay is ruined for a like reason, while the animals themselves (I do not mean now on the wild-stock ranges, but even on the trans-Missouri farms) have no roof over their heads, except the canopy of heaven, with the mercury going occasionally twenty and even thirty degrees below zero. These wasteful methods in farming are in part promoted by the United States homestead law, and the occupation of the hitherto inexhaustible expanse of cheap lands. When the ignorant, degraded, and impecunious can no longer acquire a hundred and sixty acres upon which to employ their barbarous methods, and when the land already taken up shall have risen from the low prices at which it now stands to fifty dollars or more per acre, a new dispensation will arrive. Neither the cattle, nor the food which the cattle consume, will then be raised by any such methods as now prevail: neither will they be exposed to the elements in winter. True enough, the opening up of other virgin fields in Australia, South America, Africa, and elsewhere, may retard this rise in the value of the land in the western part of our continent, and thus to a certain extent delay the passing of the land exclusively into the hands of larger capitalists and better managers; but it must be considered that not all climates are suitable for energetic, capable farming populations, and likewise that the best forage plants are restricted to temperate latitudes."

are altogether too barbarous to be much longer tolerated; and, as the result of such progress, the return of the prices of meats and cereals to their former higher rates, which many are anticipating on account of the increasing number of the world's consumers, may be delayed indefinitely. Possibly in the not very remote future, the world—as its population shows no signs of abatement in its increase—may be confronted with a full occupation of all farming-land and a great comparative diminution of product through an exhaustion of its elements of fertility; but, before that time arrives, improvements may possibly be made in agriculture which will have practically the same effect as an increase in the quantity of land; or possibly chemistry may be able to produce food by the direct combination of its inorganic elements.

CONCLUSION.

Finally, a comprehensive review of the economic changes of the last quarter of a century, and a careful balancing of what seems to have been good and what seems to have been evil in respect to results, would seem to warrant the following conclusions: That the immense material progress that these changes have entailed has been, for mankind in general, movement upward and not downward; for the better and not for the worse; and that the epoch of time under consideration will hereafter rank in history as one that has had no parallel, but which corresponds in importance with the periods that successively succeeded the Crusades, the invention of gunpowder, the emancipation of thought through the Reformation, and the invention of the steam-engine; when the whole plane of civilization and humanity rose to a higher level, each great movement being accompanied by social disturbances of great magnitude and serious import, but which experience has proved were but temporary in their nature and infinitesimal in their influence for evil in comparison with the good that followed. And what the watchman standing on this higher eminence can now see is, that the time has come when the population of the world commands the means of a comfortable subsistence in a greater degree and with less of effort than ever before; and what he may reasonably expect to see at no very remote period is, the dawn of a day when human poverty will mean more distinctly than ever physical disability, mental incapacity, or unpardonable viciousness or laziness.

But, in order that this dawning may be hastened, it is of the first importance to recognize that civilized society in recent years, and under the new economic conditions which those years have evolved, has become a vastly more complicated machine than ever before—so complicated, in fact, that, in order to make it work smoothly, all possible obstructions need to be foreseen and removed from its mechanism. Great armaments; millions of men made soldiers and removed from the work of production; laws interfering with free commercial exchanges between nations — these and many lesser interferences with the free action and interaction of industrial social forces under existing conditions, all tend to destructive irregularities or stoppages of the great machine; whereby labor is rendered unproductive and discontented, want increased, comfort lessened, social inequalities multiplied, the comity of nations discouraged, and the idea of the brotherhood of man, which constitutes the foundation of every system worthy of being called " religious," denied and repudiated.

APPENDIX.

Exhibit of the Relative Production and Prices of Iron and Steel in the United States and Great Britain, and of the Extent to which the Duties on Imports augment the Prices of these Metals in the former Country.

THERE is probably no standard by which the relative prosperity of nations can be so accurately gauged as by their relative consumption of iron and steel. The use of these metals corresponds to their conversion into rails, engines, machinery, and tools of every kind which lie at the foundation of all the arts of production and distribution.

The iron and steel industry is singular in another respect. There is probably no other art about which the statistics are so ample, so complete, and so trustworthy. The United States Census Reports of 1880, by Mr. James M. Swank, upon Iron and Steel; by Prof. Raphael Pumpelly, upon Iron-Ore and Coal Production; by Mr. Joseph D. Weeks, on the Coke Industry, leave nothing to be desired. They cover every point and are based on the sworn returns of establishments, in which the work is conducted in such a systematic way as to afford an absolute and complete picture of the condition of the business; and year by year statistical abstracts and other publications in the United States and Europe keep up the record of the world's experiences to the latest dates. No more important addition to this department of economic literature has, however, been made in recent years than the publication during the year 1888, under the auspices of the American Iron and Steel Association, of a complete collection of the statistics of the iron and steel industries of the United States for many years down to the close of 1887, embracing both production and prices, with the concurrent prices of British iron and steel from 1830 to 1887 inclusive;* inasmuch as it affords data so exact as to permit

---

* "A Collection of Statistics to the Close of 1887, relating to the Iron and Steel Industries of the United States; to which is added much Valuable Sta-

the relative prices or cost of iron and steel to the consumers of these metals in the United States and Great Britain, for the period mentioned, to be clearly exhibited.

Taking advantage of the facilities thus afforded, the following exhibit, believed to be strictly warranted by the facts, has been prepared and is here submitted; with the premise that in computing its statements of numerical results small fractions have been omitted, on the assumption that, without adding anything essential to completeness in this instance, their inclusion tends to confuse the mind and consequently weaken the impression which it is desirable should be made upon the reader.

The world's average annual production of pig-iron, from 1878 to 1887, was in round numbers 20,800,000 *net* tons of 2,000 pounds each.* In 1887 it reached 24,600,000 net tons. The average product of the United States, from 1878 to 1887 inclusive, was 4,758,000 tons.

The average annual import of iron by the United States, from 1878 to 1887 inclusive, in the form of pig, bars, rails, and plates (omitting machinery and hardware), was 1,100,000 net tons. Reasoning from the value of the imports of machinery, hardware, and other manufactures of iron and steel during the same period, the average annual import of these products for the ten years in question was probably in excess of 225,000 net tons. It is safe to say, therefore, that the consumption of iron and steel in the United States, in one form or another, each year for the ten years, 1878 to 1887 inclusive, was about 6,000,000 tons of 2,000 pounds each, or a fraction less than thirty per cent of the entire product of the world.

The consumption of the United States for the year 1887 was yet more startling. The domestic product amounted to 7,187,000 tons. The import of rails, bars, plates, and the like, was 1,997,000 tons; and by estimate from value, the import of machinery, hardware, tools, etc., must have been at least 330,000 tons additional, giving a total consumption for the year of 9,500,000 net tons, or a fraction less than forty per cent of the entire product of the world.

The pig-iron production of the United States for 1888 was 7,268,-

tistical Information relating to the Iron and Steel Industries of Great Britain, etc.," by James M. Swank, *General Manager of the American Iron and Steel Association, Philadelphia*, 1888, 8vo, pp. 24.

* In England and Russia 2,240 pounds constitute a ton of pig-iron. In all the Continental countries of Europe, except Russia, the metric ton of 2,204 pounds constitutes the standard. In the United States 2,240 pounds constitute a *gross* ton, and 2,000 pounds a *net* ton.

507 net, or 6,489,738 *gross* tons. For the twelve months ending June 30, 1889, the product was 7,993,903 *net*, or 7,137,413 *gross* tons.

The average annual product of pig-iron in Great Britain from 1878 to 1887 inclusive was 7,500,000 gross tons, or a little less than 8,400,-000 net tons. The product of 1887 (7,559,518 tons) corresponded very closely to the average of the whole period.

It therefore follows from these figures that the consumption of iron and steel in the United States for the ten years—1877 to 1887—was equal to seventy-five per cent of the average production of Great Britain during that period, and that it has now (1889) reached such dimensions as to approximate closely to the present entire annual British iron and steel product. Furthermore, as no country other than Great Britain exports iron and steel in quantities proportioned in any important degree to the total consumption of the United States, nearly every other country, with the possible exceptions of Belgium, Sweden, and Norway, importing more iron and steel than it exports, it is obviously impossible for the United States to procure a supply adequate to meet its consumption of these necessary metals except in great measure from its own mines and furnaces. It is, however, apparent that, until within a very short time, perhaps only since the Southern and Western mines and works have been established, the production of iron in the United States has been conducted at a very great disadvantage. In Pennsylvania and in many other parts of the country, the deposits of iron-ores and of coal are separated by other intervening geological formations, which interpose considerable distances and heavy grades between the points of supply of these materials, while the iron-ores of the Lake Superior region are very far removed from the sources of supply of the fuel by which they must be utilized Hence it is not surprising to find by the census figures of 1880, that the difference between the value of the ores and coal at the mines and of coke at the coke-ovens, and the cost of these materials at the iron-furnaces, amounted for that year to over $21,000,000 on a product of pig iron valued at $89,000,000, a difference of $5.60 per ton; most of which must have been expended in transporting ores or coal from widely separated mines and in assembling the materials at the points where they could be economically converted. In confirmation of this statement, the testimony of Mr. Cyrus Elder, of the Cambria Iron Works of Pennsylvania, given in a tract published in 1888 by the Industrial League, and which can be purchased from Mr. James M. Swank at 262 South Fourth Street, Philadelphia, is most valuable. In this publication, after dealing with the question of the transportation of materials, Mr. Elder states that " the books of one of the principal steel-rail manufacturing companies for the year 1887 show that the cost of transportation to its works, of the materials used in making each ton of steel rails, amounted in that year to $12.75," or to an aggregate burden or tax upon the product of the year of $1,591,332.92. Mr. Elder, in his discussion of this subject, also objects to the duty of $11 per ton which the bill reported by the Committee of Ways and Means to the United States House of Representatives of the fiftieth Congress, 1888 (and familiarly known as the " Mills Bill "), proposed to levy on the import of steel rails into the United States, on the ground that it " does not much more than compensate the American manufacturer for the excess in cost to him of assembling the materials above what is paid by his foreign rivals." The evidence, therefore, is conclusive that until a recent period about twenty-five per cent of the cost of iron, and more than twenty-five per cent of the cost of steel in the United States, has consisted in the expense of assembling the materials at the furnaces. But in these latter days the furnaces and mills are being placed where they belong, to wit, at the various points, especially in Alabama, where the materials may be said to assemble themselves—the coal, iron, and limestone lying near the surface in adjacent ridges, not separated by heavy grades or excessive distances.*

---

* In this connection the following remarks of Hon. Abram S. Hewitt at the meeting of the British Iron Trade Association, on the 7th of May, 1889 (and printed in the official record of the proceedings of that body), will be read with interest.

Mr. Hewitt said : " In Carolina there were vast bodies of magnetites, and, if not very near to the coal at present, railways were in course of construction which would bring them within sixty miles of the best coal in the world. *He had made a calculation, and believed that coal and iron could be bvought together to make pig-iron for Bessemer steel at not exceeding 40s. ($9.74) a ton.* He knew that this might astonish his hearers, particularly in view of the fact that the American mining industry was dependent upon a duty ; but they were slow to learn in the United States, and they honestly believed that they needed this protection, *and it would go on until they had fried long enough in their own fat to learn to find some other outlet in the markets of the world.* There was a vast deposit of ore, commencing in Tennessee and thickening until in Alabama, where a great physical eruption must have taken place at one time, a mountain was covered with a fifty-per-cent ore, which was, as a rule, in admirable condition to be put into the furnace. It was not low enough in phosphorus for the acid Bessemer, but could be used for the basic process. The coal and the ore were only five miles apart, and about five shillings ($1.25) would deliver at the furnace the materials for a ton of iron. Of course, this was a combination which, as far as he knew, did not exist anywhere else in the world, and he supposed he might assume that the only drawback at all

It now becomes interesting to compute the relative price or cost of iron and steel to the consumers of these metals in the United States as compared with those of Great Britain and other countries; and Mr. Swank's little pamphlet affords all the data necessary for making this comparison, for the years 1878 to 1887 inclusive. This decade includes one year of prices, in the United States, on a slightly depreciated paper basis. Specie payments were not renewed until 1879; and, during 1878, the paper-money price of iron was a very little higher than the gold price. This difference may, however, be legitimately disregarded; because, if we had the enormous figures of the consumption of 1888 to add to the previous years, omitting 1878, the results of the following computation would find more than ample confirmation. Thus, in the period under consideration, 1878 to 1887 inclusive, the average price of anthracite foundry-iron in Philadelphia was $21.87 per ton. During the same period the average price of Scotch pig-iron, as given in Mr. Swank's pamphlet, presumably in Glasgow, was $12.94, reckoning the shilling at twenty-four cents. During the last portion of this decade trans-oceanic freights were very low; considerable quantities of iron having been even carried as ballast, without charge. But, even assuming that the freight on pig-iron had been the same as that on manufactures of iron, it would not have exceeded $2 per ton. Adding this to the price in Glasgow gives us a fraction under $15 per ton, as the price of Scotch pig landed in the United States; and deducting this from the price of anthracite foundry-iron, as above stated, we find a disparity of $7 per ton in the price of all the pig-iron consumed in this country in ten years, as compared with the average price of Scotch pig for the corresponding period in Great Britain.*

If objection be taken to this comparison, it may be more fair to take a higher grade of iron. For example, during the same period the average price of the best rolled bar-iron in Philadelphia was $50.30 per ton of 2,240 pounds, while the average price in England of the best

would be in the higher rate of wages; *but there was the vast body of negro labor quite available, and he doubted whether the per-diem wage was so much as in England.*"

* "Scotch pig" is taken as a standard in these comparisons, because it is expedient to restrict their sphere to the statistics furnished in Mr. Swank's valuable report; and the average prices of no other brands of British pig-iron are given in his tables. If, however, "English pig," which represents the bulk of British production and consumption, and the average price of which is less than Scotch pig, had been taken as the British standard, the disparity between the English and American prices of iron would be much more considerable than that above indicated.

Staffordshire marked bars was $36.48, a difference substantially of $14 per ton. And this disparity in the prices of iron and steel in the two countries becomes greater the higher we go in the grades selected for comparison. But, selecting the lowest grades as the standard, and applying the difference of $7, between the price of Pennsylvania anthracite "foundry" and "Scotch pig" to the consumption of the United States of 60,000,000 tons in ten years, it will be found that the consumers of iron and steel in the United States paid, in the ten years from 1878 to 1887, $420,000,000 in excess of the cost of a like quantity of iron to the consumers of Great Britain during the same period.

In respect to steel, comparison shows the disparity of prices to be even much greater. Thus the production of steel in all its forms, in the United States, for the ten years under consideration, was 19,127,-000 net tons. The import of steel during the same time was 859,000 tons. Adding this last amount and a fair allowance for other kinds of steel imported, it becomes apparent that the consumption of steel in the United States in the ten years from 1878 to 1887 was over 20,000,-000 tons.

To determine now the difference or disparity in the prices of steel in the two countries, the lowest form will be again taken as the standard for comparison; and for so doing Mr. Swank's tables afford the following data :

The average price of steel rails in the United States from 1878 to 1887 was $44 per ton. In Great Britain, during the same period, the average was $30 per ton. At these rates the adverse difference in the cost of consumption of 20,000,000 tons of steel in the United States would have been $280,000,000. But as a difference, as respects the cost of the iron used in the making of steel in the two countries of $7 per ton, has been already allowed, the cost of the consumption of steel in the United States may be properly charged with only one half this disparity, or $140,000,000.

Taking, therefore, the lowest grades of iron and steel as a standard in this computation of the disparity of cost or price, from 1878 to 1887, the aggregate excess of cost of iron and steel in ten years, to the consumers of the United States, above that paid in Great Britain, has been $560,000,000, or at an average of $56,000,000 per annum; and on a separate computation, made in the same way, for the year 1887, the disparity in price for the United States rises for that single year to $80,000,000.

The revenue derived by the Government of the United States during the fiscal year ending June 30, 1887, was, on ores and pig-iron,

APPENDIX. 473

$3,667,000, and on manufactures of iron and steel $17,046,000; or a total of $20,713,000.

It therefore appears that in the process of collecting an amount of revenue, which constituted less than one fifth part of the excess or surplus revenue of that year, the country was subjected to an additional tax of $60,000,000, which was paid by the consumers of iron and steel in some way. Doubtless this difference was largely absorbed in the cost of assembling the materials, and by charges on the making of iron and steel in those iron-furnaces and rolling-mills which are either out of place or out of date; and it can not fairly be claimed to have been all a bounty to the owners of the works, whatever part may have gone in that direction.

Attention is next asked to the benefit that is popularly supposed to accrue from making iron and steel in the United States in preference to importing it.

The conditions of life in the iron and coal mines have been so often described that it is not worth while to here repeat them. The wages paid are low, and the conditions of employment are as bad as they well can be. In the blast-furnaces and the rolling-mills the conditions are somewhat better; but the work is arduous in the extreme and most exhausting.

In the census year 1880, in which it was estimated that the sum paid in wages corresponded to about three fourths time for the full force, the earnings of the skilled and unskilled workmen in all the rolling-mills, blast-furnaces, coke-ovens, and iron and coal mines of the United States averaged $365 each per annum. The number occupied in these industries in the census year was a fraction over 205,000; the sum of their earnings was $75,000,000. The production of the census year was a little less than the average consumption of the last ten years, and about four sevenths of the consumption of 1887. Since 1880, however, very great improvements have been made in the processes of conversion of ore and fuel into iron and steel, by the application of natural gas and by improvements in mechanism. The iron-mines of the South have also been opened, where a very much less proportionate quantity of labor suffices for the production of a given quantity of iron than in Pennsylvania. Wages have risen in daily rate, but the cost of labor in a ton of metal has been reduced; and the sum of the wages has also proportionately diminished in ratio to the value of the product. It may be safe to compute that there are now occupied in this work of making iron and steel for 65,000,000 people about 300,000 men and boys, averaging perhaps $400 a year each in wages, earning altogether $120,000,000. The people of the United

States therefore paid, in the year 1887, $21,000,000 toward the surplus revenue, and $60,000,000 excess in price, which was distributed among the owners of the mineral lands, the owners of the furnaces, and the operators of the Bessemer process, and also among the railways, for the cost of assembling the materials.

In 1880 there were 1,005 iron and steel works, rolling-mills, and blast-furnaces in the United States, whose aggregate capital, according to Mr. Swank, was $231,000,000. According to Prof. Pumpelly, the capital in the iron-mines of the country for that same year was $62,000,000 ; and from the joint reports of these two census experts it would appear that the aggregate capital invested in all the coal-mines of the country, at the same date, was $248,000,000, of which nearly $200,000,000 stood for the value of the mineral lands or royalties. The proportion of coal and the cost of coking, chargeable to the iron industry, may possibly cover the odd $48,000,000. The entire capital invested in the iron and steel industry of the United States in 1880 was, therefore, about $341,000,000 ;* and the data above submitted warrant the conclusion that the price paid by the consumers of iron and steel in the United States, in order to sustain these industries for ten years, and to enable the owners thereof to enjoy its profits—paying wages to their employés somewhat less on an average than were paid at the same time to other and outside labor—was about sixty-five per cent more than the entire capital invested in it. And, as it has been already shown that it would be impossible for any other country to supply the annual requirements of the United States of iron and steel for consumption, it further follows that the payment of $50,000,000 to $80,000,000 per annum by this country to sustain a branch of industry which can not be displaced or destroyed by any possible foreign competition, is clearly unnecessary.

It will be also pertinent at this point to consider the probable effect of the removal of all duties (taxes) now imposed upon the importation into the United States of ores of iron, and upon coal, coke, crude iron and steel, and upon tools, machinery, and implements of every kind made therefrom ; which duties now yield a revenue—not required—of from $20,000,000 to $22,000,000 per annum.

The paramount advantage of Great Britain over even Belgium and Germany long since passed away. Her mines of the finer qualities of iron-ore, while they can not be said to be absolutely exhausted, are yet

---

* Blast-furnaces and rolling-mills, $231,000,000 ; iron-mines, $62,000,000 ; coal-mines appurtenant to iron and steel and coke works, $48,000,000 ; total, $341,000,000.

worked under such bad conditions that England is forced to import iron-ores from Spain, from Elba, and from Africa.* Her coking coals are also produced under conditions of great disadvantage, which have been thus described in a recent (1886) report by Mr. Joseph D. Weeks to the United States Geological Survey. Referring to the most important British coke district—the "Durham"—from which nearly one half of the coke-supply of Great Britain is derived, he says: "The typical coke of Great Britain, as the McConnellsville is of the United States, is the Durham coke; it is high in carbon, low in ash, etc.; the veins are low, the thickest measuring but six feet; the miner is necessarily compelled to lie in a constrained and cramped condition upon his back while working, never standing upright while in the face; the pits are deep and the mines fiery, with all the danger to life and health arising from these conditions. The best coal is obtained from the lower seams." The Durham cokes are furnished at a lower price than any other in Great Britain or in Europe. The average earnings of those who work in them are from seventy cents to $1.10 per day. The cost of coke in Durham is not given. The price of coke for Bessemer pig in Cardiff, Newport, and Swansea is stated to be $3.51 to $3.57. In South Wales the cost of a ton of coke is given at $1.70, and in Belgium at $2.57. At McConnellsville, Pa., the rates of wages are considerably higher, but have been somewhat depressed of late by reason of the use of natural gas at Pittsburg. For several years, according to Prof. Pumpelly's investigations, the value of coke at the oven throughout the United States was $1.22 per ton; a striking example of production at low cost—i. e., of coke—with exceptional high wages, owing to the better conditions under which the work is performed.

The data for the cost of iron-ore and steel in Great Britain and in the United States, and for the comparison of the rates of wages, are not at

---

* The importation of iron-ores into the chief iron-producing countries of Europe dates from about the year 1866, when the Bessemer process had become fairly established. In that year Great Britain imported little or no ores, the only European countries receiving supplies of foreign ores being France, Germany, Belgium, and Austria. The aggregate imports of those four countries amounted at that time to nearly 900,000 tons, or about one seventh of the total now imported into the chief iron-making countries from outside sources. In 1868 the iron-ore imports of Great Britain were returned at 114,435 tons. In 1877 they exceeded 1,000,000 tons. In 1880 they suddenly rose to 2,634,000 tons; and for 1887 they amounted to 3,762,000 tons. That large areas of consumption in the United States also found it profitable to use foreign ores of iron is shown by importation into the country, in the single year 1888, of 1,770,947 tons, notwithstanding a duty on the same of thirty-eight per cent.

present available. It is alleged, however, that the abundance of our supply of ores and coal, lying near the surface and in close proximity, will enable the American manufacturer to pay about double wages, in comparison with Great Britain, and yet to bring out the iron at the furnace at the same cost, so far as the element of labor in it is concerned. Under the instructions lately given by Congress to the Bureau of the Statistics of Labor, and by means of the investigations which are now in progress, it may be possible at no distant day to be able to compare the cost of production of iron and steel and other crude or partly manufactured materials in the United States in terms of days' labor, or by the quality and intensity of the labor, as well as in terms of price, or by the rate of wages; the latter being an entirely fallacious standard, seldom of any value in making the comparison of the relative power of one country, as compared with another, to supply goods or wares of any kind. For, as a rule, the rates of wages in all industries to which modern machinery, tools, and inventions have been applied, are in inverse proportion to the cost of the product, so far as it is made up of the wages of labor—the lowest cost being the correlative or complement of the highest rates of wages, where the commerce between several countries, or between the sections of one country with another is free from artificial obstruction. Doubtless a sudden remission of the existing duties now levied by the United States on the importation of iron and steel would result in the suspension of some furnaces—perhaps a considerable number—which are out of date as respects location, construction, and management. Such establishments are now kept alive only by the disparity in the price of their products in the markets of the United States and of Great Britain. Concurrently, also, there might be a sudden and excessive demand upon the iron-mines and furnaces of Europe, especially of Great Britain, for their products. But this last could not be met without altering all the existing conditions of the iron industries of those countries. Miners and metal-workers are not trained in a day; and those who are in such work would immediately feel the effect of the additional demand and would call for higher wages; while the disadvantages of production in Great Britain would be rendered even greater, through the necessity of ordering larger and larger supplies of ore from Spain, Elba, and Africa. The supply in Spain being now limited, it could hardly fail to happen that a heavy advance in the price of iron would occur throughout Europe. The sudden appearance of a free customer, whose consumption is already forty per cent of the total production of the world, for any considerable part of the iron and steel supply from other countries, would have an effect on the conditions of the workmen in Europe very greatly disproportionate to the quantity called for. Such an advance in the price of these products on the other side of the ocean would immediately protect all the well-placed iron-furnaces, mines, and metal-works of the United States. Their control of their own markets would then be established; stability would be given to the conditions of business, and the American consumers of iron, who outnumber the makers of iron by twenty to one, would be relieved from their present disadvantages in competition with other countries.

It is well known and may be considered a well-established fact that, in almost all the arts of using iron and steel, the people of the United States excel those of Great Britain. Their heavy exports of locomotives, of cutlery, axes, sewing-machines, pumps, and the like, bear witness to this fact. The only reason why they have been unable thus far to build ocean steamships has been the disparity between Europe and America in the price of materials. This would be removed for all time by the heavy advance in the price of such materials in Great Britain and on the Continent, which would certainly ensue from the increased demand contingent on the abrogation of import duties under consideration; and then would follow such a participation by the United States in the commerce and carrying-trade of the world as her natural advantages entitle her to claim and expect. Holding, as her people now do, the paramount position in the production of iron and steel at low cost, but at higher rates of wages than are elsewhere paid for similar service, the time would soon come when all questions of competition in the production and supply of iron and steel would cease. The people of the United States, furthermore, are not subjected to the burden of excessive taxes in ratio to their product, their gross taxes being even much less per capita than those of any other country. They are free from the burden of standing armies, the cost of which is represented only in small measure by the amount paid to support them, but is felt in greatest measure by the withdrawal of men at the most productive period of life to waste their time in camps and barracks. They would, accordingly, assume that advantage of position to which they are entitled in the civilized world and for supplying the non-machine-using nations with every kind of manufactured products which they may require.

It may be held by those who would oppose the remission of all duties upon iron, steel, machinery, and the like, that, unless this artificial stimulus of a high tariff had been given to those branches of industry in the United States, they would not have been developed to anything like the extent which has occurred. This is a pure hypothesis. There is no foundation, in fact, for any such theory. The iron and steel industry in the United States is older than the Constitution, and its growth has been coincident with the growth of the country. Doubtless the variations in the tariff, as well as in the demand for railway purposes, have subjected this branch of industry to greater fluctuations than almost any other. Whether or not the product of iron and steel would have been as great as it is now without the interference of the Government is to-day a matter of no consequence. It is a dead issue. The question now is, What is the cost to the people of the United States of this disparity in the price of iron and steel which is due to the maintenance of a tariff—a tariff not for the purpose of building up or starting an infant industry, but for the mere purpose of maintaining the present conditions, whatever they may be? When viewed in this light, the cost of the system may prove to be much more than it is worth to the people subjected to its burden, for it is a tax upon productive capital and productive power laid at the very foundation of all industry. The disparity in the price of rails costs every mile of railway in the United States a certain amount of money over and above the cost of laying rails, for example, in India, over which wheat is to be transported that comes into direct competition with American wheat in foreign markets.

The people of the United States being deprived of the power to build steamships for ocean service, and the disparity in the price of materials increasing the cost of their railways by ten per cent and of their mills and factories by twenty, and even in some cases by fifty per cent, as compared with the cost of the mills and works of their direct competitors in other countries, the latter are thus enabled to supply the non-machine-using nations of the world with the greater part of their necessary goods and wares, and are sending to the United States a constantly increasing proportion of goods and wares for its consumption, in spite of the high taxes levied on their importation.

The American people are thus subjected to a very heavy and continuous loss. Their power of controlling their home markets is impaired; they lose the advantage of their position and of their opportunity to supply the vast non-machine-using countries of the world, containing over a thousand million population, with goods and wares made at high wages and low cost, for the reason that, in consequence of a disparity in the price of the material which lies at the foundation of all arts, they have by their own act given supremacy to Great Britain, in the lower cost of her investments, for meeting this demand.

INDEX.

RECENT ECONOMIC CHANGES.

486

many, 415; tendency for transfer to higher grades, 390.

Laborers, in Great Britain, improved condition of, 355; lowest, change in relative numbers of, 407; manual, slow advance in culture of, 77.

Land, area of cultivated, in the United States, 176; decline in value and use in France, 378; decline in value of, 423; fertile, influence on material progress, 454.

Lard, supersedure of by cotton-seed oil, 56.

Latin Union, action of, in relation to silver, 227.

Laundresses of Paris demand protection, 281.

Law of the use of metallic money, 251.

Lead, limited uses for, 148; recent production and price-experiences of, 147; world's production of, 148.

Leather, recent decline in prices of, 198.

Lexis, Prof., on recent price movements, 125.

Life assurance in Great Britain, 359.

Living, reduction in the cost of, 337.

Looms, power, displacement of labor by, 365.

Losses, occasioned by economic changes, 111.

Luxuries, increase in consumption of, 337.

Machinery, antagonism with machinery, 96; counteraction of the evils of labor-displacement by, 388; displacement of labor by, 51; effect of labor-saving, on wages, 371; epoch of efficient, 61; evolutions of from labor discontent, 327; for Panama Canal, labor power of, 50; influence of, in equalizing wages, 105; intensified influence in recent years, 61; labor-saving, stimulus to invention of, 68; most expensive of all products, 91.

Mackerel, recent price-experiences of, 163.

Madder, destruction of the business of growing and preparing, 55.

Maine, purchasing power of wages in, 412.

Malthus's views on population, 330.

Man, and animals, essential difference between, 400; change in condition of, through prices, 115.

Manchester, recent commercial policy of, 266.

Mankind, what is to be the future of, 427; recent increase in control of the forces of Nature by, 27.

Manufactures, tendency to consolidation, 96.

Manufacturing, modern system of, 93.

Marines, mercantile, of Europe, 311.

Marriage-rate, decline of, in Europe, 350.

Maryland, cost of living in, for operatives, 340.

Massachusetts, apportionment of population in, 352; cost of dietary for prisoners in, 340.

Masses, greatest accruing gain of the, 444.

Matches, increased consumption through exemption from taxation, 384.

Meat, dressed, restrictions on sale of, in the United States, 284; frozen, extent of trade in, 161; improvements in the production of, 339; new sources for supply of, 159.

Meats, cost of ocean transport, 38; recent price-experiences of, 158.

Mechanics, practical, imperfect development of, 400.

Medicine, prospective progress in, 348.

Merchandise, cost of transporting in the United States, 164; sales by samples, 110.

Metals, precious, change in relative values of, 224; inquiry respecting

THE END.